Prophet Singer

Prophet Singer

THE VOICE AND VISION OF WOODY GUTHRIE

MARK ALLAN JACKSON

UNIVERSITY PRESS OF MISSISSIPPI / JACKSON

www.upress.state.ms.us

The University Press of Mississippi is a member of the
Association of American University Presses.

Frontis: An illustration of the vigilante actions of various
"Citizens Committees," c. 1946. Sketch by Woody Guthrie.
Courtesy of the Ralph Rinzler Archives.

Print-on-Demand Edition

Library of Congress Cataloging-in-Publication Data

Jackson, Mark Allan.
  Prophet singer : the voice and vision of Woody Guthrie /
Mark Allan Jackson. — 1st ed.
    p. cm. — (American made music series)
  Includes bibliographical references and index.
  ISBN-13: 978-1-57806-915-6 (cloth : alk. paper)
  ISBN-10: 1-57806-915-7 (cloth : alk. paper)
1. Guthrie, Woody, 1912–1967. 2. Folk singers—United
States—Biography. 3. Folk music—Social aspects—United
States. I. Title.
  ML410.G978J33   2007
  782.42162'130092—dc22
  [B]   2006020846

British Library Cataloging-in-Publication Data available

Contents

ACKNOWLEDGMENTS [vii]

PROLOGUE [3]
GIVING A VOICE TO LIVING SONGS

CHAPTER ONE [19]
Is This Song Your Song Anymore?
REVISIONING "THIS LAND IS YOUR LAND"

CHAPTER TWO [48]
Busted, Disgusted, Down and Out
DOCUMENTING THE STORIES OF AMERICA'S AGRICULTURAL WORKERS

CHAPTER THREE [93]
The Poor, Hard-Working Man Blues
DOCUMENTING THE TROUBLES OF OTHER AMERICAN WORKERS

CHAPTER FOUR [127]
Skin Trouble
DOCUMENTING RACE AND REDEMPTION

CHAPTER FIVE [166]
Stepping Outside the Law
CLASS CONSCIOUSNESS IN GUTHRIE'S OUTLAW SONGS

CHAPTER SIX   [204]

That Union Feeling

TRACING A VISION OF A BETTER WORLD

EPILOGUE   [253]

THIS SCRIBBLING MIGHT STAY

NOTES   [259]

INDEX   [293]

Acknowledgments

Many people and institutions must be recognized for their help in making this book possible. I have to start off by mentioning certain friends who shared their enthusiasm about music with me. So I salute Casey Whitt, John Snyder, Cody Walker, Derek Van Lynn, Maxine Beach, Robin Becker, and David Koen in no particular order. They allowed me to see the deep places in America's music, made me think about its beauty and meaning.

I am also appreciative of the support I received from Louisiana State University and its faculty. Financial support from a Graduate School Dissertation Fellowship helped me bring this work to a conclusion. But my deepest gratitude goes to John Lowe and Frank DeCaro for their detailed criticism and unyielding support. Both these scholars challenged my ideas and my writing with sharp comments. Although I claim all faults found here, they helped make this project better than I thought possible. I never doubted their faith in my work. Thank you. I also want to acknowledge the rest of my dissertation committee—Patrick McGee, Carl Freedman, and Pat Marerro—for their contributions.

A couple of important archives and their staffs have greatly aided my research and encouraged me personally. I want to give a nod of appreciation to Nora Guthrie and the crew at the Woody Guthrie Archives, especially Jorge Arevalo and Michael Smith, for their kind assistance and permission to quote from their materials. The staff at the Library of Congress's American Folklife Center also has helped guide my research on Woody Guthrie and his songs; I owe them much credit.

A considerable amount of the research that made this project possible was aided by a Predoctoral Fellowship from the Smithsonian Institution (SI) and by the help of certain staff members. In particular, Jeff Place of the Ralph Rinzler Archives at the Center for Folklife and Cultural Heritage provided me guidance through the Woody Guthrie Papers and endless insight into our nation's music, and Stephanie Smith was extremely helpful in providing images from the archive for use in this project. I also want to thank the archive as a whole for its kind permission to quote from unpublished materials held there. While I was at the National Museum of American History, both Charlie McGovern and Pete Daniel commented on various sections of this book; they have also helped me immensely simply by being my friends. Needless to say, I owe much thanks to the SI for its overall support.

The University Press of Mississippi also offered me much support as this project came to publication. A variety of editors and advisors—David Evans, Kip Lornell, Craig Gill, Anne Stascavage—all skillfully guided my manuscript along. The careful and concerned copyediting by Carol Cox was extremely valuable and valued. Also, the design staff's creative force brought extra pizzazz to the book. All their efforts are greatly appreciated.

Finally, I want to thank my family, who stood by me even when they were not exactly sure what it was I was doing. My father, Lee Jackson, gave me compassion for all working people and their struggles and a belief that all honest labor is noble and worthy of praise. My mother gave me faith that there was good in the world—all you had to do was look for it. She endowed me with a sympathy for the human condition. Throughout my life, my parents have given me a rock to stand on. They are my church. This book is dedicated to them.

Prophet Singer

Prologue

At more than one point in his life, writer and political activist Woodrow Wilson "Woody" Guthrie (July 14, 1912–October 3, 1967) broke the world of song into distinct categories:

> There are two kinds of songs—living songs and dying songs. The dying songs—the ones about champagne for two and putting on your top hat—they tell you that there's nothing to be proud of in being a worker, but that someday if you're good and work hard, you'll get to be boss. Then you can wear white tie and tails and have songs made up about you. I like living songs that make you take pride in yourself and your work, songs that try to make things better for us, songs that protest all the things that need protesting against.[1]

Too often, Guthrie believed, the popular media of his day only offered Americans "dying songs," those voicing giddy visions of glamour and romance, a carefree image far removed from the experiences of the majority of the American people listening to their radios and phonographs. He further argues, "I did not hear any [songs of protest] on the radio. I did not hear any of them in the movie house. I did not hear a single ounce of our history being sung on the nickel juke box. The Big boys don't want to hear our history of blood, sweat, work, and tears, of slums, bad housing, diseases, big blisters or big callouses, nor about our fight to have unions and free speech and a family of nations."² Even while recognizing that much of America's commercialized music excluded dissenting voices and tranquilized the populace, he also believed that "living songs" could fight against the forces of conformity and complacency and could be a powerful means for equitable societal change. He writes, "Music is a weapon, the same as a gun, and can be used by the slave just the same as by the big boss."³ For him, songs have the potential to point out the wrongs done to the majority of Americans even as they could also express a vision of a better, more just nation.

As Guthrie was born on Bastille Day and named after Woodrow Wilson, the Democratic presidential candidate at the time, it might seem that he would be automatically inclined to mix dissent and history into his writing. But it was not an inborn sense of injustice that pushed him to make the statements he did, to protest the ills he saw. Hard experience helped direct his work. His own family, once graced with a solid middle-class position, fell into ruin in the 1920s, suffering an economic decline shared by many others in the rural South and Southwest after World War I. When the Great Depression came to the rest of America in the 1930s, the people whom Guthrie knew best had already experienced almost a decade of decreasing return on their labors. While living in Texas during the height of the Depression, he also felt the sting of black dust storms raging the land and saw the plight brought on by drought in the southwestern plains. From his travels out of this area and to the West Coast, he learned of displaced farmers from other states and regions, tying their struggles together, especially in the "factories in the field" described by social critic Carey McWilliams in 1939. Guthrie's understanding of the struggles of other working-class people grew during the early 1940s as he continued traveling the nation and encountering lumbermen, steelworkers, sailors, miners, and other laborers—eventually realizing that only a privileged few never knew hunger or hardship. During this same time period, in part due to his encounters and friendships with a variety of white and black artists with leftist political and social views, he also began to break away from the prevailing prejudices of his time and to advocate for racial groups other than his own. Educated by his experiences and companions, he came to link the entirety of America's underclass together.

In time, Guthrie slowly began to realize that the diverse and downtrodden of America had a huge story of their own to tell, one that was worth the telling. He writes,

Out of all our hard work and low pay, and tired backs, and empty pocketbooks, is goin' to come a tune.

And that song and that tune aint got no end, and it aint got no notes wrote down and they aint no piece of paper big enough to put it down on.

Every day you are down and out, and lonesome, and hungry, and tired of workin' for a hoboes handout, theys a new verse added to the song.

Every time you kick a family out of a house, cause they ain't got the rent, and owe lots of debts, why, theys another verse added to this song.

When a soldier shoots a soldier, thats a note to this song. When a cannon blows up 20 men, thats part of the rhythm, and when soldiers march off over the hill and dont march back, that's the drumbeat of this song.

This aint a song you can write down and sell.

This song is everywhere at the same time.

Have you heard it?

I have.[4]

To him, this urge to sing out an emotion-based history of the nation seems to be the only true and open expression afforded the underclass, as noted in a 1945 songbook: "I have never heard a nation of people sing an editorial out of a paper. A man sings about the little things that help him or hurt his people and he sings of what has got to be done to fix this world like it ought to be. These songs are singing history. History is being sung."[5] Throughout his life, Guthrie had discovered the history of the American people through their songs. As a youth in Oklahoma and Texas, he learned "Chisholm Trail," "Jesse James," and other folk songs from family, friends, and acquaintances. Later, others taught him songs such as "Which Side Are You On?" and "Roll the Union On," which detailed labor struggles of impoverished workers. As a result, he easily recognized that this form offered communities mired in poverty or limited by illiteracy a means to vent their frustrations and share their collective history. These songs could also transmit the suffering of the underclass to others, those who might desire or who might be persuaded to join in the fight for economic justice and social equality for all.

Beginning in the late 1930s and continuing until the onset of the degenerative disease Huntington's chorea cut short his writing career in the early 1950s, Guthrie used his lyrics to voice his views on a wide variety of American historical realities and offered his vision for creating a just future. In a short essay, Guthrie once tried to lay out the questions that his work meant to answer in his songs. Among them he asked, "What section of the American people are carrying the real load, doing the real work, the real fighting, the real living, loving, courting, and song-making right this minute? Who is keeping American history alive and moving? Who is holding progress back? Who is going forward and who is drifting backward?"[6] Through his lyrics, he worked to capture the history of Franklin Roosevelt's "Forgotten Man," to praise those who struggled daily just to make ends meet and to point out those whose greed and prejudice made life difficult for the majority of Americans. He tried to capture on paper and on recordings a part of the history of this nation's underclass for others to know in years to come and to offer a vision of what the country could be if this group joined together to demand a truly democratic and egalitarian society.

As a means of grabbing his audience's attention and their empathy, the never-ending "living song" that Guthrie describes above contains no clinical distance in the telling. Unlike many published histories, with their dependence on dusty fact rather than emotional pang, Guthrie's songs concerning such events as the Great Depression or the Dust Bowl are filled with energy and passion. The impetus behind this drive is obvious; he experienced both. As a result, many of his songs detailing these historical moments appear as autobiography, even when the song's narrator cannot vaguely be construed as the author himself. When writing of incidents even further removed from his own life, such as those only read about in newspapers, he also works to document, to remember with passion those whose stories are ephemeral, who seem forgotten by the media almost as soon as they are noted. He often picked specific events or people to focus on in his songs, refashioning them so they epitomized the injustices occurring in America even as they humanized and personalized these stories.

Additionally, much of Guthrie's lyrics compared the promise and democratic myths of the nation to the reality discovered in his travels—and noting whatever divides he found. At least one folklorist, however, argues that Guthrie's work is not informed by negativity towards America: "He protested against prejudice and financial abuse, but his songs never contained bitterness or hatred or criticisms for this country."[7] Certainly, Guthrie had much praise for the nation, as we can see in the best-known verses of "This Land Is Your Land," but he also thought it necessary to point out the wrongs he saw, just as he did in some lesser-known verses of the same song. As another critic notes, many of his lyrics point out the "hollowness of heart beneath the often hysterical pretensions to national greatness, a hollowness that bespoke the unrealized ideals of the land and its people."[8] His songs demand that the democratic vows of our own nation's founding documents be made into reality. Realizing that the songs and stories of his time would eventually come to represent his era's reality to others, he bears witness to the truth as he knew it in the writing he produced, especially his lyrics.

In his relatively short creative life, barely two decades, Guthrie wrote thousands of songs. Now, however, we can often discover only his lyrics, while their tune has disappeared, faded into time. Much of the reason for this loss is that he did not know how to write down the notes to which he put his words. As a musician, Guthrie did have some ability. He could play the guitar, the mandolin, the fiddle, and the harmonica—although he was no virtuoso on any of these instruments. Using any one of them, he could play hundreds of folk songs and other tunes that he learned in his far-flung travels throughout America. But he did not do much in the way of composing his own original music—an admission he made early on in his songwriting career. In his first songbook, *Alonzo M. Zilch's Own Collection of Original Songs and Ballads*, he confesses to a process that he would follow for the rest of his life: "At times I cannot decide on a tune to use with my words for a song. Woe is me! I am then forced to use some good old, family style tune that hath already gained a reputation as being liked by the people."[9] Later, he was even more direct in admitting his use of others' tunes. He once confided to Pete Seeger, "I steal from everybody. Why, I'm the biggest song stealer there ever was."[10] As Guthrie biographer Joe Klein has noted, "The music usually was an afterthought. The words were most important. He wrote songs at the typewriter; it was the instrument he played best."[11] In fact, almost all of his lyrics simply ride on the back of someone else's music, both folk and commercial songs. For Guthrie, the emphasis was on words, and any easily singable tune could be their vehicle.

If we only look at Guthrie's words, his lyrics, without the benefit of their music, do we lose too much? Folklorist Richard Reuss argues, "Woody's lyrics, in most cases, were written as songs, to be sung and performed in a dynamic atmosphere. Reduced to two dimensions on the printed page, they frequently suffer as do many famous traditional songs."[12] Perhaps Guthrie's lyrics do lose some of their power removed from the tunes he put them to or from the singer's own unique presentation. Through the years, many knowledgeable critics have emphasized how his personal style and timing helped empower his words. Oral historian Studs Terkel writes, "It was a nasal, dragged-out way Woody had of telling a tale. The seemingly undramatic pause, followed by what *seemed* to be a reluctantly drawled out punchline. In retrospect, we recognize the consummate artistry, the comic-tale craftiness of a Twain and, to a lesser extent because his targets were less formidable, the approach of his fellow Oklahoman, Will Rogers" [emphasis in original].[13] But does this verbal style encompass the whole of Guthrie's ability? Do his lyrics lose all power when they are found on the page instead of coming directly out of the singer's mouth?

Guthrie himself believed that "Every word is a music note," that there was grace and sound to the lyrics themselves.[14] If we agree with this assertion, the music of the words endures whether the author utters them or not, just as the meaning of the words remains with us too. Guthrie's lyrics have an inherent power and purpose, which many have noted and commented on through the years. Early on in his career, one critic hailed him as a true poet, "a rusty voiced Homer."[15] The reference here stands as a particularly appropriate and revealing one, for Homer's stories capture the history and myths of his people and nation with beauty and power. Homer sang out his vision of his own time, one that others have told and retold, century after century. Similarly, Guthrie's work also attempted to document the history and myths of our country and its citizens with moving words. His vision too has been passed on for decades as literature worthy of study and appreciation.

Early on in Guthrie's career, a few critics speculated on the singer's significance to America through his writing. In 1943, when Guthrie's autobiographical novel *Bound for Glory* appeared, it garnered generally positive reviews in such elite publications as the *New York Times Book Review* and *The New Yorker*. In particular, writer Louis Adamic noted an unusual strain of expression in both Guthrie's songs and his book:

> He is the twentieth-century troubadour whose subject is not the deeds of princes but the dreams of people. Born in the Midwest, which is too small to hold him, he roams from coast to coast, working and playing his guitar and singing for his supper. The songs are made out of what he sees and knows and feels; they are the living folksongs of America.
>
> The same quality pervades the book. It is completely American, twentieth-century American, in feeling, in experience,

in idealism and humor and rhythm. Through it one sees again the disjointedness, the inarticulation, of modern life; but—and this is so rare as to be very nearly unique—the author is not disjointed. He does not know all the answers, but he knows the right questions, and he has an unassailable grasp of the values which lead to the right answers.[16]

Here, we have one of the earliest appraisals of Guthrie's work that notes his desire to articulate the hopes of the everyday citizen, to document the world around him, and to ask pointed questions about our nation and its problems. In essence, Adamic found Guthrie's writing a worthy vessel of our country's history and a prick to our national consciousness. Unfortunately, the singer's growing inability to articulate his own thoughts brought about by the degenerative effects of Huntington's chorea lessened his literary output by the late 1940s and stopped it completely by the end of 1955.

As a result of a lack of publication of either his songs or his prose, little detailed critical notice was given Guthrie or his writing throughout the 1950s. The only major exception came in the form of John Greenway's groundbreaking *American Folksongs of Protest*, which touched on the lyrics of Guthrie and a number of other folk artists who imbued their songs with political and social criticism. But even in this work, Greenway only covered a few of Guthrie's songs, providing the complete lyrics of each and giving each a bit of historical context but little real analysis.[17] So during the early years of the cold war, with its accompanying fear of Communist influence in the entertainment industry and intellectual circles that hushed many other voices of dissent, much of his writing slid into obscurity.

Even during this quiet time, some efforts to hold Guthrie's work up for public consumption still occurred. Pete Seeger should be given much of the credit for giving a voice to Guthrie's words, bringing the now-debilitated singer a new audience. While touring college campuses during his own hard time brought about by the accusations of anti-Communists in general and the House Un-American Activities Committee in particular, Seeger performed and celebrated many of Guthrie's songs, especially "So Long," a version of which his own group, the Weavers, brought into the charts during the early 1950s. Along with the efforts of *Sing Out!*, the folk music magazine in which he had a managing hand, Seeger gave a sometimes faint but always steady voice to the idea that Guthrie's songs offered insight into America's past and a vision for its future. Driven in part by these efforts, many of the next generation of folk-style performers such as Joan Baez, Bob Dylan, and Peter, Paul, and Mary included his songs in their repertoires by the beginnings of the 1960s, finally bringing his words a greater audience than he probably could have imagined, making him the kind of poet of the people of which Walt Whitman would only ever dream.

With the energy of the folk song revival of the 1960s in full swing and a growing number of Americans voicing their dissent through the civil rights and anti-Vietnam movements, Guthrie's work again received a public hearing—not only from the many folk-style singers performing his songs but also through his own pen, from his own printed word. For during this decade, several of his major literary efforts found themselves in print, some for the first time. In 1963, Pete Seeger put together *Woody Guthrie Folk Songs*, containing the largest collection of his songs ever published.[18] Two years later, music critic and Dylan worshipper Robert Shelton collected some of Guthrie's prose and lyrics together in the volume *Born to Win*.[19] Although compiled and edited over twenty years earlier by Guthrie, Seeger, and Alan Lomax but too radical for publishers then, the protest song collection *Hard Hitting Songs for Hard-Hit People* finally came out in 1967.[20] The next year, E. P. Dutton dusted off Guthrie's autobiographical novel *Bound for Glory*, which was then long out of print, and republished it with a new foreword by Seeger.[21] By the end of this decade, not only could you hear Guthrie's songs on the radio or buy them in a record shop, but you could also stroll into your local bookstore and find his voice still alive just behind the cover of one of these books.

With this upturn in Guthrie's literary legacy also came interest from various music critics and folklorists, who started giving the singer and his work a closer and more rigorous review than ever before. Perhaps also partly driven by Guthrie's death in 1967, several music scholars began to consider his legacy. Just what, if any, was his place in our culture and what did his writing have to offer us of any lasting value? Some critics came down clearly as proponents of him as a literary figure whose written work was worthy of serious exploration. Even with his misgivings about studying the words divorced from their music, Richard Reuss believes, "Woody's creative work as literature and art has yet to be evaluated seriously. Certainly his songs and prose are an eloquent chronicle of the Depression and World War II generation, presented from a unique perspective, and might profitably be studied."[22] Folklorist John Greenway went even further in his praise: "The best of Woody was his early Dust Bowl chronicles. On these his reputation will—in my opinion—grow to a high rank even among sophisticated

American poets."[23] In much the same vein, in his introduction to *Born to Win* Robert Shelton looks forward to a time when Guthrie's lyrics and his ideas become part of the American literary canon: "His reputation as a writer, poet and philosopher is still underground and must be brought into the light. When his songs, poems, and essays are studied in our American literature classes, this omission may be righted."[24]

No matter how many accolades Guthrie's writing received during this time period, other well-versed critics of American folk song and popular culture did not believe that his lyrics or prose reached the level of competence that would allow them to be ranked among the great literature of America. Although recognizing his high ranking in the 1960's folk revival and in "American popular music," folklorist D. K. Wilgus believes, "Anyone who sees him as a major literary figure needs to be bored for the simples."[25] In a review of *Born to Win*, Ellen Stekert bluntly states, "[Guthrie] is clearly not a great literary figure."[26]

But for those wanting an in-depth discussion of Guthrie's literary or cultural significance, these commentaries—both pro and con—only offered the briefest of justification for the claims they made. They stand more as individual beliefs than as well-argued opinion. In the following decades, this situation did change somewhat, even as Guthrie's songs, prose, and legend continued to be more widely available. In the 1970s, several books came out that discussed Guthrie's politics, especially the influence of the Communist Party on his thinking. These writers looked at Guthrie's work and that of other popular folksingers from the early part of the twentieth century through a political lens, focusing on the influence of leftist thought on their attitudes and subject matter.[27] Actually, Guthrie himself discussed, among other topics, his connection to the Popular Front movement in the 1975 book *Woody Sez*, which was a collection of his Will Rogers–flavored columns for the Communist newspaper *People's World*.[28] During this decade, Henrietta Yurchenco also brought out the first biography of Woody Guthrie, *A Mighty Hard Road*. Her book does include a number of his lyrics, either excerpts or the full texts, but only accompanied with a minimum of commentary.[29] At the very end of this decade, Edward Robbin released his memoir *Woody Guthrie and Me: An Intimate Reminiscence*, which includes some useful insight into the singer's changing political development during the late 1930s and early '40s.[30] Collectively, though, these books offer only a limited examination of how Guthrie's personal experiences and his political education directly affected the content and attitude of his lyrics.

The 1980s also saw the publication of a number of books that looked deeper into the songwriter's life and work than ever before. But even in journalist Joe Klein's detailed and well-researched biography, *Woody Guthrie: A Life*, the focus remained more on Guthrie's personal life, especially his sexual antics, than on the worth of his writing and what it offered to us, although Klein did break down the meaning and the history behind several songs—making it a valuable resource for a general understanding of Guthrie's work and its context.[31] Also in the 1980s came Robbie Lieberman's *"My Song Is My Weapon": People's Songs, American Communism, and the Politics of Culture, 1930–1950*, yet another treatise on the Communist Party's influence on members of the American folk music community, including Guthrie.[32] Perhaps the best analysis to this point in time of how Guthrie's life and his political development directly shaped his songs appeared in Wayne Hampton's *Guerrilla Minstrels*, but even this scholar's comments were truncated into only one chapter of this book, resulting in a rushed approach to all of Guthrie's lyrics discussed in it.[33]

During the last decade of the twentieth century and the first of the twenty-first, more and more critical attention has turned towards Guthrie and his writing. Still, little in-depth analysis of individual songs or even thematic trends in his work appeared. In 1990, Dave Marsh edited and released *Pastures of Plenty*, a collection of Guthrie's writing containing some of the music critic's own brief musings concerning the singer's worth as a writer and activist.[34] Ed Cray's biography *Ramblin' Man: The Life and Times of Woody Guthrie* offers a useful history of the man but little insight into any particular song.[35] Even in the critical collection *Hard Travelin': The Life and Legacy of Woody Guthrie* and Bryan Garman's excellent *A Race of Singers: Whitman's Working-Class Hero from Guthrie to Springsteen*, we still can only find isolated moments specifically discussing how Guthrie's personal history and his era's cultural and political realities have directly inspired and shaped his lyrics.[36] So as more and more of his prose and songs have appeared in print or on recordings, even as other artists performed his songs, and as various critics examined his personal life and a few isolated influences, no single book-length study has appeared that looks deeply into his songs, trying to trace their creation, meaning, and significance. This goal is the one *Prophet Singer* undertakes.

The songs discussed here—ranging from the well-known to the unknown—all provide access to our national past. They become carriers of information, folk song–like, providing players, listeners, and readers a window on the history of America's underclass for those interested in looking deeply into them. Guthrie, well-founded in the folk tradition, recognized the power of song to capture a moment in time and pass it on to future generations. His songs remind us what the poll tax was, what Harriet Tubman fought for, and what tenant farmers yearned for. The situations he documents in his songs can reveal truths about forgotten, ignored, or abused Americans' lives, but only by re-establishing the history encapsulated in Guthrie's songs can they regain some of the power they have lost through the forgetting of the events that triggered their creation. If we search for the events that impulsed his "living songs," the turned earth of the past offers up many exciting discoveries, often long lost or little known but still important to anyone concerned with the history and culture of America.

This study also compares the stories he tells to the historical truth as best it can be determined, looking for divergences and investigating the possible reasons behind them. It is important to note that he was more concerned with re-creating reality than dabbling in complete fictions. Even Guthrie's autobiographical novels *Bound for Glory* and *Seeds of Man* cannot be looked at as sources of absolute fact about his personal history. Using his life as a bare skeleton, he elaborates upon his youthful reality, giving it muscle and skin of his own design. But even in his most fictive creations, he always bases his tale in a reality that he either experienced himself or that he learned of through other people's lives. He also seems much more concerned with fact in his songs than in his other writing. Although he does stray from the historical truth in a number of lyrics discussed in this work, these shifts are duly noted. But there are several important reasons that should be mentioned to help explain this divergence. First, some of the commercial sources he looked to for information or events, such as books or newspapers, were themselves misinformed or misinforming. In these instances, Guthrie did try to follow the facts as best he could. Second, when he depended upon folk or oral sources, such as other songs and personal tales, he could also get the facts wrong. Again, in these cases, Guthrie did try to draw upon others for the truthfulness of his work, which sometimes failed him in accurately documenting certain events. Third, sometimes the story itself—his desire to capture the attention and sympathy of his audience—became more important to him than any particular fact. To do so, he often pulled from the general knowledge he had of a situation and created a song to represent a group's experience through that of a fictional character who is firmly rooted in historical fact.

Rather than stand as pure history, these songs and their subject matter provide access to the past for a purpose. Guthrie wanted those who encountered his songs to take in the tale and then recognize the example of resistance inherent in each. In a brief piece eventually published as the "Foreword" to the radical songbook *Hard Hitting Songs for Hard-Hit People*, novelist John Steinbeck noted this essential element: "Harsh voiced and nasal, his guitar hanging like a tire iron on a rusty rim, there is nothing sweet about Woody, and there is nothing sweet about the songs he sings. But there is something more important for those who will listen. There is the will of a people to endure and fight against oppression. I think we call this the American Spirit."[37] Steinbeck's point is an important one. The majority of Guthrie's songs, especially those lyrics referenced in my analysis, offer up a spirit of resistance to a multitude of evils affecting everyday Americans, and the process that Guthrie went through to come to achieve the perspective and desire to record the life experiences of our nation's underclass is a complex one that *Prophet Singer* also traces.

Guthrie's writing also often contains clues to its creator's sentiments and beliefs. Like many others engaged in documentary, Guthrie gives us a distilled rather than a pure vision. For he let his politics and beliefs shape his work, yet his songs do not fall into mere didacticism. He even warns against this tendency: "I think one mistake some folks make in trying to write songs that will interest folks is to . . . make it too much of a sermon. A folk song ought to be pretty well satisfied just to tell the facts and let it go at that."[38] His work goes beyond simple candid recording. It inhabits a space straddling art, history, and politics. The term "social documentary" well represents these different drives. Just as exposé does, social documentary reports and pronounces judgment—sometimes subtly, sometimes not.

For these incidents, these stories to be fully accepted, they must be felt by his audience. To accomplish this goal, he creates specific characters, individuals whom he brings to life with words. They come to represent the many who struggled in American's vast economic and social landscape, even if a few fictive liberties are taken in their creation. This type of focused emotional appeal to express historical events often occurs in social documentary. In *Documentary Expression and Thirties America*, William Stott notes that artists use it in their work to "increase our knowledge of public facts, but sharpen it with feeling; put us in touch with the perennial human spirit, but show it struggling in a particular social context at a specific historical moment."[39] This urge to mingle facts with feeling aptly describes what Guthrie strived for in his songs about the American underclass. Taken together, his songs present a word and sound documentary of these people.

To be clear, I will not argue in this study that all of Guthrie's songs merit the status or praise of great literature; for some of the lyrics detailed in this critical work, as a whole, do fall flat. But even many of his weakest efforts contain clever lines or phrases that can draw a smile or spark indignation in a listener or a reader. His strongest efforts have the power to enliven and enthrall audiences—evidenced by their longevity—and make them important pieces of writing to ordinary Americans. They have become a part of the American experience. "This Land Is Your Land" is sung at VFW halls, protest rallies, schoolhouses, and other events where our nation's people gather. Generations of our best performers have musically reinterpreted songs such as "Oklahoma Hills," "Pastures of Plenty," "Deportee," and "Pretty Boy Floyd." Much of Guthrie's work has become part of America's soundtrack, its shared cultural memory.

I begin my analysis by discussing how Guthrie's most famous song "This Land Is Your Land" came into being, how it shifted in his revisions, how it has been embraced by our nation, and how it has been used in a variety of situations—all an attempt to lay out the history of its many and diverse versions. Starting off with an examination of this particular song is important since many of the other lyrics commented on in *Prophet Singer* are either little known or unheard-of by both the general population and those engaged in the exploration of American music. Since most readers will be familiar with the popular version of "This Land," a discussion of how the particulars of Guthrie's personal politics, the inclusion of its lesser-known verses, or the context in which it is performed can reshape our understanding of this celebrated song helps prepare us for an examination of many of Guthrie's other protest lyrics, which is the central purpose of this book.

In the next three chapters, I discuss how a great number of his songs documenting the hardships of white farm laborers, various other workers, and several racial minorities reflect how Guthrie's social consciousness shifted through time due to his own experiences, education, and friendships. As noted in chapter two, early on in life he gained an appreciation, even an empathy, for farmers and farm workers—although he did not himself personally belong to this group. Due to the ravages of the drought and the dust in the Southwest and the South, many of these people left their homes and drifted west, looking for the promise of a golden land where work and wages were plentiful. Guthrie follows them and chronicles their experiences—from the Dust Bowl and the sharecropper's shack to the Hoovervilles and the fields of California.

In time, he came to apply the same sympathetic attitude towards other groups. The third chapter traces how he ended up recording the miseries of many other working-class people in his songs. As noted before, Guthrie's family was firmly middle class until the postwar depression of the early 1920s, when they become impoverished. His personal fall allowed him an early understanding of how financial situations can easily fluctuate due to larger changes in regional and national economic structures. In his travels throughout America beginning in the Great Depression, he came into contact with nonagricultural workers and began to document their hardships and struggles. Eventually, he linked all workers together, coming to his own vision of class consciousness.

Expanding on how his experiences and sympathies could reshape his past thinking, chapter four traces how, beginning in the late 1930s and early '40s, Guthrie moved from a racist-tinged past to a welcoming of all people of color. As a result, many of his subsequent lyrics either call for racial unity or denounce racist actions and institutions, such as lynchings and Jim Crow laws.

Rather than document only the hurts and miseries of America's underclass, Guthrie also celebrated those who fought unjust laws, who demanded that the promise of America be fulfilled. Chapter five examines various outlaws appearing in Guthrie's songs—such as Jesse James, Pretty Boy Floyd, and Harriet Tubman—and works to discern how he transformed these men and women into figures of class revolt.

In his stories of heartache and hardship, Guthrie praises those who stood up for their beliefs, those who tried to live their lives unmolested but who were beaten down by the powers that be—bankers, politicians, sheriffs, and vigilantes. He even praises those who stepped outside the law looking for true justice against these forces. But the outlaw, the man or woman who steps outside the law, even for the good of their class, often ends up dead. In acknowledging this historical end, Guthrie came to realize that only through collective action could true and lasting change be made possible. Individuals have to unify to gain power, not for one but for all—democracy undiluted by the brokerage of money, prejudice, or favor. In chapter six, I discuss how Guthrie's interaction with various groups and ideologies helped shape his eclectic sense of unionization. This final chapter especially limns out his personal philosophy, for even as he tried to document certain events, he always allowed his own political and social principles to shape the telling. In addition, it traces many of his lesser-known influences, such as Populism and Christianity, to find the origins of his perspective and tracks certain of his political interests expressed in his songs, allowing a coherent pattern to emerge. But Guthrie does not limit his comments to what has happened; he also recommends directions for the future, as is noted in detail in this chapter.

In essence, *Prophet Singer* discusses Guthrie's attempt to use song as a means to record the wrongs of which he knew and to point out the paths that he thought the nation could take in order to improve the lot of its underclass. We can catch a glimpse of Guthrie's belief in the redemptive power of what he describes as "living songs" in a 1948 letter addressed to President Truman. Here, he asks, "Let everybody everywhere sing all night long. Love songs, work songs, new hope songs." This singing, he concludes, "will cure every soul in our jail, asylum, and sick in our hospital, too. Try it and see. I know. I'm a prophet singer."[40] In Guthrie's lyrics discussed in this study, we find an artist taking an account of the world around him, emphasizing the injustice suffered by the poor and the oppressed. But it also finds a man looking forward to a time and a place when and where all people have homes and jobs, plenty to eat, freedom to speak their minds, and equal status under the law—regardless of race or gender or class. His unified personal philosophy lies in wait in his songs for curious minds to discover. These expressions, captured by his voice and through his words, remain for us as a social document and populist prophecy.

CHAPTER ONE

Is This Song Your Song Anymore?

REVISIONING "THIS LAND IS YOUR LAND"

After drifting around New York for almost two months at the beginning of 1940, sleeping on a succession of friends' couches, and busking for tips in Bowery saloons, Woody Guthrie settled into the shabby surroundings of Hanover House, a hotel located near the jumble and noise of Times Square. There, on February 23, he wrote "God Blessed America," whose six verses ended in the refrain "God blessed America for me." Afterward, he did not show much interest in the song and did not perform it often.[1] Then sometime before the end of April 1944, when Moses Asch first recorded him singing it, Guthrie decided to change the title to "This Land Is Your Land" and the refrain to "This land was made for you and me."

Over the years, this song has surpassed simple popularity and found its way into our national consciousness, evidenced by a great many Americans' familiarity with the melody. Many people can sing all or part of the chorus—and some even know Guthrie wrote the song. But this recognition cannot be attributed directly to its commercial achievement. If we look to *Billboard* magazine as a typical measurement of a song's commercial status, we find that none of the many versions of "This Land" has reached the top ten, forty, or even hundred in terms of sales. Even without this type of commercial success, it has become as Clifton Fadiman describes Guthrie and his work as a whole: "a national possession, like Yellowstone or Yosemite, and a part of the best stuff this country has to show the world."[2] "This

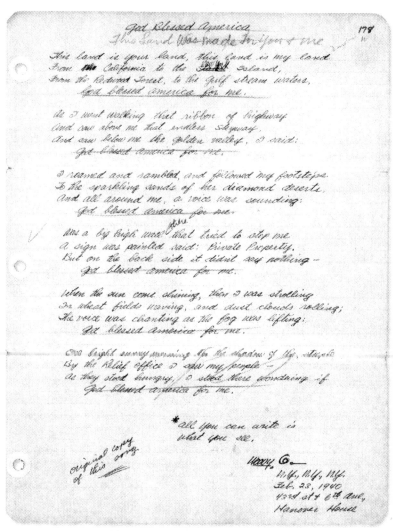

Original manuscript of "This Land Is Your Land" ("God Blessed America"), 1940. Courtesy of the Woody Guthrie Archives.

Land" has risen to the same status of such songs as "The Star-Spangled Banner," "America the Beautiful," "My Country 'Tis of Thee" ("America"), and "God Bless America." Much like these other works, through varied and sometimes subtle means, "This Land" has entered the blood stream of our nation's cultural body.

No matter how Americans first encounter the song, the version they hear always contains vivid and idyllic references to "the redwood forest" and a "golden valley," to "diamond deserts" and "wheat fields waving." If we compare the verses most of us are familiar with to those in the original version of "This Land," some differences appear. In the first rendering of the song, the fourth and sixth verses address aspects of our society Guthrie finds disturbing:

> Was a big high wall that tried to stop me
> A sign was painted said: Private Property,
> But on the back side it didn't say nothing—
> God blessed America for me.

> One bright sunny morning in the shadow of the steeple
> By the relief office I saw my people—
> As they stood hungry, I stood there wondering if
> God blessed America for me.[3]

The sentiments expressed here, detailing restriction and want, differ greatly from the celebratory vision of America shining through the popular three-verse/chorus version.[4] The omission of these lyrics also removes the song's initial dissenting and questioning voice and leaves behind a praising remnant, one that sounds more like a national anthem than its intended purpose—a musical response to and protest of Irving Berlin's "God Bless America."

Considering the prominent status "This Land" holds in our culture, it is important to those exploring the American experience to understand how one dominant version of the song came to be known by the American populace and how its meaning has been changed by different contexts throughout its life. While looking into the song's past and popularity, we also need to examine the original lyrics and those from other versions and compare them to the words of the popularized creation. This analysis will also produce new insight into Guthrie. Over the years, his image has become clouded by hyperbole from across the political spectrum. Since "This Land" remains the main means through which the American people have encountered Guthrie's voice and vision, it offers the single best vantage point to regard the man who wrote it and the country he sang about.

In that Guthrie initially intended "This Land" as a critical response to "God Bless America," a brief discussion of Berlin's song—its origin and acceptance by Americans—provides an idea of just what inspired the creation of this popular work. To find the beginning of "God Bless America," we must travel back to 1917, when a young Irving Berlin—who was in the army at the time—wrote and directed the musical *Yip! Yip! Yaphank* as a military fund-raiser. As part of this production, he wrote "God Bless America," which one Berlin biographer terms an "unashamedly patriotic anthem."[5] The unmitigated nationalism of the song was so obvious that even its creator believed it inappropriate for this particular production. The *New York Times Magazine* quotes Berlin as saying, "[E]veryone was emotionally stirred and realized what we were up against. It seemed like carrying coals to Newcastle to have a bunch of soldiers come out and sing it."[6] Because of these apprehensions, he cut it from the show and filed it away with his other unused manuscripts—where it stayed for over twenty years.

In late 1938, with another war in Europe looming ever closer, popular singer Kate Smith asked Berlin for a song that would stir patriotic fervor to use on her Armistice Day radio broadcast. After a few abortive efforts to produce a new tune, he remembered the song cut from *Yip! Yip! Yaphank* and decided to rework it to fit the current situation. First, he took the line "guide her to the right with a light from above" from the original song and changed it to "Through the night with a light from above" because when the song was originally written, Berlin says, "'to the right' had meant 'to the right path,'" but in 1938 it meant "'the political Right.'"[7] The second change shifted it away from being a war song. "Make her victorious on land and foam, God bless America, my home, sweet home" became "From the mountains to the prairies to the oceans white with foam, God Bless America, my home, sweet home."[8] Even with these changes, the opening vision of "storm clouds gather[ing] far across the sea" still remains, invoking a fearful image. Then comes the push for "allegiance" from a voice that uses "us" to establish the speaker as being unified with the listener. After asking for all to "be grateful for a land so fair," the speaker finally calls for a unifying prayer:

> God bless America land that I love.
> Stand beside her and guide her
> through the night with a light from above.
> From the mountains, to the prairies,
> to the oceans white with foam.
> God bless America, my home sweet home.[9]

Although this final version remains nationalistic, Berlin's revisions do make the song less jingoistic than its earlier incarnation.

After making these changes, Berlin offered "God Bless America" to Smith. Supposedly, she read the manuscript and blurted out, "Irving, do you realize you've written the second 'Star-Spangled Banner'?"[10] Smith first sang the piece on November 11, 1938, during her highly rated radio program on CBS. Almost immediately, the song established itself at the top of the Hit Parade and could be heard throughout America. The sheet music also did well, staying in the top fifteen in sales for almost six months in the first half of 1939.[11] But these typical signs of popularity do not show how deeply the American people accepted the song in the late 1930s. Within a few months, Smith's comment on first hearing the song seemed prophetic when "God Bless America" did actually take on some of the trappings of our national anthem. On Memorial Day in 1939, the assembled sports fans at Ebbets Field in Brooklyn stood and even took off their hats for it just as they would have done for "The Star-Spangled Banner."[12]

Not everyone held Berlin's song in such high esteem. As he traveled north from Texas to New York City in early 1940, Woody Guthrie heard Berlin's song "in Pampa [Texas], in Konawa [Oklahoma], on car radios, in diners, and it seemed that every time he stopped in a roadhouse for a shot of warm-up whiskey some maudlin joker would plunk a nickel in a jukebox and play it just for spite," according to biographer Joe Klein.[13] For Guthrie, Kate Smith was singing a song about America, a song celebrating this country, that did not completely jibe with what he had lived or had witnessed. He knew firsthand that not everyone had reason to be "grateful for a land so fair" nor that everyone experienced an America that could reasonably be called their "home sweet home."

Looking at Guthrie's personal history, one can see several important reasons for his dissatisfaction with the song's sentiments. First, he had already become a "Dust Bowl refugee," even if he had never been driven off a farm by dust, drought, or mechanization—just as he had never worked in western fields alongside his fellow Okies. But he had ridden the rails and highways with those who had left their homes in the South and Southwest for an uncertain future out west. He had also seen and talked to landless migrant laborers toiling in the fields when he toured California's farming communities above Los Angeles during the late 1930s. During these wanderings, he heard the migrants' stories of hardship and saw their weather-beaten, old-before-their-time faces, much the same as we can see in thousands of Farm Security Administration photographs taken during the Depression. Although not a photographer, Guthrie too captured their suffering and beauty, but with words: "I did keep my eyes on you, and kept my ears open when you came close to me. I saw the lines chopped across your face by the troubles in time and space. I saw the wind shape your face so the sun could light it up with thoughts and shadows. I remember your face as it was when I saw you."[14] In another prose piece, he writes even more explicitly, "I saw the hundreds of thousands of stranded, broke, hungry, idle, miserable people that lined the highways all out through the leaves and the underbrush."[15] His own eyes easily told him that these people had been little blessed by America. But the suffering he lived and saw did not end in the nation's farming communities.

During the course of his travels, Guthrie also found that America's cities had their own brand of ills, which would be another reason for his problem with Berlin's song. Just as he had in the fields of California, he saw the angry reaction to the Okies pouring into the urban and new suburban landscapes of Los Angeles. Later, after first moving to New York, he traveled down to the Bowery. According to Klein, "instead of unemployed Okies just passing through" such as those he had encountered on Los Angeles's Skid Row, he found "hard-core alcoholics groveling for pennies."[16] Flophouses, cheap bars, and relief agencies—these were the sights of the city, just as dust clouds, repossessed farms, and migrant laborers were those of the country. Human misery was a constant in both. This panorama of suffering did not add up to an America blessed for everyone.

Guthrie's once inchoate political awareness also began flowering around the time he wrote the song that would eventually become "This Land." He started connecting the poverty in the nation's fields, skid rows, and elsewhere to the unfairness of the distribution of wealth in America. For example, drawing on the melody he had used for "So Long, It's Been Good to Know You" and a sentiment similar to that found in his work "I Ain't Got No Home in This World Anymore," he finds a voice for these newfound notions in the song "I Don't Feel at Home on the Bowery No More," written in early 1940. First, he writes, "Once on this Bowery I use to be gay." Next, he juxtaposes images of the decrepit Bowery with those of opulent Fifth Avenue and ends the song with the lines "Since I seen the difference 'tween the rich and the poor / I don't feel at home in the Bowery no more." In an endnote, he dedicates the song "to the bum situation up and down every Skid Row and Bowery Street in this country."[17] To Guthrie, the great gulf between the wealthy and the poor stood out more boldly in New York than it ever had before.

This difference in class status also manifests itself in the personal backgrounds of Berlin and Guthrie. A full quarter century before "God Bless America" made its successful public debut, Berlin rose from immigrant poverty to great wealth. During the 1930s, he was part of a New York social circle left largely untouched by the Great Depression. In contrast, Guthrie and his family fell from a solid middle-class status to harsh poverty during the late 1920s boom / bust cycle of Oklahoma's oil fields. This early class shift, along with his low-budget travels across the whole of America in the mid and late 1930s, the sights that met him in the fields of California, and his time on Skid Row in Los Angeles and on the Bowery in New York, gave him a greatly different perspective on America's condition than Berlin had.

Somewhat surprisingly considering these class differences, Berlin and Guthrie held similar beliefs concerning the source and power of songs; they both believed songs represented the common discourse of Americans. In fact, their comments on this issue strongly jibe. Guthrie writes, "A song ain't nothing but a conversation fixed up to where you can talk it over and over without getting tired of it," while Berlin is quoted as saying, "A good popular song is just sort of the feeling and conversation of people set to music."[18] Both songwriters believe their work gives the people of America a voice that can speak, moan, or holler out their minds and feelings. But listening from different vantage points, Guthrie and Berlin channel wildly disparate voices.

In contrast, only Guthrie thinks that songs can point to suffering and explain how to lessen it. In late 1940, he expresses this view with poetic suppleness in a letter sent to Alan Lomax: "A folk song is whats wrong and how to fix it or it could be whose hungry and where their mouth is or whose out of work and where the job is or whose broke and where the money is or whose carrying a gun and where the peace is."[19]

By the time he first traveled to New York, Guthrie had already put the sights and experiences of the Dust Bowl into songs such as "So Long, It's Been Good to Know You," "Dust Storm Disaster," and "Dust Pneumonia Blues." He had also explored and exposed the harsh reality of the California-as-promised-land myth in "Do Re Mi" and "Dust Bowl Refugee." He performed these songs, along with less politicized material, on the radio at KFVD in Los Angeles. In response, thousands of people wrote him, many of them expressing support for his reflections on the Great Depression and sympathy for those down and out. These people told him he had spoken their words and amplified them. When he heard Berlin's paean to the unmitigated, the unmarred magnificence of America, Guthrie realized that the song neglected to address many people's pain, that it failed to document the injustices and suffering that stretched along with the land "From the mountains, to the prairies, / To the oceans white with foam." But he did not have to remain silent in his dissent; he had the talent to counter Berlin's song with one of his own.

Soon after arriving in New York, he began to transmute his feelings about "God Bless America" into song. Like many folksingers before him, he often hung his lyrics on the tunes of others. As a result, much speculation as to the source for the melody for "This Land" has arisen, with candidates ranging from the old Baptist hymn "Oh My Lovin' Brother," the Carter Family's "Little Darling, Pal of Mine," the gospel song "When the World's on Fire," or even "You Are My Sunshine."[20] Yet none of these suggestions completely satisfies—any or none could have been his musical inspiration. But this debate over the melody's origins shifts the emphasis away from an equally important part of a song—its lyrics. In fact, Guthrie believed that the words, not the music, matter most in a song. He writes, "If the tale the ballad tells is worth the telling, the tune makes very scant difference."[21] He only demanded that the music used could be easily sung and played by everyone, and "This Land" fits his own criteria. The tune he used (or even created) can be sung by almost anyone since it stays within one octave—unlike Berlin's song, which ranges over an octave and a half. In addition, not only does the song remain in a simple major key throughout, but both the chorus and verses also use the same chords and in the same sequence—so any beginning player can easily handle "This Land."

Moving away from the tune and with Guthrie's emphasis on language in mind, let us look to the words of the six-verse song originally titled "God Blessed America" to see the vision of America he created to counter Berlin's song:

> This land is your land, this land is my land,
> From California to the New York island,
> From the redwood forest to the Gulf Stream waters;
> God blessed America for me.
>
> As I was walking that ribbon of highway
> And saw above me that endless skyway,

And saw below me the golden valley, I said:
God blessed America for me.

I roamed and rambled, and I followed my footsteps
To the sparkling sands of her diamond deserts,
And all around me a voice was sounding:
God blessed America for me.

Was a great high wall there that tried to stop me
A sign was painted said: Private Property,
But on the back side it didn't say nothing—
God blessed America for me.

When the sun come shining, then I was strolling
In wheat fields waving, and dust clouds rolling;
The voice was chanting as the fog was lifting:
God blessed America for me.

One bright sunny morning in the shadow of the steeple
By the relief office I saw my people—
As they stood hungry, I stood there wondering if
God blessed America for me.[22]

Running the gamut from a laudatory to a discordant vision, these lyrics offer a far more complete depiction of America—detailing both its beauties and its ills—than does "God Bless America."

In the opening verse (which later became the chorus), Guthrie lays out the space of his canvas: "From California to the New York island / From the redwood forest to the Gulf Stream waters," which strongly suggest Berlin's lines, "From the mountains, to the prairies, / To the oceans white with foam." Guthrie then begins a catalog of beauty that includes an "endless skyway," a "golden valley," "sparkling sands," "diamond deserts," and "wheat fields waving." But in this beautiful landscape full of lush images, we find "dust clouds rolling," most likely the same ones he sings about in some of his Dust Bowl ballads. Other scenes definitely point to less pleasant realities. Verses four and six criticize the selfishness of private property and show the very real need for public relief. In bold contrast to Berlin's song, here the bad of America appears along with the good. Songwriter and activist Ernie Marrs well explains the range of the song's images: "All together, I don't know of another song so full of love for these United States, recognition of the injustices in them, and determination to do something about the latter."[23]

Unlike the hymns from which its underlying musical structure might have come or Berlin's song, "This Land" does not look to God for explanation of these differing images and definitely does not turn directly to Christianity for hope in resolving them. It offers a nation containing both beautiful vistas and people standing in shadow, hungry. The conflicts between these very different images are not resolved. Even the final refrain continues in this uncertainty since it shifts from a statement to a question through the addition of the phrase "I stood there wondering if." With this moment of doubt occurring at the very end of the song, it allows the audience the space to create its own answer, which is very different from the commanding tone of the prayer that ends "God Bless America."

Guthrie implicitly acknowledges in his song that the ills he saw in this country were but a part of the American experience as a whole; he also admits that some of his excitement came from this understanding. In a letter to his second wife, Marjorie, he writes, "The world I've seen is alive and interesting, not because its perfect and pretty and eternal, but because it needs my fixin', I need fixin', so does the land" and then adds that this realization allows his own shortcomings and mistakes to be removed: "When I let my mind dwell on such truths, I seem to float up like a balloon, way up high somewhere. And the world and the work and the trouble and the people, seem to be goin' as a bunch in such a good direction, that my own little personal lead weights and drawbacks, miscues, mistakes, and flounderin' around seem to fade away; rubbed out like a finger rubbin' out a wild pastel color."[24] An understanding of the positive and negatives of America and the people in it allowed Guthrie personal transcendence and redemption. The nation he writes of does not exclude the ugly in order to emphasize the beautiful; he links the two and works to increase the latter while decreasing the former.

Guthrie's drive for honest expression, which included criticism of the country he loved, was at odds with a powerful segment of the American political scene. At the time of the song's writing, these forces actually were growing in control and influence. In May 1938, Congress created the Dies Committee, which eventually mutated into the House Un-American Activities Committee. Another example of curtailment of freedom of expression occurred in June 1940 when Congress passed and President Roosevelt signed the Alien Registration Act, also known as the Smith Act. Through a number

An illustration of the restrictions placed on private property, c. 1946. Sketch by Woody Guthrie. Courtesy of the Ralph Rinzler Archives.

A line of men receiving relief payments in California, 1938. Photograph by Dorothea Lange. Courtesy of the Prints and Photographs Division of the Library of Congress.

of general restrictions on civil liberties and freedom of speech, this act worked to quell Socialist and Communist protest against the war in Europe and America's growing part in it. Before the act passed, the *New York Times* described it as pulling together "most of the anti-alien and anti-radical legislation offered in Congress in the last twenty years."[25] Restrictions against any type of domestic protest grew even more insidious during a desperate scramble to condemn all radicals during the Communist witch hunts of the late 1940s through the early 1960s. The challenging nature of the protest verses in the original version of "This Land" not only put Guthrie at odds with Berlin and those who gave America unadulterated support but also put him in some danger of prosecution if those in power so desired, as evidenced by later attacks on other left-leaning composers and songwriters such as Hans Eisler and Pete Seeger.

But it is doubtful that this possibility would have entered Guthrie's thoughts in early 1940, especially considering how little interest he showed in the original version of the song to become "This Land." Much like Berlin with "God Bless America," Guthrie did not immediately realize the popular potential of his new song and did not record it until the spring of 1944. During a marathon session in March and April of that year, Guthrie and a smattering of other artists including Cisco Houston, Sonny Terry, Bess Lomax, and Lead Belly recorded a number of songs for Asch Records (later to become Folkways). One was the first recorded version of "This Land." By this time, Guthrie had replaced the original title and refrain of "God Blessed America" with "This Land Is My Land" and "This land was made for you and me" respectively. In addition, he decided to use what had been the first verse as the chorus, which he also used to open and close the song. Of the protest verses, this particular version of the song contains only the one criticizing private property, although this take remained unreleased until 1997, when it first appeared on *This Land Is Your Land: The Asch Recordings, Vol. 1.*[26]

Even after this session, the song did not become fixed in Guthrie's mind; for he created another version of "This Land" that same year. From December 1944 until February 1945, he had a weekly fifteen-minute show on radio station WNEW in New York. On this program, he used "This Land" as the theme song and also included it in the mimeographed songbook *Ten of Woody Guthrie's Twenty-Five Cent Songs*, which he hawked on the show. Just as in the version recorded for Asch, Guthrie used the first verse of the original as the chorus and included variants of the second, third, and fifth verses. While subtracting the two original protest verses, he did add a new one:

> Nobody living can ever stop me,
> As I go walking my freedom highway.
> Nobody living can make me turn back.
> This land was made for you and me.[27]

The rebelliousness of this verse does place it more in the protest vein than the other three standard verses and the rousing, everybody-knows-it chorus. Still, this verse found little or no circulation for decades. Guthrie's friend Gordon Friesen, a leftist writer and fellow Oklahoman, noted in 1963 that he "has yet to hear or see anywhere outside of Woody's little mimeographed book his final verse."[28] As far as the author's intentions for this version of "This Land," we do not have to speculate. In the songbook's introduction, he writes, "The main idea about this song is, you think about these Eight words all the rest of your life and they'll come a bubbling up into Eighty Jillion all Union. Try it and see. THIS LAND IS MADE FOR YOU AND ME."[29]

Neither of these two early versions had much impact, however. Instead, another eventually became the standard. According to Jeff Place of the Ralph Rinzler Archives, which houses all of Moses Asch's recordings and papers, this particular version came out of some 1947 sessions Guthrie laid down after he returned to New York City from a trip to Portland, Oregon.[30] Only the three verses and the chorus that eventually comprise the popular version appear here. This take eventually appeared on the 1951 Folkways album *This Land Is Your Land*, the first commercial pressing of the song. Even Pete Seeger, who worked closely with Guthrie throughout the 1940s and early 1950s, states he originally heard the song on this record.[31] Subsequently, this particular version of Guthrie singing "This Land" found its way onto over a dozen other albums and CDs.[32]

Despite this landmark recording, Guthrie continued to change the song. During a brief session for Decca Records on January 7, 1952, he recorded yet another version of "This Land." Here, the chorus remains largely the same as before; and out of the three verses used here, two are variants of those already mentioned. However, the third does offer new lyrics:

> I can see your mailbox, I can see your doorstep
> I can feel my wind rock your tip top tree top
> All around your house there my sun beam whispers
> This land was made for you and me.[33]

By the time he made this recording, Guthrie showed distinct signs of the hereditary disease Huntington's chorea—resulting in a halting and somewhat disjointed performance. Consequently, Decca never issued this version although it did eventually find its way onto the extensive box-set *Songs for Political Action: Folkmusic, Topical Songs, and the American Left, 1926–1953* in 1996.[34]

The reasons for all these additions and subtractions are not readily apparent from any of Guthrie's writings, but comments made by Moses Asch to folk music fanatic Israel Young may give us some idea of Guthrie's methodology. Asch said Guthrie "would often use the words but change the tune. He'd make two or three versions of the thing 'til the right tune came to him. He always used a folk tune to the words he created." Asch somtimes had a hand in making these changes, even to Guthrie's best-known composition: "I made suggestions. 'This Land Is My Land' [*sic*] and some of the songs from *Songs To Grow On* . . . were worked on right at the studio. He had a concept, and then through discussion it evolved into something."[35] In mentioning "This Land" in conjunction with the *Songs to Grow On* selections, Asch probably refers to the 1947 sessions in particular since Guthrie recorded both these children's songs and the now-standard version of "This Land" around the same time. But with the deaths of Guthrie and Asch, we will never know just exactly the extent of or motivation for any suggested changes.

In time, the 1947 recording became the authoritative text although Guthrie may not have wanted it to achieve this dominance. In fact, several plausible reasons exist for the exclusion of the protest verses in the other recordings that have nothing to do with self-censorship. First, by the time of this first recording for Asch, the relief problem in America had largely disappeared due to the booming postwar economy. So Guthrie may have dropped the verse referring to relief because it no longer had the same relevance to the current situation in America as when he first wrote it. Second, Guthrie often forgot or changed words, depending on his mood and memory. Klein states, "Occasionally Woody might screw up the words or music irretrievably (sometimes he'd actually have trouble remembering which tune went with which set of words) and they'd [Guthrie and Asch] have to start over again."[36] Third, his overall approach does not suggest that any one performance of a song, whether recorded or not, had precedence over any other—just as the folk tradition from which he came never fully respected or acknowledged the authority of any one version of a song and expected all songs to change from performer to performer and even from performance to performance. Guthrie might have thought any version he recorded would stand among several possibilities for the song.

Around the same time as the 1951 Folkways release, the now-standard version of "This Land"—still lyrical and beautiful—began entering America's cultural blood stream from a number of sources. Not surprisingly, the protest verses were mostly forgotten, as was feared by their author. In one of the most arresting moments in Klein's *Woody Guthrie: A Life*, Woody's son Arlo speaks of one particular afternoon when his father came home to the family apartment in Howard Beach from the Greystone Park Hospital where he stayed most of the time due to the ravages of his illness. There, in the apartment's small backyard, his hands trembling uncontrollably from a disease that would eventually kill him, Guthrie taught his young son the two protest verses of the original version of "This Land Is Your Land" and the "Nobody living can ever stop me" verse for fear that if Arlo did not learn them, "no one will remember."[37] Soon after, Arlo began to sing the verse about private property, although this practice did not have much of an impact on the general perception of the song until the late 1960s.[38]

Pete Seeger also points to Arlo's story as evidence of Guthrie's dissatisfaction with the song's presentation. Seeger adds to this story that Guthrie knew schoolchildren were learning only select verses of the song while his other lyrics were ignored, quoting Guthrie as saying to Arlo, "They're singing my song in the schools, but they're not singing all the verses. You write 'em down now."[39] Indeed, one version of Guthrie's song did slowly find its way into America's classrooms.

In the late 1940s and early 1950s, several liberal private schools in the New York City area, such as the Little Red School House and the Brooklyn Community School, began to use some of Guthrie's songs as part of their general music curriculum. Harold Leventhal, who was Guthrie's manager, notes that the teachers and the students in these schools "took these songs with them when they left, particularly 'This Land.'"[40] As a result of being disseminated in these schools and by these teachers, the song became well-known in liberal circles in general. But the song's influence did not end in small private schools; it eventually became known in America's public schools, too.

In 1951, Guthrie, then noticeably experiencing the effects of Huntington's chorea, tape-recorded hundreds of his songs for Howie Richmond, his music publisher. One of these tapes contained a version of "This Land," and Richmond supposedly recognized the potential of the song.[41] Confident of its appeal, he made a version of it available without cost to some scholastic publishers producing songbooks in an attempt to make it a national standard.[42] Klein describes this plan as "a classy, low-key strategy, with the advantage of being both high-minded and astute."[43] Through Richmond's actions, the song gained enough status in the classroom to become known as an alternative anthem. By 1966 Leventhal felt confident enough to say it was "almost a second anthem to thousands of students."[44] One critic echoed and amplified Leventhal's opinion when he wrote, "Plenty of progressive-school pupils already think Woody Guthrie's populist jingle is the national anthem," although he added, "the tune is a little too Barney the Dinosaur-ish."[45] Alan Lomax had a higher opinion of the song, for he used it to open the first annual Music in Our Schools Day in 1975. By this time, the song had become a standard that most children knew and could sing. For a couple of incredible minutes, millions of schoolchildren all across the country joined together on "This Land" through the miracle of live television transmission. But the version used in this momentous broadcast, the same version used throughout the majority of American schoolrooms, left the protest verses unsung and unknown.

Along with the thrum of support due to the appearance of the song in schools came the added weight of commercial publications; for textbooks were not the only source for a hard copy of the lyrics of the shortened version. Throughout the 1950s and 1960s, printed versions of "This Land" appeared in several forms. In 1954, the song first showed up in the pages of *Sing Out!*, the well-known folk music magazine. Those who missed this issue had another opportunity five years later when it appeared in *Reprints from Sing Out! Vol. 1, 1959* and then over three decades later in the *Collected Reprints from Sing Out! Vols. 1–6, 1959–1964*.[46] All three times, the editors noted that the text followed the lyrics sung on the 1951 Folkways album, further proof that this one recorded version by Guthrie was held as the standard. Even when the published lyrics were not transcriptions from this one recording, the words captured generally adhere to it.

In 1956, Guthrie's own music publishers, Ludlow Music / TRO Richmond, finally decided to copyright the lyrics to "This Land" and put them out in sheet music. Two years later, "This Land" also appeared in the songbook *California to the New York Island*, including the entire script and songs from the first of many tributes to Guthrie. Following the March 17, 1956, show at Pythian Hall in New York, the songbook ended with the pretty but politically passive version of "This Land."[47] In 1963, Ludlow Music eventually brought out its own songbook, *Woody Guthrie Folk Songs: A Collection of Songs by America's Foremost Balladeer*, edited by Pete Seeger.[48] Here, "This Land" occupies the prominent opening selection. That same year, in the May 1 issue of *Variety*, Leventhal printed it as part of a greeting from Guthrie to the once controversial and blacklisted Weavers on the occasion of their fifteenth anniversary.[49] No matter how many magazines, songbooks, or other publications included the lyrics of "This Land" until the late 1960s, the shortened version almost always appeared.

This situation also repeats in the work created by those musicians covering Guthrie's song. The first documented instance of a group reproducing this song occurred sometime in the late 1940s or early '50s, when music director Robert DeCormier and his Jewish Young People's Folksingers Chorus began performing it.[50] Since then, a wide array of artists—whose views range across the political spectrum—have sung "This Land" in styles as varied as bluegrass and bop, country and choral.[51] Although some of these performers have revised "This Land," they largely sang and still sing only the popular lyrics in performances. The past omission of the protest verses by artists with close ties to Guthrie—such as Pete Seeger and Ramblin' Jack Elliott—is more surprising than the work produced by more commercially driven singers. These leftist performers do not fear singing controversial material. Actually, they would seem to be eager to include any politically charged verses penned by the man many consider the father of contemporary folk protest.

These omissions do become more understandable when we recognize that the protest verses were available in only three little-known sources until the 1960s: Guthrie's original handwritten lyric sheet, the unissued 1944 Asch recording, and the mimeographed songbook *Ten Twenty-Five Cent Songs by Woody Guthrie*. But none of these sources contained all three of the protest verses. Almost completely unknown and scattered, these lyrics got little notice. In contrast, the shortened version of the song began its slow drumbeat with the Folkways version, its subsequent re-releases, its place in school texts, and its exposure through various publications and a horde of artists' recordings.

As the song's recognition and reputation grew, so did opportunity for criticism, even from left-leaning musicians and writers. The earliest published reaction to "This Land" appears in *The Bosses' Songbook: Songs to Stifle the Flames of Discontent*, a 1959 collection of folk and leftist song parodies. Compiled by folk-style singer Dave Van Ronk and Richard Ellington, these songs poke fun at old-left personnel, such as Pete Seeger, and their positions—particularly those stemming out of some folksingers' past affiliations with the Communist Party and assorted unions. Some of these parodies used such well-known songs as "Wreck of the Old '97" and "Columbus Stockade" as musical structures and even copied a few lines from the originals. Although the preface to this songbook includes the disclaimer that these songs "were done for fun and meant to be sung for fun," some of the works included not only use various folk songs' melodies but also directly parody the ideas expressed in these songs. The book also contains direct parodies of three Guthrie songs. The version of "Jesus Christ" offered here depicts a savior who becomes an avid Marxist and a Judas who becomes a labor spy, while in the "Modern Union Maid," the title character fears radicals enough to stick to both her conservative union and Harry Truman.[52]

The third parody, "This Land Is Their Land," offers a take on America that strangely echoes the viewpoint expressed by Guthrie in the often-omitted lyrics of his song. The first verse of the parody opens with the observation, "This land is their land. It is not our land." It then lists the material goods and comforts the wealthy in America have, concluding that "This land is not for you and me." In the next verse, the focus shifts from a discussion of the rich to the plight of the poor and begins, "As I was walking that endless breadline / My landlord gave me a one-week deadline."[53] The image of want here is similar to that expressed in the sixth verse of the original version of Guthrie's song: "In the shadow of the steeple / By the relief office I saw my people / As they stood hungry." Of course, the author(s) of the parody probably would not have known these lyrics in that they were not readily available to the public at this time.

The parody does not end here. The final verse begins with the lines "So take your slogans and kindly stow it, / If this is our land you'd never know it," which reads as a direct rejoinder to the attitude found in the popular version of "This Land." Here, the song offers an alternative to passive acceptance: "Let's join together and overthrow it."[54] In effect, the parody's last stanza goes beyond simply pointing out some of society's ills and questioning whether "This land was made for you and me," as Guthrie's original version did, and becomes incendiary, advocating revolution. Even without the parody's similarities to the original version of "This Land" or its revolutionary ending, the rest of the lyrics would still contradict the bright vision of America found in the popularized version of Guthrie's song.

Despite any criticism of "This Land," the popular version basically remained unchanged. When Guthrie finally died on October 3, 1967, his earlier fears had definitely been realized—none of three protest verses had ever been released in wide-access recorded or published versions. As it turned out, Guthrie missed by just a few years the resurgence of these verses. Beginning in the latter part of the 1960s, they started to appear in a few publications, performances, and recordings through the efforts of some members of the folk-style community who discovered the exclusion. In a January 1968 article he wrote for the leftist musical journal *Broadside*, Ernie Marrs claims, "So far as I know, the first time anyone sang all six verses of ['This Land'] on the air was when I sang them on KPFA-FM, in Berkeley, California, in the spring of 1960." He adds in the same piece that he confronted Pete Seeger with the omitted verses: "When I came across that page in Woody's old KFVD notebook in 1959, I made a copy of it and showed it to Pete Seeger." Finally, Marrs accuses Seeger of not supporting the use of the verses, even going as far as quoting him as saying, "They're good verses. But the short version's been around so long now, and is so well known, that nobody would believe he wrote these."[55]

But years earlier, in 1961, Seeger had published all of Guthrie's protest verses from "This Land" in *American Favorite Ballads: Tunes and Songs as Sung by Pete Seeger*, although these lyrics did not gain much notoriety by their inclusion in this little-known songbook.[56] In the later months of 1968, perhaps egged on by Marrs's comments, *Sing Out!* (for which Seeger was a member of the editorial advisory board and a columnist) published the two omitted original verses along with two 1954 photographs of Guthrie looking shaggy and disheveled at Washington Square in New York City.[57] Gone is the little hobo bard; in his place appears the protohippie, a biologically but not ideologically damaged forefather of the protest singers of the sixties. These pictures and lyrics strike out from the page, demanding attention. In the final years of the 1960s, Pete Seeger, Arlo Guthrie, and other folk-style singers did begin making the protest verses an essential part of the song again.

The first time one of the lost verses showed up in a major performance occurred at the end of the 1970 Hollywood Bowl memorial concert for Guthrie. As can be heard in a recording of the concert, singer Odetta opens up "This Land" with a slow but powerful slide through one of the popular verses. Later in the song, actor Will Geer jumps in, while Odetta and the other performers back off, and recites a brief but often quoted passage from a speech Guthrie wrote for his opening show on WNEW in December 1944, the same show on which he used "This Land" as a theme song. During a moment of synchronicity, Geer emphasizes the line "I am out to sing songs that will prove to you that this is your world," while the chorus chants the refrain "This land was made for you and me." Then everyone pulls back, and Arlo takes the third and final verse of the evening alone. He sings,

> As I went walking, I saw a sign there.
> And on the sign it said, "No Trespassing."
> But on the other side, it didn't say nothing.
> That side was made for you and me.[58]

This important moment, along with several other songs and readings from both the 1968 Carnegie Hall and 1970 Hollywood Bowl memorial concerts, appears on the 1972 album *A Tribute to Woody Guthrie*, which contains the first instance of any of the song's protest verses being included on a commercially released recording.[59] As with to the 1956 tribute concert, these two memorial shows also found themselves represented in a songbook. In 1972,

Ludlow Music and Woody Guthrie Publications brought out *A Tribute to Woody Guthrie*, which followed the lead of the second concert by including the verse Arlo sang along with the other two protest verses.[60]

During this same period, Pete Seeger and other folk-style performers began adding their own verses to the song in an attempt to represent and comment on the changing problems of America. In a July 1971 article for the *Village Voice*, Seeger notes that he had created numerous verses for the song, such as the following:

> Maybe you been working just as hard as you're able
> And you just got crumbs from the rich man's table
> Maybe you been wondering, is it truth or fable
> This land was made for you and me.

In the same article, Seeger also pointed to other professionals' and amateurs' creative efforts to reshape and to keep current "This Land." He offered an added verse by Jerry J. Smith:

> We've logged the forests, we've mined the mountains
> We've dammed the rivers, but we've built fountains!
> We got tin and plastic, and crowded freeways,
> This land was made for you and me.

These lyrics do not stand alone in pointing out environmental degradation through Guthrie's song. Other new verses created by Seeger that appear in the article do much the same, along with other writers' verses that pointed out additional ills faced by America. Seeger also included two verses in Spanish by Alberto O. Martinez, showing the song's potential for crossing cultural boundaries and reaching an ever changing and multicultural national audience.[61]

Others had already discovered newly created verses and published them. Irwin Silber and Barbara Dane cobbled together a wide range of antiwar songs for inclusion in their 1969 collection, *The Vietnam Songbook*. Within the "Parodies" section, a "GI Vietnam version" of Guthrie's song appeared:

> This land is your land
> But it isn't my land,
> From the Mekong Delta
> To the Pleiku Highland,

When we get shot at
The ARVN flee,
This land was meant for the V.C.![62]

Here, the song's location is shifted from America to Vietnam. With this change comes a new group who has a claim to their own land. In this version, the narrator—the GI—becomes the interloper, the usurper, while the Vietcong become the true owners of their own land. This perspective comes in direct opposition to America's rabidly anti-Communist foreign policy, again proving that Guthrie's song had the ability to shift with the prevailing views of the nation's left and offer commentary on matters beyond America's borders.

The folk-style community seemed to welcome all of these additions, just as long as they were in keeping with the sentiments of the song's creator. Seeger believes "the best thing that could happen to the song would be for it to end up with hundreds of different versions being sung by millions of people who do understand the basic message."[63] Decades before, Guthrie himself acknowledged the need for artists to shift and add to songs so as to keep them current. He writes, "This bringing them up to date is what keeps a folk song a folk song, it says whatever needs to be said, or as much as the law allows, at the time when it needs to be said."[64] The additions mentioned above show how easily his song could be altered and reshaped so as to connect it to contemporary issues and move it further away from the American nationalist jingle it had, in part, become.

Looking back to Seeger's article again, we find not one but two new verses by Country Joe McDonald, who released a Guthrie tribute album called *Thinking of Woody Guthrie* on Vanguard Records in 1969. Here are the verses Seeger included:

As I was walking that ribbon of highway
I heard the buzzing of a hundred chain saws
And the Redwoods falling, and the loggers calling
This land was made for you and me.

As I went walking the oil-filled coastline
Along the beaches fishes were choking
The smog kept rolling, the populations growing
This land was made for you and me.[65]

One year before the publication of this article, McDonald and his group the Fish had become the center of nationwide attention due to their Woodstock performance of the Vietnam protest song "I Feel Like I'm Fixin' to Die Rag" and their signature salute, which involved spelling out the word "fuck" to the great glee of the assembled crowd. As a result, McDonald's voice became synonymous with protest in the late 1960s. Thus, his use of Guthrie's song to include his thoughts on environmental dangers in America brought together two well-known voices of protest. In fact, all the performers who added comments on the ills of 1960s and '70s America to "This Land" helped to keep it current and alive, resulting in the re-energizing of Guthrie's work. These discoveries and additions are not surprising if we look at what was happening during this time in some sectors of popular music.

Beginning in the early 1960s, more and more music that offered criticism or even displayed open hostility towards the status quo in America became available—not only to young people through college radio and little-known recordings but also, although somewhat later, to all ages through mainstream radio stations and well-established recording companies. A major source of this protest came from the pen and voice of Bob Dylan, who himself was greatly influenced by Guthrie's work. But Dylan's protests and interest in Guthrie did not stand alone. Along with Dylan, many other performers—such as Phil Ochs, Tom Paxton, Joan Baez, and Peter, Paul, and Mary—pointed out the injustices they saw around them, using song as their medium, just as Guthrie had done. These artists also often included his songs in their performances and on their recordings.

After the late 1960s and early '70s, songs containing lyrics explicitly protesting establishment values and regulations became, and continue to be, more commonplace than in Guthrie's era. Even in this environment, the once-lost lyrics of "This Land" could have a far-reaching impact, if only to challenge the authority of the popular version. From this time on, the once completely unknown verses did become more accessible in publications, performances, and recordings—providing a counterinfluence to the popular version that continued its steady and unabated drumbeat.

One source of this drive came from Guthrie's music publisher, Ludlow Music / TRO Richmond, which helped in bringing all the lyrics to public notice. The early 1970s saw a change in the sheet music of "This Land" that Ludlow Music put out; for it began to include all the verses of the song, albeit only on the middle-voice pieces, while those for high and low voice continued to include only the popular verses.[66] Beginning in 1963, this firm put out five Woody Guthrie songbooks, of which four contain all the known verses. The inclusion of the three protest verses in *101 Woody Guthrie Songs, Including All the Songs from "Bound for Glory,"* does not surprise since this songbook appeared in conjunction with the release of the United Artists film version of Guthrie's autobiographical novel *Bound for Glory.*[67] The film's soundtrack includes two of the protest verses, which is in keeping with the project's emphasis on Guthrie's leftist views.[68]

Another film project on Guthrie also used the protest verses. The Arlo Guthrie–hosted 1984 documentary *Woody Guthrie: Hard Travelin'* ends with a sing-along jam on "This Land" that overlays images of Guthrie and those interviewed during the course of the film. But what stands out the most here are the lyrics sung. Along with the well-known chorus and the verse that begins "As I roamed and rambled," all three protest verses are included. Arlo and Joan Baez trade off on the verse about private property, while Pete Seeger alone handles the verse mentioning the need for relief. Arlo finishes up with the verse beginning with the line "Nobody living can ever stop me."[69] With the emphasis on these lesser-known verses, the documentary's end focuses on Guthrie's more radical lyrics and brings attention to the song's dissenting voice.

Despite this rediscovery and dissemination of the once-lost protest verses, many recordings and publications of the song still excluded them. One of the most surprising of these instances occurred on the 1988 Grammy-winning album *A Vision Shared: A Tribute to Woody Guthrie and Lead Belly* put out by CBS Records. As performed here by Pete Seeger, Sweet Honey in the Rock, Doc Watson, and the Little Red School House Chorus, "This Land" remains fairly faithful to the version released in 1951, the only change being the repeating of the chorus between all the verses and twice at the end.[70] The continued reinforcement of the popular version left it firmly entrenched in the public mind. Some cultural forces also began shifting and molding the song's meaning by placing it in a variety of contexts.

Soon after the protest lyrics resurfaced, Pete Seeger explained the reasoning behind his belief that they should be put before the public. He writes, "I and others have started singing [the protest verses]. We feel that there is a danger of this song being misinterpreted without these old/new verses being added. The song could even be co-opted by the very selfish interests Woody was fighting all his life."[71] At the time of Seeger's writing, the cultural symbolism of the popular version of the song had already been co-opted. During the late 1960s, both the Ford Motor Company and American Airlines used the verses lauding America in their advertising campaigns, selling their wares while the song played on in seeming acceptance and agreement. Some attempts to appropriate the song have been thwarted, such as when the U.S. Army requested its use as part of their recruiting campaign. Considering their political tendencies, the Guthrie family balked at this proposal; and the plan was never carried out.[72]

Just as commercial and conservative forces have shaped the message of the popular version of "This Land," so have progressive forces. But these lyrics have the potential to offer up a protesting voice, just as the song's original lyrics do. Unlike the original version, the popular version offers this voice in ambiguous language, thus requiring a particular context to release a radical message. A radicalized setting could energize the expurgated version of this song, or any song. In *Minstrels of the Dawn*, Jerome Rodnitzky argues, "Within the subversive, righteous atmosphere that permeated their [the folk-protest singers'] performances, it mattered not what they sang. There, a simple patriotic song like 'God Bless America' could take on the colorings of a radical hymn."[73] A telling and specific example of how context can control the perception of a song as protest comes from the leftist historian Howard Zinn. He notes that during a May 1971 gathering in Washington, DC, to protest the Vietnam War, the police arrested six people who were peacefully walking down the street and singing "America the Beautiful."[74]

Simply presenting the popular version of "This Land" in certain environs could re-establish an effect similar to its original purpose and make it a powerful leftist statement of unity and pride or of environmental protectionism. When Guy Carawan performed it at National Association for the Advancement of Colored People meetings in the 1950s, the song could be heard and sung with the hope that one day America would indeed be "made for you and me."[75] Here, the refrain all at once becomes a question and a demand. More important, sung before this group and in this context, "This Land" offers an idea of revolutionary import in the 1950s: America belongs equally to black and white. Although somewhat less striking than in the last example, even the use of the song in advertisements can offer a progressive agenda. In the 1980s, country singer Loretta Lynn recorded a version that appeared on national radio and television advertisements for the National Wildlife Federation.[76] Placed in this context, the images of "the redwood forest," "golden valley," "diamond deserts," and "wheat fields waving" encourage pride in the American landscape and urge us to work to protect it and the wildlife that inhabit it. In effect, the popular version of the song becomes an environmental rallying cry.

For a more telling example of how trappings surrounding the presentation of the song can twist and shape it in different ways, we can look at "This Land" in the context of the national conventions of America's two dominant political parties. In what might be considered the high point of its use in liberal mainstream politics, the singing of "This Land" immediately followed George McGovern's famous 3 a.m. "Come Home, America" acceptance speech at the 1972 Democratic National Convention in Miami. According to one observer, the song filled the hall and helped make it "come alive with an emotion of oneness" to such a degree that her "feelings of discontent were blotted out by the music and singing."[77] Later, the song even became McGovern's theme song in his failed presidential bid. But who could disagree that the song must have taken on a completely different meaning when the 1960 Republican National Convention featured it, especially considering that Richard Nixon became the party's chosen candidate? Guthrie's political sympathies and Nixon's red-baiting tendencies are incompatible, yet it is doubtful that many at this convention would have known about the politics of the song's author. It is easy to imagine that the overwhelmingly white, Protestant, middle- and upper-class crowd would not hear the "you" of the song as referring to anyone other than Americans very much like themselves.

Even in a political environment that would have completely pleased Guthrie, the song can be interpreted in undesired ways. It could even be seen as a colonialist statement, as an incident involving Pete Seeger in June 1968 testifies. During much of that month, Seeger had been in Washington, DC, staying at Resurrection City, a camp organized by Dr. Martin Luther King as part of his Poor People's Campaign. One night there, Seeger participated in a sing-along that had a strange turn concerning "This Land." He writes that when he and singer/organizer Jimmy Collier began singing it, "Henry Crowdog of the Sioux Indian delegation came up and punched his finger in Jimmy's chest, 'Hey, you're both wrong. It belongs to me.'" Then, Collier stopped and questioned whether the song should go on. At this point, "a big grin came over Henry Crowdog's face. 'No, it's okay. Go ahead and sing it. *As long as we are all down here together to get something done*'" [emphasis in original].[78]

This incident affected Seeger noticeably. Bernice Reagon, who is Seeger's friend and a founding member of the Freedom Singers, remembers his reaction and even expresses a theory about it:

> That song was the basis of the American dream—coming in and building a country, freedom, blah, blah. I felt that in '67 and '68, all that got smashed to smithereens. . . . I remember Pete talking constantly about that exchange with . . . Collier around Chief Crow Dog, and how he then had a hard time doing "This Land Is Your Land." It felt like he didn't know *what* to sing . . . he was not sure what his function was.[79]

Not only could the "very selfish interests Woody was fighting all his life" that Seeger mentions make a mockery of the song, but history itself could make the song tell a lie—or at least point out a promise not kept and an entire people displaced. Somehow, Seeger did find a function for himself and the song, although he had to add an extra verse written by Cappy Israel to do so:

> This land is your land, but it once was my land
> Before we sold you Manhattan Island
> You pushed my nation to the reservation,
> This land was stole by you from me.[80]

After singing this verse, Seeger would tell the story about the problems the song sparked in Resurrection City. Here, Seeger recontextualizes the song by adding the above verse that strains against some of the other unity verses and by explaining how some of the song's sentiments can easily be seen as exclusionary. Considering the song's heavy use in the past decades as nationalistic jingle, a concentrated effort is still needed to push the song in a direction more in keeping with its creator's intentions, especially since Guthrie never had a chance to perform the song after its rise—or explain his intentions in writing it.

Even if Guthrie were alive today, it would be impossible for him to control the meaning of "This Land." Once an artist releases a song into the blood stream of America, it can flow anywhere and be used in many different ways. As music critic Greil Marcus notes, "Good art is always dangerous, always open-ended. Once you put it out in the world you lose control of it; people will fit it into their lives in all sorts of different ways."[81] These myriad interpretations may not match the original sentiment the artist intended for the work. Not only songs but even more contemporary artists' own images can and have been appropriated. During the 1984 presidential campaign, the Reagan re-election juggernaut briefly used Bruce Springsteen and his song "Born in the USA" for its own nationalistic purposes, completely ignoring the singer's politics and misrepresenting the song's lyrics—particularly the ironic chorus. Eventually, Springsteen felt driven to make a very public effort to regain control of his image and his song.[82] Unlike Springsteen, Guthrie did not have the opportunity to combat the shifting politics of "This Land." He remained hospitalized, with no hope of recovery, from the mid-1950s until his death in 1967. Thus, he had little or no control over the song's presentation or contextualization during the time period when it first began to flow into the consciousness of America.

The reason for the continued muting of the protest verses may not be due to the lack of access to these lyrics but rather to the American public's inability to deal adequately with the abuses that Guthrie documented in them. English songwriter Billy Bragg believes, "One of the problems America has about Woody is he don't beat around the bush—he looks America in the eye and says what he says. And these are questions America cannot bring itself to focus on today, let alone in the Thirties; the questions he asked have still not been answered."[83] The final question of the original version of "This Land" remains as relevant today as when Guthrie first put it to paper back in 1940—and just as difficult to answer.

Given that Guthrie's comments, criticisms, and questions continue to be applicable to contemporary America, then those encapsulated in the little-known protest verses of his most popular song should be brought more forcefully to the public's attention. Just as all songs, all texts, remain malleable, so does the seemingly intractable popular form of "This Land." The mere act of acknowledging all of Guthrie's verses changes "This Land" forever. Realizing how the song has come to us, how it has been changed over time, gives "This Land" new meaning. It becomes a song with a history rather than a set of lyrics to mumble through at some public occasion. Realizing that the song has shifted from its beginning may provide those who care about Guthrie's art and his complete vision the impetus to change the song once again. Simply because one of its many voices has shouted down the others does not mean that this situation is permanent—the voices of the other verses can be heard more clearly. Their volume merely needs adjusting through their inclusion in more performances and publications so that they may gain a more complete hearing—creating a situation where one version no longer has dominant status over any other and allowing the American public the opportunity to choose for itself which lyrics it wants to sing.

CHAPTER TWO

Busted, Disgusted, Down and Out

DOCUMENTING THE STORIES OF
AMERICA'S AGRICULTURAL WORKERS

Sometime after first writing "God Blessed America" in early 1940, Woody Guthrie returned to his original lyric sheet, transformed the song into "This Land Is Your Land," and added this phrase at the bottom of the page: "All you can write is what you see."[1] Considering his many experiences and travels, he had much to write about by the end of the Great Depression. During his youth in Oklahoma and Texas, he saw the results of boom/bust farm economies and the damage wrought by drought and dust storms. In the mid-1930s, he moved west along with thousands of migrant workers from the Southwest and other regions—those who looked to California as the promised land but who too often found hardship and repression there. Much of what he saw during this time, Guthrie remembered and recorded in song for others to encounter. He writes, "My eyes has been my camera taking pictures of the world and my songs has been messages that I tried to scatter across the back sides and along the steps of the fire escapes and on the window sills and through the dark halls."[2] If we look deeply into his songs from the mid-1930s to the early '40s, a telling document emerges of the lives and experiences of Dust Bowlers, tenant farmers, and migrant workers who found themselves abused by natural disasters, economic hardships, and social prejudice.

The bulk of his songs documenting the struggles of these poor southwestern and southern peoples do what music critic Nicholas Dawidoff believes all good country songs do; they tell "the experiences of people who weren't often written up in the newspapers."[3] Much of Guthrie's work moves beyond generally reporting the everyday experiences of these people and specifically documents their hardships from a personal perspective. In fact, the emotional power of many of his songs often comes from the dramatic experiences and events that impulsed their creation as expressed through a first-person narrative voice. In his work, we encounter farmers suffering from scorching heat and black clouds of dust, dealing with low prices for wheat or cotton. We meet those who fled west looking for escape but who often found a bitter welcome in California's fields. In coming to understand these people and their experiences, Guthrie followed his own advice: "The best thing [to do] is to sort of vaccinate yourself right into the big streams and blood of the people."[4] In his songs and other writings, he used the understanding this direct exposure gave him to explain their lives to the whole of America. He acknowledges this drive in a letter to Alan Lomax in 1940: "All I know how to do . . . is to just keep a plowing right on down the avenue watching what I can see and listening to what I can hear and trying to learn about everybody I meet every day and try to make one part of the country feel like they know the other part."[5] Guthrie's firsthand experiences with and understanding of Dust Bowlers, tenant farmers, and migrants gave him insight into what was happening to those not readily or honestly known by the rest of America. Instead of silently witnessing the lives of the "busted, disgusted, down and out" farm workers in America, he captured in song for all time what he saw and heard.[6]

Since a number of the songs Guthrie heard as a child contained sympathy for agricultural workers and their hardships, it does seem natural that his writing would include some related social commentary. During his early years, he heard the old populist-flavored folk song "The Farmer Is the Man," with its praise of the farmer and its condemnation of greedy merchants, lawyers, and bankers. He also heard "Pictures from Life's Other Side," which details the burdens of the rural poor and contrasts them to the bounties of the rich.[7] Even with his exposure to and appreciation for these folk songs and others like them, many of his early efforts at songwriting show surprisingly few signs of social consciousness of or underclass empathy with agricultural workers.

Songs such as those found in Guthrie's 1935 mimeographed songbook *Alonzo M. Zilch's Own Collection of Original Songs and Ballads* focus mainly on western-flavored tales of heartache or joy, farmers and cowboys. Yet a few of these early songs do include moments where his inchoate underclass sympathies flash through. His song "Old Rachel" includes a few evocative lines illustrating a farmer's uncertain future. In the first verse, the narrator laments to "Old Rachel" that "We'll starve to death together," then shifts into the reasons behind his dire predictions:

> My wheat wont stand this weather.
> When the harvest days are over—
> We'll turn the property over
> To the bank.

A quick line in the second stanza—"The rain has killed the cotton"—also points out that the wheat harvest is not the farmer's only problem. But the song's final verse has him reversing these dark predictions and descriptions by optimistically telling Rachel, "Prosperity is upon us, / So get yo'self in—the harness." This line also adds a comic touch through surprise that Rachel is a plow mule, not a woman. Together, the added optimism and comic turn at the end manage to undercut the farmer's earlier worries. In a few other moments in this songbook, Guthrie uses humor to express social criticism, especially in the sarcasm-tinted "Can't Do What I Want To" and the imaginative "If I Was Everything on Earth."[8] But as in "Old Rachel," this humor often ellipses the underlying political commentary in the songs. In future efforts, he was better able to use a humorous line or ending to help emphasize his message instead of diffusing it. This change in his writing occurred about the same time he began creating songs that came out of his own and others' experiences in the Dust Bowl region of the Great Plains.

From 1930 until 1941, a large part of the nation Guthrie describes so beautifully in "This Land" found itself in desperate conditions. But this disaster did not strike suddenly; it crept up slowly and covered the land. During World War I, much of the Great Plains faced an exploding demand for wheat, the area's dominant crop. Eventually, Herbert Hoover, then acting as wartime food administrator, helped set the price of wheat at over two dollars a bushel, an all-time high. In response, farmers increased both their wheat acreage and their output. After the war, decreased demand hit these same farmers hard due to the debt incurred in expanding their operations. To keep up with their bills, these farmers continued a high rate of production, hoping increasing volume would compensate for dropping prices. This strategy resulted in some success for several years. Guthrie even refers to the wheat farmers' situation in the 1920s in the opening verse of his "Talking Dust Bowl":

> Back in nineteen twenty seven,
> I had a little farm and I called that heaven.
> Well, the price was up and the rain came down,
> And I hauled my crops in to town.
> I got the money, bought clothes and groceries,
> Fed the kids, and raised a family.[9]

Unlike the song's assertion, the unit price of wheat actually continued its general downward slide throughout the twenties. By the harvest of 1931, wheat ended up only bringing around thirty cents a bushel. Then beginning in the fall of that year, the ecological reality of the plains again reasserted itself.

For millennia before the 1930s, the entire region but especially the southern plains experienced periods of drought and dust storms. Even after the grassland made way for the farmlands, the area experienced many dry seasons—the last great one then having occurred in the 1890s. Between the years of drought, crops greened and grew as farmers experienced some prosperity. Then in the early 1930s, the rains failed to come and record-high temperatures baked the region, killing much of the wheat. The combined effects of overplowing and drought allowed the unhampered winds to strip the precious topsoil from the earth and send it swirling across the southern plains in great clouds of dust.

During the so-called "Dirty Thirties," artists such as photographers Arthur Rothstein and Dorothea Lange, painter Alexander Hogue, and filmmaker Pare Lorentz worked to document the ravages brought on by the drought and dust storms. But these artists were not alone in their attempts to capture the destruction going on in the southern plains. From 1929 to early 1936, Guthrie lived in this dry and dusty land, providing him an intimate knowledge of the area and its people. In particular, he resided in the panhandle region of Texas in the little town of Pampa. Although never in the heart of the Dust Bowl, this town always remained well within its body. Here, Guthrie saw the desolation and destruction around him and eventually decided his own surroundings deserved to be documented in song. He writes, "There on the Texas plains right in dead center of the dust bowl, with the oil boom over and the wheat blowed out and the hard-working people just stumbling about, bothered with mortgages, debts, bills, sickness, worries of every blowing kind, I seen there was plenty to make up songs about."[10] Many of these songs eventually appeared on the 1940 Victor album *Dust Bowl Ballads*, his first commercial recording. Oklahoma folklorist Guy Logsdon calls this album "with the exception of some imaginative exaggeration, an accurate historical depiction overall, through music, of the Dust Bowl," then adds, "It is doubtful that any historical period has had comparable folk response."[11] These songs and others Guthrie wrote during this period accurately document one of the worst ecological disasters of the twentieth century and its effect on the people living in this region.

At first, these dust storms did not ravage Pampa during the early 1930s as they did other towns in Texas, New Mexico, Colorado, Kansas, and Oklahoma—although some small storms did come through, leaving a thin powder perpetually hanging in the air. Matt Jennings, who was Guthrie's friend, bandmate, and even brother-in-law, says, "We had dust come up every morning, about ten or eleven o'clock in the morning. You could look straight at the sun on a perfectly clear day, and it looked like a big orange up there."[12] This dust did not remain in the air; it settled on furniture, clothes, and food. Nothing remained untouched. Although these problems were not easily endured, the worst was yet to come.

On April 14, 1935, sometimes called "Black Sunday," the greatest dust storm of all raged across the majority of the southern plains. The dust rose up in a great wave thousands of feet high, swept over fields and towns, blotting out the sun and covering the land in darkness. Nothing could keep the dust out of homes; it crept in through every crevice until it thickened the air. According to Guthrie, "It got so dark that you couldn't see your hand before your face. You couldn't see anybody in the room. You could turn on an electric light bulb, a good strong electric light bulb in a little room . . . and [it] would look just about like a cigarette a burning."[13] During the storm, his family did their best to shut out the dust by caulking doors and windows with newspapers; when this strategy failed, they placed wet cloths across their faces to protect themselves from breathing in the dust.[14] For days following the event of April 14, townspeople throughout the region, soon to be known as the "Dust Bowl," swept and cleaned as best they could, trying to remove the dirt from their homes and the memory of the great storm from their minds. It must have struck some resilient spot in Guthrie's imagination; for soon afterward, he immortalized the storm in his first complete documentary song.

A heavy black dust cloud blots out the sun over the Texas panhandle and threatens to overtake a lone automobile, 1936. Photograph by Arthur Rothstein. Courtesy of the Prints and Photographs Division of the Library of Congress.

Using as a musical linchpin the melody from Andrew Jenkins's "Billy the Kid," Guthrie captured his thoughts on the great dust storm in a song he alternatively called "Dusty Old Dust" and "So Long, It's Been Good to Know You." His narrator begins with the line, "I've sung this song, but I'll sing it again" and presents the song as a story being told and retold, as a form of verbal history. He also connects us to time and place by adding "In the month of April, the county called Gray." Finally, he tells us "what all of the people there say" and shifts into the song's well-known chorus:

> So long! It's been good to know you.
> So long! It's been good to know you.
> So long! It's been good to know you.
> This dusty old dust is a gettin' my home,
> And I've got to be drifting along.

In the next verse, we get the narrator's only description of the storm itself. He says,

> The dust storm hit, and it hit like thunder
> It dusted us over, it dusted us under
> It blocked out the traffic, it blocked out the sun.
> And straight for home all the people did run.[15]

Considering the impetus for the song, this brief illustration of the storm itself surprises; but Guthrie does not seem to be trying for pure description of the dust here. Instead, he focuses on residents' reactions to the storm and their reasons for saying, "So long."

The first reaction he details concerns people's religious fears. In the third verse, the narrator touches upon the apocalyptic dread this event provoked in residents: "We talked of the end of the world."[16] During a spoken intro-ductory piece for "So Long" made during a 1940 recording for the Library of Congress, Guthrie voices the people's fear of the storm as the wrath of God upon a villainous race: "This is the end, this is the end of the world. People ain't been living right. The human race ain't been treating each other right, been robbing each other in different ways, with fountain pens, guns, having wars, and killing each other and shooting around. So the feller who made this world he's worked up this dust storm."[17] These kinds of sentiments do not seem to have originated in Guthrie's imagination, for many who experienced the ravages of Black Sunday also mention the religious fears this storm evoked. Detailing similar but even more heightened fears, Clella Schmidt (who lived in Spearman, Texas, during the Great Depression) recalls the reaction of a frightened young female neighbor. Before the storm of April 14th came, Clella's family tried to pick up this woman and her baby. Just as they got to her house, the dust storm hit. The young woman then became hysterical, even going as far to suggest she "kill the baby and herself because it was the end of the world and she didn't want to face it alone." Luckily, Clella's father, through the quoting of Bible verses, convinced the woman that the end was not near.[18] As Guthrie's lyrics suggest and this story confirms, the fear of God and his judgment firmly embedded itself in those experiencing the worst the Dust Bowl had to offer.

The song also depicts some Dust Bowlers' attitude towards matrimony. In the fourth verse, the narrator relates how "sweethearts sat in the dark and sparked" and how "they hugged and kissed in that dusty old dark." Despite their passion, "instead of marriage they talked like this," and then the song again shifts into the good-bye chorus.[19] Thomas Alfred Tripp, in a 1940 article in *Christian Century*, offers much the same claim. In discussing an unnamed county seat in the southern plains, he writes, "The brighter unmarried professional women between the ages of 25 and 40" do not wed because the group "among whom they might have found husbands under normal conditions have moved away." Many of the men Tripp talked to in this same town also blamed the Depression for their lack of a mate; and in fact, marriages throughout America decreased during the 1930s.[20] But even as this verse points to a historical truth, it also contains the least cutting humor in the song. Unfortunately in 1950, when Guthrie himself bowdlerized "So Long" for the musical group the Weavers to record, he not only kept this verse but made the rest of the song revolve around the narrator's impending marriage. In discussing this later version, Joe Klein writes, "It became a perky love song, with little of the humor or bite—and none of the dust—of the original."[21]

In the rest of the original version, there is plenty of bite, especially stemming from another and more dominant theme—religious opportunism. With the seeming apocalyptic nature of the dust storms, many people felt the need to get a little religion. The last two verses of "So Long" make some comic jabs at Dust Bowl preachers, even suggesting they used the storms to get people into church and then to get money out of them. In the fifth verse, Guthrie writes,

> The telephone rang, and it jumped off the wall,
> And that was the preacher a-making his call.
> He said, "Kind friend, this may be the end;
> You got your last chance at salvation from sin."[22]

Although these lyrics do not expressly condemn this preacher, in another version of this verse there can be no doubt when the preacher says in the last line, "I've got a cut rate on salvation and sin."[23] Although unfair to accuse all southwestern preachers of cashing in on the fear the storms aroused, some churches did do a thriving business after the dust clouds hit the southern plains.[24] In particular, longtime Oklahoma resident Caroline Henderson noted on March 8, 1936 that "one village church reported forty people in attendance on one of the darkest and most dangerous of the recent dusty Sundays."[25]

In verse six, Guthrie continues his attack on preachers. Once the parishioners arrive and "jam" and "pack" the churches, the story takes an interesting twist. Because "that dusty old dust storm blowed so black, / The preacher could not read a word of his text," although he does manage to take up collection just before skipping town and leaving the dust and his congregation behind.[26] Actually, some preachers did leave due to the dust. In Grant County, Kansas, a Church of God preacher left his post. According to a local newspaper, he said, "We feel it is advisable to get out of this dust bowl for our health's sake."[27] Just as the fictional Preacher Casey did in John Steinbeck's *The Grapes of Wrath*, some Holiness and Pentecostal preachers left the dust and drought of the southern plains behind and traveled to California. Some even set up new churches there.[28]

In "Dust Storm Disaster," also known as "The Great Dust Storm," Guthrie again brings us his thoughts on Black Sunday, although in a less satirically based manner than in "So Long." Other contrasts appear. First, this song examines and exhibits in great detail the dust storm itself and the area it affected. Second, Guthrie focuses more on the reaction of the song's narrator than that of all Dust Bowlers. As a result of this first-person perspective, the story appears more realistic than in "So Long." In this unity between fact and fiction, the two songs' main similarity appears—especially when Guthrie acknowledges his own experiences. Reflecting on "So Long" years later, he divulges that some of the incidents detailed in the song came from his own life. In an end note to one version of the song, he writes, "This actually happened in Pampa, Gray County, Texas, April 14, 1935. I was there. The storm was as black as tar and as big as an ocean. It looked like we was done for."[29] In a similar comment on a lyric sheet of "The Great Dust Storm," he writes, "This is a song about the worst dust storm in anybody's history book, and I was in what I claim the very center of it, the town of Pampa, Gray County, Texas, sixty miles right north of Amarillo, along towards sundown on the afternoon of April 14, 1935."[30] Thus, Guthrie boldly acknowledges the autobiographical nature of both songs and earnestly tries to establish his expertise on the Dust Bowl. As a result, we understand that these songs do not only stem from his imagination but also reflect his own history and, in effect, that of other people living in the Dust Bowl.

Much as "So Long" did, the opening of "Dust Storm Disaster" embeds the story in time and place with the lines "On the fourteenth day of April / Of nineteen thirty-five" before announcing the driving event behind the tale: "There struck the worst of dust storms / That ever filled the sky." In

DOCUMENTING THE STORIES OF AMERICA'S AGRICULTURAL WORKERS

the second verse, the narrator says the dust storm appears "death-like black" as "through our mighty nation / It left a dreadful track." Verse three then offers an interesting predecessor to another moment in one of Guthrie's songs. In lines reminiscent of those in the chorus of "This Land," the narrator here draws us a portion of America, giving us a general outline of the area affected by the dust storms:

> From Oklahoma City
> To the Arizona line
> Dakota and Nebraska
> To the lazy Rio Grande.

In other verses, he looks inside his map and points out that the destruction touched "Albuquerque and Clovis / And old New Mexico," "old Dodge City, Kansas," and "Denver, Colorado." Through these comments, the narrator gives us his estimate of the region affected by the "Dust Storm Disaster." Although his dimensions exceed the true boundaries of the Dust Bowl, they do generally cover the area hit hardest by drought. Unlike in "This Land," the very earth itself suffers in this song. The "wheat fields waving" actually disappear beneath "the dust clouds rolling." After the storm blows through, "Where the wheatfields they had grown, / Was now a rippling ocean / Of dust the wind had blown."[31]

In the fourth verse, the narrator shifts from noting the destruction of the entire region to expressing the fear around him. He says, "It fell across our city / Like a curtain of black rolled down." In the next line, he more directly includes himself among those experiencing the dust storm: "We thought it was our judgment / We thought it was our doom." Later, in verse ten, the song again touches on religious-based fears and uses much the same language as in "So Long" but shifts the focus away from the narrator and to the other denizens of the Dust Bowl: "They thought the world had ended, / And they thought it was their doom."[32] Again, Guthrie plays on the theme of Black Sunday being a sure sign of the Apocalypse.

Moving away from religious-based fears but back to language unifying him with other Dust Bowlers, the narrator again includes himself among those who suffered the disaster by the use of "we" in verse five. When the radio reports about the "wild and windy actions / Of this great mysterious storm," he says, "we listened with alarm." The narrator continues to relate the events through his eyes in verse nine, giving more particulars concerning the toll the storm inflicts on others:

> Our relatives were huddled
> Into their oil-boom shacks,
> And the children they were crying
> As it whistled through the cracks.[33]

By using the word "our," the narrator again connects himself to the events in the Dust Bowl; but this time he moves away from his own personal experience to that of his family, also victims of the storm. In essence, we get to see an interlocking group of people's miseries. The language Guthrie uses causes the storm to cease being an event that happens to someone else, bringing it home and making it personal.

At other points in the song, the narrator removes himself from the narrative and brings in others to comment on the storm. Using "they" to signify various and unknown speakers, he has people "From Albuquerque and Clovis / And old New Mexico" report "it was the blackest / That ever they had saw." Again in verse eight, other Dust Bowl residents, this time "From Denver, Colorado," are heard from, telling us that the storm "blew so strong, / They thought that they could hold out," although "They did not know how long." Others' stories are brought in, but they give even less hope:

> In old Dodge City, Kansas,
> The dust had rung their knell,
> And a few more comrades sleeping
> On top of old Boot Hill.

These comments work to substantiate the story and support what the narrator tells us, thereby reinforcing his particular tales of woe. No matter what perspective offered here, all the verses document the harsh reality created by the blowing dust. After the storm has passed, the residents then survey the full extent of the damage: "When we looked out next morning / We saw a terrible sight." Wheat fields are missing, covered up by the dust. But the dust does not limit itself to the crops: "It covered up our fences, / It covered up our barns, / It covered up our tractors."[34]

With so many people's homes and other possessions buried by the dust and their fields devastated, some decided to escape. More than once,

Guthrie notes this push away from the Dust Bowl region. In the last verse of one version of "Dust Storm Disaster," the narrator reports the residents' final reaction to the storm:

> We loaded our jalopies
> And piled our families in,
> We rattled down that highway
> To never come back again.[35]

These lyrics resemble those found in an alternative ending to "So Long": "Most everybody they took to the road, / They lit down the highway as fast as could go."[36] This image of people fleeing the southern plains appears at the end of many of Guthrie's Dust Bowl songs. But all the reason for flight did not stem from the storms; one came from an illness the dust brought.

From the dirt in the air, some people (especially children and the elderly) became ill or even died from what locals called "dust pneumonia," a respiratory pneumoconiosis caused by accumulation of dust in the lungs.[37] Guthrie knew about this disease, in part, because his own younger sister Mary Jo had a mild case of it.[38] Just as he did with much of what he experienced and saw in the Dust Bowl, Guthrie wrote a song about the illness called "Dust Pneumonia Blues." Again, he involves the narrator in the action—or sickness in this case. He begins with a lamentation, "I got that dust pneumony, pneumony in my lung." Despite his announced illness and the doctor's prognosis, "you ain't got long, not long," the narrator still proclaims, "I'm a gonna sing this dust pneumony song."[39]

Considering the very real dangers dust pneumonia presented, Guthrie gives this song a humorous focus, albeit a dark one. In the third stanza, he takes a gentle dig at the blue yodeler and the first country-western legend, Jimmie Rodgers, who suffered from tuberculosis. The narrator says, "There ought to be some yodeling in this song / But I can't yodel for the rattlin' in my lung." In an alternative version of the song, he gives an even more striking reason for his singing limitations: "Now when I sing this Dust Pneumonia song / It don't sound good, 'cause I only use one lung." Other verses also use humor in discussing this illness. In a joking misery-loves-company line, the narrator acknowledges that his sweetheart "loves me 'cause she's got the dust pneumony too."[40] At the end of the best-known version of "Dust Pneumonia Blues," he even includes an old Dust Bowl joke: "Down in Texas my gal fainted in the rain / I throwed a bucket of dirt in her face to bring her back again."[41] By using downhome humor, the narrator works to undercut his suffering even as he offers an earthy resistance to the misery the dust created.

Although they often include humor, Guthrie's songs of the southern plains do not offer an optimistic vision. The dust comes and the preachers run, lungs clog, and hope sometimes vanishes. Everyone living in Pampa, in the Texas panhandle, and in the greater Dust Bowl region during the 1930s to some extent experienced the hardships engendered by the drought and the dust. In his Dust Bowl songs, Guthrie wanted to reproduce these people's stubborn resistance to defeat in the face of one of America's greatest ecological disasters. Nowhere is this defiance found in more abundance than in "Dust Can't Kill Me." Here, his narrator lists all the destruction that the storms have wrought: they "killed my baby," "killed my family," and "might kill my wheat." But all this death does not crush him; for at the end of all these verses, he proclaims, "But it can't kill me, Lord, / And it can't kill me."[42] Through his lyrics, Guthrie explores the hardships and privations, the humor and defiance of the residents of the Dust Bowl. Taken together, these images, descriptions, and denunciations do make a great document of the region's happenings and its people's experiences—all shaped through Guthrie's imagination but true in essence and grittily so.

As Guthrie asserts in many of the songs, the drought, the dust storms, and their accompanying burdens did drive some people out of the southern plains. But these ex–Dust Bowl denizens did not make up the majority of the people heading west. No more than a quarter of those living within the borders of this region eventually left, and one sociologist even asserts that fewer than sixteen thousand of these Dust Bowlers actually resettled in California.[43] Yet the mistaken idea that all or most of the migrants traveling to this state came from the Dust Bowl did hold wide sway. Even Carey McWiliams, an informed observer of the labor situation in California, states that the greater portion of the migrants to his state during the 1930s came "from the stricken dust-bowl areas."[44] The fact remains that the majority who left Oklahoma during this time period formerly resided in the eastern, non–Dust Bowl portion of the state. They were joined in this westward journey by those who came from other cotton country in eastern Texas, northwestern Arkansas, and southeastern Missouri. Guthrie briefly suggests this mix in "Dust Bowl Refugee" in the lines "From the Southland and the drouthland / Come the wife and kids and me."[45] The dust did not drive these people from their homes (although drought did provide a strong push for some), just as not all those who left the southern plains did so because of the harsh environmental conditions there. Many of these people were driven west by the hardships of and changes to cotton-tenant farming, which Guthrie also documents in song.

Just as wheat farmers had, cotton farmers overproduced during the twenties and thirties, resulting in price depression. During World War I, cotton brought in almost thirty-five cents a pound. By 1932, the price per pound of cotton had plummeted to only around five cents. Even before the Depression hit, cotton's low price received commentary and criticism in song. Written by Bob Miller and Emma Dermer in 1928, "Eleven-Cent Cotton and Forty-Cent Meat" points out the lack of parity in the price of the cotton that farmers sold and the cost of goods that they bought. The song, which Guthrie knew and sang, offers detail after detail of poverty and hardship, with each verse ending in the couplet, "No use talkin', any man's beat / With 'leven-cent cotton and forty-cent meat."[46] With cotton prices swinging between five cents and twelve cents for much of the 1930s, meat remained difficult to come by for cotton farmers. In Macon County, Georgia, in the summer of 1937, one cotton tenant told sociologist Paul Taylor and photographer Dorothea Lange that it had become such a rarity, "A piece of meat in the house would like to scare these children of mine to death."[47] Already stretched to their limits, many small farmers in the Southwest and the South could not stay in business due to low prices for their cotton crops and the general misery of the 1930s. Those who could least endure these burdens were tenant farmers.

Although large-scale cotton production only came to the Southwest during the early 1900s, this region quickly caught up to the South in terms of tenant farmers. In the cotton regions of Oklahoma and Texas, tenants made up 60 percent of all farm operators by 1930.[48] With this growth in tenancy came an increase in poverty. Never an easy proposition, cotton tenancy became more crippling than ever during the Depression. One sharecropper in this region, with a wife and five children, talked to Taylor and Lange about his hardships: "There's lots of ways to break a man down. In 1934 I give a year's work for $56.16 sharecropping 16 acres of bottom land in Love County, Texas. Had to leave 4 to 6 bales of cotton standing in the field, with not a mattress in the house and we couldn't gin our own cotton to make one. I got my brother-in-law to give me the money to get the gas to bring me back from Love County."[49] Many of the southwestern tenants were not sharecroppers, the least lucrative form of tenant farming. Since many had their own horse or mule teams and farming implements, they were share or even cash tenants—meaning that they could keep much of their crops or merely pay rent on the lands they farmed. But sharecroppers had to rent both the land they farmed and the tools and animal teams they used. Sharecroppers also bought food, clothing, and furnishings on credit given against their portion of the crop. Some ended up owing more than their share brought in, leaving them in debt to the landlord and compounding their miseries.

After the Civil War, tenant farming in the South slowly but steadily began its rise. By 1935, over 1.8 million tenant farmers worked the southern fields.[50] More so in the South than the Southwest, American farmers found themselves working other people's land for little pay, especially if they were sharecroppers. At the beginning of the Depression, nearly eight hundred thousand southern tenant farmers were sharecroppers, with an almost even split between blacks and whites.[51] But the institution offered no real hope of advancement, as Federal Emergency Relief Administration's chief investigator Lorena Hickok notes: "The truth is that the rural South never has progressed beyond slave labor. Their whole system has been built up on labor that could be obtained for nothing or for next to nothing. When their slaves were taken away, they proceeded to establish a system of peonage that was as close to slavery as it possibly could be and included Whites as a well as Blacks. That's all a tenant farmer is—or has been, up to the present time—a slave." She also argued that this system often resulted in a "situation where half-starved Whites and Blacks struggle in competition for less to eat than my dog gets at home, for the privilege of living in huts that are infinitely less comfortable than his kennel."[52] Although overstating the case here, for many farm laborers' situations were better than any slave's, Hickok does correctly point out that in general the southern tenant system left its workers with little to show for their labors.

Although neither he nor his father farmed, Guthrie learned of the cotton farmers' trials and tribulations from his encounters with them in his youth and his travels. He grew up in the town of Okemah, a southeast Oklahoma community that for all its oil-boom energy was still surrounded by prime cotton country. From the high porch of one of his childhood homes, he could "see the white strings of new cotton bales and a whole lot of men and women and kids riding into town on wagons piled double-sideboard-full of cotton, driving under the funny shed at the gin, and driving back home again on loads of cotton seed."[53] In an autobiographically based song called "High Balladree," he mentions having learned of cotton and other important Oklahoma staples from Okemah's residents: "At a drunk barbershop where your boots I did shine / I heard about cotton and cattle and booze."[54]

Guthrie also learned about the plight of tenant farmers from his travels through parts of the cotton region in Oklahoma and Arkansas during the early 1940s. The cotton farmers he met during this tour knew that they were being unfairly treated. Years before, in 1934, some tenants in Arkansas organized the Southern Tenant Farmers Union (STFU) to offset this abuse. The group even had its own bard in the form of John Handcox, an African-American sharecropper, organizer, and singer. One song he wrote and performed was "Raggedy Raggedy," with its stirring descriptions of the miserable conditions faced by tenant farmers. In the first four verses, its narrator tells us that since "We don't get nothing for our labor" the tenants end up "raggedy," "hungry," "homeless," and "landless." In addition, the narrator says, "the planters don't 'low us to raise" cows, hogs, or corn. Altogether, these conditions and restrictions leave them "So pitiful, pitiful as we, / Just as pitiful as pitiful can be."[55] By 1939, this song and the union's activities had spread beyond Arkansas; for the STFU had a membership of thirty-five thousand and chapters in Oklahoma, Missouri, Tennessee, Mississippi, and Alabama. In particular, the Oklahoma branch of the organization had more than seventy-five hundred members by 1935.[56] Guthrie knew well of these burgeoning union members' struggles, for he praises their efforts and Handcox's songs in particular in the radical songbook *Hard Hitting Songs for Hard-Hit People.*[57]

Using what he knew about cotton tenants, Guthrie added his voice to those discussing the hardships they faced. In "Down in Oklayhoma," he specifically notes the abundance of cotton in his home state and its resulting heartaches. He writes, "Cotton sprouts up from every post / Down in Oklayhoma" but then also adds in the last lines "Everybody I know goes in the hole / Down in Oklayhoma."[58] Using a more specific image in the song "I'll Say It's Hard Times," this narrator says, "My brother's a-havin' a hard time" because "He's been a-pullin' that cotton sack," resulting in "debt up to his neck."[59] Although the hardships of cotton farming alluded to in these songs characterize that experienced by many during the Depression, it is important to note that the cotton farmers Guthrie traveled with and whose stories he knew best came from Oklahoma, Texas, and Arkansas—the same three states where the majority of agricultural workers who migrated to California during the Depression originated.

Although singing of the hardships that cotton farmers faced in general, Guthrie spent more time and energy attacking the institution of sharecropping in particular. Aware of the adversity facing sharecroppers from his time in Oklahoma and Texas and from the stories displaced persons in California told, he denounced the practice in song and prose. In 1939, he wrote his earliest specific comment on these farmers' plight in the little-known "Sharecropper Song." His narrator says, "Folks need to work but it ain't worth cropping / Cain't pay for seed way prices are dropping," again pointing out how decreasing farm prices adversely affected farmers. In the opening verse, the narrator sits "around my cabin door" asking the listener, "Ain't it a shame we got to live so pore?" He then shifts into fantasy about food. But he imagines no elaborate meal—he wishes for "Hot bread. Chicken. Butter and cream." But in the next line, he admits, "This ain't nothing but a sharecropper's dream." In the third verse, the tone of the song shifts when we see the narrator's flash of anger directed at his family: "Make that baby stop its bawling." Soon we learn the reason for this reaction, for there is "Nothing to eat on the place this morning." However, he does recognize the unfairness of his position: "I got blisters and you got the blues / Kid needs medicine. Boys need shoes," while the "Boss got a toilet and a new cook stove. / Big new house full of liquor and clothes." Considering their current situation, the family's only option is escape. They go to Illinois, find it "Just as bad here," then travel south, where the police abuse them and other dispossessed people. But the song ends with the narrator working to "make this country the promised land" through group unity and action. In an afternote to this song, as if his lyrics do not fully express his distaste for and displeasure in sharecropping, Guthrie writes, "One of the worst things wrong with this country right today is this infernal sharecropping system."[60]

Probably his best-known views on sharecropping appear in the song "I Ain't Got No Home in This World Anymore." Taking for inspiration the old gospel song "I Can't Feel at Home in This World Anymore," popularized by the Carter Family in the early 1930s, Guthrie recasts the tune to document the harsh realities the sharecroppers experienced. Like Wobbly songwriter Joe Hill, Guthrie rejected any type of religious song that urged listeners to passively accept the wrongs in this world in the hope of receiving heavenly rewards, "pie in the sky," when they died. The result of his meditations on this subject is "I Ain't Got No Home in This World Anymore." In an afternote, he reveals the reason for creating the song: "I seen there was another side to the picture. Reason why you cant feel at home in this world any more is mostly because you aint got no home to feel at."[61]

After detailing some of his hardships out on the road, the song's narrator begins in the second verse to explain how he found himself without a home. He says, "Rich man took my home and he drove me from my door / And I ain't got no home in this world anymore." In the next verse, he explains just how he lost not only his home but his wife:

> Was a-farmin' on the shares, and always I was poor,
> My crops I lay into the banker's store.
> My wife took down and died upon the cabin floor
> And I ain't got no home in this world anymore.

Due in part to low prices for crops, high prices at landowner-owned stores, or outright duplicity on the part of landowners, many sharecroppers found themselves in debt at the end of the season. In the end, the conditions the narrator lives under finally cause him to recognize the irony of the situation:

> Now as I look around and it's very plain to see
> This world is a great and funny place to be
> The gambling man gets rich and the working man gets poor
> And I ain't got no home in this world anymore.[62]

But the narrator finds no solace in this newfound knowledge. In an end comment to an alternative version of this song, he has a joyless realization. Prophetically and almost threateningly, he remarks, "You think they's lots of us out loose on th' roads? River's a risin' an' it's gonna be more."[63]

More and more sharecroppers did find themselves stranded out on the road due to increasingly scarce positions during the Depression years. In June of 1938, one tenant farmer said, "Was waiting to see what would be the outcome of my hunt for a place, and the outlook right now is that I will move to town and sell my teams, tools, and cows," a situation that would move him from being a cash or rent tenant to being a sharecropper or even day laborer. But it is uncertain if he would even find these positions. He added, "I have hunted from Childress, Texas, to Haskell, Texas, a distance of 200 miles, and the answer is the same."[64] With no job and no prospect of one, he feared that he would soon have to go on relief. One important reason for this lack of tenant positions in cotton country was increasing mechanization.

This trend toward mechanization in the fields really did not strongly affect cotton production until the early 1920s, when the all-purpose tractor was introduced. In 1920, our nation's farmers used around 250,000 tractors. By 1937, mechanization had infiltrated most of America's fields, and the number of tractors rose to over 1.1 million. In particular, tractors in Oklahoma increased from 26,000 in 1929 to 32,500 in 1936, with 1,000 of these new machines appearing in the state's five leading cotton-producing counties alone. With this new technology, a few men on tractors could do what had taken hundreds with hoes, plows, and mules to accomplish in the cotton fields of the Southwest and the South. As a result, fewer tenants were needed, although day labor remained a low-paying employment option, especially during cotton-picking season. One ex-sharecropper in the cotton-producing county of Ellis, Texas, said, "The big fellows are working their farms with tractors and day labor. The peoples is walking the road looking for places. I don't know what's going to become of this here world."[65]

In several of his songs, Guthrie comments on how new labor-saving devices took jobs away from these people. His most concentrated denunciation of mechanization appears in "Poor, Hard-Working Man Blues," where machines take over all manner of laborers' jobs. In the final verse, the narrator says,

> I always thought of a big machine
> As the way the Lord His people blessed;
> But in the hands of a selfish man,
> The more you're blessed, the worse it gets.[66]

Guthrie saw this drive towards mechanization, especially concerning tractors, as destructive as any other force. In "Dust Can't Kill Me," two verses discuss the damage caused not by dust storms but machines:

> That old tractor got my home, boys,
> But it can't get me, Lord,
> And it can't get me.

> That old tractor run my house down,
> But it can't get me down,
> And it can't get me.

Tractors force out tenant farmers in the cotton country of the Texas panhandle, 1938. Photograph by Dorothea Lange. Courtesy of the Prints and Photographs Division of the Library of Congress.

The book *The Grapes of Wrath*, its film adaptation, and even Guthrie's "Tom Joad" all point to tractors as one of the main pushes for the fictional Joad family traveling to California. For when Tom gets home from the McAlester pen, he finds his family has been "tractored out by the Cats," a poor homecoming at best.[67] We can see the historical truth behind these claims in one of Dorothea Lange's more famous Farm Security Administration (FSA) photographs, which shows an abandoned sharecropper shack sitting alone among tractor furrows that run right up to it.

In his songs focusing on southwestern cotton tenants, Guthrie began to document hardship somewhat removed from his own direct experiences. These songs also represent the singer himself. Writer Studs Terkel makes this point well: "Though [Guthrie's] sharecropper songs deal with sharecroppers, they deal with the poet himself; though his dustbowl ballads deal with other Okies, they deal with this Okie."[68] As in all social documentary, the artist asserts his politics and principles in the work itself—so Guthrie becomes as much a part of his songs as his subjects. They become inseparable; they become one. But his documentary impulse does not begin and end in the wheat fields of the Dust Bowl or in the cotton fields of the Southwest and the South. After all the injuries and hardships stemming from environmental disasters and economic injustices, many of these farmers decided to revisit their pioneer roots, step out on that road, and make the trek west. Guthrie followed these workers and recorded their experiences.

In going west, these migrants followed a well-worn path and perception. America was born looking westward, towards the distant Pacific shore. As a result, the West as a whole found itself as the projected promised land, the place where all Americans could fulfill their destiny and the nation's promise of prosperity and opportunity for all. Of all the western destinations of which travelers could dream, California stood as a place of especially high expectation. A full eighty years before the Great Depression, the Golden State had been the focus of a powerful myth of plenty. In 1848, the discovery of gold made the state the destination of a rush of people from throughout the Union. Tales abounded of the poor, through the luck of a good claim, transforming themselves into the rich. Even songs spread these tales and pointed to the state's golden bounty. In the 1849 song "Ho! For California," written and performed by the Hutchinson Family Singers, a famous close-harmony group from New Hampshire, the state becomes "the promised land" where gold can be had in "lumps as heavy as brick" with little effort.[69] Stories and images detailing California as a place of green lands and opportunity continued their influence into the twentieth century, all of which led people to believe that life there could be better than even imagined elsewhere. In fact, a 1920s booster pamphlet entitled "California, Where Life Is Better" encouraged millions of people to come to the state.[70] Even the produce box labels from California, where much of the nation's foodstuffs were then being grown, depicted an everlasting bounty springing from a lush green land.[71]

Nowhere were these songs, stories, and images better appreciated than in southwestern America. Although many of those who poured out of the Dust Bowl and the whole of the southern plains did end up in Washington and Oregon, the majority of these migrants went to California. From 1930 to 1940, somewhere between three hundred thousand and four hundred thousand people from Oklahoma, Texas, Arkansas, and Missouri came to California, driven out by their hard luck and drawn in by the promise of good times. In songs and poems, some of these people even explicitly point to stories of the state as a place of beauty and bounty as drawing them to California. Imogene Chapin, a migrant worker living in the Arvin, California, FSA camp in August of 1940 wrote a song entitled "The Job's Just Around the Corner" containing the following verse:

> They said in California
> That money grew on trees,
> That everyone was going there,
> Just like a swarm of bees.

In a poem titled "Why We Come to California," Flora Robertson, who lived in the Shafter FSA camp in 1940, creates another vision of California as paradise:

> California, California,
> Here I come too.
> With a coffee pot and skillet,
> I'm coming to you.
>
> Nothing's left in Oklahoma,
> For us to eat or do.
> If apples, nuts, and oranges,
> And Santy Clause is real,
> Come on to California,
> And eat and eat till you're full.

Other migrants performed songs that pointed to less mythic but still exaggerated opportunities that supposedly existed in California. Jack Bryant sings "Sunny Cal," which includes this verse:

> You've all heard the story
> Of old sunny little Cal.
> The place where it never rains,
> They say it don't know how.
>
> They say, "Come on, you Okies,
> Work is easy found,
> Bring along your cotton pack,
> You can pick the whole year round."[72]

California had at this point become a leading cotton-producing state only two decades after this crop's introduction. Although cotton picking did not last "the whole year round," the fertile lands there did yield almost three times as much cotton as produced on equal acreage in other regions, creating work opportunities in California's cotton fields for many southwestern and some southern dispossessed pickers.[73] The state also had many other crops that needed seasonal labor, whereas back home little work existed for these migrants. As drought, dust, depression, and mechanization provided a strong push away from the southern plains, images of California as a dreamland, a land of ultimate opportunity, created a strong pull to the West Coast and gave the dispossessed a place to look to and to dream about.

Guthrie believed that golden tales of sunshine and jobs drew people to California. In a 1940 interview, he says, "Most of the people in the Dust Bowl talked about California. The reason they talked about California was that they seen all the pretty pictures about California and they'd heard all the pretty songs about California." During this session, he even points to one particular song as helping to draw people to California: Jimmie Rodgers's "Blue Yodel #4," also known as "California Blues." Guthrie actually blames this song for encouraging people from the Dust Bowl and the South to migrate to California. When introducing it, he says, "This ... one here attracted several hundred thousand families to go from the Dust Bowl to California." Then after singing it, he says people heard the song "all down through Oklahoma, and it went all over Texas, and went over Georgia and Alabama and Tennessee and Mississippi and Kansas." He adds, "I've seen hundreds and hundreds of people gang up around an electric phonograph and listen to Jimmie Rodgers sing that song." Then these people would jab each other and say, "Boy, there's the place to go. That old boy's singing the truth."[74]

In the version Guthrie sings, the lyrics do point out the ills of Oklahoma and Texas while emphasizing the shine of California. The first verse tells us that loving comes hard back home, for "them Oklahoma women, / Why they just ain't treatin' me right." In the second verse, the narrator would rather suffer anywhere other than in the Lone Star State:

> I'd rather drink muddy water
> And sleep in a hollow log
> Than to be down here in Texas
> And be treated like a low down dog.

When we find out in another verse that "Oklahoma waters taste just like turpentine," even muddy water sounds good in comparison. In contrast to that found in Oklahoma, "Them California waters / Taste like cherry wine." Also, sleeping in a hollow log does not seem necessary in California, since there everyone can "sleep out every night."[75] With these conditions, who would not want to leave home for California?

Looking at Rodgers's "Blue Yodel #4," we find that Guthrie's takes great liberty. The original 1927 version of the song only refers to California in two verses: the first and the third, with their respective repeated lines "I'm going to California, where they sleep out every night" and "I've got the California blues, I'm sure gonna leave you here." Also, Rodgers's recording does not even mention Oklahoma or Texas. In his version, the narrator mostly admonishes a "mama" who does not treat him right.[76] Instead of horrible conditions at home driving the narrator towards California as in Guthrie's version, here we find Rodgers's narrator running from an unhappy love affair, with little reason given for his choice of destination.

Even more surprising considering his comments about Rodgers's song, Guthrie himself participated in promoting California in his lyrics. In "Dust Pneumonia Blues," he suggests that only through California dreaming can you get to an Oklahoma woman's heart: "If you want to get a mama, just sing a California song." Another of his songs is even more explicit in its praise. "California! California!" contains an impressive description of the state's vistas:

Your mountains so high
Take your golden poppies
To the land of the sky.
Your wide peaceful ocean
Your bright colored sand
Your sunkist green valleys
Are the best in this land.

The narrator does not just describe the land, for the people of California "are healthy / All happy and free." So wonderful is the state that "When heaven's on earth / This is where it will be."[77] The praise and exaggeration here especially surprise in that Guthrie promoted this song after he came to the state, experienced some of its many drawbacks firsthand, and knew that it did not resemble the promised land it had been made out to be. But this song is an exception. For almost all of his other work about the trek to California, Guthrie's views on the conditions there were myth-breaking instead of myth-creating.

Perhaps as James N. Gregory asserts in *American Exodus: The Dust Bowl Migration and Okie Culture in California*, the majority of the thirties migrants did not suffer in the extreme on the road to the new paradise called California.[78] Certainly, many did encounter setbacks: old cars did break down, the desert heat made day travel unbearable, scant money ran out. Guthrie even humorously details the hardships of automobile travel in "Talking Dust Bowl":

> Way up yonder on a mountain road,
> I had a hot motor and a heavy load,
> I was going pretty fast, I wasn't stopping,
> Bouncing up and down like a popcorn popping.

> Had a breakdown,
> A sort of a nervous bust down of some kind.
> There was a fellow there, a mechanic fellow,
> Said it was engine trouble.[79]

Some families did not even have the relative comfort of travel afforded by jalopy and had to ride in wagons or even walk westward. These types of travails were not new. Americans have suffered out on the road to new territory since the beginning of our nation, and they have always sung about these travels and their associated hardships.

For well over a hundred years, various migrants have sung the "Lonesome Road Blues," which goes by a number of names such as "I'm Goin' Down That Road Feelin' Bad" and "I Ain't Gonna Be Treated This Way." Along with its many titles, this song also has many verses, although a variant of the following almost universally opens the song:

> I'm going down the road feeling bad,
> I'm going down the road feeling bad,
> I'm going down the road feeling bad, Lord, Lord.
> I ain't gonna be treated this a way.

In the 1930s, the migrants from the southern plains and the southwestern cotton fields also gave it voice. As the folk song collectors Charles Todd and

Robert Sonkin note, it "has become almost the theme song of the Okies, the 'Oh, Susannah' of the migration of the Nineteen Thirties."[80] In a nod to its popularity among this new group of migrants, a version of the song appears in the film version of *The Grapes of Wrath*. It includes the above verse and one other: "They fed me on cornbread and beans."[81] In one introduction to the song, Guthrie even claims he suggested that Warner Brothers use this piece in the film, although this story seems unlikely.[82] What is certain, though, is that John Ford wanted to use a traditional and easily recognizable song for a group scene where the Joads spend the night in a travel camp while on the road to California. According to John Greenway, "[Ford] asked the Okies whom he had recruited as character extras to sing something that was known to every Okie, Arkie, and Mizoo. Without hesitation, they began singing 'Goin' Down the Road Feelin' Bad.'"[83] In an interview with Alan Lomax, Guthrie refers to the manner in which the song was performed in the film: "In the picture, they sing it pretty classical," then adds, "I don't know if the Okies or the hoboes will recognize it or not."[84]

Whatever its style, the song would have been recognizable to Guthrie. In his autobiographical novel *Bound for Glory*, he mentions hearing migrants singing it.[85] He also sang and recorded it himself, even adding several individual touches to it in typical folk fashion. Sometime in 1939, he also created his own version called "Blowin' Down This Road," which generally focuses on the hardships and hopes of the Dust Bowl migrants who found themselves out on the road. He begins and ends the song with the following verse:

> I'm blowin' down this old dusty road;
> I'm blowin' down this old dusty road;
> I'm blowin' down this old dusty road, Lord, Lord.
> And I ain't a gonna be treated this a way.

He also throws in two others specifically referring to the Dust Bowl: "I'm a going where them dust storms never blow" and "They say I'm a dust-bowl refugee." Three verses he wrote for this song but never recorded do contain a defiance well beyond the usual "I ain't gonna be treated this a way" refrain. They begin and repeat their respective lines: "I ain't afraid of no goddam deputy sheriff," "I'll get me a cop if they get me," and "You bastards, you better leave me alone."[86]

Although the migrants who sang the "Lonesome Road Blues" in the thirties blew down a number of different roads on their way to the promised land of California, a majority picked Highway 66 (also known as Route 66, Lincoln Highway, and Will Rogers Highway) as their main pathway. Officially opened in 1926, Highway 66 began in Chicago, swept across the Southwest, and ended in Los Angeles. By 1937, the entire length had been paved and offered a speedy path to the West Coast.[87] During much of the Great Depression, the road became more than a means of access; it became an avenue of escape from the deprivations many experienced in the southern plains and elsewhere, as John Steinbeck aptly describes:

> 66 is the path of a people in flight, refugees from dust and shrinking land, from the thunder of tractors and shrinking ownership, from the desert's slow northward invasion from the twisting winds that howl up out of Texas, from the floods that bring no richness to the land and steal what little richness is there. From all of these the people are in flight, and they come into 66 from the tributary side roads, from the wagon tracks and the rutted country roads. 66 is the mother road, the road of flight.[88]

Most of these people's flight had a definite direction: California. This state's border station inspectors estimated that over half a million people traveling by car and needing "manual employment" came into their state from 1935 to 1940. Of these people, slightly over 275,000 came from the plains states (with about 195,000 coming from Oklahoma, Texas, Arkansas, and Missouri alone); and the majority of them drove into the state on Highway 66.[89] For the people soon to be labeled "Okies" no matter their point of origin, this road became a main artery, pumping people into the heartland of California.

In 1946, Bobby Troup immortalized this road in song when he penned the energetic hymn "Get Your Kicks on Route 66." But his was not the first time Highway 66 appeared in a song, for Guthrie discusses this road in some detail in three of his songs. Unlike in Troup's song, the only kicks Guthrie's characters get on Route 66 are to their posteriors. In one song, he wanted to distinguish between those who drove this highway for "kicks" and those who drove it out of dire necessity. In a brief introductory passage, he writes that the song "Hard Travelin'" details "the hard traveling of the working people, not the moonstruck mystic traveling of the professional vacationists." In the song itself, after detailing a litany of difficulties found out on the road, the narrator says,

> I been hittin' that Lincoln Highway
> I thought you knowed
> I been a hittin' that sixty six
> Way down the road

Then he adds in the refrain, "I been a havin' some hard traveling lord."[90] No one could mistake this wanderer out on Highway 66 for a pleasure traveler.

In the song "66 Highway Blues," the rigors associated with traveling this famous highway appear in greater detail than in "Hard Travelin'." In the spring of 1940, Guthrie and Pete Seeger collaborated on this song as they actually traveled down the highway itself, although they mistakenly write that it stretched "from coast to the coast, / New York to Los Angeles." Despite this error, the song does satisfy in its story of why the narrator has the blues. But who could blame him for being down when everywhere he goes, "The police in yo' town they shove me around"? He is not alone, for "Ten million men like me" get shoved along also. In the last three verses, he thinks about striking back at those who push him: "Sometimes, I think I'll blow down a cop" (he even mentions the caliber of gun in this fantasy), all because they "treat me so mean." Still, he realizes that suffering on Highway 66 is better than having "a number for a name." The last verse does offer some nonviolent, positive action, however. He says,

> I'm gonna start me a hungry man's union,
> Ainta gonna charge no dues,
> Gonna march down that road to the Wall Street walls
> A singin' those 66 Highway Blues.[91]

Here, a rebellion of hungry people marches to the economic center of power and wails out its suffering, demanding attention. This ending points to the collective action Guthrie advocates in his union songs as the only true resistance to power and the solution to inequity.

In another song about Highway 66, Guthrie again points to the hardships he saw out on the road and in America but spins them out in conjunction with one of his heroes, Will Rogers. Guthrie wrote "Will Rogers Highway" sometime before March 1940, when he recorded it for Alan

Lomax. In the first verse, the narrator again mistakenly notes, "There's a highway that goes from the coast to coast / New York town down to Los Angeles." But other verses offer an accurate account of the situation on Highway 66 during the Great Depression. Verse two opens with the highway "lined with jalopies as far as you can see," all of them "with a mighty hot motor and a heavy old load," a line also found in "Talking Dust Bowl." Even those who get off Highway 66 find little comfort, for the narrator sees "ten thousand people you see every day / Camped under the bridges and under the trees." Parked alongside are their "rattle trap cars that have come apart / From old Oklahoma to Los Angeles." When they finally get on the road again, they still find trouble. In verse five, the narrator says, "It's a mighty hard / All day you're hot all night you freeze / But we've got to have work so we're takin' a chance" so they stay out on that "66 Highway."[92]

To some extent, Guthrie points to Will Rogers as being the catalyst for these migrants traveling Highway 66, for the narrator says a "hundred thousand . . . followed him" out on that road, although no historical evidence supports this claim. But Guthrie does not condemn him as he did Jimmie Rodgers. In the final verse, the narrator moves away from discussing Will Rogers and points to some of the reasons for these people being out on this road to California:

> That wind it blowed and the dust got black
> And now we're known as refugees
> We're stranded now on that 66 Highway
> From old Oklahoma to Los Angeles.[93]

In essence, all Guthrie's songs of the highway to the promised land of California point not to joy of escape but to the difficulties found out on the road.

Even after all the hardships of being displaced by drought and dust, poverty and tenancy, then picking up and moving across half of the American landscape, the migrants' difficulties did not come to an end. When they arrived in California, they often found economic hardship and prejudice, even becoming the social pariahs of those already living in the state. A powerful example of this rejection occurred on the California border itself. Beginning on February 3, 1936, one hundred and twenty-six Los Angeles police officers under direct orders of Police Chief James Edgar Davis created sixteen checkpoints where main highways or railroads entered the

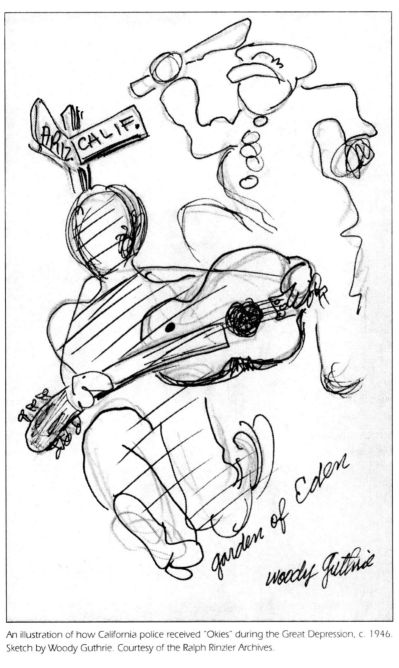

An illustration of how California police received "Okies" during the Great Depression, c. 1946. Sketch by Woody Guthrie. Courtesy of the Ralph Rinzler Archives.

state. These officers then allowed only those who had money or who were state residents to enter. Hundreds were turned away in just the first few days. This so-called "bum blockade" had political support for a time since a growing bias against the influx of migrants into the state had unified public opinion. Soon the nation's press ridiculed this practice of exclusion, and the American Civil Liberties Union filed a lawsuit opposing it. Due to this pressure and cost concerns, the blockade ended quietly in April after two and a half months.[94]

In 1936, Guthrie first visited California, hoboing into the state on a railroad car during the last section of his journey from Pampa, Texas. Although he did not get stopped by Davis's blockade, he certainly would have heard about the police checkpoints from other newcomers. Much as he did with other incidents that touched his sense of injustice, he transformed his thoughts into song. Sometime before 1937, using the tune to "Hang Out Your Front Door Key," he wrote "Do Re Mi."[95] During his lifetime, he played and recorded the song often—which may help explain why it is one of his best-known songs.

"Do Re Mi" opens with a tale of the western migration: "Lots of folks back east, they say, leavin' home ev'ry day, / Beatin' the hot old dusty way to the California line. / Cross the desert sand they roll, getting out of that old dust bowl." The narrator then alludes to the migrants' expectations: "They think they're going to a sugar bowl," a belief similar to those of the migrants mentioned earlier. As noted above, Guthrie's main drive in his songs of California is to dispel the state's myth of plenty for all. His narrator achieves this goal easily with a depiction of the police counting and rejecting those who come to the state without the universal passport of money. He says, "Now the police at the port of entry say, / 'You're number fourteen thousand for today'" then quickly shifts into the cautionary chorus:

> Oh, if you ain't got the do re mi, folks,
> If you ain't got the do re mi,
> Why you better go back to beautiful Texas,
> Oklahoma, Kansas, Georgia, Tennessee.
>
> California is a garden of Eden,
> A paradise to live in or see.
> But believe it or not, you won't find it so hot,
> If you ain't got the do re mi.[96]

DOCUMENTING THE STORIES OF AMERICA'S AGRICULTURAL WORKERS

Again, we find California being described as a "paradise," but here it becomes one that can only be accessed through money. Although in the beginning he mentions the Dust Bowl as the place the migrants are running from, the narrator also refers to people from the South in his warning, thus expanding the spectrum of those seeking relief in California from the troubles back home.

In the second verse, the narrator shifts the focus a bit and urges those thinking about leaving their homes for California to reconsider:

> If you want to buy you a home or farm
> That can't do nobody harm
> Or take your vacation by the mountains or sea,
> Don't swap your old cow for a car,
> You'd better stay right where you are.

He then offers a warning about the misplaced trust in the California dream, saying, "You'd better take this little tip from me / Cause I look through the want ads every day. / But the headlines on the papers always say," and shifts into the chorus again.[97] In an alternative version of verse two, the last two lines move away from personal experience; instead, a prominent right-wing, red-baiting political figure in California offers the migrants a warning: "Governor Merriam on the radio one day, / He jumped up to the microphone" and offers the cautionary and, from this speaker, slightly threatening chorus.[98]

In an endnote to the song, Guthrie expands on the song's warning but tempers it somewhat:

> For years people have been pickin' up and leavin' out of the
> drought country and dust bowl parts of the Middlewest, a-comin'
> to California by the streams. I ain't a-discouragin' nobody not
> to come west and try their luck. I like to see people with spunk
> enough to go through anything to try and reach a goal they have
> in mind. But to those who are just a-comin' to be comin', or sorta
> frivolously a-swappin' off a farm to come to they know not what,
> I present the above song.

He also adds a final comment and establishes his authority along with his unity with his intended migrant audience: "It ain't so much on poetry, but it tells a LOT of truth. I rattled thru from Pampa, Texas, on a hot and dusty freight train last March, I know."[99]

Even after these roadblocks were removed and the migrants had freer access into the state, they still found obstacles. One of the most trying had to be the difficulty of finding a worthwhile and long-term job in the state's lush and bountiful fields. As they do in Steinbeck's novel, Ford's film, and Guthrie's song, the Joad family looked at the abundant and fertile fields and believed work would be easy to find:

> They stood on a mountain and they looked to the West,
> And it looked like the promised land.
> That bright green valley with a river running through.
> There was work for every single hand, they thought.
> There was work for every single hand.[100]

But the fictional Joads and the very real migrants found the farming situation in California unlike what they had left in the Southwest and the South.

The two most important differences were the lack of permanent housing and a shortened work season. Some owners did provide limited and often unappealing housing for the migrants—but only until the crop was picked. Then these workers had to move on. Back home, whether they farmed wheat or cotton, whether they had owned, rented, or sharecropped, these agricultural workers generally lived on the land while tending the crops and in the off-season. In California, most were reduced to day laborers. The hardships involved with a lack of housing were compounded because work gathering pears, grapes, cotton, or any of the other almost two hundred crops generally lasted a few weeks at a time.[101] The short harvest seasons for each of these varied crops left most migrants with work for about two-thirds of the year. With their hopes of permanent homes and employment dashed, the migrants ceaselessly traveled in search of work.

During their travels, they encountered prejudice, expressed even in the names given them. Often Californians called the migrants "Okies" no matter what their home state. In the fictional realm of *The Grapes of Wrath*, we find the assembled Joad men learning about this name. Just after the family crossed the desert and hit California, they stop at a migrant camp beside the river just outside the town of Needles and meet a Texan who had come from the "Panhandle, come from near Pampa" (where Guthrie lived for several years) and who was returning there. This man sharply defines the word for them, saying, "Well, Okie use'ta mean you was from Oklahoma. Now it means you're a dirty son-of-a-bitch. Okie means you're scum. Don't mean nothing itself, it's the way they say it."[102] Resident Californians also called them "Dust Bowl refugees." Guthrie uses the term in several of his songs and even employs it as a title in one. During his recording session for the Library of Congress in March 1940, he discusses (with a bit of surface humor but an undercurrent of bite) how prevalent the term was: "They called us Dust Bowl refugees. All the newspaper headlines was full of stuff about Dust Bowl refugees. Refugees here, refugees yonder, refugees, refugees, refugees everywhere you look."[103] But instead of letting the term remain a badge of shame, he re-encodes it by explaining the story behind the migration and thus makes it into a name deserving of sympathy instead of disdain.

In the song "Dust Bowl Refugee," Guthrie laments the transitory nature of the migrants even after they came to California and documents their plight. In the first verse, the narrator tells us where the "refugees" come from and where they went: "Just a Dust Bowl refugee / From that dust bowl to the peach bowl." His family comes "from the southland and the drouthland" and went "Cross the mountains to the sea" by way of the "hot old dusty highway." But their travels have not helped them; for in the West, they still find the world "Hard, it's always been that way / Here today and on our way." They "wander" and "work / In your fields and in your fruit." Since they can find no steady place to live, "the highways is our home / It's a never ending highway." As a result, they are called "ramblers" who "travel with the seasons." The narrator even accepts the pejorative label: "We're the Dust Bowl refugees." In the final verse, he—like many other migrants—remains without a permanent home and wonders whether this will always be his fate:

> I'm a Dust Bowl refugee
> I'm a Dust Bowl refugee
> And I wonder will I always
> Be a Dust Bowl refugee.[104]

The lack of steady work often kept the migrants traveling even after they had reached what they thought would be their final destination. In that they had to be mobile, any shelter had to be accepted, much of which would not likely be termed "home."

Since many of the migrants could find no set place to live when they came to California, they had to make do wherever and however they could. Some ended up building shacks out of trash from the dumps at the edges of towns. These places often earned the name "Hoovervilles," in dishonor of the former president. In the book and film versions of *The Grapes of Wrath*, the Joads stay in one of these makeshift camps just outside Bakersfield when they first come to the state. This fictional representation accurately reflected the reality of many displaced persons in California during the Great Depression. In fact, Florence Thompson, whose image in Dorothea Lange's "Migrant Mother" visually represents the pain and struggle of these people and this time, lived at the same Hooverville as did the fictional Joads. She says,

> When Steinbeck wrote *The Grapes of Wrath* about those people
> living under the bridge at Bakersfield—at one time we lived
> under that bridge. It was the same story. Didn't even have a tent
> then, just a ratty old quilt. I walked from what they'd call the
> Hoover camp at the bridge to way down on First Street to work
> in a restaurant for 50 cents a day and leftovers. They'd give me
> what was left over to take home, sometimes two water buckets
> full. I had six children to feed at that time.[105]

In the migrants' living quarters in California's Imperial Valley during 1934, the National Labor Board's Leonard Commission found "filth, squalor, an entire absence of sanitation, and a crowding of human beings into totally inadequate tents or crude structures built of boards, weeds, and anything that was at hand to give a pitiful semblance of a home at its worst." In their report, they also added, "Words cannot describe some of the conditions we saw."[106] These Hoovervilles did not only exist in the hinterlands of sunny California. Some migrants from Oklahoma had already experienced the hardships of such living quarters in their home state; for one sprang up just outside Oklahoma City. Hoovervilles were also a nationwide disgrace, appearing like mushrooms after a rain in Detroit, Michigan; Youngstown, Ohio; Chicago, Illinois; St. Louis, Missouri; and many other industrial and metropolitan areas.

In 1969, these migrant camps found themselves being represented in song by a second-generation Okie, Merle Haggard. His mother, father, and two siblings came out to California from Checotah, Oklahoma in 1934,

A desperate migrant laborer and mother of seven, 1936. Photograph by Dorothea Lange. Courtesy of the Prints and Photographs Division of the Library of Congress.

three years before the singer was born. There his family lived in labor camps and eventually moved up to an abandoned boxcar (much like the one the Joads live in for a while). They made it as home-like as possible, and there Haggard grew up. When he sings of the California squatters' camps—

"a canvas-covered cabin, in a crowded labor camp"—in his autobiographical song "Hungry Eyes," personal knowledge drives the song. His mother says, "Almost every word of it really happened like that."[107] Nearly three decades before Haggard documented his experiences and that of his family in song, Guthrie had already described the ugly reality of Hoovervilles.

Guthrie knew of the conditions and people found in these places, especially those in California. As he traveled back and forth between the Southwest and this state, he saw how many of the migrants lived "outside, like—coyotes." He saw the camps they made and shacks they built. He also admits that the situation was so bad that he would not have believed it if someone had told him about it:

> If people had set and tell me that there was hundreds and hundreds and hundreds and hundreds and thousands of families of people a living around under railroad bridges, down along the river bottoms in the old cardboard houses, in old rusty beat up houses that they'd made out of tow sacks and old dirty rags and corrugated iron that they'd got out of the dumps and old tin cans flatten out and old orange crates that they'd been able to tear up and get boards out of, I wouldna believe it.[108]

But he did see the Hoovervilles and knew their squalor. He did not have the refuge of ignorance that some Americans did about the conditions in which many migrants and other citizens lived every day.

Over time, these impressions of the poor housing of the migrants formed a barb that pricked a song out of Guthrie. In the simply named "Hooversville," the opening verse works on building a visual image of the ugly reality of the squatter camps. Here, the narrator offers a bleak vision: "Ramblin', gamblin', rickety shacks" made out of "Rusty tin an' raggedy sacks" located "On the skeeter bit end of the garbage dump," where "30 million people slump / Down where the big rats run an' jump." In the next verse, the people of the Hoovervilles appear in their ragged truth. We see the "Kids that aint knowed too much fun" and "Kids that bed on the old wet ground / An' eat old rotten grub that's found / Diggin' the great big dumps around / Hooversville."[109] The fictional conditions of the children in the song depict the reality of the migrant children, who sometimes died of malnutrition and disease in the richest agricultural region of America. Their parents bitterly resented their children's woeful situation. One writer interviewed a migrant father living in a Hooverville who acknowledged his disappointment in not being able to provide what he had growing up: "My children ain't raised decent like I was raised by my father. There were no rag houses then, but I can't do no better."[110]

In the third verse, the narrator confronts the audience about other harsh realties found in Hoovervilles and offers some inhabitants' feelings about their condition. The narrator asks, "Maybe you just didn't know" and "Guess you didn't never go / To Hooversville." But the next question surprises and disturbs:

> Maybe you ain't never seen
> The little girls around fifteen
> Sold for the price of a bowl of beans
> In Hooversville.

Here, the "kids" mentioned in other verses find themselves, through dire necessity, engaged in the ugly dealings of adults. These living conditions create little affection for the Hoovervilles. In the last verse, the narrator tells us,

> Feller hates like hell to live
> In Hooversville;
> Gonna get the hell out first chance I get
> From Hooversville;
> Kids need 3 square meals a day,
> Man need honest work an' pay;
> Woman'll die if she's got to stay
> In Hooversville.[111]

Only hardship and degradation thrive in Hoovervilles as presented in this song, and no remedies exist except escape.

Relief from these conditions was hard to come by without steady work and with the rising prejudice; for this flood of poor, working-class people created resentment that went beyond simple name calling. This negative reception had not always been Californians' reaction. Just a decade before, migrants from the South and Southwest had been accepted and, in some cases, had even been welcomed to the state. One Oklahoma woman recalled, "The farmers would meet you at the trains. Naturally people came out."[112]

The reason for this earlier positive reception came from California's need for skilled cotton pickers. During the twenties, cotton production in the state rose greatly; and only skilled workers—such as those from Oklahoma and Texas—could effectively and economically work this relatively new crop. In the thirties, migrants from the Southwest and the South again traveled to California but found a different reception from those who came the decade before. One easily identifiable reason for this change in attitude is the Great Depression itself. Unemployment in California, although lower than the national average, still remained well above ten percent throughout the thirties. By 1933 almost 1.25 million residents received some sort of public assistance.[113] With the added relief needs of the migrants in between harvesting seasons, the drain on California's resources grew.

This answer does not completely account for the particular resentment that these migrants encountered. Another factor that strongly affected the populace's attitude came out of the state's 1934 gubernatorial election. During novelist Upton Sinclair's close but unsuccessful run for the California governorship, groups resistant to the candidate's progressive policies created a media blitz near the end of the campaign that offered up the image of thousands of hoboes scurrying to the Golden State to seek easy public relief. Sinclair had given his critics this opening by stating that if his End Poverty in California programs came to fruition, then many of the country's unemployed would come there to escape the privation in other states. Newspapers owned by powerful and conservative media moguls, such as William Randolph Hearst, played up this boast with misleading articles and fictional photographs. The Republican-sponsored California League against Sinclairism even published and distributed a parody of "California, Here We Come" that warned of the consequences of Sinclair's plan:

> California, here we come!
> Every beggar—every bum
> From New York—and Jersey
> Down to Purdue
> By millions—we're coming
> So that we can live on you.
> We hear that Sinclair's got your state.
> That's why we can hardly wait
> Open up that Golden Gate
> California, here we come![114]

DOCUMENTING THE STORIES OF AMERICA'S AGRICULTURAL WORKERS

By the time the Okies arrived, Californians already had the image of out-of-state relief cheats beaten into their consciousness. Their own economic interests and fears thus played upon, Californians could easily be made to castigate this new migrant group's very real request for refuge and relief. Beginning around 1935 and lasting until the end of the decade, various people and groups proposed the idea that the new arrivals came only to soak up tax dollars from the state's tax-made relief funds.

In one of the little-known protest verses penned for the song that was eventually to become "This Land," Guthrie conjures a dark vision of people standing "in the shadow of the steeple / By the relief office," a sight that causes his narrator to wonder "if God blessed America for me." Yet Guthrie never castigated the people receiving relief. He knew that most of those looking for help, including the migrants, took it out of necessity rather than avarice. When one California reporter whipped up a diatribe against the migrants asking for relief, Guthrie even defended them in one of his "Woody Sez" columns in the Communist newspaper *People's World*:

> The Times carried quite a story about the flood, drouth, an' dust-bowlers a comin' to Calif. in their rickety, rundown jallopies, their little handful of belongin's, an' their children . . . only, says the Times, to dig into some of the Relief Gold.
>
> The tale, written by Kenneth Somebody, an' paid for by Mr. Somebody Else, was wrote up for the one purpose for givin' the Refugees another black eye.[115]

"Kenneth Somebody," who was reporter Kenneth Crist of the anti-migrant *Los Angeles Times*, had earlier described the living conditions in the Hoovervilles and how the police broke them up for public safety and health reasons, along with his denunciation of the Okies' desire for relief.[116]

Guthrie dissects the author's argument by re-explaining the situation and the notion that people would subject themselves to the hardships under which the migrants lived just for the less-than-adequate relief payments California offered:

> Scenes or Life in a Trailer Camp City were painted to call your attention to the untold, inhuman suffering that these people are willing to go thru—just for some of that "Easy Relief Money."

How the Sheriff's Force "cleared out the Jungles," and drove the Shack-dwellers out of the River Bottom, set fire to their Cardboard Houses, and destroyed their patch-work shelters—was told about—not to make you feel in your heart a genuine sorrow for your brothers and sisters of our American Race that's got to live in such places, but to try to make you believe that these Underprivileged people are designing in their hearts to "Dig some Easy Gold"—off you Taxpayers.

The Author was trying to make you believe that these weatherbeaten, browbeaten, homeless people are really robbers at heart and he gave some typical conversations of some Oklahoma people who were living like wild hogs in a boggy river bottom for a whole year in order to get some of that easy Relief Gold.

Guthrie then shifts into a comparison between the writer and the migrants in an attempt to show the latter to be equal to the former:

No, Kenneth . . . it ain't the "Easy Relief Money Us Folks Is After"—it's jest a chanct to work an' earn our livin' . . . sorta like you earn yore livin'. You've got youre Gift of Writin'—an' that's the way you work an' earn yore meal ticket here in this old world. An' each one of us has got our little Job thet we hope to do in order to pay for our keep.

Finally, the singer turns his humor directly on "Kenneth Somebody," uses himself as a stereotype-breaking example, and ends with a shaming jab:

'Course we ain't as educated as you are—'cause you're a mighty smart feller. But we'd like fer our children to grow up an' be big, smart, educated fellers like you. ('Course if any of 'em ever got so educated thet they took to a robbin' or a runnin' the rest of the folks down, or a makin' fun of the pore folks—well, we jest naturally wooden't claim him no more.)

Personal, I've ben in Calif. 2 years—'cause the dust and the cold, run me out of Texas . . . an' I ain't never applied fer relief of any kind yet. An' for the past year I've averaged a makin' less than $1 a day.

But before I'd make my livin' by writin' articles that make fun
of the Hungery Folks, an' the Workin' folks,
    I'd go on Relief.[117]

In response to the hostility toward the migrants that peaked in 1939, Guthrie
defended those with little access to any media source.

Within a year, the state's and the nation's attitude towards these
migrants changed drastically. One major reason for this shift was the publication of John Steinbeck's novel *The Grapes of Wrath*. The long-suffering
Joad family found much sympathy from a national audience. With the
release of director John Ford's film version of the book, support for the
migrants grew further. Fact, along with fiction, also helped change public
opinion concerning the Okies. Cary McWilliams's 1939 book *Factory in the
Fields* presented the hardships that various migrant groups had experienced
in California since the agricultural industry began there in the late 1800s.
In addition, the Tolan Committee of the House of Representatives and the
LaFollette Committee of the Senate began their investigations of abuses
of agricultural laborers in California around this same time. Finally, and
most important, with the growing demand for America's products due to
war elsewhere, industry nationwide needed workers—especially in the burgeoning field of airplane production and in the once stagnant shipbuilding
industry in California. Thus, the once condemned "relief cheats" suddenly
transformed into needed and valued workers.

Nevertheless, Guthrie continued to write songs into the early 1940s
about the migrants from the Southwest and the South, even after their negative image began to fall away. After relocating to New York City in early 1940,
he writes in an opening piece to the song "Govt Road" that "Us Oakies are
out of jobs, out of money, out of drinking whiskey, out of everything, except
hope."[118] In response to this continuing impulse, music critic Dave Marsh
notes, "[Guthrie] was still addressing himself to fellow Okies even though
he'd relocated to the East Coast, where there were few, if any, Dust Bowl
refugees besides himself."[119] Later, when he worked for one month in 1941 for
the Bonneville Power Administration in Washington state, Guthrie wrote his
last great song about the Okie migrants: "Pastures of Plenty." Unlike most of
the songs he wrote during this brief but productive time, this piece's content
connected it to much of his other work discussing the migrants' situation.

Using the folk song "Pretty Polly" as a musical structure, "Pastures of
Plenty" works to tell the continuing story of the Dust Bowl migrants. In

the first verse, the narrator explains that these migrants come "Out of your Dust Bowl" and down a "hot dusty road." In a later verse, he says that these migrants "come with the dust and we go with the wind." In an alternative verse, he adds, "I think of the dust and the days that are gone." Soon this wistful lament shifts into a hopeful moment when he reveals he also thinks of "the day that's to come on a farm of our own." Unfortunately, this farm remains in the realm of dreams, for the narrator and others like him must "ramble" around, working "a mighty hard row" by day and sleeping "on the ground in the light of your moon." They travel from California to Arizona to Oregon, "working in your orchards of peaches and prunes" and gathering "your hops," digging "your beets from the ground," and cutting "the grapes from your vines, / To set on your table your light sparkling wine."[120]

All of the traveling and suffering documented here seems to have a purpose other than just eliciting sympathy for these people's sacrifices; the song also shows how the migrants' sacrifices serve all Americans. The migrants not only provide us "sparkling wine" but also "work in this fight, and we'll fight till we win." They protect the land they work so hard on: "My land I'll defend with my life, if it be, / 'Cause my pastures of plenty must always be free."[121] Of course, these last lines can be read in a number of ways. The fight mentioned could be against the people of California who wished to repress and marginalize the migrants, and the land referred to could be communally owned land that has nothing to do with property rights but everything to do with essential human rights, like food and shelter. In light of the time when the song was written, the fight more probably refers to the coming war in Europe and the Pacific, making the land that of the nation as a whole. In this interpretation, "Pastures of Plenty" documents the bounty of America, the hardships of those who work it, and the migrants' patriotism in the face of despotism—quite a lot to accomplish in just one song.

Considering its sympathy for suffering Dust Bowlers, disenfranchised tenant farmers, and abused migrant workers, Guthrie's work could be denounced as being biased. Where, critics might say, are the bums and drunkards, layabouts and louses in his description of these people? How is it that all those whose suffering Guthrie captures in these songs appear as noble poor who have had their fortunes and rights unjustly denied? True, Guthrie does not focus much effort on depicting the evils of these agricultural workers. In fact, the criticism Lionel Trilling offered James Agee's *Now Let Us Praise Famous Men* can be equally applied to most of Guthrie's songs about the downtrodden: "[Agee] writes of his people as if there were no human unregenerateness in them, no flicker of malice or meanness, no darkness or wildness of feeling, only a sure and simple virtue, the growth, we must suppose, of their hard, unlovely poverty."[122] In fact, similar criticism has been directed against Guthrie before. Joe Klein believes Guthrie "simply refused to acknowledge that they [the common people of America] could also be selfish and petty and fearful. He willfully blinded himself to all but those who suffered the hard times with dignity."[123]

Believing that all too often the media presents members of the nation's underclass negatively, Guthrie consciously made a point to document the positive aspects of these and other groups in the American landscape. He succinctly and passionately states this belief in one of his most often quoted pieces:

> I hate a song that makes you think that you are not any good. I hate a song that makes you think that you are just born to lose. Bound to lose. No good to nobody. No good for nothing because you are too old or too young or too fat or too slim or too ugly or too this or too that . . . Songs that run you down or poke fun at you on account of your bad luck or hard traveling.
>
> I am out to fight those songs to my very last breath of air and my last drop of blood.
>
> I am out to sing songs that will prove to your that this is your world and that if it has hit your pretty hard and knocked your for a dozen loops, no matter what color, what size your are, how your are built. I am out sing the songs that make your take pride in yourself and in your work.

He adds that he cannot write songs "that knock you down still farther and the ones that poke fun at your even more and the ones that make you think you've not got any sense at all" because "the radio waves and your movies and your jukeboxes and your songbooks are already loaded down and running over with such no good songs as that anyhow."[124]

In effect, Guthrie wanted to express the other side of the situation in his song lyrics by describing the dehumanizing, demoralizing conditions that the Dust Bowlers, the tenant farmers, and the Okie migrant laborers suffered under in America during the Great Depression. By providing these stories in a sympathetic voice, he not only exposes the unfulfilled promise of the "Land of Opportunity" and other national myths but urges his audience to feel for the people who inhabit his songs. In doing so, Guthrie rewrites (or at least re-focuses) our nation's history. In many of Guthrie's songs of the late 1930s and early '40s, those who normally found themselves bit players in history become its stars. Their stories and hardships become the focus of his art, which attempts to capture our nation's history even as it implicitly asks us to embrace those who were too often forgotten or ignored.

CHAPTER THREE

The Poor, Hard-Working Man Blues

DOCUMENTING THE TROUBLES OF
OTHER AMERICAN WORKERS

Towards the end of the Great Depression, Woody Guthrie's songs recounting the hardscrabble lives of Dust Bowlers, tenant farmers, and Okie migrants helped launch his professional music career in both Los Angeles and New York City. Additionally, in July of 1940, Victor Records released his most famous album, *Dust Bowl Ballads*, containing songs documenting the experiences of those planting and picking cotton in the South or Southwest or vegetables and fruit under the California sun. Having known agricultural workers since his youth, Guthrie naturally drew upon these people when he started writing songs about the struggles of America's underclass. Then through his own travels across America in the late 1930s and early '40s, he began to have direct access to a wider spectrum of working people, adding their hard-luck stories to those he already knew. These encounters contributed to his understanding of the nation's working class and directed his depiction of labor troubles in his work.

While coming to sympathize with and then writing about the difficult lives of farmers and laborers, Guthrie sharpened his own ability to look through others' eyes. Although he suffered through poverty and other hardships in his youth while in Oklahoma and Texas, he never saw his crops succumb to drought, dust, or both. Nor did he have to pack his family up in an old Model T and drive out to an uncertain future picking crops on the West Coast. But many of his early songs' narrators do have these experiences.

To speak in a believable voice from a perspective not actually his own, to make the farmers and migrant laborers in his songs come alive, he had to strongly identify with his narrators and the stories they told. At the very tail end of the 1930s, using the same poetic imagination that transformed the Okie experience into song, he continued creating social documentaries in his lyrics by detailing the real-life hardships of a broader range of American workers than those sweating in our nation's fields.

Often, past discussions of Guthrie's songs have presented him primarily as the voice of Dust Bowlers and Okie migrant laborers—both agricultural workers. Critic James Curtis notes this focus when he writes, "Despite his association with the labor-radical movement of the 1940s and the songs which were born of that affiliation, he is perhaps best remembered as a spokesman for the Dust Bowl migrants."[1] But remembering Guthrie mainly as a "spokesman" for this group leaves his songs exposing the difficulties and degradation of a number of other workers underappreciated. Therefore, an in-depth exploration of his lyrics about nonagricultural workers provides specific insight into how he expanded his understanding of the nation's working class beyond that of agricultural workers and yields a better overall understanding of his views on labor abuse.

Sometime in the late 1930s, Guthrie began contrasting the poverty of workers with the luxury of the rich. As noted in earlier chapters, he points out this disparity in both "I Don't Feel at Home in the Bowery Anymore" and "I Ain't Got No Home in This World Anymore." Some of his others songs from this period continue to point out and denounce the gap between the rich and the poor. Just as in "I Ain't Got No Home," he uses the sharecropper as an embodiment of the abused worker in the song "Farther Along." But the contrast between the two classes appears starkest in how a worker's poverty directly affects his family: "Working Man has no home for his children; / Rich Man he dwells in his mansion so high."[2] The working man also has other worries facing him—such as losing his job and being imprisoned for his privation. In "Been in Jail," the narrator is locked up "for vag 'cause they won't give me work no more." As a result, he ends up "sleep[ing] down on the floor" of the jail house the "rich man" built.[3] In other songs written around this time, Guthrie moves beyond the general term "rich" and uses more specific titles and names to define the group that lives in comfort or builds prisons for the poor. For example, we find "bankers" and "Mr. Randolph Hearst" filling their pockets while the "working folks" cannot even get an even break in the song "I'm a-Lookin' for That New Deal Now."[4]

That Guthrie focused criticism on the gap between workers and the wealthy at this point in time does not surprise. During the 1930s, the nation separated into two very disparate camps: the haves and the have-nots, with the richest fifth of America's citizens having an income equal to that of the other four-fifths.⁵ With the divide between the two wider than ever before and the times being harder than usual, anyone willing to look had an easy time seeing the ugly truth behind our nation's grand illusion—the majority does not realize the American Dream. Eventually, he also came to recognize that his country did not hold out the same opportunities for all, no matter what promises were made in school history books and civics lessons, no matter what the politicians said or our own national mythos claimed. Through his own travels and encounters with those who were stranded out on that road with him in Depression America and afterward, Guthrie saw that the working class as a whole suffered from poverty and prejudice. This realization must have been all that more compelling considering it came to him, in part at least, through his own experiences during the 1920s and '30s.

In his earliest years, his perspective was far removed from those laboring with their hands in Okemah. This early lack of class consciousness becomes more understandable considering he did not actually come from a working-class background; he was born into a middle-class family that eventually fell into ruin. His father, Charley, began his working life as a cowhand in the Oklahoma Territory around the turn of the twentieth century. But he had ambition and a thirst for self-improvement. Through his own efforts, Charley moved into various administrative jobs around Okemah, eventually even running for district court clerk in 1907 and winning.⁶ Although never reaching higher political circles, he did build a fairly successful real estate business, buying, renting, and selling farms in the area until the early 1920s. As a result, Guthrie's early life was one of small-town prosperity. Only with Charley's business failure did the Guthries drop into America's underclass. When the oil boom hit Oklahoma after World War I, Charley's fortunes faltered and then fell abruptly, leaving the family to suffer through the general depression that hit agricultural regions around America during that same time. In the spring of 1927, after Charley was burned in an accident and his wife, Nora, sent to the state asylum due to the ravages of Huntington's chorea, young Woody was left without a home and had to fend for himself, picking up and selling junk or playing tunes on a mouth harp for coins. When the Great Depression swept up the majority of other workers in the 1930s, he had already known privation for years before. But his personal hardships would not stand alone as the only force driving his growing understanding of the plight of workers who also faced a lack of comfort or security.

While in Los Angeles during the late 1930s, Guthrie met writers, actors, and other artists involved in America's labor movement. Some of these people befriended him and helped broaden his understanding of underclass unity beyond what he had developed on his own. One person who helped him expand this class consciousness was Will Geer, an actor and earnest left-winger. Geer not only knew the hardships suffered by workers in California's fields, those whom he supported and performed for during a 1939 cotton strike, but he also championed all workers in their efforts to gain equality. Throughout the Depression, he participated in various efforts to educate others about America's labor problems, such as his role in Mark Blitzstein's famous first production of the labor-protest musical *The Cradle Will Rock* in 1937. Geer was not the only friend who influenced the singer's growing class sympathies during his time on the West Coast. Both Ed Robbin and Mike Quin became close friends with Guthrie and provided him access to current labor strife and struggles. These two men wrote for *People's World*, the West Coast version of the Communist newspaper *Daily Worker*, just as Guthrie did for a while. In fact, Robbin helped Guthrie get a column with the paper. In addition, Quin's eclectic columns about all manner of workers certainly helped Guthrie to understand how the injustices perpetrated on one group of laborers was really an affront to all those who sweated for their livelihoods. As a result of these relationships, he began to see the general abuse of labor beyond that of agricultural workers and his songs began to reflect his new realizations. When he moved to New York City in the early 1940s, he continued to strengthen his connection to the labor movement. There, he met other musicians who detailed workers' hardships in song. Guthrie's relationships with these songwriters also inspired his work documenting labor strife. Through his own experiences and the efforts of his leftist friends, Guthrie came to better understand that all workers were connected in their struggle to have a home, a family, a future. As a result of this awareness, when he found out wages were down or conditions were hazardous, Guthrie would recast these situations in song so others could hear this news.

Biographer Joe Klein suggests that Guthrie began writing more politically aware songs during his time in California because he often played for leftist groups there: "He began to devote more time to the serious, political songs his new audience—which was virtually his sole source of income—enjoyed."[7] Klein's claim suggests that this desire to document the political injustices and worker abuses Guthrie saw and read about came from a monetary incentive. But this impulse does not jibe with the singer's character. Although sometimes shifting his material to please an audience, he would not do it if it went against his own beliefs. For example, he could have had a long-term and lucrative contract singing for Model Tobacco in 1941; instead, he quit the show due to producers' constant restrictions on the material he wanted to play. A much more plausible reason than Klein's for his change in the focus of his songs during his time in Los Angeles comes from Guthrie's own realizations about how many of society's institutions and powerbrokers united to repress workers. As Guthrie notes himself, "I never had been able to look out over and across the slum section nor a sharecropper farm and connect it up with the owner and the landlord and the guards and the police and the dicks and the bulls and the vigilante men with their black sedans and sawed off shot guns" until he was educated by experience and the teaching he received from his own travels and the insights of leftist activists in America during the late 1930s and early '40s.[8]

Beginning in the spring of 1939, Guthrie first included terms and phrases such as "worker," "working man," and "workin' folks" into his songs and moved away from his earlier focus on agricultural laborers. Looking at one of his songbooks from this time period, we find a number of examples of this change, such as in "Indian Corn Song" and "I Looked at the World."[9] These songs refer to workers in general rather than just those who toiled in the fields of America. Even in "I Ain't Got No Home in This World Anymore," which details the hard life of a sharecropper, the narrator calls himself "just a wandering worker."[10] An alternative version of this song also includes the lines, "a working man is nothing but a slave. / And a slave he'll be till they lay him in his grave."[11] Yet the majority of the songs Guthrie wrote before 1939 merely mention workers as a general class or detail the hardships of agricultural laborers. Only in one case does he stray from this norm: "Poor, Hard-Working Man Blues," written on April 3, 1939.

In the first two verses, the song's narrator stays true to past form and discusses working men in general and agricultural workers in particular. Both have troubles because "a machine come along and took" their jobs. As noted in the previous chapter, Guthrie saw how various machines, especially tractors, had taken the place of men in the fields of America and had already denounced agricultural mechanization in such songs as "Dust Can't Kill

Me" and would continue this theme in "Tom Joad." But in "Poor, Hard-Working Man Blues," his narrator expands his condemnation of the move toward mechanization to include nonagricultural industries. In the third verse, we find machines taking over the most basic of jobs—ditch digging. He looks back at a better time: "A hundred men used to dig a ditch, / You could hear them work, and sing." But this idyllic past comes to an end when "Along come a big ditch-digging machine / And done the work of the whole shebang." As a result, "Boss man fired us—one man run it, / And ninety-nine men went hungry."[12]

This pattern repeats itself again and again in other industries with little variance. The ubiquitous narrator gets jobs in a "packing plant," "a big steel mill," and "a big coal mine." From the wages received for these positions, some good does come. The packing plant job allows him to begin "a-paying out a little house." The other jobs bring in needed money, too. But in each case, an unnamed "they" invent "a big machine" that replaces the men or that changes the market. Both the packing plant and the steel mill bring in machinery and eliminate jobs. In the coal mine, the situation differs slightly; the increased use of machines that "burn oil and gas" decrease the demand for coal. However, the result in all three cases is the same: the employers "Stopped our salary." This loss leaves the narrator with no money for his mortgage and results in the "Finance man [getting] the little home." Others are equally affected, for the lost jobs leave "a hundred thousand on the bum," push "a million men" into "the poor house," and force "a million more men . . . down the line— / Busted, disgusted."[13]

In fact, mechanization did take jobs from men who desperately needed them during the Great Depression. Even Public Works Administration jobs during the 1930s were not immune from machines replacing men. Federal Emergency Relief Administration investigator Lorena Hickok contrasts two work projects in Sioux City, Nebraska, where we explicitly see the effect of mechanization: "On one, 40 men were at work with teams and shovels, building a road. On the other, the contractor had moved in $75,000 worth of road-building machinery that was doing the job twice as fast. EIGHT MEN WERE EMPLOYED."[14] In Baltimore in November 13, 1934, National Reemployment Service employee and ex-coal dealer George Smith told Hickok that others complained to him of the Bethlehem Steel plant in Baltimore "constantly installing new machinery—and every time they install a new machine, they throw a couple of hundred men out of work—for good."[15] In addition, just as Guthrie notes, the coal industry found its wares in a state of declining demand, although this situation began in the years following World War I rather than in the 1930s.[16] Although not mentioned in this song, mechanization also came to America's mines, resulting in layoffs in that industry.[17]

While continuing to acknowledge "working folks" in general in his songs, Guthrie more typically documented the specific hurts of different groups of workers from this point onward, especially miners.[18] This shift does not defuse his energy but expands his interests and his concerns as he began to see all workers as a group already dear to him—migrants. In his autobiographical novel *Bound for Glory*, he explains this idea by creating a new definition of crops and a new perception of the migrant worker: "the people that follow the sun and the seasons to your country, follow the buds and the early leaves and come when the fruit and crops are ready to gather, and leave when the work is done. What kind of crops? Oil fields, power dams, pipe lines, canals, highways and hard-rock tunnels, skyscrapers, ships, are their crops. These are migrants now."[19] After these realizations, he inevitably pointed out what he saw as the abuses of them by employers. The people whom he works to understand and to write about move from those he knew in the fields—either in Oklahoma or in California—to those found laboring throughout the nation.

Considering the proliferation of cowboys and songs about them in Oklahoma and Texas, it seems natural that these workers would capture Guthrie's interest early on. However, in the songs he penned himself that discussed the life of the wranglers in any depth, he spent little effort in detailing their hardships. In looking at one of his earliest songs, "Cowboy's Philosophy," written in March 1935, we find an unnamed narrator asking an 'old cowpuncher / For his plain unwritten law— / For the laws among the cowboys." Of all that the old cowboy says, only one comment points to hardship and evokes some sympathy:

> There ain't no fancy doctors
> Here to bind the cowboys hurt;
> We jest warsh it at th' waterhole,
> Then we dry it on his shirt.[20]

Otherwise, the old buckaroo expresses his pride in cowboys' simple life and its pleasures. After the mid to late 1930s, this worker appears less and less in Guthrie's original songs until he eventually disappears altogether.

Nevertheless, Guthrie continued to play and record traditional cowboy songs such as "Chisholm Trail" and "I Ride an Old Paint" throughout his life. Among these songs, some of his versions from the early 1940s and on do actually contain instances of complaint or even outright protest. One of these is "Whoopie Ti Yi Yo" ("Get Along Little Doggies"). As folklorist Guy Logsdon points out, "Woody rewrote portions of the song to reflect the struggles of the cowboys on the trail drives."[21] In a line that appears original to Guthrie, the narrator tells us, "That cattle trail is rough and a hard road to travel." A later verse also includes the comment, "Some boys hit this old cow trail for pleasure/But that's where they get it most awfully wrong."[22] Although general in nature, the complaints expressed in Guthrie's version of this folk song do not present the cowboy profession as being ideal in nature. Another Guthrie favorite, "Buffalo Skinners," provides much more detail to decry the hardships accompanying life on the range. Like most others, his version explicitly relates the abuses of several cowboys by a conning trail boss. After a buffalo hunting season where lightning storms, cactus needles, and outlaw attacks make for a less than pleasant experience, the trail boss claims that all the cowboys owe him for their expenses. Thinking this debt unjust, they "left that drover's bones to bleach on the plains of the buffalo."[23] Logsdon calls this piece "an authentic cowboy protest song."[24]

Tracing the origins of "Buffalo Skinners" leads us to another group of workers whose troubles Guthrie documented in song. Apparently, the song originated as an English sea ballad. Once in the Americas, it had a change of profession as well as location, becoming a lumberman's lament in the form of "Canaday IO" before migrating west in the mid 1800s, where it retained its theme but acquired new titles, such as "Michigan IO" and "Colley's Run IO." Although it is doubtful that he actually knew of this conjunction, Guthrie did come to know and write of the plight of lumbermen in the early 1940s.

Guthrie came to know of this breed of worker from several sources. He got a fleeting understanding of the logging industry and the men who worked it while just a youth. Oak, pine, and even a little hickory grew around Okemah, and "King Timber," as Guthrie called it, came to reign in Oklahoma around the beginning of the twentieth century.[25] While traveling in the Pacific Northwest toward the end of the Great Depression, he came to a much more fully formed impression of lumbermen and their travails. His most intensive study of these laborers occurred in the summer of 1941, when he worked for the Bonneville Power Administration (BPA) as an "information consultant," writing songs for a documentary film on the development of this government program.[26] During his short tenure there, he wandered around work sites, talking to the people he met and learning about their labors. Then he would turn some of what he learned into songs such as "Roll On Columbia" and "The Grand Coulee Dam." Although many of his most famous works came from this time, his songs touching on the lives and troubles of lumbermen are much less known and have not been discussed in depth.

In the later months of that same summer, Guthrie returned to this area with Pete Seeger as a truncated version of the newly formed Almanac Singers. As they drove back to New York, they stopped off in Duluth, Minnesota, where they met Irene Paull, who wrote for a lumberman's newspaper under the pseudonym "Calamity Jane."[27] From her, Guthrie learned more about the troubles of lumbermen in America. He even praised her efforts on their behalf in song. In "Calamity Jane," the narrator details her travels through "the crummy lumber camps" where she tells the men she meets a few home truths—"Your bunks and beds are flea bit, / And your wages they're too low"—in an attempt to organize them against such miserable conditions.[28]

Along with this tribute to Calamity Jane, Guthrie crafted other songs documenting lumbermen's work and troubles. For example, among the many jobs taken on by the roving narrator in "I'm a Rounder's Name," he eventually "grappled my clamps in y'r lumber camps; / I wrestled an' rigg'd with the' timbers."[29] But Guthrie's most detailed song about this type of worker is "Lumber is King" ("Lumber's th' Life"), written on May 30, 1941, while he worked for the BPA.

The song opens with the narrator, "Tree Top Tom," singing the praises of a lumbering life. Through his and others' efforts, "It's ties and rough lumber for the whole world 'round."[30] Several verses expand on Tom's prowess, reading much like a frontier tall tale. In one version of the song, his bragging rises to the point where he attributes Paul Bunyan–like ability to himself: "At one swing of my axe th' best of y'd fall / One swing of my blade an' this forest comes down."[31] After emphasizing his exploits, Tom remembers his forefathers and establishes their legacy: "My father before me a logger was he, / He cleared out all the forests in Minnesotee; / My grandfather logged it from Maine on down."[32] This generational listing of logging regions follows the history of the industry, which moved from the northeast lumber camps in the mid-1800s to the Great Lakes region, then ended up in the Pacific Northwest's forests of Douglas fir around the turn of the century. Those wishing to remain employed as lumbermen during these shifts did truly become migrants following a crop needing harvesters.

The logging industry's demand for workers in the Pacific Northwest in the early part of the twentieth century resulted in some potential for good wages. In verse five, Tom looks back into his own past to a lucrative demand for his labors: "Back in the 20's I worked every day, / It's $14 I drawed for my pay." He reports that relative good times lasted until 1929 when "the Timber towns boomed" and "A billion board feet of the fir and the pine" were cut. But with the deepening of the Great Depression "In 19 and 30 the mill shut down." Even the great Tom loses his job, vainly searches for work, and ends up bumming around "on the old skid row" for a while.[33]

In these verses, Guthrie hits and misses some of the lumber industry's true history of the 1920s and early '30s. Although he points to a lumber production boom in 1929, one did not occur either in the Northwest or anywhere else in the nation at that time. The western logging industry did hit a high point in production in the mid-1920s, bringing in millions of board feet but nowhere near the "billion board feet of the fir and the pine" as stated in the song. By the end of this decade, production in all lumber regions had dropped to its lowest point in a decade. In her final report as the chief investigator for the Federal Emergency Relief Administration, Lorena Hickok writes, "The lumber industry did not profit from the prosperity of 1926–1929. In fact, the industry had experienced a steady decline for several years prior to 1929, and lumber production that year was actually 20 per cent under that of 1919."[34] But Guthrie does correctly point to the early 1930s as the time when unemployment in the lumber industry shot up. Between 1924 and 1933, over half of America's lumbermen lost their jobs, and the majority of those who managed to remain employed only worked an average of thirty hours a week. By the summer of 1933, "the industry was at the lowest ebb in over sixty years," according to Hickok.[35]

The lackluster employment situation remained in effect in the Northwest's lumber industry when workers from the South and the Southwest came looking for jobs cutting timber and milling lumber during the Great Depression. As Tom observes, "Folks from the plains, and folks from the east, / Folks from the Dust bowl" appear but can find no work. In "Washington Talkin' Blues," another song written during his BPA tenure, Guthrie again touches on these laborers' fruitless search for employment in the

DOCUMENTING THE TROUBLES OF OTHER AMERICAN WORKERS

Northeast woodlands. In "Lumber is King," Tom pointedly asks, "What you gonna do 'bout these hard working Men, / Whole families, and women, and kids pouring in?" Although no answer comes in reply to this angry question, in several succeeding verses, he takes to predicting the demise of "King Lumber" due to "the day when the land is cut o'ver."[36]

In time, the lumber industry and the economy as a whole recouped their losses with the end of the Great Depression due to increased demand attributable to the expanding conflict in Europe. In recognition of this change, Tom announces, "Times gettin' better, th' big papers shows." This general prosperity hides some unsettling truths concerning the increase in clear-cutting and the decrease in jobs due to mechanization. He points to what he sees as the new rapacity of the lumber industry, which is "Cutting the timber twice fast as it grows; / The trees will be gone when the years roll 'round." After this criticism of clear-cutting and in a familiar Guthrie mode, the narrator blames mechanization as the main culprit in this desolation of America's woodlands. Tom points to "the Mechanical fellers," "high power saw," and "fast diesel cats" as the main force behind the destruction of the forests and lumber jobs.[37] Certainly, technological advances in logging camps and sawmills did speed up the removal of trees from throughout America's woodlands, just as they had been doing for decades. Machines first came to the forests in the late 1800s in the form of steam engines that allowed for quick hauling of logs, later evolving into large machines run by diesel or electricity to do the same. By the time Guthrie began exploring the northwest woods, Caterpillar tractors (the "cats" mentioned above) had appeared. In time, Guthrie would shift his opinion enough to actually praise the "guys that skin the cats" (run the tractors) in a revised version of "The Biggest Thing Man Has Ever Done" ("The Great Historical Bum"), but in "Lumber is King," the machines are the source of labor's ills.[38]

Nevertheless, Tom does not just point his finger at the lumber companies' destructive policies and machines. His fellow workers find themselves included in the indictment, even as Tom indicates that only they can save the forests through their own conservation efforts. In a later version of the song, he denounces his fellow lumbermen's participation in the efforts to devastate the trees: "My big trees are goin', an' us lumber jacks / We're a-droppin' 'em down, an' not plantin' 'em back." Also in this version, Tom promises to do his part to stop this depiction. He says, "I'll cut me down one tree, I'll plant me back Two." For "I know, if I don't, lumber's gone out and down," taking with it the livelihood of many workers.[39]

In addition to lumbermen, Guthrie became well-acquainted with other workers who were relatively new to him during his stint with the BPA. Of these laborers, those who handled the dangerous blasting operations impressed him enough to be immortalized in the song "Grand Coulee Powder Monkeys." Using the tune from Jimmie Rodgers's "Muleskinner Blues," Guthrie sets his story of a powder monkey (demolition man) who brags of his skill to gain a job. In a tall-tale moment offered as proof of his ability, the powder monkey creates a single explosion with some impressive results: "The marble was finished and loaded and the loose dirt" that came down from the explosion filled in the hole. As a result of this miraculous demonstration, the boss says, "I'll give ye the job." Unfortunately, the powder monkey has made a crucial mistake and ends up "buried way down dead."[40] Even though the song comes across as fanciful story, the powder monkey's death undercuts the bragging with a surprise jolt of harsh reality at the end.

Many of the songs that Guthrie wrote during his time with the BPA celebrate certain workers with the same energy and exaggeration found in traditional songs and stories. Both Tree Top Tom and the unnamed powder monkey have ability beyond that of mortal man, yet they suffer also: Tom with unemployment and the realization that his livelihood is limited and the powder monkey through death. Much the same holds true with the worker who made the greatest impression on Guthrie during this time: the jackhammer operator. This worker looms large in the song pictures that he paints in the early 1940s. For the most part, all the jackhammer operators we find in Guthrie's songs appear more like mythical heroes than flesh and blood men found in his songs about sharecroppers and migrant laborers. In both "Jackhammer John" and "The Girl in the Red, White, and Blue," the man who wields the jackhammer has physical power beyond belief. In the latter of the two songs, he even challenges such legendary figures as Paul Bunyan and John Henry to battle. Although their conflict is resolved through peaceful means, Jackhammer John still comes to stand as Guthrie's most fully realized original tall-tale character.[41]

Nevertheless, Guthrie also explores a more realistic representation of this worker. The figure of the nonlegendary jackhammer operator appears in passing in "I'm a Rounder's Name." Written during the mid-1940s, this song covers many occupations; the narrator seems to be a jack of all trades or the everyman of the working class. But at one point in his varied career, he works for the Tennessee Valley Authority, where he labors mightily with a jackhammer in his hands:

> I whimmed an' I whammed on yore Tennessee dam;
> I frogg'd an' I frigg'd with th' boulders;
> I cobbled their jocks on the jaggery rocks
> Till a jackhammer jostled my shoulders.[42]

In another song from this era, Guthrie again details the reality of this worker. One of the earliest versions of "Jackhammer Blues" ("Jackhammer John") opens with lines evoking the folk song "John Henry": "Jack Hammer John was a Jack hammer man / Born with a Jack hammer in his hand." But John's powers only bring him to the best of positions some of the time, for he announces, "I've hammered in the best, and I hammered in the worst." Even in the midst of the bragging that fills this song, he admits that he had "Been in jail a thousand times" and complains that he is "always broke when my job is through." The uncertainty of this job also plays a role in the song "Columbia Waters." Here, the narrator is just a normal man. In the past, he did his job well and was recognized for it: "Back in my hometown I was a man of some renown; / When I take a jackhammer down in a hole, gonna be some rock come down." Now out of work and with others dependent on him, he admits, "Ramblin' around from place to place is hard on a family man." Still, he remains proud: "I aint a gonna beg and steal." At the song's end, through the opportunity to work steady on the Grand Coulee Dam, he again regains his self-esteem and excitedly pledges to "settle down and live my life by the C-O-U-L-double E!"[43]

But even as Guthrie sympathized with this worker, he did not know much about the difficulties of the profession from direct personal experience. In fact, fellow Oklahoman and friend Gordon Friesen used to cow Guthrie when he got a bit uppity about his proletarian background by saying, "You're an intellectual, a poet—all this singin' about jackhammers, if you ever got within five feet of a jackhammer it'd knock you on your ass."[44]

During his short term with the BPA in the summer of 1941, Guthrie managed to compose songs that covered several different types of workers, not just those who handled jackhammers. One of these songs was "Hard Travelin'," which through its appearance on albums and in songbooks has become one of his better-known compositions. The original version focuses on the "hard travelin'" of various migrant laborers, but the song later expanded to include a verse discussing steelworkers.[45] The exclusion of these workers in the first version of the song is understandable. At the time, Guthrie had had no contact with them, although this situation would change soon after he left the BPA. Almost as soon as he hit New York from his cross-country journey from the West Coast, he joined the Almanac Singers on a national tour. These pro-union troubadours had a lot to do in that strikes had swept across America along with the prosperity that war production had brought. Almost two and a half million workers were on strike in 1941, more than any previous year except 1919.[46] Along the way, the Almanacs stopped in Pittsburgh to sing for steelworkers. In a section edited from his final version of the introduction to *American Folksong*, Guthrie writes of their "hit[ting] our first union hall stopoff, the Smokey old Town, the Iron Town, Pittsburgh, stole by Jones and Laughlin's steel. We made up songs. From the Alleghaney to the Ohio she's all gonna melt up CIO, Pittsburgh! Lord God! Pittsburgh!"[47] Using the tune to "Crawdad Hole" and containing much of the same rhetoric in the aforementioned prose piece, the group immortalized their impressions of the town in the song "Pittsburgh." Among its observations about the town and its history appear these lines: "All I do is cough and choke / From the iron filings and the sulphur smoke / In Pittsburgh, Lord God, Pittsburgh."[48]

One of the many incarnations of the Almanac Singers (from left—Woody Guthrie, Millard Lampell, Bess Hawes, Pete Seeger, Arthur Stern, and Sis Cunningham), c. 1942. Courtesy of the Woody Guthrie Archives.

DOCUMENTING THE TROUBLES OF OTHER AMERICAN WORKERS

At the time of the Almanac Singers' visit, steelworkers in Pittsburgh were working to unionize their profession as money from the steel-hungry war industry started rolling in. This influx of cash was a welcome shift from the starvation days of the Great Depression years. In 1935, the industry nationwide operated at only 40 percent of its capacity, which was actually a hundredfold increase from the latter part of the previous year. But even this Depression-era jump did not strongly affect job opportunities; from 1934 to 1935 employment in the industry only saw a ten percent increase.[49] By the late 1930s, steelworkers still had little to celebrate. So the sharp increase in production of the early 1940s encouraged steelworkers to demand a corresponding increase in their salaries.

Armed with his encounters with steelworkers and an understanding of their conditions, Guthrie embraced them and documented their hardships. He rewrote "Hard Travelin'" during his stay in Pittsburgh so as to include these workers. In an added verse, he opens with "I been working that Pittsburgh steel." Then come the specifics; he has been working pouring "red hot slag," along with "a-blastin'," "a-firin'," and "a-duckin' red hot iron."[50] All this effort has made for "some hard traveling, Lord." Steelworkers also appear in other of his songs. In "I'm a Rounder's Name," the descriptions of the job come across as less than pleasant. The narrator "rocked an' I reeled in th' iron an' steel" where he "fumed in their fiery blast."[51]

During his time with the Almanac Singers, Guthrie also began documenting in song the plight of another group of laborers, oil workers. As a youth, he came into direct contact with these workers in the oil fields surrounding Okemah, which he describes as "one of our first Oil Boom Towns," and those around Pampa, Texas.[52] Although familiar with the oil industry early in life, he only began featuring oil workers in his lyrics after the Almanacs received a songwriting commission in 1942 from Edwin Smith, who was the organizing campaign director of the Oil Workers International Union (OWIU).[53] Guthrie wrote two pieces for Smith. One was "Boomtown Bill," which follows the tune to "The Wabash Cannonball." Its narrator opens with the common "Come ye" device and asks "oilfield workers . . . [to] listen to my tale." Guthrie's personal experience comes into play in this song when the narrator, Boomtown Bill, says he "lit in Oklahoma in the boom called Seminole." But Bill does not stay put there; he also "worked . . . the Alegehaney field" in Pennsylvania, "slushed in Louisiana," and "bailed the shale in Illinois and West Coast's Signal Hill." Although the story he unfolds does not much focus on the hurts suffered by oil workers in these wide-ranging places, one moment of injustice does appear: the narrator suffered through "wind and weather of rain and sleet and snow" in his work while "John D got the dough."[54] John D. Rockefeller and his company unions appear again in the other commissioned song, "Keep That Oil A-Rolling." Here, the narrator admits, "the company union made a fool out of me" and adds that it leaves the oil workers "singing them Rocke-feller blues."[55] The oil magnate appears in these songs for several reasons. For one, his fortune and fame (or infamy) resulted primarily from his oil ventures. The other reason is less obvious: his organization invented the company union in 1914 as a means to avoid more meaningful worker repre-sentation. Indeed, Guthrie's songs primarily denounce company unions and celebrate oil workers, their efforts to defeat the Nazis, and the CIO. In effect, the songs are propaganda for the OWIU, and recordings of these songs were used for that purpose at the group's thirteenth convention in 1942, where "playing of these records at union meetings and elsewhere has created a lot of enthusiasm for the Union."[56]

Other of Guthrie's songs documenting workers' troubles also come out of specific needs, even if these works were not commissioned. One of these is "Hard Times on the Subway," which details New York subway drivers' job woes in the early 1940s. The history behind this particular labor strug-gle starts in the summer of 1942, when members of New York's Transport Workers Union (TWU) began a unified push for improved conditions and wages. The city's Board of Transportation (BT) resisted these efforts from the beginning, and negotiations completely fell apart in October, eventually resulting in the TWU's threat to strike. Since New York Mayor Fiorello La Guardia backed the board and did not intervene on the side of the union, he fell into disfavor with TWU leaders and members. At an early January 1943 rally, the president of a TWU local even went as far as calling La Guardia and BT Director John Delaney "Hitler lovers" since the two obviously were trying to force the TWU to strike and thus slow down the war effort.[57] In time and through arbitration, the union and the mayor worked out a pay increase in the summer of 1943.

On first coming to New York City, Guthrie found the subway fascinat-ing, and it gave him much material for the comical "Talking Subway Blues" and "New York Town." Unlike these songs, "Hard Times on the Subway" does not contain any lilting humor. Instead, it deals with the complaints of subway workers against their unsafe working conditions, their low pay, and Mayor La Guardia's resistance to improving both. The song opens by categorizing the story to follow as "A mighty sad" one "concerning the mayor and the T.W.U." The narrator stakes out his desires early by stating, "I want to haul workers to win this war / That's what I work on this subway for." He then mentions the two main obstacles to his stated goal. First, he complains, "The people so crowded and the train so packed / My wheels can't turn and they're jumping the track."[58] Although these lines overstate the danger, overcrowding on New York's subway did draw complaints during the war years. Due to the rationing of gasoline and rubber at this time, more people than ever before crammed the city's rapid transit system, resulting in drastic overcrowding and the possibility for disaster. In a letter to the *New York Times*, one woman expressed her fears due to overcrowding in the subway by first telling of an elderly man who had been trampled and then confessing, "I am personally petrified every time the train becomes so jammed, thinking that if by chance something should go wrong the worst panic ever would result."[59]

The narrator's second complaint draws his concern more than overcrowding. He says, "My wages so low" that "I can't feed my belly [and] my wheels can't go." His reduction in wages results in more than one empty stomach: "My family don't eat." His and the other subway workers' money problems have larger repercussions than hunger. Since "The war plants and factories are giving more pay," many "trainmen are quitting and stopping the trains," and without the trainmen, "Five million workers will walk on the street." Thus, the narrator lays out the trainmen's dilemma: stay at an important low-paying job or leave for better pay and strand millions of workers. In an endnote to the song, Guthrie writes that the TWU workers' pay "was so low that lots of them were quitting and going to work in war factories."[60]

His comments on this subject do adhere to facts. Even BT Director Delaney admitted, while resisting a pay raise, that over a thousand transit workers quit to take higher paying jobs in private industry.[61] Some transit workers, Guthrie notes, decided to hold "down two or three jobs, one in the subway and others in war plants." Of this last course, the singer warns, "A subway worker that's half asleep or dead tired when he comes down to work is certainly too dangerous to handle." In a dispute over transit workers moonlighting in 1944, Mayor La Guardia agreed with this claim, saying, "Now, these men need their rest. They just can't work at two jobs."[62] However, Guthrie and the mayor do not seem to agree otherwise.

Although Guthrie did not go as far as stating that the mayor was a "Hitler lover," his narrator does place both La Guardia and Hitler in opposition to the union and fair pay. Since a subway slow-down would hurt the war effort, the narrator believes "fascists are working to keep my pay low," and the mayor is clearly linked with them. Although the union brought its grievances to him, "The mayor he stalled and it certainly exposes / That our little flower is not all roses." As a result of the mayor's inactivity, the continued resignations of workers, and the overcrowding, "The trains are stalling all over town."[63] Thus, the final image is one of gridlock—but as noted, soon after the composition of this song, the TWU and the city administration worked out a deal and pushed the song into history. "Hard Times in the Subway" stands as the only example of Guthrie expressing sympathy in song for this particular type of worker, but it shows him writing topical material and attempting to comment directly on the immediate issues affecting the working class. Other groups found their way into many of Guthrie's compositions. Of these, miners held his interest more than any other American workers except those in agriculture.

Beginning in the early 1940s, Guthrie began including miners in the long list of workers whose hurts he documented. But before he wrote of their lives, he had learned of them and their songs. Although the area he grew up in was never known as a major mining region, Guthrie writes, "The soft coal mines, the lead and zinc mines around Henryetta, [Oklahoma,] were only seventeen miles from my home town, Okemah."[64] Folklorist John Greenway believes that this proximity has to do with the singer's interest and adds, "Next to the migratory crop pickers, the miner has been the worker closest to Guthrie's heart."[65] Actually, migrant farm laborers and miners had some points in common. For one, many miners once had been farmers themselves before being uprooted by changing times and enticed by work in the mines. For another, they too suffered mightily. In particular, many of them eked out a bare living in the hills of Kentucky, Pennsylvania, and West Virginia during the Great Depression, although they had earned little better than starvation wages since coal production decreased after World War I.[66] Guthrie knew Oklahoma's miners originally came "in search of elbow room on the ground, room to farm the rich topsoil; but, hushed and quiet, they dug into the private heart of the earth to find the lead, the soft coal, the good zinc." In writing of coal mining in his home state just before the end of the war and the coming of the 1920s, he points back to Henryetta's yearly "King Koal Karnival" to muse, "in a year or two King Koal would die and his body would be burned to ashes and his long twisting grave would be left dank and dark and empty under the ground."[67]

Along with these understandings of his state's miners in particular and coal industry in general, he also "heard their songs of people killed in the mines."[68] In particular, from the miners, the radio, or even a record, he learned "Dream of a Miner's Child" when only a child himself.[69] In this song, while sleeping, a miner's little girl envisions destruction: "I dreamed that the mine was a-seething with fire; / The men all fought for their lives." Then in the chorus, she begs her father,

> O daddy, don't work in the mines today,
> For dreams do so often come true.
> O daddy, my daddy, please don't go away;
> I never could live without you.

Although the song's theme and basic lyric structure originally come from an English dance hall piece by Will Geddes and Robert Donnelly titled "Don't Go Down in the Mine," Guthrie most probably knew "Dream of a Miner's Child" from Andrew Jenkins's penned and Vernon Dalhart's popularized 1925 release. In support of this assumption, we can look to one of Guthrie's songbooks, which included a version very similar lyrically to Jenkins's.[70]

The miners he met and their songs he heard in his youth did not provide him his only access to these workers' lives and hardships. After moving to New York in the early 1940s, he encountered many mining songs, such as "Only a Miner" and Florence Reece's classic "Which Side Are You On?" But his most important source for insight into miners and their lives came from Aunt Molly Jackson and from her half-siblings Jim Garland and Sarah Ogan. All three had been involved one way or another in the bloody coal mine strikes in Harlan County, Kentucky, during the early 1930s. Eventually, they left their native state to come to New York City, where they all sang traditional songs and their own original material about the lives of miners. Guthrie met them there in early 1940. First, he sang with Jackson at a benefit show in March of that year. Through her, he met and then played with both Garland and Ogan on radio station WNYC that summer.[71] In a section from *American Folksong* he discusses their songs and singing: "Aunt Molly Jackson would sing us an hour or two of Bloody Harlan County, songs of organizing the coal miners to beat the [sheriff's] thugs...." Of Jim Garland, he notes, "He tried to tell us with his songs and ballads the stories of the ones that went down fighting. Half a song would be a clear story of how the murderous gunthugs hid in the brush and killed the union organizer, Harry Simms, and the other half of the song would be Jim's slo-gans, his sermons, his plea, his newspaper editorial, his whole appeal for you to come over onto the union side and fight." However, Guthrie's strongest praise went to the youngest of the three: "Singing to us as she had sung into the rifle fire of Sheriff Blair's deputies, Sarah Ogan got the house of people to keep so still that the cat licking his hair sounded like a broomstick rubbed against a washtub."[72] From them, he learned such songs as "Ragged Hungry Blues," "Fare Ye Well Old Ely Branch," "I Am a Girl of Constant Sorrow," "Come All You Coal Miners," "The Murder of Harry Simms," and "Welcome the Traveler Home." By the early 1940s, he had many examples of miners' hardships in stories and songs to help him give his mining songs shape and authenticity.

Surprisingly, his first original song focusing on a miner's woes was far from the work he would eventually turn out about the dangers of the min-ing industry. In his 1935-era song "Californy Gold," a miner tells of a "girl living high in the city, /. . . living in luxury untold," all due to his money. As it turns out, he fell in love with this girl, romancing her by fireside, accepting her kisses, listening to her sad tales until she "set me free from my Californy gold." After the relationship has ended and his "Californy gold" ends up in the hands of his former love, "I am back in the mountains, / With my pick and my shovel in my hand." But even here, in this lovelorn song, Guthrie briefly hits on the miner's suffering, even if only to accent his lover's betrayal: "There is frost on my face this fair morning, / And my little old log cabin is so cold."[73]

In some of his later works, Guthrie included moments that more point-edly address miners' difficulties. In his well-known piece "Hard Travelin'," his narrator explains, "I been working in a hard rock tunnel." There, he has "been a leaning on a pressure drill" with "Hammer flyin', air hose suckin', / Six feet of mud I sure been a muckin'."[74] As a result of all this work, he has "been having some hard traveling, Lord." We also find a passing comment in "I'm a Rounder's Name" where the narrator tells us, "Like an' eyeless mole I grubbed f'r coal / In th' belly of ole Pennsylvania."[75] But even after he began noting miners' difficult lives in song, Guthrie could still create toothless pieces about these workers' lives. A prime example of this type of song is "Miner's Song" ("Dig My Life Away"). As Guy Logsdon notes, this piece actually "gives a 'first impression' of being a children's song," a feeling that comes out of its whimsical nature.[76] In searching for "precious metal," "a perfect ruby," and "a good-shaped diamond," the narrator "Go[es] in the hole both day and night" and ends up "dig[ging] my life away-o."[77] These lines, which could be read negatively, are undercut by the jaunty tune to which they are set and Guthrie's happy deliverance. But to suggest that this song represents Guthrie's typical presentation of miners would be misleading. For the most part, he used his songs touching on miners' lives to point to the abuses they suffered as a result of the greed of the mine owners.

Long before Guthrie began writing about their plight in the early 1940s, miners had been eking out a marginal existence throughout America. In fact, two of Guthrie's best-known songs about miners focus on events taken out of the past instead of current events. To find the impetus behind these songs, we can look back to New York City in the early 1940s, when he read Ella May "Mother" Bloor's autobiography *We Are Many*. Bloor, who was Will Geer's grandmother-in-law, was an activist and all-around rabble rouser in various progressive, Socialist, and Communist causes throughout the first four decades of the twentieth century. Although never as famous as her counterpart Mother Jones, Bloor also worked as a labor organizer, as well as a journalist for various liberal and socialist periodicals. In the fall of 1940, she revealed much of her efforts on behalf of America's workers in her autobiography. Out of the many tales of class strife and union action, one of the book's chapters, titled "Calumet and Ludlow—Massacre of the Innocents," grabbed Guthrie's attention and spurred him to action.[78] Considering the dramatic and tragic nature of these stories, his interest is understandable.

On July 23, 1913, around fifteen thousand copper miners led by the Western Federation of Miners began a strike in Michigan's Houghton County, which the Calumet and Hecla Mining Company largely controlled. The next day, due to pressure brought about by the mine owners, Governor Woodbridge Ferris called out over twenty-five hundred members of the Michigan National Guard, stating, "Property and life must be protected."[79] They were joined in the protection of the mine owners' interests by armed private detectives—some of whom trained local deputies and killed at least two miners. Local businessmen also joined in against the strike by creating the Citizens Alliance in November. Although Ferris eventually decreased the National Guard contingency, the number of deputies increased at the same time, reaching over two thousand men at one point.[80] Under this protection, some of the nonstriking miners returned to work, joined by scabs from the East brought in by the mining companies. Nevertheless, thousands of strikers held out during the summer, fall, and early winter.

Michigan workers handling cars loaded with copper ore at a Calumet and Hecla Company mine, c. 1916. Courtesy of the Prints and Photographs Division of the Library of Congress.

Although low on funds, the Calumet Ladies' Auxiliary organized a Christmas party for the striking miners' children in the Italian Benevolent Society's hall in the heart of the village of Red Jacket. In the late afternoon of Christmas Eve, over five hundred children and some of their mothers and fathers crowded the hall, opening their meager gifts and listening to music.[81] A short time after 4 p.m., someone yelled, "Fire," and a panic resulted in the packed hall. A mass of children and some parents scrambled down the stairwell leading to the main entrance, got trapped there, and smothered in the press of their own bodies. After the stair was cleared, Mother Bloor "saw the marks of the children's nails in the plaster, where they had desperately scratched to get free, as they suffocated."[82] Fifty-nine children and fourteen adults died as a result of this frenzy.[83]

In response to reading Bloor's detailing of this tragedy, Guthrie wrote the song "1913 Massacre" sometime before May 24, 1945, when he first recorded it. It opens up with an unnamed narrator requesting that the listeners "Take a trip with me in nineteen thirteen / To Calumet, Michigan in the copper country." Then we enter the Italian Hall and go up the "high stairs" to the Christmas party. There, "Singing and dancing is heard ev'ry wheres" as we meet the miners and "watch the kids dance 'round the big Christmas tree." The joy of the season is so great that we are taken in as neighbors:

> There's talking and laughing and songs in the air.
> And the spirit of Christmas is there ev'ry where.

DOCUMENTING THE TROUBLES OF OTHER AMERICAN WORKERS

Before you know it you're friends with us all
And you're dancing around and around in the hall.

While joining in on the happy festivities, we learn about the conditions the miners face: "They'll tell you they make less than a dollar a day, / Working their copper claims, risking their lives."[84] But these thoughts only momentarily draw attention away from the party, and soon all eyes focus on a girl as she plays the piano for the gathered crowd.

But all is not well. For while miners and their families enjoy the party, "the copper boss thug men are milling outside." They soon break the quiet of the girl's performance by yelling, "There's a fire." Some realize that "it's just the thugs and the scabs" trying to trick the partygoers, but not all heed this warning. First, "A man grabbed his daughter and he carried her down," but "then others followed, a hundred or more." Unfortunately, they cannot get out because "the thugs held the door." As "The gun thugs . . . laughed at their murderous joke," the sheer press of the struggling bodies smother the trapped children. In the aftermath, the miners carry seventy-three little bodies "back up to their tree" while "The scabs outside still laughed at their spree." Now "the piano played a slow funeral tune" as "the town was lit up by a cold Christmas moon." The warm spirit encountered at the beginning of the song evaporates, leaving mothers and fathers behind with their grief and their anger at the company and its murderous minions: "The parents, they cried and the miners, they moaned, / 'See what your greed for money has done?'"[85]

While the first-person narrative here drives the story along to its tragic end and makes for effective anti–mine boss propaganda, all the song's details do not follow established history. As noted, the incident actually occurred not in Calumet but in nearby Red Jacket. In addition, the dead numbered one more than in Guthrie's account and were made up of both adults and children. But the most important mistake involves the cause of the disaster; for the majority of the testimony from eyewitnesses (many of whom were striking miners or their families) does not support the claim that "gun thugs" hired by the company raised the alarm or held the doors closed at the bottom of the stairs. Although rumors immediately following the incident did point to either deputies or private detectives as the ones who caused the panic, the coroner's inquest, at which many of the party survivors testified, found that the person who first called "Fire" could not be determined and that only union-affiliated persons entered the hall on the fateful day. In addition, testimony proved that the doors to the hall were open and that the crowd fell upon itself, resulting in the deaths.[86] Nevertheless, the song's story has overshadowed the truth, with some critics who have discussed the piece continuing to perpetuate these factual errors.[87]

In the other song inspired by Bloor's book, Guthrie comes closer to mirroring the historical truth. On September 23, 1913, over nine thousand coal miners went out on strike in southern Colorado, primarily against the Rockefeller family–controlled Colorado Fuel and Iron Company (CFIC). Since the miners lived in company housing, evictions occurred soon after the strike was called. With help from the United Mine Workers of America, the strikers persevered by building tent cities near the mining towns of Trinidad, Walsenburg, and Ludlow. Immediately, the mine operators brought in armed private detectives to assist mine guards in harassing the striking miners and in protecting scabs. The strikers resisted these efforts, and numerous casualties occurred on both sides of the conflict, although the well-financed CFIC-backed forces gave more than they got. On October 28, Governor Elias Ammons succumbed to the pressure brought to bear on him from the mining interests and ordered in a 1,100-man-strong contingent of the Colorado National Guard under the command of General Chase, whom labor organizer Mother Jones described as "a monster . . . whose veins run with ice water."[88] Ostensibly sent to keep the peace, the soldiers often joined the company's gun thugs in protecting the scabs and harassing the striking miners and their families. As a result of this threatening situation, some miners dug pits under their tents where their wives and children would be safe from the gunfire that occasionally ripped through the tent cities.

As the strike dragged on into 1914, the two forces came to an uneasy stalemate. Then in mid-April, the governor withdrew all of the National Guard units except Company B, which was made up almost entirely of mine guards and private detectives still in CFIC's pay. In addition, men loyal to the mine operators formed a volunteer company after the other guardsmen were recalled. These two units stationed themselves above the largest tent colony, located just outside the town of Ludlow. On the morning of April 20, a small group of militiamen searching for a missing person imperiously entered the camp, harassed some of the miners and their families, and then promised they would return later. This intrusion provoked the miners, who positioned themselves for an attack. Seeing this move by the miners, the soldiers opened fire with machine guns into the tents below.

The onslaught lasted throughout the day, leaving six men and one child dead.[89] That night, the military force moved in and set fire to the tents; and the next day, eleven children and two women were discovered dead in a pit dug beneath a burnt-out tent. This slaughter eventually came to be known as the "Ludlow Massacre."

In his song detailing this incident, Guthrie again uses a first-person narrator who jumps into the story at "early springtime," just at the moment when CFIC's minions "drove us miners out of doors. / Out from the houses that the company owned." As a result, the striking miners "moved into tents up at old Ludlow." But there they are not safe since the guards stationed above the tent city occasionally let "bullets . . . fly, / [That] kick up gravel under my feet." Worried about the safety of the children, the narrator and others "dug us a cave that was seven feet deep, / Carried our young ones and a pregnant woman / Down inside . . . to sleep." But even this measure cannot protect the innocent, for the miners did not guess that the soldiers would set the tent city on fire and "pull the triggers of your gattling guns" at the fleeing strikers and their families. This onslaught keeps the narrator from rescuing the hiding children, and thirteen die. Afterward, miners bury their murdered but not their own misery:

> I never will forget the look on the faces
> Of the men and women that awful day,
> When we stood around to preach their funerals
> And lay the corpses of the dead away.[90]

But even after the events of the massacre are related, Guthrie's song does not end. It goes on to detail the miners' reactions to the killings.

The miners try to rid themselves of the guardsmen by beseeching the governor to have President Wilson call them off. However, the narrator tells us, "But the National Guard belonged to the governor, / So he didn't try so very hard." With the pain of the killings still fresh and the authorities unwilling to act, the miners decide to fight back. Their women sell potatoes at the nearby town of Walsenburg to buy guns, which they smuggle back and "put . . . in every hand." When the soldiers next attack, they meet with a violent surprise, for the "miners mowed down these troopers, / You should have seen those poor boys run." After the battle, the miners return to the site of the massacre, where they create a makeshift monument to the dead. In the final moment of the song, the narrator links this sacrifice to the formation of his union and weeps for the murdered: "I said, 'God bless the mine workers union,' / And then I hung my head and cried."[91]

As alluded to earlier, unlike "1913 Massacre," much of what Guthrie reports in this song does adhere to the facts that can be established about the strike and the attack on the tent colony. The reason for this accuracy may be that Guthrie had several sources for information about this tragic incident from America's labor history. In addition to what he learned from Bloor, Guthrie also knew about the troubles at Ludlow from Earl Robinson and Alfred Hayes's song "Ludlow Massacre" and from Edwin Smith of the Oil Workers International Union.[92] However, he still gets some of his details wrong. For one, twelve children died, not thirteen. Guthrie also omits any mention of the adult casualties. But it is in his comments about the actions occurring in the aftermath of the Ludlow Massacre where he strays from the truth and instead follows the tale related in Bloor's autobiography. For example, in the histories on this incident, no source other than Bloor's mentions the potatoes-for-arms scenario. Her story also distorts the truth in other parts of the song. Well before April 20th, the striking miners had weapons; they even used them on the day of the attack. In addition, according to most histories of this incident, after the massacre, survivors and striking miners from other sections of southern Colorado attacked mine employees and burned mining facilities in the area. They even engaged several hundred Colorado National Guardsmen in raging gun battles until President Wilson sent in federal troops at the beginning of May to restore order. But by this point the strikers had suffered too much to achieve victory against CFIC and the other mine operators; and on December 10, the strike ended in defeat.[93]

Although these two songs draw upon past events, most of Guthrie's mining songs focus on current cases where those who labored underground had their lives discounted by their employers. Of all professions, mining has long been one of the most dangerous, and folk songs have long documented disasters in this profession. One of the earliest such songs in America is "Avondale Mine Disaster," which details the deaths of 110 men and boys on September 6, 1869, in Pennsylvania's coal fields. But the dangers to miners did not end in the nineteenth century. From 1900 to 1946, official U.S. government documents note 71,030 fatalities due to mine accidents, resulting in an average of 129 deaths per month.[94] Although some improvements resulted from federal and state mandated mining inspections by the mid-twentieth century, death remained a constant threat in America's coal mines, with almost 900 fatalities officially reported in the 1940s.[95] The largest single death toll during this time occurred in 1947 at Centralia, Illinois.

On March 25th, around 3:30 p.m., a great explosion rocked Centralia Coal Company Mine Number 5. In the aftermath, rescuers brought out eight wounded miners, but over a hundred workers remained underground, their condition unknown. In freezing weather, rescue teams worked around the clock to free those still enclosed while their families gathered at the mouth of the mine. In the end, these efforts and the families' prayers went unrewarded; all of the missing one hundred eleven miners were found dead. But the body count alone did not attract national media attention, for it soon came to light that both state and federal mine inspectors had warned of the mine's hazardous condition less than a week before the disaster.[96] In fact, the state inspector accused Illinois Department of Mines and Minerals Director Robert Merrill of ignoring repeated negative reports on the Centralia mine.[97] As a result of the disaster and the controversy about it, a Senate subcommittee investigated. At the end of these hearings, the chair stated, "If there has been one thing shown to this committee, it has been that there was gross negligence here in the handling of safety conditions" at Centralia.[98]

In a spurt of creative energy on April 1, 1947, Guthrie wrote three songs detailing this disaster and published them the next month in the progressive folk song magazine *People's Songs*.[99] Although based on newspaper reports, these songs do detail the historical facts even as they include fictional voices to express the miners' and their families' feelings. In explaining how he could speak from these miners' perspective, Guthrie writes that even though he did not actually see the disaster, the similar hardships shared by workers around the world unify the underclass no matter their nationality or individual job and give them insight that the overclass cannot access:

> I was there the same as you was there and seen the same things
> that you did. And you was here the same as I was here and you
> felt the same things I felt. This is the trick of human nature
> that is going to outwit and outfight our owners and their hired
> bosses, this way . . . that we've got of being on the spot at places
> like Centralia, both in body and in spirit, like being on a manure
> street in India and seeing the eyes of good folks hungry and
> starving to death. You see, our landlords and our owners don't
> make full use of this eye of ours that sees around the world, not

like us miners and tongbuckers and shipscalers and riggers do
when we risk our lives to get the work done.[100]

Guthrie believed that his own connection to the underclass gave him the power to speak for the miners and their families. In effect, he thinks that all workers can channel the voice of others who labor, who sweat, who risk their lives for bread and board.

In looking at these three songs, we can judge for ourselves how well he achieved his own stated goal. First, let us look at "Talking Miner" ("Talking Centralia"). Again, Guthrie creates a narrator who speaks from personal knowledge. In this case, he is a miner involved in the accident. He announces his profession and then adds, "I did like a mole in a hole in the ground / When the sun comes up till the sun goes down." For him the day of the explosion begins like any other:

> I got up this morning in my same old way
> Drunk my hot coffee to start off my day
> My wife give me breakfast in her stocking feet,
> I kissed the kids in bed, then I walked up the street

As he trudges to work, he loses himself in observation and thought. First, he briefly describes his fellow miners as "Some joked, some teased, some argued, some sung" while joining in on the march to the mine. Then he considers his own weariness, wishing for the day "I'll quit mining . . . and I'll sleep about a week" and "Dream up myself a lot of pretty dreams" of a perfect work place and a caring boss. But this fantasy dissipates before his reflections on the fear that lingers in his and all miners' minds:

> Most men don't talk what's eating their mind
> About the different ways of dying down here in the mines
> But every morning we walk along and joke
> About mines caving in and the dust and the smoke
> One little wild spark of fire blowing us skyhigh and crooked.
> One little spark blowing us crosseyed and crazy.
> Up to shake hands with all of the Lord's little angels.

But these foreboding images are driven away when they finally reach the mine. There, they ride the elevator into the dark bowels of the earth and

DOCUMENTING THE TROUBLES OF OTHER AMERICAN WORKERS

"scatter and kneel and crawl different places." Once at their positions, even before the explosion, they suffer from "fumes in our eyes and dust on our faces / Gas on our stomach. Water on the kneecap. Aches and pains. / Rheumatism." As a result, they drift off into a kind of feverish swoon, with "All kinds of crazy pictures flying through our heads."[101]

Unfortunately, the ugly dangers they joked about earlier come to pass in verse six. Here the narrator announces the explosion with rather matter-of-fact language: "Well, this spark did hit us in Number Five." But unlike in the other two songs Guthrie wrote about the Centralia disaster, this miner does have some luck and only "got carried out with a busted head." Most of the other miners did not fare so well; for "A lady said a Hundred and Eleven was dead." But then we learn that the narrator is a veteran of many a mine disaster and numbers the dead he has seen: "I come through two cave-ins and one more fire before this one. / Twenty Two dead down Ohio. Thirty Six in Kentucky's green hills."[102] In the last verse, he laments, "It seems like the very best men go down / And don't come back in these mining towns."

After this reflection, the narrator muses on the easy way that officials ignored the warnings that mine inspectors made about the number five shaft. He also imagines what would happen if our national legislators had the same danger as did the miners:

> I keep on a wondering how things would be
> If a cavein would come to a Senator's seat
> Or if a big explosion of some kind was to go off in Congress halls.
> What words and messages would they write on the walls?
> Wonder if they'd hire anybody to come to the Senate's Chamber
> And put in any safety devices?

Then, in a moment of humor amid the serious tone of the rest of the song, the narrator says, "I think there's just about enough loose gas around the Capitol dome / To make a mighty big blow if a spark ever hits it."[103]

Most of the miners at work that day did not fare so well as this narrator. Such is the case in the song "The Dying Miner" ("Goodbye Centralia"), which uses the tune to "Give Me Three Grains of Corn, Mother" and which has as its narrator one of the doomed miners. In the first verse, this worker sets the scene by telling us that only an hour ago "The gas caught fire from somebody's lamp / And the miners are choking in smoke."[104] Although the explosion actually resulted when an overcharged blast set off excessive coal dust in the mine, this error stands as the only major one in the song.[105] Part of the reason for the song's accuracy comes from Guthrie's use of the miners' notes to their families; for of the one hundred and eleven miners who died, fourteen survived long enough underground to write notes to their families and friends.[106] In an endnote to this song, Guthrie explains, "I got the idea for writing these words as I turned into the papers and read some of the words to the letters the trapped miners wrote to their families and friends."[107] In fact, this song generally follows the form of a last letter. In it, the narrator says good-bye to his children and wife, then to the rest of his family, and finally to his town itself:

> Goodbye to Dickey and Honey
> Goodbye to the wife that I love
> A lot of these men are not coming home
> Tonight when the work whistle blows.
>
> Dear sisters and brothers, Goodbye,
> Dear mother and father, Goodbye,
> My fingers are weak and I cannot write
> Goodbye, Centralia, Goodbye.

The men realize that their end is near and write out their final thoughts: "We're all writing letters to children we love, / Please carry our word to our wives." To get to a short-lived safe haven, they "crawled and drag ourselves here." But still "the smoke is bad and the fumes coming in / And the gas is burning my eyes."[108]

In his letter, the narrator asks, "Forgive me for things I done wrong / I love you lots more than you know." But the theme he returns to again and again is that the ones left behind need to work to make sure that no other miner will die. He asks, "Just work and fight and try to see / That this never happens again." Then in the final verse, he begs, "Please name our new baby Joe / So he'll grow up like big Joe." This child, he wishes, will "work and he'll fight to fix up the mines / So fires can't kill daddies no more."[109] Much like the writer of "Dream of a Miner's Child," Guthrie uses a child as a means of grabbing sympathy for the miners, although Joe's children do not have a premonition that keeps their father from suffering from death in the mine. In another of his Centralia songs, Guthrie focuses even more on the children than here.

Not surprising considering its title, "Miners' Kids and Wives" ("Waiting at the Gate") places its emphasis on the families left behind. In the first verse, the unnamed narrator says, "Tell the miners' kids and wives / There's a blast in Number Five." Soon, he points out that the disaster has been foretold, although by a mine inspector rather than by a prescient miner's child: "The Inspector years ago / Said Number Five is a deadly hole." Verse two continues in this vein with more details:

> The Inspector told the boss
> It was more than a year ago
> You are risking these mens lives in Number Five
> This hole's full of fumes and dust,
> Full of high explosive gas
> But the boss said we'll just have to take the chance.

As already noted, both state and federal inspectors documented the mine's dangers less than a week before, but here Guthrie's pronouncement about the mine's danger, as expressed by inspectors, is exactly right. In fact, not only the inspectors but "Everybody told the owner / That this deadly day would come." But all these pleas have no effect, for in verse three "he said we had to work to pay our bills."[110]

Most of the song does not place blame, no matter how well deserved. Instead, it works to make the disaster a personal one by focusing on the community that must deal with the deaths of friends and family. The song's chorus first pushes towards this goal when the perspective expands so as to include the miners' families along with the unnamed narrator:

> Waiting at the gate
> We are waiting by the gate
> Smoke and fire does roll and boil
> From this dark and deadly hole
> While the miners' kids and wives
> Wait by the gate.

As a result, the song affects the listener by including all those experiencing the fear that accompanies the explosion. Although the miners appear in the song, they only do so as a means to ground the grief felt by the children and wives left in the wake of the disaster. We see them "Kiss their wife and kids good-bye / Then they walk with their lunchkits up the hill," into the mine, and to their deaths. Here, they are anonymous, faceless people who draw our sympathy. In verse four, the dead miners are brought out of the mine; still anonymous, now they merge together as a dramatic symbol of wasted lives:

> I try to get a look
> Of a face I ought to know
> As the men are carried out wrapped up in sheets
> I can hear the church bells ringing
> For the Hundred and Eleven dead
> I can hear the families weeping in the streets.

Here, the narrator becomes a member of the community; he becomes part of the group that would be mourning the miners' deaths. But still the focus comes back to the families, the ones who would most strongly feel the loss. In the last verse, with days passing between the explosion and the discovery of the bodies, the perspective changes again, pulling away from the unnamed narrator, to the families, finally to focus in on one child and his or her lesson, one given from the grave:

> They laid my daddy out with the other men
> In the pocket of his shirt
> I found a little note he wrote
> I'll never go in a dangerous mine again.[III]

This move from the anonymous narrator, to the community, and then to the child allows for a diverse emotional effect, ending with a miner's final warning to another generation. Here, Guthrie gives us both vivid storytelling and social commentary.

Although explosions and cave-ins remained the most dramatic dangers in the mines, less obvious perils existed. Those who labored in the nation's mines faced a number of industrial diseases, especially those associated with air conditions. Black lung, the ailment brought about by breathing in years of coal dust, killed miners and brought on other life-threatening respiratory diseases. The coal miners could not escape the dust when at home, for it hung over little mining towns like the dirt that filled the air in the Dust

Bowl. Noted folklorist George Korson describes the extent of the problem that existed in mine towns when he writes, "Coal dust was everywhere, like sand on the desert. It was in their food. Their clothes grated with it. The rasping dust was underfoot. It rubbed deep into their skin."[112] While visiting West Virginia in August 1933, Lorena Hickok notes, "I don't suppose anybody really knows how much tuberculosis there is in the state. Tuberculosis and asthma are common among miners."[113] In her report, she did not explicitly connect these illnesses to their occupation; however, Guthrie did realize that dust could kill.

On September 21, 1949, Guthrie wrote "Dead from the Dust."[114] This song has a few predecessors. For one, Guthrie was familiar with the song "Silicosis is Killing Me," detailing the sickness often suffered by those digging in earth heavy in silica.[115] This song is similar to "Dust Pneumonia Blues" in that it touches on respiratory illnesses and related troubles—but unlike this Dust Bowl song, it has no humor. For the sickness is not due to dust blown up by wind whipping across a dry, barren plain. This illness comes from dust that could be removed from the mines if only owners would put in filters. Guthrie also became aware of respiratory diseases during his travels through his home region, where he describes "the silicosis death that blows off the high piles of shale and slag from the lead and zinc mines."[116] But his most direct understanding about the respiratory illnesses that affected miners came from Sara Ogan. He writes, "Sara's father is dead, Sara's husband is dead. Her little baby boy is dead. The dust from the coal mines gave them that deadly disease called, 'Silicosis'—gets your lungs."[117]

To humanize his subject, Guthrie holds "Dead from the Dust" together by concentrating on the loss of life caused by breathing the dust and the simple solution to the problem. His narrator opens up the song at graveside, with his "kinfolks and friends . . . hold[ing] the brass handle" of a casket. Then he reveals, "My mother's cold clay is wrapped in this pine box." She, along with his father, sisters, and brothers, are all victims of "the dust that blows from the mine." After dealing with so much loss and pain, the narrator realizes "I'd rather dig coal than to stand digging grave holes" and decides action must be taken:

> I can't stand here now around these cold grave mounds;
> I've prayed and I've cried till my tears have run dry.
> I've got to go ask that coal operator
> Why he lets my folks die from that dust from his mine.

While "running wild down the street with fire in my eyes," he passes a policeman who might mistake his sorrow for insanity because "that trooper won't know about my folks in this grave hill / Killed by that dust that blows from the mine." There is even the danger that the "dicks [will] cut me down on my way" to tell the mine owners, "You can build a machine for a few silver dollars / That would clean all this dust as it flies in the skies." Even if he cannot make the changes necessary, he asks, "My good union sistren and brethren, don't cry. / Make him put you to work and build that big cleaner / So you will not die, choked by dust from the mines."[118] Guthrie's denunciations of the dangers brought about by breathing dust place him in the vanguard of those raising the alarm of this condition. For not until the 1960s did the mining industry finally admit the destructive nature of breathing in coal dust, day after day and year after year. Later, other songwriters also captured the harm of black lung disease. For example, Hazel Dickens, herself the daughter of a coal miner, wrote "Black Lung" and "Clay Country Miner," both detailing the human toll of this preventable illness.

The songs presented in this chapter represent only a small sample of the large body of work that Guthrie produced on the hardships and hurts of the working class. Taken together, they become his unabashed chronicle of their oppression, one that could not be silenced. As John Steinbeck notes in the foreword to *Hard Hitting Songs for Hard-Hit People*, "You can burn books, buy newspapers, you can guard against handbills and pamphlets, but you cannot prevent singing."[119] Although all of Guthrie's songs documenting workers' troubles may not have found their way into tradition to the degree that they can be called folk songs, they were made to go out into the world as news, as history, as truth that needed to be told. Guthrie wrote them as a denunciation of the wrongs against the great mass of America, those who labor for their bread and bed. With his words, he wishes to draw blood—not from them but their oppressors. He points his finger, sometimes subtly and sometimes not, but with full conviction. He amasses evidence against the great legion of the rich and powerful while detailing the lives of those people who raise our food, build our cities, mine our fuel. These men he honors with songs, even as he points out how they are dishonored by the ruling class. In this effort, he attains Walt Whitman's definition of greatness: "The attitude of great poets is to cheer up slaves and horrify despots."[120] This attitude permeates all of Guthrie's songs that tell of the "hard-working man blues."

CHAPTER FOUR

Skin Trouble

DOCUMENTING RACE AND REDEMPTION

To gain insight into Woody Guthrie's racial attitudes, we can look to a striking moment in his 1943 autobiographical novel *Bound for Glory*. While riding a freight train, one bum takes offense at having to share space "with a dam nigger." But before the young black man named Wheeler can answer the insult with blows, a white rider named Brown deals with the racist by using a few rough but pointed words. After this show of solidarity, Brown says, "I've run onto this skin trouble before," then explains his views on race hate in general:

> I got sick and tired of that kind of stuff when I was just a kid growing up at home. . . . God, I had hell with some of my folks about things like that. But, seems like, little at a time, I'd sort of convince them . . . ; lots of folks I never could convince. They're kinda like the old bellyache fellow, they cause a lot of trouble to a hundred people, and then to a thousand people, all on account of just some silly, crazy notion. Like you can help what color you are.[1]

Although spoken by a character, these comments represent Guthrie's own thoughts. In a 1940 interview with Alan Lomax, the singer admits some people from his hometown had "a crazy way of looking at the colored situation."[2] Like Brown, Guthrie also attempted to convince others of the wrong of racial hate.

Beginning in the late 1930s, Guthrie decided that the public needed to hear songs about the hardships of America's minorities so as to expose the destructive power of racism. Some of these lyrics only briefly address the race issue. For example, by creating a highly ironic narrator in "Talking Meanness" ("Mean Talking Blues"), he offers some amusing blows against those who would encourage various forms of hate and, in one verse, takes a none too subtle slap at those who would "get colors to fighting one another / Friend against friend / Sister against brother" or even "the stripped against the polkadots."[3] But many of his songs, such as "Poll Tax Chain," denounce racism throughout. Taken together, his lyrics touching on "skin trouble" create a wide-ranging look at race relations in America. This work speaks of the suffering of several minority groups, such as Chinese, Japanese, and Mexicans; but most of his work commenting on racial hate focuses on African Americans, whose plight he understood best.

Looking back into his life, we can find several reasons for this expansion in his sympathies. In both Okemah and Pampa, Guthrie witnessed the second-class citizenship of African Americans. After he traveled to the West Coast, he encountered and began to sympathize with other abused racial groups—Chinese, Japanese, and Mexicans—all of whom had labored and sweated in the state's fields before the Okie migrants arrived. The fact that many Californians turned their prejudices on these white migrants during the mid-1930s increased his education on these matters. Through his encounters with various leftist groups and people who espoused racial tolerance as part of their ideology, he also expanded his understanding of race relations during his time in Los Angeles. These associations and friendships continued when he moved to New York City in early 1940. There, he also formed close personal relationships with several black musicians who influenced his racial understanding by giving him firsthand tales of discrimination.

For Guthrie, already skilled in documenting pictures from life's other side and educated by his travels, friendships, and political associations, was it such a great leap to empathize with racial groups different from his own? Did these people not also number among those he knew best: the busted, disgusted, down and out? In truth, Guthrie did not always express identification with nonwhites. Although some have speculated that he had an innate lack of racial prejudice, he has exhibited a biased attitude.[4] Considering the overall prejudice of his nation and his region during the first three decades of the twentieth century, this youthful racist turn seems part and parcel of his early social and cultural environment. Nevertheless, he rejected this behavior in the late 1930s as he came to understand the lives and difficulties of other races and then used his songs to detail their sufferings.

However, much of the past discussion of Guthrie's work has centered on his songs of the Dust Bowlers and Okies, who were primarily white. This focus has resulted in the underappreciation of his songs exposing the difficulties and degradation of other racial groups. Only recently has race representation in his work been explored to any degree, such as in some of the essays in *Hard Travelin': The Life and Legacy of Woody Guthrie*. Even in one of these commentaries, music critic Dave Marsh argues, "Woody did not write that many songs that directly commented on 'race' issues in the United States" and claims that only eleven of Guthrie's songs touch on race in a direct or indirect fashion.[5] But this estimate is far too low. As noted, many of his songs mention race relations in brief while others specifically document the suffering of minority groups, especially African Americans. To broaden the discussion of his work beyond its normal borders, an in-depth exploration of Guthrie's lyrics about the difficulties of racial minorities will yield a better overall understanding of his efforts to denounce this bigotry. In addition, by discussing the singer's own attitudes within the context of America's racial history, we can trace how he shucked off some of his own prejudices and documented a range of wrongs perpetrated upon some of our nation's ethnic minorities.

The earliest example of Guthrie penning a song with negative racial overtones occurred sometime around 1937, when he wrote "The Chinese and the Japs," which exhibits a strong disregard for Asians and their struggles. In the chorus, he dismisses the invasion of China by Japan's Imperialist forces as a "disputin' o'er the bound'ry wall," all the while using the derogatory terms "Japs" and "Chinaman" in referring to the combatants. But the last verse stands out as the most disturbing moment in the song. In the first two lines, the narrator moves from "I" to "we" in an attempt to project his thoughts onto the listener: "We don't know just who will ever win the battle / And as far as we're concerned we do not care." Then he adds, "If they bombard good old Tokio— / Well, I guess that's okie dokio / But let's pray they don't go droppin' 'em over here."[6] Essentially, the song uses racist-tinged humor to send up a war where thousands of Chinese were dying defending their homeland from invasion by the Japanese Imperialist juggernaut.

Years after, Guthrie realized some portion of the ill he created in "The Chinese and the Japs." In a handwritten notation on a copy of the song, he writes, "When I made this one up, the war between China and Japan had just got started a few days and I didn't have sense enought to know that I was on China's side 10,000 percent."[7] Although he never directly apologized for his comments about the Japanese people in this song, he does include a scene in *Bound for Glory* where he and others defend a bar owned by Japanese Americans from a mob caught up in post–Pearl Harbor rage. He even has his singing partner and friend Cisco Houston make a speech to the assembled throng: "These little Japanese farmers that you see up and down the country here, and these Japanese people that run the little old cafes and gin joints, they can't help it because they happen to be Japanese. Nine-tenths of them hate their Rising Sun robbers just as much as I do, or you do."[8] In his rejection of negative attitudes towards Japanese Americans, Guthrie stood in the minority in the early 1940s. The most egregious example of anti-Japanese sentiment in America during this time came as the result of Executive Order 9006. Empowered by Franklin Roosevelt's presidential edict, our military forces interned over 120,000 people of Japanese descent beginning in March 1942 and confined them for the duration of the war due to race-based prejudice and fear.

Around the same time he wrote "The Chinese and the Japs," Guthrie also expressed a less than enlightened attitude towards Mexicans, although he did change his views later. An early example of his negative comments about this group occurred in early 1938. While appearing on Station XELO in Tijuana for a couple of weeks, he called Mexicans "pepper bellies," among other unflattering comments.[9] But during the mid-1940s, he ended up defending Mexican Americans. In a July 1945 postcard to his friend Ed Robbin, Guthrie pities his ex-wife Mary's characterization of Mexicans: "She talks anti mexican awful bad. I feel sorry for her."[10] A year later, he also expressed a deep felt sympathy with their plight as migrants: "The other races all have their troubles, but I would judge that the Mexicans catch the roughest end of it all. They are allowed to come in, make their trip north, and then are herded back out as aliens and undesirables every year as the birds fly; only the birds are lots more welcome and better fed."[11] Considering the similar experiences Okie and Mexican workers had in California, his eventual empathetic connection to this migrant group seems an understandable reaction.

Mexicans labored in California's fields before the Okies arrived and after they left. Throughout the 1920s and even the very early '30s, the state's growers favored a Mexican work force over all others, believing them to be malleable and willing to accept low pay. When the Great Depression began to affect the state's economy, this immigrant community found itself represented as a drain, through relief payments, on county and state governments' limited resources. In addition, these laborers began to unite to demand improvements in working conditions and a raise in pay; their unionizing effort started in the late 1920s and cumulated in the large strikes in San Joaquin Valley during 1933 and the ones in Imperial Valley the following year. As a result of Californians' growing fears and the migrants' increasing union activity, state officials hatched a plan to repatriate a portion of their Mexican laborers. In February 1931, state administrators worked out a deal with the Southern Pacific Railroad to begin shipping them back across the border. By 1933, the monthly numbers of those returned to Mexico ranged from thirteen hundred to six thousand.[12] Although greatly reduced, Mexican laborers remained a presence in California's fields throughout the Great Depression.

During the same time period, the state's growers feared the resulting labor shortage would leave produce rotting in the fields. Then the arrival of white migrant laborers from the southern plains and the South in the mid-1930s essentially guaranteed that enough hands would be available for the harvest seasons, although Californians in general did not share the growers' glee. Just a few years earlier, migrants from these same areas had been welcomed for their cotton-picking skills. But attitudes had changed in the Depression years, and the Okies did not generally receive any higher economic or social status than their Mexican counterparts had. Actually, Californians often shifted their prejudices from one group to the other, resulting in the white migrants receiving much the same treatment as had Mexican migrants. One observer of the agricultural situation during this period describes the situation succinctly: "Since rural California had displaced onto the Okie the prejudices that had been applied to the Mexicans, it was natural that the migrants would be subjected to segregation and other external signs of their supposed inferiority."[13] In addition to or as a result of this prejudice, some citizens of California began to worry that these white migrants would also become a burden on the state's relief funds, as discussed at the end of chapter two. As a result of these negative perceptions, the newcomers found themselves the butt of public ridicule and abuse, just as the Mexican laborers had.

Eventually, attitudes towards these migrants from the Southwest and the South did change. In part, this shift came from the spotlight of public attention being shined on their plight beginning in 1939. The federal government weighed in on the subject with some of the findings of the Tolan Committee Report and the La Follette Committee. Additionally, two nonfiction pieces concerning the plight of these migrants came out in 1939: *Factories in the Fields* by Carey McWilliams and *An American Exodus* by Paul Taylor and Dorothea Lange. But the most devastating discussion of the Okies came not in the form of fact but of fiction. In 1939 John Steinbeck's *Grapes of Wrath* appeared and exposed the conditions Okie agricultural workers experienced to a horrified public. The following year, John Ford's film based on the novel further imbedded the migrants' miseries in the minds of Americans. Historian Walter Stein also believes that the fact those working for a pittance and in squalor were white helped unify Anglo-American outrage:

> No *Grapes of Wrath* would have been written; no migrant problem would have attracted the nation's gaze; no novel, however brilliant, which chronicled the migratory route of the Pedro Morenos in California's valleys could have become a best seller. The tribulations of the Joads received attention, however, because the nation found intolerable for white Americans conditions it considered normal for California Mexicans. . . .[14]

For certain, the combined effect of these works' revelations, especially Steinbeck's, created a vast public sympathy for this group of white laborers.

Even as the public became more aware of these white migrants' conditions, pressing historical events abroad conspired to create demand for workers in the defense industry in California, which the Okies gladly filled. As this group left the fields for factory jobs in the early 1940s, the public outcry and debate about working conditions in California's agricultural industry abated. Nevertheless, growers still needed laborers in the fields—especially with demand increasing as the war progressed. When the Okies moved to war industry jobs, larger numbers of Mexican laborers were again lured back to California—still unwanted after the crops had been picked but valued, or at least needed and tolerated, during the harvest. Guthrie himself noticed this shift during a trip he took through the fields of the San Joaquin Valley in 1941. After having been away from the West Coast for a little over a year, he found the Okies gone, replaced by imported Mexican workers.[15] Beginning in 1942, the federal government even allowed some Mexican nationals to legally come and work in the fields of California and a handful of other states as part of the *Bracero* program, which continued in one form or another until 1964. Other Mexican farm laborers continued to come to America illegally to find work. Meanwhile, state and federal authorities throughout the

1940s continued to send both groups, legal and illegal, back across the Mexican border—but only after they had brought in the lucrative harvest.

Sometime in 1948, Guthrie read a newspaper report of a repatriation effort that went horribly wrong. Twenty-eight Mexican migrant farm workers being flown back to their home country died when their plane crashed near Coalinga, California, on January 28.[16] The newspaper account left Guthrie cold in that its author kept collectively referring to the people who died as "deportees." After reading the article, the word used to describe these Mexican workers continued to haunt him. Perhaps he remembered how the migrants from the Southwest and the South had been stripped of their individual identity when Californians had called them "Dust Bowl refugees" and "Okies." These Mexican migrants had names and families too, and they had experienced great difficulties coming to this country for work. But their names and these realities did not appear in the article. So Guthrie decided that a rebuttal was in order. On February 3, 1948, he wrote "Deportee" ("Plane Wreck at Los Gatos").[17]

As the song opens, we find the harvest so plentiful that "the peaches are rotting" and "the oranges are piled in their creosote dumps." But now the Mexican laborers who brought in this bounty are no longer needed. In a later verse, the narrator says, "Some of us are illegal and some are not wanted" because "Our work contract's out, and we have to move on / Six hundred miles to the Mexican border." As "They chase us like outlaws, like rustlers, like thieves," the Mexicans move from being needed as laborers to being treated like criminals. As a result of their perceived uselessness, "You're flying them back to the Mexican border / To pay all their money to wade back again." Who is the "you" here: the listener, the state, the nation? Perhaps Guthrie indicts all of white America. In the chorus, he moves into territory where his meaning is more certain as he provides a few names of those fated to be unnamed in their deportment and maybe even their death:

> Good-bye to my Juan, good-bye Rosalita,
> Adios, mis amigos Jesus y Maria;
> You won't have a name when you ride the big airplane,
> All they will call you will be deportee.[18]

Here, Guthrie highlights the impersonal nature of the treatment these laborers receive. The sentiments expressed in this song harmonize with the migrants' own perceptions; they realized that they were being denied their personal identity. For example, in the early 1950s, a Mexican *Bracero* migrant laborer told a government interviewer, "In this camp, we have no names. We only have numbers."[19] Whether through the term "deportee" or a *Bracero* identification number, these migrants were often not given the dignity of their own names.

But the song does not express sympathy with the migrants through an abstract affection. Verse two shows that the narrator's identification with the "deportees" comes out of his own past. He says, "My father's own father, he waded that river." Thus, the narrator offers a family story here and goes on to tell of the hardships that befell them. First, his grandfather pays dearly for the privilege of slaving away in our nation's fields: "They took all the money he made in his life." Then, the rest of his family follows the migrant trail from Mexico to America, where they fare even worse: "My brothers and sisters come working the fruit trees, / And they rode the truck till they took down and died."[20]

This theme of death continues in two other verses. In a Whitman-like moment, the narrator catalogs some of the places where Mexican laborers have lost their lives:

> We died in your hills, we died in your deserts,
> We died in your valleys and died on your plains,
> We died beneath your trees and we died in your bushes,
> Both sides of the river—we died just the same.

The sixth verse details the event that sparked this song. He says,

> The sky plane caught fire over Los Gatos canyon—
> A fireball of lightning which shook all our hills,
> Who are all these friends all scattered like dry leaves?
> The radio says they are just . . . deportees.[21]

These verses show the migrants dying along the border as they struggle through the landscape to American jobs and then dying as they are brought back home after their usefulness in the fields is over. But no matter whether in the wilderness of their country or ours, whether in a modern "sky plane" or not, these migrants perish in their quest for work in America.

In the last verse, the narrator appeals to our sense of justice. He asks, "Is this the best way we can grow our big orchards? / Is this the best way we can grow our good fruit?" Next he points out how these migrants "fall like dry leaves, to rot on my topsoil." Realizing all these Mexican migrants have done and all that they have suffered, he wonders why they do not deserve their own individual identity and asks how could they "be called by no name except deportees?"[22] Through the song's lyrical power, singer / songwriter Nanci Griffith believes, "Woody put [the migrants'] story into the hearts of America and the world, so that these people would never be forgotten."[23] With Griffith and other artists performing and recording it as often as they do, "Deportee" does not seem in danger of disappearing. Through these efforts, it also stands as Guthrie's best-known comment on racial injustice.

However, the bulk of Guthrie's work focusing on race details the abuse suffered by African Americans. During much of America's early history, the majority of this group had been held in bondage. Even after emancipation, legally sanctioned or community-accepted prejudice against African Americans existed nationwide. In the aftermath of the Civil War, the promise of equality quickly came undone, especially in the South. African Americans barely moved from slavery to second-class citizenship, with their rights rarely manifest in full. Soon after the adoption of the Fifteenth Amendment, poll taxes, white-only primaries, and literacy tests were used to disenfranchise African Americans. As they were kept from the ballot box, they found themselves held back from gaining social equality due to widespread Jim Crow laws and economic discrimination. The ugliest signs of America's prejudice could be seen in the lynched, mutilated, and burnt bodies of thousands of black victims. Even when illegal lynching faded, legal execution took its place as the final punishment of thousands of blacks under the white-controlled judicial system.

Although this prejudice against African Americans existed nationwide, each state manifested restrictions and abuses in its own individual fashion. Guthrie's home state of Oklahoma was no exception. Only three years after Oklahoma achieved statehood in 1907, the electorate amended its constitution to restrict the black vote through a literacy test although this measure eventually failed before the Supreme Court in 1915. Some segregation existed in the territory in the 1890s, but widespread Jim Crowism raised its hydra head soon after Oklahoma became a state, resulting in segregated housing, schools, streetcars, bathrooms, mines, and even telephone booths. Oklahoma historian Jimmie Lewis Franklin notes, "For most of the state's history Jim Crowism occupied a central place in the life of Oklahoma's black community."[24] In addition, restrictions on black behavior went well beyond these legal restrictions. In speaking of how white people in Oklahoma expected

African Americans to act and speak, Guthrie admits, "It was a common custom down in that country . . . that the Negro people more or less come to the back door when they went to see you, and take off their hat when they meet you on the street, and say, 'Yesum, Mister. . . . Yes, Ma'am.'"[25]

Any black men or women who did not follow or were perceived to move beyond these legally or socially prescribed forms of behavior would often suffer severe penalties. According to official records, forty-one lynchings took place in Oklahoma in the first three decades after it became a state, with the largest number occurring between 1910 and 1918.[26] Then during the early 1920s, the Ku Klux Klan expanded their numbers nationwide but especially in Oklahoma. Noted historian C. Vann Woodward even goes as far as writing, "Oklahoma . . . [was] for a time almost completely under the domination of the Klan."[27] In light of the state's racist past and the Klan's growing power throughout the early years of the 1920s, it does not surprise that the single most egregious attack on African Americans in Oklahoma's history occurred in 1921 when one of the nation's largest race riots ripped across Tulsa on May 30th, leaving over twenty black citizens officially confirmed dead and with many more fatalities probable.[28]

Repression against blacks, even that of a violent nature, occurred in Guthrie's hometown of Okemah; and Charley Guthrie, Woody's own father, involved himself in racist behavior there. In this region, as was the case in many others, African Americans who did not adhere to white-sanctioned behavior were severely dealt with, and those who committed violence against whites often found themselves at the end of a rope. An example of this situation occurred in mid-May 1911. A white officer named George Loney attempted to arrest a black man named Nelson for theft. Going to the man's home, Loney found only Nelson's wife, Laura, and his son, Lawrence, there. Believing Loney pulled a pistol, young Lawrence shot the officer, who bled to death in the Nelsons' frontyard—reportedly begging for water. A week after the entire family was arrested as a result of this incident, a mob broke in to the local jail and abducted Lawrence and Laura—by this time the father had already been sent to prison for livestock theft. The angry mob may have then raped the mother—but it is certain that they took her and her son to a bridge outside of town and hung both of them over the Canadian River. Although his exact role is uncertain, Guthrie's own father, Charley, attended this lynching, as observer or even as participant.[29] Later, just as many other Oklahomans did, Woody's father joined the local chapter of the KKK and became what Joe Klein characterizes as "an enthusiastic member."[30] Charley's racial attitudes came to him, at least in part, as a legacy of his family, who Guthrie biographer Ed Cray notes were "fervent Confederates."[31]

Considering the mass of prejudices toward African Americans in his nation, state, town, and family, it would be surprising if Guthrie grew up unbiased. In fact, we can find an example of his youthful prejudice, one that was completely socially acceptable throughout the South. Folklorist Richard Reuss points out that according to sources in Okemah, a young Woody Guthrie and some of his friends put on blackface, then gave an impromptu minstrel show in the middle of town.[32]

Although no racial slurs against African Americans appear in the few surviving examples of his work from the mid-1930s, his racist tendencies came out in some of the language Guthrie used in California in the latter part of the decade. On radio station KHVD in Los Angeles, he performed songs containing the words "darkie" and "nigger."[33] But the majority of evidence concerning Guthrie's early negative attitude towards African Americans can be found in his writing. The most striking example of his racist language occurred after a confrontational episode with some black bathers on the beach of Santa Monica. He documents the incident in the *Santa Monica Social Register Examine 'Er*, a homemade newspaper he whipped up. Along with racially offensive cartoons, jokes, and articles, this little paper contains a seventeen-verse parody of Longfellow's "Hiawatha" entitled "Clippings from the personal diary of a Full-Fledged son of the beach." He writes that his pleasures at the beach were interrupted by a shout: "What is that Ethiopian smell / Upon the zephyrs, what a fright!" In answer comes the line "Africa was overflowing." Later, he describes these blacks as "chocolate drops" and "monkeys." One verse outstrips the others in its racist description:

> We could dimly hear their chants
> And we thought the blacks by chance,
> Were doing a cannibal dance
> This we could dimly see.
> Guess the sea's eternal pounding
> Like a giant drum a-sounding
> Set their jungle blood to bounding;
> Set their native instincts free.[34]

Overall, this language does not exactly place Guthrie on the side of the racially enlightened. However, he soon changed due to a variety of reasons.

Beginning when he first hit the West Coast in 1936, Guthrie witnessed the Okies suffering in the fields and streets of California. Even as these migrants desired equal status, many white Californians—some of whom had also come to the state as migrant laborers themselves and had lived there less than a generation—lumped the underclass, white or not, together. Historian Walter Stein explains some of the reasoning behind Californians' negative identification of the Okies thus: "The malnourished physique of the migrants, the deplorable settlements along the ditch banks, even the slightly nasal drawl which had come with them from the southern Plains were the touchstones for a stereotype of the Okie as a naturally slovenly, degraded, primitive subspecies of white American."[35] These white migrants—who, like Guthrie, often held their own prejudice against blacks—found themselves being discriminated against and, at least in part, losing some of their white-status privileges. An example of how this loss manifested itself comes from Carey McWilliams, who notes, "In the summer of 1939 a sign appeared in the foyer of a motion picture theatre in a San Joaquin Valley town, reading: 'Negroes and Okies Upstairs.'"[36] Living in California while all these ill feelings about Okies existed, Guthrie had an explicit example of how those in power could unfairly discriminate against minorities, even white ones.

This understanding came in addition to other lessons. In response to one of his shows on KFVD, Guthrie received a letter in October 1937 from an irate listener who writes, in part, "You were getting along quite well in your program this evening until you announced your 'Nigger Blues.' I am a Negro, a young Negro in college, and I certainly resented your remark." The writer went on to note, "No person or persons of any intelligence uses that word over radio today."[37] This letter upset Guthrie so much he apologized on air for his thoughtlessness and tore the offending song out of his notebook, along with any other that used the word "nigger."[38] Years later, the event remained solidly in his mind. Sometime in the early 1940s, he writes, "A young Negro . . . in Los Angeles wrote me a nice letter one day telling me the meaning of that word [nigger] and that I shouldn't say it any more on the air. So I apologized."[39] Additionally, in an early draft of his autobiographical preface to *American Folksong*, he relates, "I took time out several times to apologize to the Negro people [for] frothings that I let slip out of the corners of my mouth."[40] These comments show that Guthrie's racial attitude in the late 1930s began to shift away from that he absorbed in his youth to one forged on his own when faced with the hurt his bigoted language could cause.

Also while in California, Guthrie first encountered and sometimes befriended members of the left, who helped educate him on the subject of racial equality. One was Will Geer. Nora Guthrie believes her father did not even have the language to describe racial issues before meeting Geer: "I don't think he [Guthrie] ever heard the word 'That's racism,' until he heard it from Will Geer."[41] Guthrie made his connection to Geer through his association with leftist writer Ed Robbin, who wrote for *People's World*. The singer eventually contributed to this paper and met other columnists there, such as Mike Quin. All of these figures had affiliations with the Communist Party (CP) and either wrote or spoke out on the evils of racism. Guthrie kept up this type of politically charged association after he moved to New York City, where he met other Communists, such as Mike Gold, and wrote for the *Daily Worker* for a while. During this time period, especially in New York City, the CP in particular and the left in general reached out, in both rhetoric and action, to African Americans—although this effort failed in a number of ways and for many reasons.[42] Nevertheless, these encounters with CP members, writers, and propaganda gave Guthrie some education on the complexities of race relations beyond what he had been able to formulate on his own.

Also while in New York, Guthrie first came into contact with white musicians who sang about the evils of racism. In the early 1940s, he met Earl Robinson, who wrote and sang a number of songs with a sympathetic view on race, such as "Free and Equal Blues." A more important relationship had begun in March 1940, when Guthrie ran into Pete Seeger, whose family (including the ethnomusicologist Charles Seeger) had long supported equal rights for all races. Later, Seeger joined up with Lee Hays and Millard Lampell to begin the folk group the Almanac Singers. Hays had just arrived in New York from Commonwealth Labor College, a racially mixed union-organizing school in Arkansas, while Lampell had involved himself in progressive causes on the East Coast. Even before Guthrie joined the group in early July 1941, these left-leaning musicians denounced racial discrimination in song.

But the most significant reason for his shift away from racist rhetoric came through his friendships with black bluesmen living in New York City. After first moving there in the winter of 1940, Guthrie often visited and even briefly lived with the legendary bluesman Lead Belly and his wife, Martha, in their cramped walkup apartment on the lower East Side. This apartment became a multicultural mixing place, for bluesman Brownie McGhee says

Woody Guthrie and Lead Belly in Chicago, 1941. Photograph by Stephen Deutsch. Courtesy of the Chicago Historical Society.

Lead Belly "had Italian friends, Jewish friends, white friends—he had all types of people at his house."[43] Here, Guthrie learned at the foot of a master bluesman and not only about music. Through his admiration for Lead Belly's ability and with an understanding of the older man's life, Guthrie gained access to the dragging weight of racism. "It was Lead Belly . . . who really educated him mentally and emotionally and psychologically about the black movement and about oppression," says daughter Nora. As a result, she adds, "He could really begin to embrace a whole other contingency of people in the United States."[44]

Black bluesmen Sonny Terry and Brownie McGhee also became close to Guthrie in New York. In the autumn of 1941, Terry and McGhee briefly moved into the Almanac Singers' cooperative house.[45] Soon after, Guthrie began performing with them in an on-again, off-again group that would last into the early 1950s. They also recorded together several times in the mid and late 1940s for Moses Asch. Through his relationships with these men, Guthrie continued to learn about the struggles of black Americans. By 1946, he would even try to articulate what Terry had shared with him: "He knows that his people can see a world where we all vote, eat, work, talk, plan and think together and with all of our smokes and wheels rolling and all of our selves well dressed and well housed and well fed."[46] Due to all these relationships, Guthrie's views towards African Americans changed dramatically. For example, when he, Terry, and McGhee toured in late 1942, an organization in Baltimore they played for did not want the three to eat together after their performance. Guthrie countered by pointing out that he had just sung with them, but their hosts would not relent. In response, he had the other two leave before calmly flipping a banquet table over and disappearing himself.[47]

Eventually, Guthrie's new attitude towards African Americans appeared in his lyrics. By late summer of 1946, he had a whole album's worth of material focusing on race. In an August 15th letter, he asks Moe Asch to record and release these songs, even suggesting the title "Documentary Supremacy." He planned to include the songs "People's Army," "Poll Tax Chain," "Killing of the Ferguson Brothers," "Blinding of Isaac Woodward," "Long and Lonesome Chain," and "Don't Kill My Baby." He also suggested three other choices: "Better World a Coming," "Fascists Bound to Lose," and "End of Every Row." By releasing this album, Guthrie predicted, Asch's label would "win the friendship of not only 13 million Negroes, but with that many other Nationalities and colors, poor White folks, and others." He also explained to Asch that these songs came out of him due to "these lynchings, hangings, tarrings, featherings, and blindings . . . taking place around over our good nation."[48] Indeed, the songs on this proposed album and others like them do document some of the injustices suffered by African Americans, ranging from the ills of slavery during the beginnings of the nation to the results of Jim Crow justice during the 1930s, '40s, and '50s.

Considering its pivotal role in instilling institutional racist behavior and attitudes in Americans, it is unsurprising that slavery is mentioned in several of Guthrie's songs, such as "On Bloody Rags" and "Slavery Grave." But his most detailed and moving description of slavery appears in "A Tale a Feller Told Me." Here, a mother tells her son of "the Ebo / Land in Africa" and "a slave ship loaded down with locks irons / Black folks loaded in like sea fish." In later verses, the perspective shifts to second person and transports the listener to the hold of the slave ship:

> Your head struck back against an iron bolt;
> You squirmed with bodies of men and women
> You felt all wet with sweat and blood that
> Trickled down on the slaves beneath you.

At the end of the smothering journey, the slaves, "chained around and shackled together," are dumped at "some south land's cotton stalk river mouth." There, they work the cotton fields under the whip, in sickness and hunger—in a place where weakness results in unmarked death:

> You seen along these watery lowlands
> Lots of graves, but never no tomb stone;
> If you fall weak, you'll sleep down under
> These crackling twigs the strong ones walk on.[49]

Guthrie never denounced America's slave past with such language and at such length again, although he does proclaim the end of slavery as one of the greatest achievements of the human race in his bragging song "The Biggest Thing that Man Has Ever Done" ("The Great Historical Bum").[50] When envisioning America's future in "People's Army" ("You Are the People's Army"), he also refers to the past injustices that must be overcome. Although "a thousand races" make up the "people's army," they first have to march "Out of the hell of slavery, / Out of the storm of darkness" and "Through these fields of history / Over this mountain of sorrow" before reaching "the city of light."[51] Other of Guthrie's songs move from the past to the present to comment on the current ills facing African Americans.

One effective tool that kept African Americans from their full rights was the poll tax. Resisting early efforts to stop them from voting, this group voted en masse and swayed local, state, and federal elections after the Civil War. As C. Vann Woodward notes, "It is perfectly true that Negroes were often coerced, defrauded, or intimidated, but they continued to vote in large numbers in most parts of the South for more than two decades after Reconstruction."[52] Then beginning with Georgia in 1889, southern states started using the poll tax as a means of disenfranchising African Americans. In a little over a decade, all the secessionist states had enacted a poll tax, often accompanied by literacy tests and white-only primaries, to deny African Americans' access to the ballot box. Overall, the tax immediately affected electoral participation; in all ten states, voting rates fell an average of thirty-six percent in the presidential elections following its addition.[53] Although the tax affected poor white voters, they sometimes avoided this fee through grandfather clauses, which gave them free access to the ballot if they or their forefathers had the right to vote before the enactment of the Fifteenth Amendment. Undoubtedly, the tax fell heaviest on the shoulders of African Americans. Louisiana was a prime example; the number of registered

African-American voters there dropped by ninety-nine percent after the introduction of the tax.[54] Southern states as a whole remained committed to this tax until the 1920s due to its effectiveness. Then, under duress from court challenges, North Carolina led the way by repealing its poll tax, with Louisiana and Florida following soon after. By the end of the 1930s, only eight southern states—Alabama, Arkansas, Georgia, Mississippi, South Carolina, Tennessee, Texas, and Virginia—still used this tax, which resulted in low voter turnout overall. In fact, these states averaged only twenty-four percent of those of legal age actually participating in the 1936 presidential election.[55]

Although part of public discussion since the late 1880s, the poll tax debate flared especially hot in the late 1930s and early '40s. During the Great Depression, the burden of the poll tax on the poor—whether black or white—could not be denied. Although the tax generally ranged between one and two dollars by 1940, the average per capita income of the poll tax states only reached around three hundred dollars at this same time, with tenant farmers in particular rarely having any cash money during the year. Guthrie notes the relative costs of the poll tax in a letter to Alan Lomax in September 1940: "Some states charge you $1.75 to vote they call it poll tax, that takes a weeks groceries."[56] As evidence of this particular injustice mounted, left-leaning groups and individuals, such as the National Association for the Advancement of Colored People (NAACP) and Senator Claude Pepper, fought back against right-wing, pro–poll tax demagogues such as Senator Theodore Bilbo and Representative Martin Dies.[57] Due to this heated controversy, Georgia, South Carolina, and Tennessee also stopped using the poll tax as a barrier to the vote in the early 1940s.

Considering the publicized nature of these political wranglings, especially in the pages of the *Daily Worker*, it does not surprise that Guthrie would cobble his thoughts on the poll tax into a song around this time. Using the melody from "The Wabash Cannonball" in 1944, Guthrie wrote "Poll Tax Chain" ("Bloody Poll Tax Chain"). Immediately, this title ties the poll tax to an image of slavery, and this connection continues in the last two lines of each verse. Nevertheless, the end of verse one makes this point more vividly than any other moment in the song:

> But a man is chained and shackled;
> And our freedom we can't gain;
> Until we beat from off our legs
> This awful poll tax chain!

In the next verse, the narrator moves somewhat away from the slave image and imagines those who cannot vote due to the poll tax as prisoners in their own bodies—trapped in silence, darkness, and deformity:

> If your voice cannot speak out the things
> That's going through your mind,
> Your ears are filled with dead man's clay;
> Your eyes just well be blind.
> Your feet just well be withered,
> And your hands drawn down in kinks,
> If your voice is chained and hobbled
> In that poll tax slavery links.

The use of the second person here, and in subsequent verses, also helps the listener identify with those suffering the injustice of the poll tax. In the third verse, the narrator moves beyond simply addressing listeners and asks us to get involved. Believing Americans will help when confronted with the truth, he says, "I know you know the right thing / When you see it with your eye." Then he suggests sights to prick us to action: "the crazy killing lynch mob / And the ones that hang and die." But if we witness these horrors and do nothing to end the poll tax, the narrator warns us that others will continue to die:

> The skeleton tree and river bridge
> Will see a blood red rain
> If you do not swing your hammer
> To break that poll tax chain.[58]

This device also draws in listeners in that it asks us to be more than voyeurs; it asks us to be activists, to save others from death.

The penultimate verse points the finger of blame at those who will do the killing and gives us villains. We encounter "The hangknot in the coward hand / Of a ghost robed K.K.K." followed by "the black sedans that skim the road / And hunt you night and day." Both the Klan and the riders are "low as the human race can fall." In the last lines, the narrator connects this "fascism" to the "poll tax chain."[59] These lyrics exhibit a radical change from Guthrie's earlier stance on race. In attacking the Ku Klux Klan, he repudiates his racist legacy by directing a blow at the organization to which his father had belonged. In this same stance, other of his songs refer to the group the "Kleagle Klucking Klan" and "Kluck Kluck Klan."[60] Also by yoking fascism to racism, Guthrie undoubtedly sees the same hate at home as that being fought in Europe. In the first verse of "Poll Tax Chain," his narrator evokes the war in the opening lines, "Say, there's freedom, freedom, freedom / Cryin' round this warring world," then refers to "fascism" and "fascist" in later verses. In other songs, Guthrie makes an even more direct connection between racism at home and fascism abroad. For example, in "Gotta Keep 'em Sailin'," Guthrie goes a step further and accuses foreign fascists of spreading racism in American as a means to weaken our country: "Oh, the dirty rotten lies / Spread around by fascists spies / To divide us and kill us one by one."[61]

Although the narrator of "Poll Tax Chain" realizes that oppressive forces "would like to harness me and you / And take our soul away," he does offer some hope in the last verse, even while pointing out the work that must be done. To offset the efforts of the "fascist K.K.K.," the "folks that thinks together," a diverse group that includes "Us blacks, us brown, us red, us white," will have to realize "One blood runs in our veins." Nevertheless, the final two lines explain, "But our feet can't walk to victory / Till we break this poll tax chain."[62] So as the song concludes, the narrator again urges us to become involved in the struggle for equality by ending the poll tax, whose repercussions went beyond restricting the black vote.

By the beginning of the twentieth century, white politicians, empowered by white voters, crafted laws putting legal force behind the color line—thus began the era of Jim Crow. Interestingly, the phrase that became synonymous with these racist restrictions has its origins in a minstrel song. Beginning sometime around 1829, white entertainer Thomas Dartmouth Rice danced around wildly in black face while he sang the song "Jim Crow," which includes this chorus:

> W'eel a-bout and turn a-bout
> And do just so
> Every time I w'eel a-bout
> I jump Jim Crow[63]

Within a few years, this name became the best-known designation for legal and social policies separating the races. Initially, widespread Jim Crow segregation was the rule in the North rather than in the South, where slavery and its crushing racial hierarchy reigned supreme until after the Civil War. As one prominent historian notes, "In so far as the Negro's status was fixed and proclaimed by enslavement there was no need or occasion to resort to segregation to establish his caste and his subordination."[64] Only after the removal of the Reconstruction administration did Jim Crow come full force to the South, where it quickly outpaced that in the North and where it remained enforced by law and threat for almost a full century.

Although he had grown up in Jim Crow states, Guthrie called it "a disease as bad if not worse than the cancer." In a move similar to his comments in "Poll Tax Chain" and other songs, he also came to believe, "Jim Crow and Fascism are one and the same vine."[65] He also saw the roots of this oppression running back in time, for he writes, "The slave war was fought and little pieces of it are still being fought. Jim Crow still makes the Negro people slaves to all kinds of things, mean and low treatment, hard work and starvation wages, and mistreated by all kinds of narrow minded bosses everywhere."[66] But before writing a single song of his own about this racial injustice, he had already heard Lead Belly's "Jim Crow Blues" and sung the Almanac Singers' "Jim Crow." Simply titled and constructed, the Almanacs' song (written by Pete Seeger and Lee Hays) uses the African American call and response pattern to explain the injustice of Jim Crow. For example, when one singer steps out to ask, "Lincoln set the Negro free, / Why is he still in slavery?" the other members would shout out, "Jim Crow."[67]

Beginning in the mid-1940s, Guthrie began expressing his thoughts on Jim Crow in song. He refers to it as a societal ill that needs to be removed in "Join That A.F. of L." and "Slavery Grave."[68] Then in one of his many versions of "This Train Is Bound for Glory," both "Jim Crow and discrimination" find themselves excluded from riding the train—unlike in the real world of 1940s' America.[69] He even sees an anti–Jim Crow stance as a major reason behind his 1948 presidential endorsement of Henry Wallace. In the blues-sermon "Bet on Wallace," Guthrie praises the Progressive Party candidate for his antisegregation efforts and dismisses Harry Truman, Tom Dewey, Robert Taft, and Fred Hartley because they cannot "whip" or "lick" Jim Crow."[70] Although these generalized denunciations do not provide many specifics for Guthrie's strong dislike for America's segregationist policies, one of his songs does explore a specific incident of violence where he saw Jim Crow as the central motivating force.

In the early hours of February 5, 1946, Officer Joseph Romeika of Freeport, New York, shot and killed two brothers, Charles and Alfonso

An illustration of a policeman killing two of the Ferguson brothers, c. 1946. Sketch by Woody Guthrie. Courtesy of the Ralph Rinzler Archives.

Ferguson. These two men, along with their other brothers, Joseph and Richard, believed they were refused coffee at the bus station's tearoom in Freeport because they were black. After an exchange between Charles and the tearoom owner, the four men left. When they later returned to the bus station so they could go home, Romeika, who had been alerted to the altercation, stopped them and lined them up against a wall with their hands up. When Charles threatened to pull what turned out later to be a nonexistent .45 pistol and made movements towards his waist, Romeika shot him and then Alfonso after he moved towards the officer. Joseph was also wounded by the bullet that killed Alfonso. An inquiry by the district attorney of Nassau County before an all-white grand jury concluded that Romeika acted justly, and no charges were brought against him. Soon after, the shooting became a cause among New York leftists. Eventually, a number of groups— such as the American Jewish Congress, the CP, and the American Civil Liberties Union—asked Governor Thomas Dewey to appoint a special investigator to the case. But this second inquiry also discovered no wrongdoing on the part of Romeika, the district attorney, or the grand jury.[71]

A month after the Ferguson killing, Guthrie weighed in on the case. Using the tune to "The Streets of Laredo," he wrote a twelve-verse piece titled "The Ferguson Brothers Killing." The song opens with the brothers celebrating because Charles has "reenlisted for quite a long time." In the second verse, the narrator focuses on Charles's military past, "You've been over the ocean and won your good record," and mentions his rank, "A Private First Class." Next, we find the brothers dropping into a bus station's "Tea Room" for a warm-up cup of coffee. But "The waiter shakes his head, wipes his hands on his apron, / He says there's no coffee in all that big urn." The brothers disagree and note "that glass gauge there it looks like several inches / It looks like this Tea Room's got coffee to burn." After this observation, the brothers decide to directly address what they see as a racially motivated denial of their request: "We made him a speech in a quiet friendly manner, / We didn't want to scare you ladies over there." However, the waiter does not agree and "calls for a cop on his fone on the sly." After arriving, "the cop come and marched us out through the night air."[72]

Once outside, events move swiftly. First, "The cop said that we had insulted the Joint man" and "made us line up with our faces to the wall." But the brothers do not understand the dangerous situation they are in, for "We laughed to ourselves as we stood there and listened / To the man of law and order putting in his riot call." Almost immediately, their laughter dies, as do Charlie and Alfonso:

> The cop turned around and walked back to young Charlie
> Kicked him in the groin and then shot him to the ground
> This same bullet went through the brain of Alonzo [Alfonso]
> And the next bullet laid my Brother Joseph down.

In the aftermath of the shooting, further injustice occurs when "My Fourth brother Richard got hauled to the station / Bawled out and lectured by the judge on his bench" and then ends up being "lugged . . . off for a hundred day stretch."[73]

The last four verses move away from the first-person reporting that dominates the rest of the song and allow the narrator to comment more generally on the brothers' deaths. Attempting to surprise his audience in the next to last verse, the narrator—with more than a hint of bitterness—notes the town where these killings occurred:

> The town that we ride through is not Rankin Mississippi,
> Nor Bilbo's Jim Crow Burgh of Washington, D.C.,
> But it's Greater New York, our most fair minded City,
> In all of our big land and streets of the brave.

The other three verses continue in this editorial vein but use the family, especially Charles's children, to emotionalize the comments. As the mourners ride to the funeral, we see "Charles' wife, Minnie, . . . her three boy children, / And friends and relatives. . . ." However, the truth of the days' events are kept from some:

> Nobody has told these three little boys yet
> Everybody rides crying and shaking their head
> Nobody knows quite how to make these three boys know
> That Jim Crow killed Alonzo [Alfonso], that Charles, too, is dead.

In the last verse, the narrator again asks how the truth will be revealed to the boys. This truth not only includes the horror of their father's death but also the fact that his efforts to "whip the Fascists and Nazis to death" have gained him no rights in Jim Crow America. Additionally, the narrator asks how the boys will be told that the fate of their father has been shared by others: "Who'll tell these three sons that Jim Crow coffee / Has killed several thousand the same as their dad?"[74] The emotionalism and the questioning of the ending make it seem that we are coming to our own conclusion even as Guthrie directs our thoughts. As in many of his songs, Guthrie makes the narrator a part of the event rather than an outsider reporting on it. In fact, he seems to be all of the Ferguson brothers. By using the first-person plural throughout and changing perspectives among the brothers, we get a panoramic view of the events surrounding the killing.

At the time of the song's writing, not all of the details of the case had been established; so the story we get here strays from the facts as later determined. For one, the police became involved not only due to the argument at the tea shop but also because Charles had kicked in the window of a nearby business. Other information that became public in the summer of 1946 made the case against Romeika weaker than in Guthrie's song. For example, the Fergusons were looking for more than coffee on the night of the killing. According to the testimony of the two surviving brothers, all of them had been drinking heavily that night. It was in this state that they went to the tea shop, where several witnesses stated that Charles did not make a "speech in a quiet friendly manner." It also came to light that Charles threatened to pull a pistol and shoot both the waiter who refused him coffee and the tearoom manager, which his brother Joseph affirmed in his testimony. Finally, even an NAACP investigator states, "It does not appear that the killing occurred because of the race of the Ferguson boys." However, even these additional facts do not excuse the killings, and some disturbing accusations regarding Romeika's actions that night still remained. For example, just as in Guthrie's song, some testimony notes that the officer both hit and kicked Joseph and Charles moments before the shooting occurred.[75]

On February 12, 1946, another attack on a black veteran occurred and similarly moved Guthrie to capture the incident's injustice in song. Only a few hours after being discharged from the army at Fort Gordon, Georgia, Isaac Woodward stepped aboard a bus bound for his wife in Winnsboro, South Carolina. During the ride, he became engaged in an argument with the driver. When the bus reached Batesburg, South Carolina, the driver stepped off and told Police Chief Lynwood L. Shull that Woodward was making a disturbance. Shull took him off the bus, struck him, and twisted his arm as they walked to the jail. When Woodward did not address him as "Sir," Shull began beating him with his nightstick. The two struggled, and Woodward took the weapon away, only to have a deputy subdue him with a gun. Back in control, Shull continued the beating, even knocking Woodward out. In the privacy of the jail, Shull again viciously attacked Woodward, bludgeoning both his face and eyes. The next day, Woodward could not see. Taken to court, he was found guilty of disturbing the peace and resisting arrest, then given the choice between a fine of fifty dollars or thirty days in jail. Eventually, Shull became concerned enough to drop his now-blind prisoner off at the Veteran's Hospital in Columbia. Later, an all-white federal jury in that city deliberated less than twenty minutes before finding Shull innocent of violating Woodward's civil rights.[76]

Much like the Ferguson brothers' killing, this incident caught the attention of the leftist press; they in turn made it a public cause. As a result of this publicity, a benefit for Woodward was held at Lewisohn Stadium in New York on August 18, 1946. Many of the day's biggest black stars appeared, including Cab Calloway, Louis Jordan, Count Basie, Pearl Bailey, and Billie Holiday. A little out of place with these luminaries, Guthrie also appeared. But he thought the others did not include enough social commentary in their acts. He writes, "For two whole hours I didn't hear nine words of fighting protest. Isaac was the last one on the program and I sung right after he made his little talk."[77] In contrast to the other performers, Guthrie decided to detail and personalize the attack on Woodward in the simply titled song "The Blinding of Isaac Woodward," whose tune follows that of "Dust Storm Disaster."

Guthrie immediately works to gain some emotional currency by making Woodward the narrator. After telling listeners his name and purpose, Woodward warns that his tale will "sound so terrible you might not think it true." Before shifting to the heart of the matter, he establishes his credibility as a patriot and a combat veteran by briefly laying out his military past: "I joined up with the Army, they sent me overseas; / Through the battles of New Guinea and in the Philippines." After the war has been won, the army sends Woodward to America and discharges him. Unfortunately, he has to ride through the heart of Jim Crow Dixie before reaching the safety of his home and the embrace of his wife. When the narrator asks to go to the restroom, the bus "driver started cursing and he hollered, 'No!'" In response Woodward "cussed back at him, and really got him told." Reluctantly, the driver finally allows Woodward's request. Back on the bus and back on the road, the narrator looks out the window and thinks of his waiting wife. Soon, these thoughts are interrupted; for at the next stop, "the driver he jumped out; / He came back with a policemen to take me off the bus."[78]

Once removed, Woodward runs into real trouble. Even as the ex-soldier explains his innocence in causing a commotion on the bus, the cop hits, then curses him: "Shut up, you black bastard." His military service also offers no protection. When the officer asks, "Have you your Army discharge?" and Woodward answers yes, the cop "pasted me with his loaded stick down across my head." Finally, with his patience at an end, "I grabbed his stick and we had a little run, and had a little wrastle." But another cop rushes up, puts a gun to Woodward's head, and says, "If you don't drop that sap, black boy, it's me that's dropping you." After the surrender, the cops beat him so that his wounds "left a bloody trail / All down along the sidewalk to the iron door of the jail." As a final blow, they "poked me in the eyes," he says.[79]

The aftereffects of this beating soon become apparent: "When I woke up next morning, I found my eyes were blind." Then adding insult to injury, a southern judge fines him "fifty dollars for raising all the fuss." After much delay, a doctor finally arrives—although he proves little concerned: "He handed me some drops and salve and told me to treat myself." In the last verse, Woodward half asks, half tells us, "there's one thing I can't see, / How you could treat a human like they have treated me." Along with blindness comes insight; in particular, he realizes his efforts in the Pacific have not ended race hate at home: "I thought I fought on the islands to get rid of their kind; / But I can see the fight lots plainer now that I am blind."[80] Not Guthrie's most subtle bit of wordplay, perhaps, but even as the politics of its author stand out, so do the details of Woodward's story.

Just as he did in "The Ferguson Brothers Killing," Guthrie gets some of his facts wrong, such as the exact date and location where the beating occurred. However, it must be added that Guthrie learned all his information about this case from newspapers, especially the *Daily Worker*, which also got some of the facts wrong. Unlike Guthrie's songs about the Dust Bowl, tenant farmers, and migrant laborers, songs like "The Blinding of Isaac Woodward" and "Deportee" depend on stories Guthrie read about rather than ones he knew from direct experience. Of course, some of these songs are more successful in fact and execution than others. Both John Greenway and Joe Klein note that many of Guthrie's songs inspired by newspaper reports fail to score highly as art or touch deeply.[81] These criticisms apply when Guthrie tried to use newspaper articles to document a particular incident, such as in "The Ferguson Brothers Killing" or "The Blinding of Isaac Woodward." Nevertheless, when the same source gave him the impetus to create a song that offered a general picture of an injustice, such as in "Deportee" or "Poll

Tax Chain," the results would often be emotionally moving, raising the work above such criticism.

If a veteran like Isaac Woodward, acting in accordance with the law, received such treatment from the police and the legal system, then it should not surprise that those African Americans who actually broke the law would receive extremely harsh punishments. In fact, many blacks who transgressed white America's rules ended up on a chain gang or a work farm. Southern penal institutions such as Angola in Louisiana and Parchman in Mississippi punished black convicts with grueling days working long hours in the southern sun, hoeing and picking cotton or planting crops for the prison's own kitchens. Southern chain gangs offered an equally brutalizing system. In describing one prisoner's future, journalist John L. Spivak damns one southern state's chain gang system:

> In the chain gang he will live in a cage like a wild animal, a cage crawling with vermin; he will be worked on the Georgia roads from sunrise to sunset. He faced an iron collar around his neck and chains around his feet. He will be left hanging in stocks from wrists and ankles, until he becomes unconscious. And should he escape death by torture . . . and I found no record of any prisoner who lived out ten years on the Georgia chain gang . . . he may be shot . . . trying to escape.[82]

Through the twin hell of chain gangs and prison farms, southern authorities tried to keep African Americans submissive.

From many sources, Guthrie would come to sympathize with men in prison, especially chain gangs. Even as a young man, he admitted, "[I] like jail house songs as much as anybody."[83] He heard and eventually performed prison songs from the country side of the musical fence, such as "Birmingham Jail," "The Prisoner's Song," and "Twenty-One Years." He also learned of prisons and chain gangs from other sources. As early as March 1935, he wrote his first prison song as a parody to "The Isle of Capri."[84] In spring of 1940, he recorded "Chain Around My Leg" for the Library of Congress. Before playing the song, he explains to interviewer Alan Lomax what inspired the song:

> I was looking through a magazine here a while back, and it was showing conditions down South. Where I come from and all

around there in McAlister, Oklahoma, the state penitentiary there, they have what they call "chain gangs." All the southern prisons do; I guess all of them do everywhere. Anyway, I was looking at all these pictures. . . . They was laying out in the sun, just completely exhausted. . . . [But] the biggest thing in the pictures was the chain. Goes around one of the boy's leg and went around all the boys' legs.[85]

He also recorded other songs on the subject, such as "Chain Gang Special" and "It Takes a Chain Gang Man."

Guthrie also learned about chain gangs from black musicians. Sonny Terry taught him the harmonica instrumental "Lost John," which Guthrie introduced in one recording by saying, "Gonna tell you the story about old Lost John . . . the guy who got away from a Louisiana chain gang."[86] His most important and moving understanding of prison and their associated punishments came from Lead Belly, who spent time on a Texas chain gang in 1915 and also worked on three prison farms—Shaw and Sugarland in Texas and Angola in Louisiana. Lead Belly documented some of these experiences in his songs, such as "Angola Blues" and "Thirty Days in the Workhouse." Taken together, these songs, pictures, and stories would give Guthrie a strong understanding of the southern prison system facing African Americans.

Although they do not contain explicit comments on race, Guthrie intended to include both a chain gang and a prison farm song on the proposed album for Asch. In "Long and Lonesome Chain," the narrator, "Looking for a job, walking around with my stomach sick and hungry," steals a chicken and is caught.[87] The law falls hard on him; as punishment, a hard-edged judge hands down a long stint on a chain gang. Perhaps this sentence seems unrealistic, but in fact a prison term was allowed for stealing a chicken in both North Carolina and Virginia.[88] While on the road gang, the narrator has time to contemplate his chain, even to the point of madness: "Yes, it's made of rusty iron, and it's heavy and it's long, / . . . Every link in my chain burns a hole in my brain, / I have counted Twenty links a million times." After the deprivations of the chain gang—the blisters, the dirty clothes, the teasing, the threats—he dreams of escape and declares, "Iron and steel can't win out over flesh and blood and spirit."[89]

In a somewhat darker moment, Guthrie comments on prison farms and their staffs' bloodlust in "At the End of Every Row," where threat of murder becomes the song's unifying theme. During his twenty years on the chain gang, the narrator has "counted all the dead men" his "big mean riding boss" has shot down "at the end of every row." Fearing that the riding boss might "draw his sights on me" and "ask my feet to dance," the narrator says that he will "tell my feet keep still" so as not to give his tormentor any satisfaction. If killed unjustly, he asks—much like Joe Hill did—for no mourning, "don't you cry; / Don't you weep," but for action: "Just do everything you can, / To get rid of this mean boss man."[90]

African Americans who committed violence against whites, who challenged white supremacy, or who were even perceived to be stepping outside white-sanctioned behavior often received punishment even harsher than any prison or chain gang offered. According to conservative figures, from 1882 to 1940, 4,694 people were lynched in America. Of these, 3,403 were black. The zenith of African American lynchings occurred in the late 1880s and early '90s.[91] But by the early 1940s, lynchings in general had dropped to only a few isolated incidents—due mainly to the efforts of such groups as the NAACP, the Southern Commission on the Study of Lynching, and the Association of Southern Women for the Prevention of Lynching. Nevertheless, this brutal reality still remained a possibility in the South.

In the 1940s, Guthrie had several sources in particular from which to learn about the horror and fears of lynching in America. He would have heard Josh White, or even Billie Holiday, singing the antilynching anthem "Strange Fruit," which Abel Meeropol wrote in 1936 after seeing a photograph of a lynching. The song made and still makes some people uncomfortable. The impulse to squirm is understandable, for it immediately confronts listeners with the lines,

> Southern trees bear a strange fruit,
> Blood on the leaves and blood at the root,
> Black body swinging in the Southern breeze,
> Strange fruit hanging from the poplar trees.

The other lyrics provide no escape, no sanctuary from the grim truth of lynching. In verse two, we find "bulging eyes and the twisted mouth," along with "the sudden smell of burning flesh" within and in contrast to the "Pastoral scene of the gallant South." The last line of the third and final verse concludes, "Here is a strange and bitter crop."[92]

Along with the story this song told, Guthrie may also have learned about lynching in a more direct fashion through Lead Belly or Josh White. After assaulting a white man with a knife in Louisiana, Lead Belly almost found himself in the custody of a lynch mob. According to the Shreveport *Times* of January 16, 1930, "Huddie Ledbetter . . . is in the parish jail charged with assault with intent to murder and only the prompt response of the sheriff's office for help saved the negro from mob violence at the hands of a band of men who stormed the Mooringsport jail Wednesday night." Local officers held this group back until two deputy sheriffs arrived and managed to disperse the angry whites.[93] As a child in rural Georgia, Josh White witnessed a lynching one night. Remembering the event years later, he describes what he saw from his hiding place: "There were two figures. They were stripped other than their shirts. Like on tiptoe. I don't think I could see them dangling, but what I could see and what I can't get out of my eyes: I saw kids, ten, twelve years old, girls and boys my age, mothers, fathers, aunts, adults . . . the kids had pokers and they'd get them red hot and . . . and . . . it was a hell of a thing to see." Indeed, White references this experience as the reason "why I sing 'Strange Fruit,' 'cause I know what I'm singing about."[94] Both White's and Lead Belly's stories would give Guthrie firsthand knowledge about the very real threat of lynching that African Americans faced.

Guthrie encountered other art that also inflamed his antilynching passions. In a column he wrote for the *Daily Worker* on April 22, 1940, he muses on a painting he had recently seen: "Stayed a few nights with a artist and painter by trade, and he's got a mighty good picture of a lynching a hanging on . . . [his] wall. . . . it shows you one man, a Negro man, already hung for excitement and entertainment, and another'n being drug in and beat up with clubs and chains and fists and guns." Perhaps it seems strange that Guthrie came across such an unsettling representation hanging in a New York City apartment. However, by the mid-1930s, two major exhibits of art depicting lynching had already appeared in the city, one sponsored by the NAACP and the other by the CP. In paintings, drawings, and prints, such well-known artists as Thomas Hart Benton and José Clemente Orozco used their creative powers to capture the horror of lynching in work meant to shock and educate. The piece Guthrie saw had this effect, for he notes in the same column, "This painting is so real I feel like I was at a lynching, and it . . . takes all of the fun and good humor and good sport out of you to set here and realize that people could go so haywire as to hang a human body up by a gallus pole and shoot it full of Winchester rifle holes just for pastime."[95]

More than just dimming Guthrie's spirit, this painting also brought up a disturbing memory from his own youth: "It reminds me of the postcard picture they sold in my home town for several years, a showing you a negro mother, and her two young sons, a hanging by the neck from a river bridge, and the wild wind a whistling down the river bottom, and the ropes stretched tight by the weight of their bodies . . . stretched tight like a big fiddle string."[96] Just as noted in James Allen's book *Without Sanctuary: Lynching Photography in America*, images of lynchings often found their way onto popular post-cards, while others appeared in newspapers sanctioning the deed—graphic reminders that these brutal acts often occurred as public displays and with community approval. As it happens, the picture on the postcard Guthrie saw first appeared in the *Ledger*, a newspaper in his hometown of Okemah, Oklahoma. Along with the origin of this photograph, the story behind its grisly subject can be traced. For this lynching is the very one Guthrie's own father attended in 1911.

Decades after this event but around the time he encountered his friend's painting, Guthrie began creating songs condemning lynching, using images as graphic and moving as in any work by Benton or Orozco. Since his under-standing of this particular form of racial violence began through his expo-sure to a single photograph, it does not surprise that Guthrie personalizes his distaste for lynching through indirect and direct references to this image. Often, the Nelsons' end only has the most oblique impact on Guthrie's songs in that the victims in his scenes meet their ends hanging from bridges rather than the more pervasive image of a figure hanging from a tree. We see this influence in the song "A Tale a Feller Told Me" where a "lynch bunch" takes a young black man who stood up against an abusive boss from jail.

> The mob then
> Swung him down over the river
> Where that rusty bridge bends yonder
> On that long iron
> Hanging down, there.[97]

As we have already seen, the song "Poll Tax Chain" also contains a moment that briefly echoes the Nelson lynching: "The skeleton tree and river bridge."[98] But we easily can surmise from these examples that Guthrie had the image of the Nelsons in his mind when he referenced lynching considering his explicit connection in many other moments in his writing.

A stylized image of numerous lynching victims hanging from a bridge with a wasted city set in the distance, c. 1946. Sketch by Woody Guthrie. Courtesy of the Ralph Rinzler Archives.

The connection between the Nelsons' end and his lyrics becomes much more certain in the song "Slipknot." Here, the narrator twice asks, "Did you ever lose a brother in that slipknot?" Then comes the answer, "Yes. My brother was a slave . . . he tried to escape, / And they drug him to his grave with a slipknot." This question and answer pattern is repeated in the second verse:

> Did you ever lose your father on that slipknot?
> Did you ever lose your father on that slipknot?
> Yes, they hung him from a pole an' they shot him full of holes
> And they left him hang to rot in that slipknot.[99]

As noted by Oklahoma folklorist Guy Logsdon, "The power of this song indicates how far [Guthrie] had come in his idea about race relations and how deeply he felt about the evil of lynching."[100] But by only looking at the lyrics, you would find no specific trace of the Nelsons' murder. However, an endnote to this song does directly reference this incident when Guthrie writes, "Dedicated to the many negro mothers, fathers, and sons alike, that was lynched and hanged under the bridge of the Canadian River, seven miles south of Okemah, Okla., and to the day when such will be no more."[101] Obviously, he sees his antilynching work as a way to rectify the wrong that occurred in his hometown.

Other moments from Guthrie's writing directly reference the Nelsons' deaths. Among its other invocations of Guthrie's youth, the autobiographical song "High Balladree" offers this striking remembrance:

> A nickle post card I buy off your rack
> To show you what happens if you're black and fight back
> A lady and two boys hanging down by their necks
> From the rusty iron rigs of my Canadian bridge.[102]

Here, the postcard referenced earlier appears in full, just as he remembered it. But of all Guthrie's antilynching songs, "Don't Kill My Baby and My Son" (also titled "Old Dark Town" and "Old Rock Jail") most fully re-creates the Nelsons' end.

In this song, the narrator returns to "the old dark town . . . where I was born" and almost immediately hears "the lonesomest sounding cry / That I ever had heard." Investigating, he discovers "a black girl pulling her hair" in jail and hears her lament, which becomes the song's chorus:

> Don't let them kill my baby,
> And don't let them kill my son!
> You can hang me by my neck
> On that Canadian River's bridge!
> Don't let them kill my baby and my son!

In another verse, we find that she sits in jail and faces death because "A bad man had pulled his gun / To make her hide him away." Soon after these revelations, the narrator walks into a store and finds a disturbing scene on a postcard: "I saw my Canadian River's bridge, / Three bodies swung in the wind." As he stares at the card, he hears her mercy plea once again.[103]

Guthrie also wrote songs commenting on lynching that did not draw on the image from the Okemah postcard. One of these is "When the Curfew Blows," which focuses on the fears of a man caught out beyond the prescribed time. Although this song may not focus on the lynching of African Americans, it certainly alludes to the threat of punishment and hanging and easily applies to the situation that this minority group faced. Before the Civil War, groups of armed whites—often called "patrollers"—imposed curfews on slaves. If any were found out beyond the set time, they would be punished and could even be killed.[104] During the time Guthrie wrote this song, some southern towns still enforced curfews for African Americans. In this song, the setting may be in the past or in the present—but in either case, the narrator announces how the coming of the curfew puts him in a dejected state:

> The lonesomest sound, boys,
> That I ever heard sound, boys,
> Was on the stroke of midnight
> As the curfew blow.

Justifying this fearful reaction, the next verses outline the penalty for violating the curfew. However, the punishment varies. Using the second person to pull the listener in, the second verse warns, "If they catch you, / They will jail you / In the city lock-up." But for the narrator, capture is more certain and more costly. Not only are "The sheriff's men ... on my trail," but "If they catch me, / My body will hang, boys, / On the gallus pole."[105]

Not all of the lynching victims depicted in Guthrie's songs are brought to their fate by mobs. Some end up being hung by legal means, for he points out that many African Americans met their end due to capital punishment. By including questions about legal executions in the last verses of the song "Slipknot," Guthrie connects the death penalty and lynching. The narrator asks, "Who makes the laws for that slipknot?" and "Who says who is goin' to the calaboose / And get the hangman's noose of the slipknot?" However, the narrator does not come to any conclusion about the lawmakers: "I don't know who makes the laws for that slipknot." Yet he is certain that "the bones of many a man are a-whistlin' in the wind / 'Cause they tied their laws with a slipknot."[106] This awareness follows the truth of the shift from illegal to legal lynching.

After public pressure in both the North and the South began to be felt, lynchings stopped being part of an illegal public spectacle and became a legal private function. As illegal lynchings decreased in the 1920s, legally sanctioned executions just as surely took the lives of African Americans. As one observer of this time notes, this "process of 'legal lynchings' was so successful that in the 1930s, two-thirds of those executed were black."[107] Often, the court of public opinion found accused African Americans guilty before any trial could be held. For example, after a black man barely escaped a lynching in Natchez, Mississippi, he was quickly tried and hung. According to one observer, the young black man's fate had always been certain: "Of course they hung him legal after the trial. There was so much feeling that he was bound to hang. You couldn't get a jury not to convict him."[108] As noted sociologist Arthur Raper pointed out in *The Tragedy of Lynching*, this situation was typical of the time: "After being kept from the overt act of killing, the mob members have successfully demanded of public officials that the accused person be tried in the local county, that the death sentence be imposed, and that no delay of execution be sought by the defendant's counsel—in most cases a local lawyer appointed by the court."[109] Nationwide statistics from the 1920s and '30s buttress Raper's accusations here, for all-white juries convicted and sentenced over twenty-five hundred people to death during this time, a little more than two-thirds of whom were black—a percentage far out of line with their numbers in the general population.[110]

During the 1920s and '30s, the issue of legal lynching most famously manifested itself in the case of the Scottsboro Boys. In March 1931, nine young black men were taken from a train, along with two white women dressed as male hoboes, Ruby Bates and Victoria Price. To protect themselves from prosecution for riding the train illegally, the women accused the nine of raping them. After a rather quick trial in Scottsboro, Alabama, all but the youngest received death sentences. At this point, the International Labor Defense, the NAACP, and other progressive groups got involved in the case. But even after Bates became a witness for the defense, the Scottsboro Boys' conviction held. The legal fracas continued until 1950, when the last of the nine gained release from prison. All the while, this case kept the interest of America's left. Certainly, Guthrie knew of the case by the early 1940s and may have encountered others' artistic response to it, such as Mike Quin's poem "They Shall Not Die" or Lead Belly's song "Scottsboro Boys."

Through the attention addressed to this case and other incidents of court-sanctioned racism, Guthrie came to understand that lynching continued in a new guise. In fact, sometime in the late 1940s, Guthrie took up the song "Slipknot" again and revised it so that it more directly comments on how African Americans unfairly receive the ultimate penalty. The new song, entitled "Death Row," opens by questioning listeners, "Did you ever spend a night along the Death Row?" Each subsequent line in the first verse ups the time—moving from a week, to a month, to a year, and then life. The next verse also asks some questions: "Did you ever take a walk," "smell the cells," or "hear the moans and sighs and the cries" on death row? Later, we find "many an innocent man along my Death Row." If you can get these prisoners to talk, "the tales that they tell will melt your heart with sorrow" because they have been "framed up to die along that Death Row." Yet some still have a chance at beating their unjust convictions. Unfortunately, race has much to do with their chances:

> If you're white you've got some chance to beat this Death Row;
> If you're white you might get loose from off this Death Row;
> But a man that's partly black, partly dark, chocolate brown
> He ain't got an earthly chance to beat this Death Row.

In the next verse, the narrator gives us some examples of places where legal lynchings occurred: "You can march to old Virginia, you can walk to Trenton's Town, / Or most any old town around to find this Death Row."[III] In indicating these different points on the map, the narrator touches on at least one specific case that Guthrie wrote two songs about himself.

On August 6, 1948, an all-white jury sentenced six black men to die in the electric chair for robbing and killing William Horner, a white Trenton, New Jersey, junkshop owner. Due to the actions of the NAACP and the Civil Rights Congress, the case did not end here. Along with these groups, other New York leftists supported an appeal and labeled the case "A Northern Scottsboro." Accordingly, a benefit performance on June 5, 1949, of John Wexley's play *They Shall Not Die*, dealing with the Scottsboro case, raised money for the Trenton Six's defense.[112] Just a few days before this performance, Guthrie decided to weigh in with his opinion.

In "Buoy Bells for Trenton," the narrator says the defendants are "marked to die / Just for having dark skin on your hands and face." All the while, the chorus repeatedly tells us that they are "boys framed up to die." In explaining the reasons behind the decision, the narrator says, "The race hate Fascists are at work." He ends by explaining that the "same old race hate" that condemned famed labor martyrs Sacco and Vanzetti has "ruled the judge and jury's heart" in the Trenton Six case.[113] In a less editorializing fashion, the song "Trenton Frameup" allows a description of the case to denounce the six's convictions. After setting the details of the crime, the narrator points to repressive police pressure: "Po' cops did ride / With a finger on their slick Tommy guns / Past the black peoples homes that cop squad did roll." Later, these same police pick up six suspects illegally: "Like stormtrooper men they laugh at the law, / For stormtroopers do not need a warrant." After being "beat up, and doped, and beat some more," all sign confessions. Then an all-white jury ("Not a black man allowed to take the box") finds the six guilty and sentences them to death.[114] Here, Guthrie again condemns the white privileged legal system that condemns innocent blacks to death.

Some of Guthrie's songs touching on legal and illegal lynching do offer hope. In "Death Row," the narrator predicts he will one day "go strolling down 'long that Death Row," "turn that key of liberty," and free "my innocent brothers."[115] But the strongest moment of optimism occurs in the song "This Could Never Happen in My Dear Old Sunny South," which tells the tale of Hugh Burleson and his exoneration from the charge of sexual assault on a white woman. After "escaping / From some crazy Southern state," he gets picked up for "a raping charge" in San Francisco. But after a doctor testifies in his behalf and Burleson's accuser turns out to have "downed a whole half-a-pint" before picking him out as her attacker, a benevolent and just judge sets him free—a fate unlike the one he would have received in the South, "Where a black man gets the hanging tree / When a girl shoots off her mouth."[116]

Even after Guthrie changed his attitude about American minorities and composed songs documenting the harsh injustices faced by them, his writing could still contain racially troubling moments. In both of Guthrie's published autobiographical novels, stereotypical ethnic minorities dot the cultural landscape. In looking at the Chinese characters in *Bound for Glory*, we find that they speak in a barely understandable English—usually while denying Guthrie a job or food. For example, when he tries to make a trade for a bowl of chili, a Chinese restaurant owner rejects his offer: "You keep. You see, I got plentee sletee [sweaters]. You think good sletee, you keep sletee. My keep chili bean." Even while explaining the subtleties and hurts of racist language, black characters do not fare much better in their speech: "When I calls my own se'f a niggah, I knows I don' mean it. An' even anothah niggah calls me a 'niggah,' I don' min', 'cause I knows it's most jes' fun. But when a white pusson calls me 'niggah,' it's like a whip cuts through my ol' hide."[117] In Guthrie's other and lesser-known autobiographical novel *Seeds of Man*, all the Mexican characters stumble clownishly through the English language. For example, after he helps stop a stalled truck from rushing downhill and saves the day, an unnamed Mexican rider warns another character not to get too close to his horse: "No. You scare. Hoss jump. Car fall. Rope slip. Nooo. You back. Me hoss."[118] Afro-American Studies professor Craig Werner refers to moments like this when he writes, "[Guthrie's] representations of the spoken language of Mexicans and blacks too often descend into near minstrelsy."[119]

But even in these moments, Guthrie seems to be trying to capture the sound of a people. In that they are not his own, he depends on stereotypes to approximate their language, his ear apparently not exactly able to trace out the nuances of these minorities' speech patterns. Although sometimes guilty of reinforcing stereotypes through this language, he often makes these same characters noble people. He molds them into shapes pleasing to the moral soul, even if their words are bent, stiff, or even offensive by today's standards. In all the work that Guthrie created after 1939, not one moment where he obviously tries to discount the people of any race appears. Quite the contrary—his work documents their oppression and calls for their rights.

Through his songs, Guthrie clearly wanted to offer whites removed from the struggles of America's underclass insight into another world. In an afternote to "When the Curfew Blows," he writes,

> To a soda jerker on a fast college corner, a song, or a program of
> songs like this, might cause him and his customers to look up and

ask themselves "what is wrong with the radio?" But, even there, in just such a crowd, if this kind of music was properly understood, everybody would get a lot of deep enjoyment out of listening, for a little while. I don't claim this kind of music should crowd the other kinds out; but, certainly, this would sound no more out of life, no more disassociated, no more cut off from experience which is truth, than to hear our soap operas and chewing gum symphonies drifting through the weather-leaking walls of 16,000,000 Negroes in the south, yes, and that many more Browns, Whites, and Red Men, to boot.[120]

After Huntington's chorea had confined him to a hospital and made writing extremely difficult, this desire for racial equality did not diminish. In a letter dated October 4, 1956, he writes, "Eisenhower can't be my big chiefy bossyman till he makes alla my United States alla my races equal."[121] Even at the end of his writing career, he could not keep from commenting on the skin trouble that he saw dividing his country.

Overall, Guthrie's songs and other writings focusing on race work to document the hardships and horrors faced by minorities during his time. But they don't expose these truths simply for the dynamic subject matter; they also include the hope that they will reveal the awful truth to a public not fully aware or understanding of those hurts suffered by other races. In effect, he hoped to use his knowledge of the abuses of racist laws and actions to explain the biting lives of African Americans and other ethnic minorities to the whole of America. He wanted to share the stories and facts in his songs with a public he believed would act justly if they truly understood and felt the harm of racism, just as he himself had been transformed by his exposure to these same truths about the plight of America's racial minorities. He used his art in an attempt to educate others, just as he was educated. In fact, he stands as his own best example that being confronted with injustice through personal experience, friendship, and art could undo people's racist beliefs. Just as he believed that songs have the power to educate minds and move hearts, his work touching on race is his offering to America to make such change possible.

CHAPTER FIVE

Stepping Outside the Law

CLASS CONSCIOUSNESS IN GUTHRIE'S OUTLAW SONGS

In early 1940, the Library of Congress's Archive of American Folksong sponsored Charles Todd and Robert Sonkin's journey to California to collect songs from the Okies in Farm Security Administration camps there. Among various other song types, the two young folklorists noticed this group's fondness for old and new outlaw ballads such as "Bold Jack Donahue," "John Hardy," and "John Dillinger." In their essay "Ballad of the Okies," Todd and Sonkin speculate on the driving force behind these displaced people's admiration for law breakers:

> The popularity of the "outlaw'd" songs among the Okies might give rise to some theorizing on the part of the sociologists if it were not for the fact that most ballad-makers from the time of Robin Hood have been partial to public enemies. Some commentators have used the "rob the rich and give to the poor" theme of many of these songs to prove the class consciousness of folk singers, but such reasoning seems a little forced. The Okies are rugged individualists of the old school, and any legend that deals with a gallant brigand who robbed a Chicago bank or stood off a posse single-handed is bound to be a popular one.[1]

Perhaps they rightly categorize the Okies as "rugged individualists of the old school." Some sociologists and historians have made similar claims concerning this group's penchant for individual rather than class identity.[2] But any comment about "folk singers" who perform outlaw songs lacking "class consciousness" would certainly not apply to Woody Guthrie. Just as other Okies did, he enjoyed and performed traditional songs detailing the lives and actions of outlaws of old. Unlike some of his fellow Okies, he often intentionally added a layer of class consciousness to the outlaw figures in these songs. He also continued this impulse in some of his original work celebrating the exploits of men and women from past and present who stepped outside the law.

Guthrie's and other Okies' interest in outlaws may initially seem strange, for most of them stand as unlikely heroes in that they robbed and killed—behavior far removed from that usually associated with those held up for public approbation. But their often violent actions appear, both in various folk songs and some of Guthrie's original songs, as an understandable response to various unjust situations and systems. In several songs that Guthrie wrote or performed, instead of taking from farmers and other working people, outlaws rob greedy bankers who steal "with a fountain pen" and shoot down the "deputy thugs" who act as the enforcers of an unfair but legal system.[3] In effect, Guthrie often depicts various men and women as stepping outside the law to gain justice—for themselves or for the underclass as a whole—from those who unfairly wield economic or legal power. Thus, they could be called outlaws even when committing admirable deeds, such as giving money—albeit stolen—to the needy. Historian Eric Hobsbawn refers to these characters as "social bandits" and describes them as "outlaws whom the lord and state regard as criminals, but who remain within peasant society, and are considered by their people as heroes, as champions, avengers, fighters for justice."[4] Although none of the outlaws appearing in the folk songs Guthrie sang or the lyrics he created himself technically come from a "peasant society," the majority of them were poor themselves or at least sprang from regions made up of rural populations frequently on the edge of poverty. Often, these communities did laud the outlaws' crimes against perceived repressive agents.

Guthrie's impulse in these songs agrees with an idea inherent in social documentary, for this particular expressive form "shows man at grips with conditions neither permanent nor necessary, conditions of a certain time and place."[5] Some of Guthrie's outlaw figures work to overturn the unjust "conditions" they saw in their own society. In fact, he states that an outlaw song helped him recognize that he too could document the struggles of the underclass for future generations. He writes that after playing the traditional tune "Jesse James" one night, he "decided right then and there to keep on going with my job of turning out such kind of balladsongs for folks a hundred generations from us to learn how things were with our bunch here."[6] In another piece, Guthrie further explains how he knew outlaw songs fit into a larger public history: "I sing songs about the outlaws that the people loved and the ones that the people hated. I sing any song that was made up by the people that tells a little story, a little part, of our big history of this country, yes, or that tells a part of the history of the world."[7] In essence, he sees his songs as a means of recording the struggles of the poor in his time for future generations. However, the history that he reveals in his songs often depends on his own ideas of truth rather than an attempt to ferret out fact-based particulars of an outlaw's life or actions.

Many of the outlaws who appear in Guthrie's songs already had gained public renown and had achieved varying popular status years before the songwriter's birth. These outlaws had had their stories told and retold—creating a spectrum of possibility rather than a single and unified history. Because of the repetition and revisioning of their stories in various popular media sources such as songs, pulp fiction, and film, the actions and attitudes of these outlaws have with time moved beyond easily determinable truth and have become legendary. Guthrie well knew of this situation himself. When talking of Jesse James in an interview with Alan Lomax in 1940, he notes how the popularity of this outlaw in Oklahoma had led several men from that region to go so far as to claim to be him: "Jesse's talked about so much and liked so good down in there that there's about ten or fifteen guys in every town that claims to be him."[8] With such a striking example of how this outlaw's legend had been shaped and warped by popularity, Guthrie would be well aware of the difficulty of determining absolute truth about such figures. Instead of automatically accepting others' sentiments, he often took certain figures condemned by various legal authorities in their own time and, using his own political views, shaped their stories so they could be seen as unabashed people's champions. As folklorist John Greenway noted, "For his heroes of history [Guthrie] wrote songs of praise long on truth and short on fact."[9]

Certainly, shaping these outlaws' stories to jibe with his own ideology was not his initial impulse when Guthrie first began learning songs about various characters who stepped outside the law. Well before he would have developed any definable class consciousness, he encountered outlaw songs.

Early in his life, family members taught him ballads of this type that had come from the British Isles. From his years in Oklahoma and Texas, he came to know several stories and folk songs about western outlaws, many of whom operated around Guthrie's home region. Another source for outlaw songs in both his youth and in his maturity came from the African-American folk song tradition. When he left Texas in the late 1930s, he took these song traditions with him to California and even began to write songs about contemporary criminals who worked and robbed in his home state. Later, after traveling to New York City in the beginning months of 1940, he continued to create songs about people who stepped outside the law. Around this time, he edged away from writing solely about stereotypical outlaws. In some of his original songs from this period, those who defied the law no longer robbed banks or shot deputies. Instead, they directly helped the poor by working to change the systems that hurt them. Realizing that the abusive situations documented in his songs of America's underclass grew out of social "conditions neither permanent nor necessary," Guthrie could imagine the undoing of current unfair laws and institutions. Consequently, some of his songs detail the lives and efforts of men and women who rebelled against the status quo. In effect, Guthrie may have started out singing outlaw songs because they appealed to the "rugged individualist" tradition from which he came. But by the early 1940s, he had moved beyond this perspective and had created several outlaw ballads showing both men and women struggling to right the wrongs occurring around them and exhibiting the author's own growing social consciousness.

One of the earliest sources for Guthrie's interest in outlaws and songs about them came from his own family members. Some of these songs harken back to an earlier time in another country. In a brief 1946 autobiographical piece, he mentions learning folk songs of the British Isles from his mother, Nora, who was well versed in this tradition. She, in turn, had "learned all of the songs and ballads that her parents knew," both of whom were descended from Scotch-Irish stock. His father also had Scotch-Irish roots, and Guthrie may have learned songs from this tradition through him or his side of the family.[10] Along with such songs born in the British Isles and imported to America as "Barbara Allen" and "Gypsy Davy," Guthrie learned at least one well-worn outlaw ballad: "Bonnie Black Bess" ("The Unwelcome Guest").[11]

Throughout Guthrie's version of this folk song, its outlaw protagonist appears nameless. But his horse's name, the Bess of the title, gives him away;

he is Dick Turpin, an outlaw from eighteenth-century Britain who rustled, poached, smuggled, and robbed. Eventually, English authorities captured him while he was living under an alias and hung him on April 7, 1739. Even before his death, various legends grew up around Turpin and his exploits, the most famous revolving around a twelve-hour ride he made on Black Bess from London to York so as to avoid capture. This escape and other deeds of daring help make up the story woven into the well-known folk song about him, which first came to be published in the mid-1800s. When looking through the thousands of songs held by the Woody Guthrie Archives for a CD project, British musician Billy Bragg recognized the history behind the song and decided to record it with the band Wilco as a means of connecting Guthrie back to an earlier tradition.[12] Although it is unlikely that Guthrie was acquainted with the origins of the song or even the name of its criminal subject, the fact that he knew the song and played it ties his celebration of those outside the law to a centuries-long tradition of outlaw ballads.

Guthrie's version of this folk song generally follows the story related in early variants found in both Britain and America.[13] An unnamed outlaw rides "the road / To plunder the wealthy and relieve my distress." Helping him in this endeavor is his horse, "bonnie black Bess." Since she aids the outlaw willingly, even "bound[ing] at my call," he spares her any of the usual methods for getting speed out of a horse; he says, "no vile whip nor spur did your sides ever gall." With her help and companionship, the outlaw would find "the rich man's bright lodges" where he would be "an unwelcome guest." She would stand silent while he took "their gold and their jewels." The outlaw does not rob or abuse all: "No poor man I plundered, nor e'er did oppress / The widows or orphans." However, his impulse to rob only the wealthy puts him in jeopardy with the law. In the best-known example of Turpin's exploits, "The rangers of justice did me hot pursue / From Yorktown to London." But with Bess "like lightening we flew," making the journey in only twelve hours. Unfortunately, Turpin's luck does not hold out forever, and the outlaw realizes that he will soon be captured—even with Bess's help, for she is "worn out and weary." Certain that the law will soon have its revenge, he praises her best qualities and then states her fate: "You're noble, you're gentle, and so brave, but must die." For although "it does me distress," Turpin shoots his horse to keep her from being captured by those who will soon take and hang him.[14] As we see, the criminal here comes across as a caring individual who spares the poor and who values his horse as a companion. Although neither the authorities nor the wealthy appear as repressive or evil, Turpin seems more heroic than notorious for his actions in avoiding the former or robbing the latter. With the aid of trusted Bess, he achieves legendary stature untainted by the crimes he commits.

Not all the songs Guthrie learned early in life whose narrative forgives their criminal subjects originated abroad. Most were decidedly homegrown in creation, and unlike "Bonnie Black Bess," a few described the dramatic actions of common cowboys and frontiersmen who stepped outside the law rather than the exploits of famous criminals. An example of this type of folk song that Guthrie knew is "Buffalo Skinners." In his version of this well-traveled song, a "famous drover" lures the narrator and other cowboys out to "the trail of the buffalo," where they "got all full of stickers" and dodge outlaws. But when the season ends, the drover says, "You're all in debt to me." The cowboys think otherwise, so they "left that drover's bones to bleach" in the sun.[15] Here, the cowboys mete out a judgment that is apparently rough justice since they are presented positively and are not punished for this murder. We hear their hardships, realize their hurt, and then forgive the murder they commit. Not all outlaw songs or stories that Guthrie learned from his family would focus on such ambiguous figures as the cowboys in "Buffalo Skinners." In fact, most of the outlaws appearing in Guthrie's songs had already been so established in the public mind of Oklahoma or even America as a whole that they could be considered legendary.

As Guthrie revealed, his mother sang "tales and stories" about criminals that led him to envision "a thousand reels of moving pictures . . . [of] outlaws, fugitives," and other denizens of the untamed West.[16] Since Oklahoma has a long history as a haven for outlaws, it seems only natural that his mother and other family members would know various songs about criminals who had operated in the area. From just after the Civil War and until its acceptance as a state in 1907, the region that would become the state of Oklahoma had very little law enforcement. From around 1865 to 1889, white outlaws could easily escape into Indian Territory and thereby elude officers since a limited process was in place to extradite lawbreakers for crimes committed elsewhere. Even after the opening of parts of this territory to non–Native American settlers, outlaws thrived since federal legislation empowering this move did not immediately authorize the establishment of local government, let alone provide for law officers, jails, or courthouses.[17] As a result of this limited legal authority, various outlaws, such as the Daltons and Belle Starr, either robbed in or escaped to this area in the last three decades of the nineteenth century. In fact, Guthrie's own family could have had or did have encounters with such figures. The Dalton gang supposedly had a hide-out near Guthrie's hometown of Okemah, and Guthrie claims that "foamy ponied outlaws" visited his mother's childhood home.[18] In light of this history, it seems natural that Guthrie wrote songs about the criminals who once roamed the region around his birthplace.

We can see the influence of this local history in Guthrie's little-known song discussing the Dalton gang. Consisting primarily of the brothers Bob, Grat, and Emmett Dalton, this gang robbed trains and banks with impunity in the early part of the 1890s in the Indian and Oklahoma territories. Before their turn to crime, both Bob and Grat had been lawmen in the region, and even young Emmett had ridden in legally empowered posses with his brothers. After they turned outlaw, the Daltons used their skills from this early time to their advantage, along with their personal and family ties in the area. Even with these advantages, the gang came to a disastrous end on October 5, 1892, when they tried to rob two banks at once in Coffeyville, Kansas, a town in which the Dalton family had once lived. When the outlaws attempted to escape after committing their twin crimes, law officers and townspeople opened fire, killing Bob and Grat Dalton, along with gang members Bill Powers and Dick Broadwell. Although severely wounded, Emmett Dalton survived and ended up serving fourteen years in the Kansas state penitentiary.[19]

In March 1939, Guthrie wrote the first version of his song "The Dalton Boys." In it, he establishes the outlaws as being denizens of his home region by stating that the Daltons used a cave as a hideout that was "close to the town of Bristow," located about twenty miles north of Okemah. As for the outlaws' exploits, the song contends that they "Shot their ways from Santa Fe / To the Indian Territory."[20] According to Emmett Dalton, the brothers did begin their outlaw career in New Mexico—but in a nameless little mining town located somewhere between Silver City and Santa Rosa.[21] Nevertheless, they did rob the Santa Fe train—twice, in fact. For the most part, though, the Daltons practiced their criminal activities in and around Indian Territory, where they did have various hideouts. But the main gist of Guthrie's song does not deal with the gang's criminal deeds; instead, it speculates on the eternal results of these actions. Twice the song asks whether Bob Dalton has "gone on to Glory" or "to Pur-ga-tory." As a result, the answer to this question pivots on whether or not listeners believe that Bob's actions were motivated by greed.[22] If he is seen as a social bandit, one who takes from the unjust, then his place would certainly be heaven. But if he appears only as a greedy robber, then hell would be his destination. Since Guthrie offers up this twofold possibility, perhaps he had not decided for himself whether the Daltons should be celebrated as folk heroes. For certain, he does not automatically justify and laud the actions of this outlaw. Instead, he leaves the decision up to us, leaving our own biases as guide instead of his.

Another outlaw who roamed the region around Guthrie's hometown in the late 1800s was Belle Starr. Although born in Missouri in 1848 and raised in Texas, Starr eventually settled down in Indian Territory in the 1870s. She owned a ranch there around sixty miles east of Guthrie's hometown of Okemah. Several of her biographers note that her criminal career included horse theft and robbery; but although indicted several times, she was convicted only once, serving just nine months of a one-year sentence.[23] Yet she was never the rogue some made her out to be; for some of her notorious reputation stemmed out of her relationships with male outlaws. Actually, the majority of Guthrie's song about Starr focuses on her only through her association with these men.

Since Starr lived near Okemah, Guthrie would easily have had access to stories and legends about her that must have encouraged his interest in this female outlaw although it seems that he did not write about her until he came across a newspaper article on her.[24] Drawing upon the romantic connections it made, in March 1946, he wrote "Belle Starr" and included it in one of his commercially released songbooks, although he never recorded it. In this ballad, the narrator speaks directly to Starr after her death and asks if it is in "Heaven's wide streets that you're tying your reins" or if she is "singlefooting somewhere below," which echoes the question asked in "The Dalton Boys." Unlike that song, the majority of this song's lyrics do not focus on Starr's crimes but on her paramours. Here, the narrator remembers the eight male lovers who "combed your waving black hair," "knew the feel of your dark velvet waist," and "heard the sounds of your tan leather skirt." Not all memories of her relationships appear as romantic as these since all her past lovers also heard "the bark of the guns you wore." As listed in the song, all these men would be quite familiar with the sound of gunfire; for they include Cole Younger, William Clarke Quantrill, and Jesse James. Just as Starr did, the eight men listed in the song all ranged around the middle border states of Missouri, Kansas, Texas, and Arkansas from the 1860s to the 1880s.[25] Guthrie wrote a couple of songs about one of the outlaws he lists as being a lover of Starr, a man who did visit the territory that would eventually become the state of Oklahoma—Jesse James.

Of all the outlaws who captured Guthrie's imagination, James was held in particularly high esteem by the people of Oklahoma. In an interview with Alan Lomax, Guthrie said that he had heard about this outlaw "all my life" and that people in the state "talk about him almost like he was one of the family."[26] Born on September 5, 1847, in Clay County, Missouri, Jesse Woodson James first tasted life outside the law during the Civil War as a pro-Confederate guerrilla riding under the command of "Bloody" Bill Anderson in the Kansas-Missouri border area. After the war, he and his brother Frank, who had also been a guerrilla, returned home and farmed for a time, but soon they began to use their martial skills to successfully rob banks, trains, and stagecoaches for their own private gain. On April 3, 1881, recent gang recruit Robert Ford, urged on by the promise of reward money from state authorities, shot Jesse in the back of the head while he adjusted a picture on the wall of his home in St. Joseph, Missouri. Although solid proof points to James killing clerks, conductors, law officers, and others who got in his way during the course of his many robberies, no solid proof exists that he gave money to poor farmers to stave off foreclosure. As one of his better biographers has noted: "In all the voluminous material that pertains to Jesse James and the James band, evidence of specific acts of generosity toward the poor, even with funds stolen from the vaults of banks and safes of express cars, is practically nonexistent." Nevertheless, the author continues, "The impression that Jesse James robbed the rich and gave to the poor lives on."[27] In particular, most of the songs composed about James encourage the belief that he was a Robin Hood figure. When Guthrie first wrote his own song about the exploits of this outlaw, he continued in this tradition.

Regardless of the true actions and nature of James during his criminal career, Guthrie seems to greatly appreciate the idea of an outlaw who "took from the rich and ... gave to the poor" since this idea is a central theme to all the different versions of his song "Jesse James and His Boys." Although all versions mention some of the outlaw's robberies, especially his holdup of "the midnight Southern Mail," and point out that "every Sheriff" was powerless to capture the James gang, they offset these images with an emphasis on the outlaw's gentle nature through some variation on the statement that he would never "frighten a mother with a child."[28] Since this depiction positions James as a folk hero, it only follows that the man who killed him would be demonized, especially since Ford also shot the outlaw in the back while enjoying his hospitality. Since his song follows the general outline of and even copies lines from the best-known folk song about James, Guthrie must have encountered a variant of it sometime before 1938 when he created the first of many versions of "Jesse James and His Boys."[29] Nevertheless, Guthrie did not merely ape the sentiments he encountered in various folk songs about outlaws. In particular, he wrote a unique song about Jesse James that emphasizes his bloody side and unjust deeds.

Simply titled "Jesse James," this song opens up with the narrator telling us that "just about the worst gun battle ever out on the Western plains" occurred when "me and a bunch of cowboys had a run in with" the Missouri outlaw and his brother Frank. During the "bloody battle" with the two James boys that follows, "guns went off like thunder and the bullets fell like rain." Apparently, the two bandits outgun the cowboys, for the narrator tells us that "my partners fell around me / With bullets in their brains." In the end, the song stands as a warning: "If you're afraid to die, / You'd better stay out of the badlands" and "out of Jesse's path."[30] Although a few folk songs about this outlaw use his life and murder as a moral example, Guthrie's stands alone as tale of Jesse's murderous tendencies.[31] From this example, we can see that Guthrie does not mindlessly follow the line that all outlaws—especially Jesse James—are heroes; he can buck tradition and offer us a vision of the extreme violence that this outlaw truly engaged in during his career.

In one song that he performed but did not write, although he did revise it significantly from the original, Guthrie again offers up a story of an outlaw from the Old West. Unlike the folk songs he drew on for some of his own outlaw ballads, Guthrie's "Billy the Kid" stems from a commercial recording. Although several songs about this outlaw existed by the time Guthrie began performing and writing, the one penned on January 20, 1927, by blind songwriter Andrew Jenkins quickly became dominant through its recording by popular cowboy singer Vernon Dalhart. A possible reason for the prominence of this song, as noted by music critic Bill Malone, is that it "sounds like a traditional cowboy ballad."[32] Jenkins's song depicts Billy the Kid as a man deserving no compassion. Here, Billy commits "desperate deeds" in his time out west. When only "twelve years old," he "went to the bad" and "killed his first man." By the time "his young manhood had reached its sad end," he "had a notch on his pistol for twenty-one men," one for each year of his life. Billy's thirst for violence leads him to threaten the life of Sheriff Pat Garrett, who kills the outlaw and ends his "trail of blood." In the last verse,

Jenkins's narrator warns that the outlaw's fate could be shared by others who are not willing to stay within the limits of society:

There's a many a young men with face fine and fair
Who starts out in life with a chance to be square.
But just like poor Billy, he wanders astray,
And loses his life in the very same way.[33]

In no uncertain terms, Jenkins's song condemns Billy the Kid and his ways. The song becomes a moral lesson about the danger of innocent youth falling into evil ways and paying the ultimate penalty.

It is certain that Guthrie knew Jenkins's song. In 1935, he used its melody for his song "So Long, It's Been Good to Know You." He also attempted to play Jenkins's song for Alan Lomax in March 1940, but could only remember a couple of verses.[34] By April 19, 1944, Guthrie had taken Jenkins's work and recast it for a recording session with Moses Asch. Although titled "Billy the Kid" and using Jenkins's melody along with some of his lyrics, most of Guthrie's version of this song came from his own creative imagination, one that celebrates this outlaw as much as it condemns him. In fact, the editors of one album containing Guthrie's "Billy the Kid" disagreed with his depiction of the outlaw so much that they felt compelled to note, "Billy the Kid, a stoop-shouldered, squinty cretin, was romanticized in this song."[35]

The difference between Jenkins's song and Guthrie's appears in the very first verse. Although both songs promise to tell us the story of Billy the Kid, Jenkins's describes his adventures as "desperate deeds" while Guthrie's uses less specific, thus less damning, language: "I'll tell of the things this young outlaw did." Yet both Guthrie's and Jenkins's narrators repeat the often-mentioned story (probably untrue) of how the outlaw murdered twenty-one men during his lifetime. Both songs also note that Billy and Garrett had once been friends, and Guthrie and Jenkins use similar language in explaining how Billy's threat against the life of Pat Garrett led to the outlaw's death. But even in these moments, contrasts appear. When Garrett shoots down Billy, Jenkins's narrator notes their past connection. Consequently, the killing becomes a testament to the guilt that Garrett must have felt for felling a man who was once close to him—even if that man threatened his life without cause. Although Guthrie's song does not present the Kid as an innocent, other details are added to complicate the outlaw's death. Here, Garrett listens outside while Billy "told his tale / Of shooting the guard at

CLASS CONSCIOUSNESS IN GUTHRIE'S OUTLAW SONGS

the Las Cruces jail" and plans the sheriff's own death. But Garrett does not stand as a symbol of justice since he shoots the Kid in the back. Thus, both Garrett and the Kid betray their past friendship in Guthrie's song. Unlike Jenkins, Guthrie does not present Billy as a "young lad" who "went to the bad" but as a "young outlaw" who threatened the wrong man.[36]

Along with those from other traditions, Guthrie also picked up songs and stories from African-American sources, including several focusing on badmen who would not follow society's conventions or laws. In looking at Richard Wright's *Black Boy*, Ralph Ellison speculated on the possible attitudes that African Americans could express towards white society's restrictions in the South of the early twentieth century:

> They could accept the role created for them by the whites and perpetually resolve the resulting conflicts through the hope and emotional catharsis of Negro religion; they could repress their dislike of Jim Crow social relations while striving for a middle way of respectability, becoming—consciously or unconsciously— the accomplices of the whites in oppressing their brothers; or they could reject the situation, adopt a criminal attitude, and carry on an unceasing psychological scrimmage with the whites, which often flared forth into physical violence.[37]

Perhaps the African-American folk song "Stagger Lee" best represents this third type of reaction. Although several possibilities exist, music critic Greil Marcus explains the story behind this song well: "Somewhere, sometime, a murder took place: a man called Stack-a-lee—or Stacker Lee, Stagolee, or Staggerlee—shot a man called Billy Lyons." He continues, "It is a story that black America has never tired of hearing and never stopped living out, like whites with Westerns."[38] Here , Marcus implicitly connects the story of this African-American outlaw with Anglo-American tales of western outlaws. Just as those men had their stories extended and exploded by legend, so has Stagger Lee. In some versions, he loses at gambling and kills in anger, only to be haunted by regret and punished for his crime. In others, he sells his soul to the devil and murders Billy Lyons with premeditated joy. Indeed, one critic sees Stagger Lee as a folk hero who defies the racist system that keeps him from having access to any possibilities other than those outlawed by that selfsame system.[39]

Guthrie recorded the song "Stagolee" several times in his career. However, in none of these versions does Stagolee come across as a folk hero. Just as in most other performers' versions, Guthrie's Stagolee kills Billy Lyons in a dispute over a hat even after the victim pleads for his life and invokes the image of his children and "a darling loving wife." This wanton killing elicits a strong reaction from the narrator and the assembled crowd as Stagolee goes to the gallows: "We was glad to see him die." Just as in some of Guthrie's Anglo-American outlaw songs, Stagolee does not receive celebration or any level of appreciation. Certainly, Guthrie's lyrical ability offered him ample opportunity to praise this outlaw if he so desired, just as he did with Jesse James. Instead, he decided to follow a certain direction set by the song's dominant tradition and present this outlaw as "a bad man, that mean old Stagolee."[40]

Just as folk song collectors Todd and Sonkin note in general about Okies, Guthrie took his enjoyment of outlaw songs with him when he escaped from the dust and drought of the Great Plains during the Depression of the 1930s. Seeking new opportunities, he moved to the West Coast in 1936 and then to the East Coast in 1940. Although he continued during this time period to sing folk songs or his own creations based on the exploits of legendary outlaws from America's distant past, he also began writing songs that expressed support for contemporary figures who stepped outside the law. During the late 1920s and early '30s in Oklahoma and the surrounding states, famous outlaws again operated. Instead of Jesse James or Belle Starr, the area now had such criminal luminaries as "Machine Gun" Kelly, the Barker gang, Bonnie and Clyde, and others. Two of these contemporary outlaws became the subjects of original Guthrie songs.

Along with his brother George, Ray Terrill, and Herman Barker (of the infamous Barker gang), Matthew Kimes robbed banks across the western plains during the late 1920s. Both the Kimes boys were born on a small farm just outside of Van Buren, Arkansas. Although they committed petty offenses throughout the early 1920s, they quickly moved on to bigger crimes immediately upon Matthew's escape from the jail in Bristow, Oklahoma, in late June 1926. In fact, the day after this jailbreak, Matthew and his brother robbed their first bank in Depew, only fifteen miles away. They soon joined up with Ray Terrill, an experienced bank robber who had already gained infamy with the Barker gang. Together, the Kimes-Terrill gang went on a two-year spree of robberies in the Oklahoma, Missouri, and Kansas border area. During this time, they suffered setbacks, including George's capture and imprisonment. Matthew was also taken into custody and held at the Sallisaw jail but escaped with the help of gang members on November 21, 1926. However, his criminal career finally came to an end on June 24, 1927, when authorities captured him near the Grand Canyon. Sent back to Oklahoma to face multiple charges, he was committed to the state penitentiary in McAlister, where he joined his brother George and other former members of his gang.[41]

In March of 1940, Guthrie commemorated the exploits of this outlaw in the song "Matthew Kimes." In an introduction to this song, Guthrie describes Kimes as "undoubtably Oklahoma's fanciest jailbreaker" who "broke every jail they laid him in." Not only does Guthrie express support of Kimes's actions but also others' escapes from legal captivity: "When any living creature walks out of a jailhouse, I like it. It's wrong to be in and it's right to be out." But Guthrie does not shy away from laying out some of the crimes that Kimes committed. In the second verse, the narrator notes that Kimes "robbed some banks / And he killed some men." Nevertheless, the song mainly celebrates his ability to escape from jails and make fools out of lawmen. The chorus emphasizes officers' troubles with Kimes: "It's a hard and hard old time / That the police had with-a Matthew Kimes." Although captured several times in the course of the song, each time Kimes quickly escapes. In verse four, he even "bet the jailer ... / That he would beat him to the edge of town." Good to his word, Kimes "in fifteen minutes ... was free." Using "string and nails and knives and soap," he gains his freedom again and again in the song. But due to his continuing criminal exploits, the "deputies he played his pranks" on eventually track him "down on the government road / And they shot him down like a dirty dog."[42]

It is in the introduction of the song that Guthrie most forcefully presents Kimes as a kind of folk hero. The songwriter notes that the outlaw not only "used all kinds of tricks, too, to get the locks open" but that he also "sometimes turned everybody else out of jail." Perhaps due to this largesse, to his winning personality, or even to people's general hatred of bankers and prisons, "Matthew had so many friends on the outside that he walked out of jail about as fast as they could turn the key."[43] Here and in the song itself, Kimes comes across as a likable rebel who laughs at the law and those who enforce it. Certainly, Guthrie does not present him as an enemy of the people; he is accepted and helped by the community even though he was an acknowledged bank robber and killer. But this song exhibits its celebration of Kimes without any direct denunciation of bankers or any explicit class consciousness—unlike Guthrie's other original song from this time period about a contemporary Oklahoma outlaw, Pretty Boy Floyd.

As noted in earlier chapters, Guthrie truly began to manifest a new political ideology in the late 1930s. A number of factors helped shape his views, especially his own experiences traveling across America on the cheap—by riding the rails, thumbing rides, or beating his heels from Oklahoma to California. During these journeys, law officers often accosted him since being poor and unemployed had become a criminal offense in many communities during the Great Depression. After he arrived in Los Angeles, he began to connect his own experiences with that of whole groups of people through the education he received from various writers, actors, and artists who had leftist political views. People such as Will Geer, Ed Robbin, and Mike Quin befriended Guthrie and helped broaden his understanding of class unity and economic injustice. Some of the political issues of the day that came to his attention during this time would also demonstrate how innocent people could be regarded as criminals for various unjust reasons. He learned about the Scottsboro Boys and about Tom Mooney, a San Francisco labor leader wrongly jailed for a bombing in that city in the summer of 1916. In fact, when the newly elected liberal governor of California, Culbert Olsen, pardoned Mooney on January 7, 1939, Guthrie wrote a song commemorating his release, "Mr. Tom Mooney Is Free."[44] Around this same time period, some of Guthrie's original outlaw songs also began to contain moments that allowed him to express his changing political views.

In 1939, Guthrie combined his burgeoning class consciousness with his love of outlaw songs in his original song "Pretty Boy Floyd," which represents the title figure as a man driven to lawlessness and who not only robs for himself but also for others' benefit. But if we look back to what Depression-era law officers and the news media said about the Oklahoma-born bank robber Charles "Pretty Boy" Floyd, he does not appear as a hero but as a vicious, murderous thug. FBI Director J. Edgar Hoover called him "a skulking, dirty, ill-clothed hobo" and "just a yellow rat who needed extermination."[45] The FBI even named him Public Enemy No. 1 in September 1934. In an article documenting Floyd's death at the hands of federal agents including famed G-man Melvin Purvis, the *New York Times* referred to him as "the most dangerous man alive."[46] In fact, the negative media representations of Floyd were so pronounced that crime writer Jay Nash notes, "Pretty Boy got the worst press of any outlaw in the 1930s."[47] In contrast, Guthrie, who grew up in the same section of Oklahoma as Pretty Boy, celebrates the outlaw in his song. He turns Floyd into a fighter against the abusive powers that be—unjust law officers and thieving bankers. Floyd also appears as a benefactor to the poor, becoming a Robin Hood. At the song's end, Guthrie even includes a touch of political commentary concerning the difference between outlaws and businessmen, with the latter getting the worst of it.

Of the song, oral historian Studs Terkel writes, "How much of Pretty Boy's goodness was true and how much myth doesn't matter too much. His life was the stuff of which folklore is made."[48] True, Pretty Boy has passed into the realm of folklore, or perhaps popular culture icon is a more appropriate description since his image is one not restricted solely to folklore. He has been represented in numerous films, novels, biographies, and other media. Guthrie's song in particular has become a part of the legend-building apparatus surrounding Pretty Boy. Over the past thirty-five years, many well-known performers—including the Byrds, Country Joe McDonald, Ramblin' Jack Elliott, Joan Baez, Kinky Friedman, Pete Seeger, Arlo Guthrie, and Bob Dylan—have covered Guthrie's "Pretty Boy Floyd." The song has also found its way into most writings on Floyd. For example, many recent works discussing the American outlaw in general have referenced the song; and every major critical writing on Floyd since 1970 includes either the full text or a reference to this song.[49] It also appears in the 1994 novel *Pretty Boy Floyd* by well-known western author Larry McMurtry and Diana Ossana. Michael Wallis quotes from it in his excellent 1992 biography *Pretty Boy: The Life and Times of Charles Arthur Floyd*, as does Jeffery S. King in his *The Life and Death of Pretty Boy Floyd*, published in 1998. In effect, the song has come to represent the outlaw's true history—even though it strays from fact in a number of essential points.

In the first verse, Guthrie moves away somewhat from the traditional folk song's come-all-ye opening and presents his song as a tale told to children, actually making the exploits of Pretty Boy Floyd a part of the nation's history that should be handed down to another generation:

> If you gather round me children,
> A story I will tell
> Of Pretty Boy Floyd, an outlaw
> Oklahoma knew him well.[50]

As noted earlier, Guthrie desired to sing songs focusing on particular people and incidents foremost in the minds of average Americans. So seeing the song "Pretty Boy Floyd" as history—or some version of it—actually corresponds to what Guthrie desired to achieve with his songwriting as a whole.

After this opening gambit to establish his song as part of the history that should be passed on, Guthrie gives us his version of the origin of Pretty Boy's lawless days. But here the law is unjust; for the listener is offered a tale of a man defending his wife's honor:

> It was in the town of Shawnee,
> It was a Saturday afternoon,
> His wife beside him in the wagon
> As into town they rode.
>
> There a deputy sheriff approached him
> In a manner rather rude,
> Using vulgar words of language
> And his wife, she overheard.[51]

Perhaps not quite satisfied that the seriousness of this matter was explained in enough detail here, Guthrie elaborates on this encounter and its significance in a spoken introduction to a 1940 recording of this song.

As Guthrie describes this incident in this introduction, Floyd and his wife rode into Shawnee, Oklahoma, where he tied his horses to a hitching rack. However, the town "had made a new ruling since Pretty Boy had been in town the week before about tying your horses" to the hitching rack since "automobiles were getting pretty thick down there." This unknown criminal act brings down the ire of an officer of the law on the hapless Pretty Boy. Guthrie explains, "They was a deputy sheriff come out and proceeded to bawl Pretty Boy out for tying his team up there. And his language wasn't quite suited to the occasion." Guthrie goes on then to elaborate on the deputy's offense: "One thing that Oklahoma and Texas and all that country is pretty strict about is the language you use in the presence of the women."[52] As a result of the deputy's language, "Pretty Boy's temper just got away from him," and a fight ensues between the two:

> Pretty Boy grabbed a log chain,
> And the deputy grabbed a gun,
> And in the fight that followed
> He laid that deputy down.

After defeating (perhaps killing) the foul-talking deputy, Pretty Boy "took to the trees and timber, / To live a life of shame."[53] Thus, Guthrie offers us in his song and its accompanying tale a vision of a man treated unjustly and a husband defending the honor of his wife. As a result of his understandable anger, Floyd is forced to flee his home and its comforts for the sanctuary of the Oklahoma wilderness.

Yet the beginnings of Pretty Boy's life of crime differ greatly from the depiction that Guthrie gives us here. As a youth, Charley Floyd bootlegged and brawled in and around his hometown of Sallisaw, Oklahoma. Along with some friends, he burglarized a local store that also served as the town's post office. The group netted themselves $350—all in change. But because this robbery occurred in a post office, federal authorities came to town to look for the culprits. When they realized the magnitude of their crime, the youthful robbers threw their ill-gotten gain into a well. With the evidence disposed of and through the alibi Floyd's father presented to the authorities, no charges were brought against Charley or his accomplices. He was not so lucky with his next major crime—the one that truly started him off into becoming Pretty Boy Floyd, America's Public Enemy No. 1.

On September 11, 1925, Floyd and two other men robbed the payroll of the Kroger Grocery and Baking Company in St. Louis, Missouri. A few days later, Floyd and one of his accomplices drove a new Studebaker into Sallisaw while wearing stylish new clothes. Their transportation and appearance immediately raised the suspicions of the local constabulary since the two young men had left town only three weeks earlier by hopping a free ride on a freight train. A search of the two yielded a couple of money rolls still banded with paper wrappers labeled "Tower Grove Bank of St. Louis." Armed with this evidence, the police arrested Floyd and his partner in crime—quite a different story than the one Guthrie tells.

Other sections of Guthrie's song do adhere more closely with the actual history of Pretty Boy's life. At the end of verse four, we find the line "Every crime in Oklahoma / Was added to his name."[54] In fact, Floyd did find himself accused of many crimes he did not commit. Charley's son Dempsey speaks of this situation: "Sometimes it was actually humorous, because at the same time Dad was supposed to be in a bank hundreds of miles away, he was right there at home with us. We all knew that he had absolutely nothing to do with many of those bank jobs."[55] Other of Floyd's relatives and friends also tell similar stories about Charley being blamed for crimes they knew he did not commit. As a well-known outlaw, Floyd joined others in being blamed for what they did not do. Even the notorious Bonnie Parker (of Bonnie and Clyde fame) complains of this phenomenon in a poem she sent to the Dallas police, which was later published in the Dallas *Morning News* on May 23, 1934. She writes,

> If a policeman is killed down in Dallas,
> And they have no clues for a guide,
> If they can't find a friend they just wipe the slate clean
> And hang it on Bonnie and Clyde.[56]

What Bonnie does for herself and Clyde, Guthrie does for Floyd—representing him as being unfairly condemned by unjust authorities for crimes that he did not commit.

In the next four verses, Guthrie begins a long list of stories detailing Floyd's largesse to those who could not help themselves. Thus, in a third of the song, Floyd comes across as a Robin Hood-type character. Two of these verses focus on the help that Pretty Boy offered the hard-hit farmers of Great Depression-era Oklahoma:

> There's many a starvin' farmer,
> The same old story told,
> How this outlaw paid their mortgage,
> And saved their little home.

> Others tell you of a stranger,
> That came to beg a meal,
> And underneath his napkin
> Left a thousand-dollar bill.[57]

Apparently, these types of stories do have some basis in fact. According to Elmer Steele, who briefly drove for Pretty Boy, "It was no joke. [Floyd] would destroy mortgages and, more than once, I saw him give money to people who needed a boost."[58] Guthrie's song not only offers us tales of Floyd's generosity to rural folk but also details an incident where the outlaw gives to poor city dwellers. Guthrie writes,

> It was in Oklahoma City,
> It was on a Christmas Day,

> There come a whole car load of groceries,
> With a letter that did say.
>
> "Well, you say that I'm an outlaw,
> You say that I'm a thief;
> Here's a Christmas dinner
> For the families on relief."[59]

Although there is no evidence that Floyd actually did this service to the poor of Oklahoma City, several other stories of his generosity to his family, friends, and farmers do exist. For example, Ruth Morgan, a cousin of Floyd's wife, remembers the outlaw's charity to a needy family.

As she tells the tale, some time in the early 1930s her mother told Floyd about a family who had hit on hard times and gave him a list of groceries to buy for them. Ruth went along, and they "drove to a little country store in Boynton [Oklahoma] and he filled up a bushel basket with all kinds of food and put it in the car. Then I showed Charley where the people lived. My mother had also told him that these folks were so poor that their kids had no shoes and had to lay out of school." After Charley put the groceries on the porch, "He got back in the car and sat there for a minute. Then he took out some money, rolled it up, and put it in my hand. He said, 'Go give this to the man and tell him to buy his kids some shoes.' I went up and knocked and the man came out and I did just what Charley said to do and the man thanked me. Years later I heard that one of the boys in that family not only finished school but went on to become the superintendent of all the schools in the state of Kansas."[60] Nevertheless, if Guthrie is working to establish Floyd as a Robin Hood type, he misses half of the "rob from the rich and give to the poor" story. For not once in the song does he mention where or how Floyd got all the money that he gave to the poor.

Alan Lomax also noted this omission during a recording session for the Library of Congress in 1940; he asks, "How did [Floyd] get those thousand dollar bills, Woody?" The singer then explained that after Pretty Boy escaped to the "trees and timbers" of Oklahoma, the bankers started using him as a convenient scapegoat to cover up their own embezzlements. After a while, the outlaw's "temper got the best of him, and it is said that he said, 'They're making me an outlaw. They're getting the money, and I'm getting the advertisement.' He said, 'I'll think I'll reverse the deal and take the cash and let the credit go.'"[61] Thus in this story, the perfidy of the bankers drives Floyd to robbery.

However, the lack of direct reference to these robberies in the song itself seems significant. Since Floyd was a bank robber—a very successful and well-known one—perhaps Guthrie thought it unnecessary to include any references to his crimes in the song. Or perhaps he intended this shape-shifting as a response to Floyd's negative press. Nevertheless, if his song is intended as a complete history, then this exclusion is telling. Here Floyd becomes sanitized; he even becomes saintly. Without any mention of his crimes, which definitely included armed robbery, kidnapping, and murder, Pretty Boy's image becomes as warped as the one offered by J. Edgar Hoover. Yet the motivation for this exclusion may not simply be an attempt to alter Floyd's reputation in particular but to focus attention on the actions of those the outlaw robbed, the bankers. For the song does contain ample evidence of Guthrie's own prejudice against this group.

In the song, this prejudice appears in its most obvious form in the final two verses. Here, Guthrie moves away from the specific story of Floyd and his exploits and compares the actions of all outlaws to those of the monied men:

> Now as through this world I ramble,
> I see lots of funny men,
> Some will rob you with a six-gun,
> And some with a fountain pen.

> But as through this life you travel,
> And as through your life you roam,
> You won't never see an outlaw
> Drive a family from their home.[62]

Thus, Guthrie seems to prefer the illegal activities of social bandits to the legal robbing of bankers. One critic dismisses the last verse in particular "because it is out of place and relies on a prejudice in the reader but not developed in the song."[63] But this bias did exist in the audience for whom Guthrie wrote this song.

Others also saw the financial wranglings by bankers and financiers as robbery and were prejudiced against this group. Many Oklahomans and

CLASS CONSCIOUSNESS IN GUTHRIE'S OUTLAW SONGS

other people, especially the poor, shared these attitudes—and for understandable reasons. Many of those condemning the outlaw were themselves suspect by much of the populace during the Great Depression. While bankers in and around Oklahoma were demanding Floyd's capture or even his death in the early 1930s, their institutions were failing in record numbers and leaving families penniless. Even if they survived, the banks often foreclosed on the holdings of the poor and truly did drive them from their homes. Examples of this kind of prejudice appeared in another Oklahoma writer's work. In Edward Anderson's Great Depression-era novel *Hungry Men*, protagonist Acel Stecker says, "I've thought that the difference between a bank president and a bank bandit is that the robbery of the banker is legal. The bandit has more guts. I think that's the reason bandits are made heroes by the public, because people sort of sense that there isn't much difference."[64] As has already been noted above, some of this impulse to laud the outlaw and boo the bankers or monied men comes from a tradition—especially in music—that Guthrie was exposed to at an early age.

It seems that he took this impulse to heart, for in the introduction he wrote for the leftist songbook *Hard Hitting Songs for Hard-Hit People*, Guthrie expresses contempt for the selfishness of the wealthy and admits his own desire to rob them. He describes seeing rich travelers wearing expensive jewelry, driving "a good high rolling car," and carrying easy money—while he remains poor and with "my head hanging down, broke, clothes no good, old slouchy shoes." At moments, he admits thinking that robbing was "a mighty tempting thing, mighty tempting."[65] His frustration comes across with even more force in an introductory piece to the song "When You're Down and Out": "I thought about a couple of big pearl handled 44s . . . and about the money in the banks, and about the hungry people," although he admits "I never did get around to robbing or shooting."[66] As Guthrie sees it, Floyd and many other outlaws fought against the same unfair system that the singer bristled against. Guthrie says, "[Pretty Boy] did have something in his system that fought back."[67] This rebellious spirit that he saw in the story of Pretty Boy Floyd and some other outlaws made them into heroes, while the bankers and other wealthy people become the villains.

Around the same time that he began to write songs about outlaws fighting against what he saw as an unfair economic and political system, Guthrie also began to pen songs that pointed a finger at those he saw as the real villains, those who robbed and stole with impunity, those who did so within the law but outside of any justice. A brief early example of this impulse appears in his song "If I Was Everything on Earth," written in May 1935. Here we find Guthrie's narrator inverting the norm by suggesting that, if he had the power, "I'd turn out all the prisoners, / And put in all the rich," although he admits, "it don't look like my cowboy life / Will ever come to sech." However, this narrator continues to dream of flouting the law by "shoot[ing] the first big oil man / That killed the fishing creek."[68] In this song, the narrator envisions achieving justice by committing a crime and also depicts those who stand within the law as not acting fairly—thus implicitly justifying the imagined crime committed against them. Often in the world Guthrie later constructed in his outlaw songs, the rich become the real villains rather than Billy the Kid or Pretty Boy Floyd.

In several of his songs, Guthrie is particularly hard on bankers and on the law enforcement officers who protected them and their unjust actions. As noted in chapter two, a banker kicks a widower out of his sharecropper shack in his song "I Ain't Got No Home in This World Anymore." But the most detailed denunciation of this profession appears in the lesser-known song "Jolly Banker," written in the fall of 1939. Here, the narrator is a banker, and all we know of him he tells us himself. His name is Tom Cranker, and he asserts, "I safe guard the farmers and widows and orphans." His hypocrisy looms large in the next verse when we find him "bring[ing] down the mortgage" on those he supposedly protects. True, he will give money for food but then will "plaster your home with a furniture loan." In return for his loans, he demands, "Bring me back two for the one I lend you." If you do not pay, "I'll come and foreclose / Get your car and your clothes." All through dust storms, cotton crop destruction, or any other kind of hard times, he remains "the jolly banker." To enforce his will against those who would resist, he will even "send down the police to keep you from mischief."[69]

Just as in this line, the idea that the police act as the enforcers of the rich and corrupt appears repeatedly in Guthrie's writing during this time period. In one of his "Woody Sez" columns from the summer of 1939, he writes, "A policeman will jest stand there an let a banker rob a farmer, or finance man rob a working man. But if a farmer robs the banker—you wood have a hole dern army of cops out a shooting at him."[70] We can also see denunciations of the police appearing in many of his songs. The narrator of "Vigilante Man" asks, "Why does that deputy sheriff carry that gun in his hand? / Was that a vigilante man?"[71] In many of Guthrie's original songs from the late 1930s and early '40s, the men who were supposed to uphold the law and to ensure justice instead appear either as subjects of ridicule

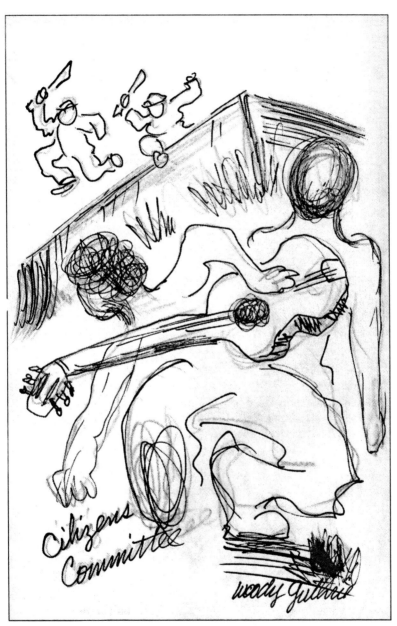

An illustration of the vigilante actions of various "Citizens Committees," c. 1946. Sketch by Woody Guthrie. Courtesy of the Ralph Rinzler Archives.

or as heavies for the monied men. Thus, lawmen lose their credibility and degenerate into criminals themselves.

When John Steinbeck's novel *The Grapes of Wrath* stormed into public view in 1939, Guthrie immediately recognized that it mirrored many of his own thoughts on bankers and lawmen. After reading the book, he writes that it tells the true story of how "the small farmers, an dustbowlers, an drowth bowlers, got run off their land by big land banks."[72] When the film came out the next year, Guthrie went down to the Rivoli Theater in March and watched it a couple of times. Again in his column "Woody Sez," he exclaims that the film is the "best cussed pitcher I ever seen" and again points out the story's villains. He writes, it "[s]hows the dam bankers men that broke us."[73]

That same year, at the urging of Victor Records, Guthrie wrote the song "Tom Joad" based on Steinbeck's novel. Although no denunciation of bankers appears in the song, we certainly find a negative representation of lawmen. First, "a deputy sheriff fired loose at a man" and accidentally "shot a woman in the back." Later, after the character Preacher Casey begins speaking out about underclass unity, "deputies" and "the Vigilante thugs" beat him to death with clubs.[74] The song even has a hero who can also be seen as an outlaw.

Here, the figure of Tom Joad rises above the classification of criminal—even though some of the actions he has taken in the past and some he takes in the song place him firmly outside the law. In both the first and second verse, the narrator reveals Tom's past. He gets "out of the old McAlester Pen," where he has spent "four long years on a man killing charge." During a ride with "a truck driving man," Tom admits that he was paroled from "a charge called homicide."[75] Unlike the novel or the film, the song does not divulge that the murder charge resulted from a fight where Tom's opponent "got a knife" in him. In response, Joad "knocked his head plumb to squash."[76] Whatever the reason for this omission, Joad comes across as a just man in the song, even when he kills again. In retaliation for the brutal murder of Preacher Casey, "Tom Joad he grabbed that deputy's club / Hit him over the head," then runs off, leaving us with the image of "a deputy and a preacher lying dead." Once again, Joad becomes a criminal. But this time we know why he killed—and we sympathize with his actions even though the victim in this case is a deputy, a supposed defender of the law. Afterward, Tom quickly takes the place of Casey. Unlike the preacher, Joad believes in fighting against the powers that be with more than words. He will use violence

CLASS CONSCIOUSNESS IN GUTHRIE'S OUTLAW SONGS

against those who would attack the underclass for demanding justice and equality. He tells his mother at the song's end, "Wherever people ain't free, / Wherever men are fighting for their rights, / That's where I'm gonna be."[77] As a result, he comes to be the omnipresent defender of the poor, the down-trodden—even if he has to break the law to do so.

When deciding to write this song, Guthrie chose to set it to the tune of the folksong "John Hardy." Two reasons made this song a likely choice. First, while staying with Alan Lomax just a month or so before the Victor sessions when he first recorded "Tom Joad," Guthrie had listened over and over again to some of the music collector's Carter Family records, espe-cially their version of "John Hardy."[78] As a result, the tune was still very fresh in his mind when he chose to use it for his own song. Second, "John Hardy" also tells the tale of an outlaw, for the title character was a black rail-road worker hung for killing a man in a gambling dispute in West Virginia in 1894.

In fact, Guthrie recorded a version of "John Hardy" himself years later. However, he tinkered with the song, renaming it "Johnny Harty," and included some of his own political beliefs in the tale.[79] Perhaps the most interesting verse of the version he recorded in 1944 is the last one, where Johnny Harty says,

> You got guards to the east and guards to the west
> You got guards this whole world around
> But before I'd be a slave, I'd rot in my grave.
> You can take me to my hanging ground, Mister Jailer,
> Take me to my hanging ground.[80]

Here, Harty makes the entire world a prison and everyone in it a prisoner. Knowing that escape does not exist and unwilling to serve, he would rather die. Actually, this line harkens back in time to another song and connects Harty's fight with that of all African Americans; for the antislavery spiritual "Oh, Freedom" contains the lines "Before I'd be a slave, I'd be buried in my grave, / And go home to my Lord and be free." Thus, Guthrie links his song about an individual outlaw resisting authority to a whole people's resistance to a legal system of repression.

As discussed in the last chapter, Guthrie became well aware of the difficulties of African Americans by the early 1940s and even began to doc-ument their struggles in song. In pieces such as "Poll Tax Chain," "The

Blinding of Isaac Woodward," and "Slipknot," he seems quite knowledgeable about African Americans' lack of access to justice under the American system of law. This knowledge came not only from current events but also from America's past. Looking back into history in such songs as "On Bloody Rags," "Slavery Grave," "A Tale a Feller Told Me," and others, he presented the hardships and evils of a system that stole people from their homeland, spirited them away in discomfort and disease in the holds of ships, and sold them into bondage in a foreign land. But Guthrie also celebrated the idea of freedom in song, even when it manifested itself as a crime. In particular, one of his songs, "Harriet Tubman," looks back in time to a woman who stole herself and others out of slavery—eventually becoming a criminal of such stature that she had a reward of forty thousand dollars on her head.[81]

Sometime around 1944, Guthrie came across the pamphlet *Harriet Tubman: Negro Soldier and Abolitionist* by Earl Conrad.[82] The story must have struck him hard, not surprising since as Harriet Tubman's first biographer Sarah Bradford states, "The story of Harriet Tubman needs not the drapery of fiction; the bare unadorned facts are enough to stir the hearts of the friends of humanity, the friends of liberty, the lovers of their country."[83] Afterward, he composed "Harriet Tubman" on September 18, 1944, using the tune to the folk song "Kansas Boys."[84] The song stands as a brief biography of Tubman's life and achievements. Actually, it becomes a fictive autobiography since Harriet Tubman herself appears as the narrator.

The song opens with her simply explaining her purpose: "I'll tell you of the beatings and of the fighting / In my 93 years I spent." Then, she reveals, "I was five years old in Bucktown, Maryland, / When into slavery I was sent."[85] This comment not only points out her birthplace but also her early entry into the harsh reality of her place as another human being's property. Tubman came into the world as one of eleven children of the slaves Benjamin Ross and Harriet Green. Even though her parents' union had no official sanction, the newborn girl was given the name Harriet Ross, linking her through words to both her mother and father. Although Guthrie does not specifically detail Tubman's introduction to slavery, her master Edward Brodas first hired her out to a woman who used harsh measures to control her new servant. For any breach of conduct required by her new mistress, Tubman received brutal whippings that left her scarred for life. Later, Tubman was made a field worker, which left her subject to whippings by an overseer. However, these early hardships and abuses did not daunt her courage, as she explains in verse two.

CLASS CONSCIOUSNESS IN GUTHRIE'S OUTLAW SONGS

A portrait of Harriet Tubman, c. 1870. Photograph by H. B. Lindsley. Courtesy of the Prints and Photographs Division of the Library of Congress.

Only around fifteen years old at the time, she made a choice and "helped a field hand make a run for freedom," although she suffered for her actions. One afternoon, a slave went to a local store without his owner's permission. As she explains in the song, "The guard he caught him in a little store / In a little slavery village town." When the "boss made a grab to catch the field hand, / I jumped in and blocked the door." In the song, as punishment for disobedience, "The boss then hit me with a two pound iron scale / And I went black down on the floor." As a result of this awful wound, Tubman lay "On a bundle of rags in our log cabin" while "My mother ministered to my needs." But her grave condition only reinforces her decision to resist slavery: "It was here I swore I'd give my life blood / Just to fight to turn my people free."[86] Since Guthrie's story follows that told by Conrad, it generally runs very close to the truth. Tubman did witness a slave running from his overseer and then blocked the door through which the fugitive had run. In an attempt to stop the slave, the overseer picked up an iron weight and hurled it at him. Instead, he hit Tubman and knocked her unconscious. As a result of this wound, she lingered near death for many weeks and was not expected to live. Although it took many months, she recovered but had a deep scar in her forehead and suffered from fainting spells for the rest of her life.[87]

Considering her spirit and the conditions under which she lived, one might wonder why she did not make her run to freedom sooner than she did. One reason for her reluctance to leave may have been her first husband, for "In '44 I married John Tubman," she says.[88] He was a freeman in a slave state, not an uncommon situation at the time, but Harriet remained someone else's property. Thus, she could still be sold, as two of her sisters had been to a Georgia planter. The same threat haunted Tubman's thoughts to the point one of her biographers states that "she never closed her eyes that she did not imagine she saw the horsemen coming, and heard the screams of women and children, as they were being dragged away to a far worse slavery than they were enduring there."[89] In 1849, the persistent rumor of her impending sale finally convinced her to flee her home, family, and husband. As she relates in verse five, "I loved [John] well till '49 / But he would not come and fight beside me, / So I left him there behind."[90]

Two of her brothers accompanied Tubman because it was also said that they too were to be sold south. However, in verse six, she tells us that "they got scared and went back home." But Harriet would not yield: "I followed my Northern star of freedom / And walked in the grass and trees alone." She continues to relate some incidents from her escape in verse seven, saying, "I slept in a barn loft and in a haystack, / I stayed with my people in slavery's shacks." Although these slaves warn of her end, she continues: "They said I'd die by the boss man's bullets / But I told them, I can't turn back."[91] In these last two lines, Guthrie seems to be echoing one of Tubman's most famous pronouncements concerning her decision to escape to the North: "I had reasoned dis out in my mind; there was one of two things I had a right to, liberty, or death; if I could not have one, I would have de oder; for no man should take me alive; I should fight for my liberty as long as my strength lasted, and when de time came for me to go, de Lord would let dem take me."[92]

The reward of her travels and dangers comes when Tubman finally reaches sanctuary and marvels at her freedom. In verse eight, as "the sun was shining in the early morning," she "finally come to my free state line." Almost unbelieving of her release from bondage, she says, "I pinched myself to see if I was dreaming / I just could not believe my eyes."[93] Here, Guthrie definitely paraphrases Tubman's own stated reaction to having reached the safety of the free state of Pennsylvania: "I looked at my hands to see if I was de same pusson. There was sucha glory ober ebery ting; de sun came like gold through the trees, and ober the fields, and I felt like I was in Heaben."[94] In fact, Tubman's original comment far outstrips Guthrie's attempt at re-creation in its emotional intensity.

Having gained her own freedom, Tubman did not soon forget her family members left behind. As noted by her first biographer, she said, "To this solemn resolution I came; I was free and they should be free also."[95] Beginning in December 1850, she was able to first make good on this promise and helped one of her sisters to escape before she could be sold at auction. Later, she also assisted another sister, several of her brothers, and their families to also escape to the North. But the most important family members she freed were her own parents, and it is this particular familial rescue that Guthrie included in his song. In a matter-of-fact fashion, Tubman says in verse nine,

> I went back home and got my parents
> I loaded them into a buckboard hack;
> We crossed 6 states and other slaves followed,
> And up to Canada we made our tracks.[96]

She also returned to Dorchester County, Maryland, to bring her husband north, only to find he had remarried. Regardless of this betrayal, she used his name for the rest of her life.

Tubman's family members were not the only benefactors of her heroic efforts. Within a ten-year period, she made almost twenty trips south and brought away as many as three hundred slaves with her. Tubman and her passengers on the Underground Railroad faced many dangers, and sometimes those escaping lost their nerve. Repeating an often-told story, Guthrie focuses on an incident where one escapee decided to give up. After lying without food in a swamp for many hours, one slave refused to go on and even planned to return to his master rather than continue the harrowing journey.[97] In verse ten, Tubman tells us how she motivated him to continue his journey to freedom: "I pulled my pistol in front of his eyes. / I said, get up and walk to your freedom / Or by this fireball you will die."[98] Apparently, this type of encouragement was necessary on more than one occasion; however, Tubman was no less strict with herself. During every rescue, she carried a pistol and vowed to end her own life if capture was inevitable.

Tubman did not stand alone in the struggle to free her people from the yoke of slavery. Her abolitionist friends included Frederick Douglass, William Lloyd Garrison, Wendell Phillips, William Still, and Lydia Maria Child. Of these allies, she admired John Brown above all others. She met him in early 1858 near Niagara Falls, where she was living nearby. The two got along quite well, and Brown would refer to her as "General" Tubman due to her spirit and experience. Brown had come north during this time to gather support for an assault on the federal arsenal at Harper's Ferry in Virginia. When the raid finally came off in October 1859, she had intended to be part of the assault party. But due to illness, she could not make it to Virginia in time and was spared the fate of Brown, who was hung along with several of his conspirators in December. In referring to this episode in the song, Tubman tells us, "When John Brown hit them at Harper's Ferry, / My men were fighting right at his side." As to his fate, she says, "When John Brown swung upon his gallows, / It was then I hung my head and cried."[99] Tubman did in fact grieve for him and later said, "It was not John Brown that died at Charlestown—it was Christ—it was the savior of our people."[100]

As a war between northern and southern states loomed ever closer, it was Brown whom Tubman revered rather than Abraham Lincoln, who she thought needed more resolution concerning the freeing of the slaves. In verse twelve, she says, "To Abe Lincoln this I said. / You've just crippled the Snake of Slavery / We've got to fight to kill it dead!"[101] Actually, Tubman made a similar statement to the abolitionist writer Lydia Maria Child rather than to Lincoln. According to Child, Tubman said,

Massa Linkum he great man, and I'se poor nigger; but dis nigger can tell Massa Linkum how to save de money and de young men.

CLASS CONSCIOUSNESS IN GUTHRIE'S OUTLAW SONGS

He do it by setting de niggers free. S'pose dar was awfu' big snake down dar, on de floor. He bite you. Folks all skeered, cause you die. You send for doctor to cut de bite; but snake he rolled up dar, and while doctor dwine it, he bite you agin. De doctor cut out dat bite; but while he dwine it, de snake he spring up and bite you agin, and so he keep dwine, till you kill him. Dat's what Massa Linkum orter know.[102]

Tubman believed that freedom for the slaves would necessitate violence and that those slaves would fight for their freedom. In verse twelve, she says, "Give the black man guns and powder."[103] Just as she herself carried a pistol during her time on the Underground Railroad and a rifle while working with the Union army as a spy and a scout, Tubman also believed that freed slaves should be armed in order to fight for their nation.

During the Civil War, Tubman backed up her words with action and participated in several battles. For example, she helped lead a raid down the Combahee River in South Carolina on June 2, 1863, which resulted in the release of over seven hundred slaves and the destruction of thousands of dollars in Confederate property. But the battle that she remembers in the song concerns the federal assault on Fort Wagner outside of Charleston, South Carolina. Led by Colonel Robert Gould Shaw, the African-American regiment of the 54th Massachusetts launched a near suicidal assault on the fort and suffered high casualties because the black soldiers would not fall back when met with the firmly entrenched Confederate forces. In verse thirteen, Tubman says,

> When we faced the guns of lightning
> And the thunders broke our sleep,
> After we faced the bloody rainstorms
> It was dead men that we reaped.[104]

This verse closely follows Tubman's real-life and striking description of this battle that she shared with historian Albert Bushnell Hart. She told him, "Then we saw the lightning, and that was the guns; and then we heard the thunder, and that was the big guns; and then we heard the rain falling, and that was drops of blood falling; and when we came to git in the crops, it was dead men that we reaped."[105] In spite of this harsh reality, Tubman believed that the fight was a just one, no matter the losses suffered. This sentiment appears succinctly in verse fourteen, where she says,

Yes, we faced the zigzag lightning
But was worth the price we paid;
When our thunder rumbled over
We'd laid slavery in its grave.

The song then skips a number of years and closes in on her story even as her life comes to an end. She asks us to "Come and stand around my deathbed" so that we can hear her "sing some spirit songs." But she does not mourn her own passing; she looks forward to a new life: "I'm on my way to my greater Union."[106]

Nevertheless, Tubman's place in history has not always been posited in the radical outlaw tradition to which she rightly belongs. As Earl Conrad notes in the pamphlet Guthrie read, "The South was an armed camp" during the time that Tubman worked as a conductor on the Underground Railroad, for "The slave states were patrolled by uniformed police, by county and state authorities, and by plain-clothes vigilantes" who were all operating with the sanction of law.[107] After the enactment of the Fugitive Slave Law in 1850, even northern citizens in free states were compelled to assist in the capture of escaped slaves. In essence, Tubman's actions were crimes—but they were more than that. Although freeing herself could be seen simply as an act of self-preservation, returning to the South again and again, in the face of federal, state, and local law, was as revolutionary an action as John Brown's raid on Harper's Ferry.

At the time of Guthrie's writing, the public's vision of Tubman did not often match this revolutionary reality, although she did gain some public attention for her many exploits and achievements in the early 1940s. For example, in 1943, to great praise, CBS's hour-long wartime series *The Spirit of '43* included an episode focusing on the contributions of African-American women, especially Tubman.[108] Then in 1944, Eleanor Roosevelt christened a Liberty ship the USS *Harriet Tubman*, canonizing this African-American hero. Nevertheless, Tubman's place in history was still not posited in the radical tradition to which she rightly belongs. Even as late at the 1970s, one historian notes, "Harriet Tubman has been portrayed as a heroine of folk history rather than a major figure of radical tradition" and goes on to add that her "life spans an entire range of black experience and is a radical statement of that experience."[109] But if we look at Guthrie's song in the context of his past prejudices and his unmitigated praise of Tubman, then he stands at the vanguard of those who celebrated Tubman's criminal but heroic exploits.

The most striking of Guthrie's representations of a person as both an outlaw and a radical figure has to be Jesus Christ. Although not raised up in any particular church, Guthrie became interested in Christianity while a young man and admits to reading "the bible and the life of Jesus almost day and night" in the mid-1930s.[110] It seems he found the example of Christ an appealing one that continued to interest him throughout his life. When Will Geer asked him whom he most admired, Guthrie said, "Jesus Christ and Will Rogers."[111] We can also see this interest manifest itself in more than one of Guthrie's artistic efforts. In *Bound for Glory*, he discusses some oil paintings he made in the early 1930s that included "a couple of dozen heads of Christ, and the cops that killed him."[112] Here, we already see him establishing Christ as a victim of legal authority. At some point in the late 1930s, Guthrie first began using Jesus's example—his denunciation of greed and his selfless attitude—as a means of attacking the greed of the wealthy.

As Guthrie represents the situation, the views of Christ put him at odds with the authorities of the day, making him an outlaw. In some moments, Guthrie was quite explicit in expressing this view. For example, in introducing this song to Alan Lomax during a 1940 interview, Guthrie says, "[Christ] was called an outlaw." Later, Guthrie even combined his view of Christ's politics with his outsider status by referring to him as "a socialist outlaw."[113] Another indication of Guthrie's thoughts about Christ as an outlaw figure appear upon realizing that he set his lyrics to "Jesus Christ" to the tune of his outlaw ballad "Jesse James." This decision does not seem a random one. Both James (the legendary version) and Christ advocated shifting wealth from one group to another, and both suffer death as a result of this stand, each betrayed by one of his own followers. But these outlaws' methodologies greatly differ.

Like most of the outlaws in Guthrie's songs, Christ comes from the underclass. The song "Jesus Christ" emphasizes that he was not only a carpenter but also "a hard working man." Instead of using physical strength or weapons to separate the rich from their money as Jesse James did, Christ uses words to urge them to do so. He tells them, "Sell all of your jewelry and give it to the poor." Although "the working people followed him around, / Sang and shouted gay," the powers that be were not ready for such a message of charity and end up killing the carpenter for his ideas. Betrayed by "One dirty coward called Judas Iscariot," Christ was turned over to the authorities. Then the "Bankers and the preachers," "the landlord," and the "cops and the soldiers" in their employ "nailed him on the cross" and "laid Jesus Christ in his grave."[114]

All the actions mentioned above occur in the past, but the song ends by making a comment about the present, for Guthrie also believed that Christ's message would be equally disturbing to the wealthy in 1940, when he first wrote this song. In a written introduction to the song, he explains the genesis of the song's creation:

> I wrote this song looking out of a rooming house in New York
> City in the winter of 1940. I saw how the poor folks lived, and
> then I saw how the rich folks lived, and the poor folks down and
> out and cold and hungry, and the rich ones out drinking good
> whiskey and celebrating and wasting handfuls of money at gam-
> bling and women, and I got to thinking about what Jesus said,
> and what if He was to walk into New York City and preach
> like he used to. They'd lock Him back in jail as sure as you're
> reading this.[115]

In fact, he felt that Christ would meet the same fate if he did return, an idea that the song reflects. For in the last verse, after telling us that the song was written in New York City, the narrator speculates, "If Jesus was to preach what He preached at Galilee, / They would lay Jesus Christ in His grave."[116]

According to one critic, Guthrie's Christ is "more Steinbeckian than Marxian, reflecting not a revolutionary dialectic but a sentimental exalta-tion of the working class, which was his interpretation of the Depression era's Popular Front Americanized radicalism."[117] But how is the song not revolutionary? It includes a figure who urges the rich to give away their pos-sessions to the poor. Certainly, if this reversal did happen, the change would be drastic, even revolutionary, in its effects. Sounding like Guthrie's own personal editorial, a character in *Bound for Glory* tells some assembled men exactly what advice Christ would give them:

> If Jesus Christ was sitting right here, right now, he'd say this very
> same dam thing. You just ask Jesus how the hell come a couple

of thousand of us living out here in this jungle camp like a bunch
of wild animals. You just ask Jesus how many million of other
folks are living the same way? Sharecroppers down South, big city
people that work in factories and live like rats in the slimy slums.
You know what Jesus'll say back to you? He'll tell you we all just
mortally got to work together, build things together, fix up old
things together, clean out old filth together, put up new buildings, schools and churches, banks and factories together, and own
everything together. Sure, they'll call it a bad ism. Jesus don't care
if you call it socialism or communism, or just me and you.[118]

Like this character, Guthrie did not think of his Christ as adhering to one
particular political perspective or ideology. His Christ advocated an economic, a political, a moral unity that transcends any label such as Communist
or Socialist. His Christ offers a possibility of the brotherhood of man.

Guthrie certainly did not see his Christ as a sort of despot, imposing
his views on others. He felt that Christ truly represented the positive ideas
that people would gladly follow since it would lead to true equality and justice. In fact, Guthrie offered up Christ as a candidate for the highest office
in America in his song "Christ for President." Editorializing for a moment,
the narrator says,

> Every year we waste enough
> To feed the ones who starve;
> We build our civilization up
> And we shoot it down with wars

But this situation can be overcome "with the Carpenter on the seat." In fact,
with Christ "Away up in the capital town / The U.S.A. would be on the way /
Pros-perity bound!"[119]

In effect, Guthrie sees this outlaw as offering a better future than the
one posited by the official dictators of political and economic policy. Actually, most of Guthrie's outlaws stand as morally superior to those who do
control the nation's money and create its laws. It seems greatly unfair to
argue, as Todd and Sonkin did about all Okies, that he represents these
outlaws as heroic simply because this perspective was part of a long tradition in folk song. For Guthrie was too intelligent a creator to simply follow a
tradition that he did not believe in himself; he could never content himself

with repeating what he heard, never satisfy himself following others' thoughts that did not mesh with his own perspective. Throughout his life, he re-examined his views and adjusted them to fit new experiences, new knowledge. Otherwise, he would have continued to spout racist thoughts or would have never empathized with workers other than those he knew personally. He may have begun singing outlaw songs out of his exposure to a certain tradition, but eventually his own experiences gave weight to songs condemning bankers rather than the people who robbed them. He made the choice rather than simply inheriting this perspective. Many of his other original songs also exhibit his own distrust of the status quo and the people who benefited from it or enforced it.

For the most part, the outlaw figures in Guthrie's songs were indeed criminals who often committed cold-blooded murder in the course of their robberies. As noted in the beginning of this chapter, although Guthrie states that he wanted his songs, especially his outlaw pieces, to give "folks a hundred generations from us" a means to "learn how things were with our bunch here," he does not seem driven to diligently research any of these outlaws' true histories. Unlike many of his documentary songs about the Dust Bowl, Guthrie does not have firsthand knowledge of the outlaws he writes about here. Even when his lyrics match their true histories, it seems arbitrary, such as his representation of Harriet Tubman due to reading Earl Conrad's pamphlet. Instead, he seems to want to represent his own vision of history rather than to simply document it. His own ideas of right and wrong, good and bad control these songs much more than in any other of his work discussed so far. Thus, outlaws could become populist heroes—even radical ones. No matter whether singing a folk song or one of his originals, Guthrie often takes well-known characters and puts his own personal spin on them—making them reflections of his own ideology, his own beliefs.

Although he did not agree completely with all of the actions the outlaws take in the songs he wrote, Guthrie did see them as people who deserve to be a part of America's history. But in his view, outlaws also deserve a positive representation in this history as figures who rebelled against social injustice that did in fact occur. To accomplish this goal, Guthrie's songs weave together fact and fiction to create a cultural legend where the hero also happens to be a criminal. Events are often shaped or created to support a particular image of the outlaw as a man or woman unjustly abused who then justly helps others. But this shaping does not end with the outlaw.

In Guthrie's songs, the whole social order often becomes inverted: the outlaw becomes the hero, while the police and the bankers become the agents of injustice. Thus, Guthrie's fictive history lesson works to teach us a revisionist view of our own past, where a solitary figure struggles against a system that creates "starvin farmers" and "families on relief." But it also shows that one person can fight against this system to help the poor and downbeaten—even if the lone figure is only an outlaw.

CHAPTER SIX

That Union Feeling

TRACING A VISION OF A BETTER WORLD

Although he composed or performed "songs about robbers and about outlaws and people that try to take it away from the rich and give to the poor," Woody Guthrie balanced these Robin Hood–flavored tales with others "that tell you why you can't help the people that are poor just by grabbing a club or a knife or a gun and going out to be an outlaw."[1] Reflecting on the defeat and deaths of outlaws documented in his own songs, he predicts,

> Every time a man gets disgusted with trying to live decent in
> the rich man's system, and jumps out with a couple of forty fives
> on his hips to try to shoot his way through—the outlaw is beat.
> Beat to start with. The whole world is against him. Reason why is
> because he's not organized. He's just by his self. Wants to holler,
> cuss, fight, work to change the world around a little bit better . . .
> but he's by his self. Bound to lose. Police will shoot him down like
> a mad dog on the country road.

Explicitly, he tells us that only collective action, getting "organized," can overcome "the rich man's system." His suggestions become clearer later in the same piece when he urges dissatisfied workers to unite to correct injustice through group rather than individual effort: "Join the union and bring your complaints to the shop steward, or from the floor of the union meeting.

This keeps your job, and you dont have to turn out to be a bad man to get some changes made."[2] Believing that all individual action eventually fails to overturn entrenched and systematic inequity, he envisioned a great coming together of all Americans, a great awakening of generosity and a fulfillment of the promise that was our nation's basis—a country where all are created equal. In particular, Guthrie's union songs point forward to a world still uncreated but recognizable in our own national myth of democracy and justice.

Although Guthrie formed his vision of unionism from varied sources, there has been much speculation over the years concerning one particular influence on his political ideas in general—Communism. One historian of the cold war characterizes Guthrie as "unabashedly Stalinist," then adds that he "cultivated an ardent pro-Communism by the late 1930s and did not waver thereafter."[3] Yet a number of family, friends, and supporters argue that he was too undisciplined to follow any particular political ideology. Guthrie's second wife, Marjorie, claims, "Woody learned to believe in a world of sharing. He constantly talked of organizing and unions, but he would never have been able to fit into the Communist party and follow a political line."[4] Although certainly influenced by communism in general and the Communist Party in particular, he was not interested in following lock step with any particular ideology not of his own creation. An iconoclastic thinker, he constantly challenged his old assumptions and listened to new ideas. Leftist musician Billy Bragg believes Guthrie "was non-ideological. He wasn't a Marxist, he was a humanitarian. He felt more strongly about people than about ideology. He didn't hate rich people, he just hated to see people treated like shit, whoever they were."[5]

Through the years, this focus on Guthrie's interest in communism has left his other ideological influences—such as socialism, Christianity, and trade unionism—largely or completely ignored by those commenting on his personal philosophy. He did not need any one particular ideology or political party to help him understand that the world around him needed changing if all workers were to achieve the American Dream, a standard of living like the one called for by labor leader John L. Lewis in March 1937: "We demand for the unskilled workers a wage that will enable them to maintain themselves and their families in health and modern comfort, to purchase their own homes, to enable their children to obtain at least a high-school education and to provide against sickness, disability and death."[6] By the early 1940s, Guthrie had pulled elements and ideas from various political and social movements around him to compose his own unique vision of union-ism, one which would bring guaranteed land and labor to all Americans, regardless of their creed, color, or sex.

Even when well informed about Guthrie's eclectic influences, some commentators have criticized his lack of an elaborate political ideology. Biographer Joe Klein dismisses his "philosophy [as] comic-book dialectics," while music critic Dave Marsh writes, "God knows, you can learn absolutely nothing of political theory from Woody's writings."[7] Rather than being seen as simplistic, Guthrie's direct and unadorned ideas about justice or the lack of it should more appropriately be thought of as mirroring those of the majority of Americans of the time. As historian Robert McElvaine notes, "Most 'ordinary' people are *never* ideological in a way that would suit an ideologue. This does not mean, of course, that their thoughts and actions are not based upon a set of underlying assumptions and values but only that they are not conscious adherents of a systematic approach to the world"[8] (emphasis in original). In an admiring manner, Guthrie's friend Ed Robbin refers to the singer's ideology as originating out of a private faith in the heal-ing power of unity. He writes, "It didn't matter whether [Guthrie] was talk-ing about Harlan County, Jerusalem, Oklahoma, or Cairo. He didn't bother to read what Karl Marx had written, or Lenin. Woody believed that what is important is the struggle of the working people to win back the earth, which is rightfully theirs. He believed that people should love one another and organize into one big union. That's the way he saw politics and world affairs."[9] Although Guthrie was not nearly as untutored as Robbin suggests, all of the singer's political beliefs did begin as a personal desire for all to have equality under the law and to give the poor dignity through homeownership and job security. These demands, which he believed should be made collec-tively, represent the basic tenets of his own brand of unionism.

As we shall see, some of the underpinnings of his eclectic and direct vision of the union of the world came from a variety of sources ranging from the populist and socialist-tinged agrarianism of his home state to the labor unionism of the National Maritime Union during World War II. The good he took from these political philosophies and organizations then con-tributed to his particular idea of unionism. Beginning in the late 1930s and continuing until he could barely hold a pen due to Huntington's chorea, Guthrie charted his own evolving and expansionist personal politics and philosophy concerning the meaning and power of unionism. An exploration of these ideas in his writing, especially his lyrics, offers us insight into those "underlying assumptions and values" that make up this vision—one that may easily be termed by one of his own songs, "That Union Feeling."

Considering that Guthrie hails from Oklahoma, perhaps his unification spirit came as a cultural gift to him though the region's allegiance to various groups urging the coming together of members of the working class. In looking back through the history of the Sooner State from the late 1880s to the 1930s, we discover the influence of the Populist Party, the Socialist Party, and the Industrial Workers of the World. Although all these groups voiced their ideologies to their constituents through speeches, pamphlets, and newspapers, many of their adherents did not come to support them through an overt intellectual analysis. The majority were small farmers, field hands, or oil workers with little time to meditate on the subtleties of any political party. Instead, these people often stood united in their realizations that the often harsh reality of their situations belied the myth of America. They worked hard yet did not find the upward mobility promised to those who did earnest labor—so they decided to unite their voices against the forces they saw keeping them from their fair share of the American Dream, a dream much like the one described by John L. Lewis. It is this defiant, egalitarian spirit that Guthrie encountered during his early years growing up in the region. Through these many strains of working-class unity, he began to empathize early on with ordinary people facing hard times on the nation's farms and in its fields, citizens wondering whether the American political and economic systems were just.

From 1889 to 1906, the federal government opened up parts of Indian Territory to white settlers, and neighboring citizens in Kansas and Texas rushed in to take up land claims, including some from both sides of Guthrie's family. Both states were bastions of the People's Party (PP), also known as the Populists, so many of these settlers brought their sympathy for this political group with them. Throughout the 1890s and even into the early twentieth century in Oklahoma, the PP supported a number of initiatives focused on bringing about debtor relief for farmers, on whom the Populists drew heavily for constituents. This group suffered mightily under the burdens of crop liens and the farm tenancy system. Under the lien system, cash-poor landowning farmers borrowed against an account at a local merchant for goods needed to raise a crop and to live, a deal often necessitated due to a legal restriction keeping homesteaders from mortgaging their lands for the first five years of a claim. After the crops were in, farmers would then settle up with the merchant for money owed. Farm tenancy offered an even more exploitive situation where landowners demanded as much as a quarter or a third of the crops raised on their property. At the end of the harvest, this system often left both types of farmers further in debt due to a combination of low commodity prices, high interest rates, and sometimes unfair manipulations on the part of lien holders and landowners. But even during the PP's greatest political representation in the Oklahoma Territory's legislature in 1897, party leaders only had marginal success in getting any of their bills passed due to the resistance of their Democratic counterparts and the frequent veto of the territory's governor.[10]

With certainty, Guthrie shared some sentiments with the Populists as expressed through his appreciation and performance of the song "The Farmer Is the Man," a ditty associated with their movement although it may have been written as early as the 1860s.[11] In it, the lawyer, banker, mortgage man, middleman, preacher, butcher, and even the cook all get their piece from the farmer as soon as he comes to town, leaving him with so little that he "lives on credit til the fall" even though he is also "the one who feeds them all." Although it is uncertain where he first heard this song, Guthrie definitely found other Okies singing it during cotton strikes in late 1930s California. In fact, he described one version he encountered there "the best I ever heard this song sung.'"[12] Regardless of whether he had any idea of this folk song's political history, he found the lyrics to be true to the facts as he saw them in his own time.

After the de facto demise of the party in 1902, some of the Oklahoma Populist vote went to a relatively new political group, the Socialist Party (SP).[13] By the year of Guthrie's birth in 1912, the SP's influence resulted in their presidential candidate Eugene V. Debs polling sixteen percent of the state's vote against the singer's namesake, Woodrow Wilson, resulting in the largest Socialist turnout in the nation. During this same election, citizens in Guthrie's home county of Okfuskee gave thirty-one percent of their vote to Socialist candidates. Drawing primarily from a rural constituency, the SP focused on many of the same issues the Populists had advocated earlier—especially those designed to help tenant farmers, whose number had grown dramatically since 1900.[14] During World War I, the SP's power declined due to a combination of its opposition to this conflict and of increasing farm prices. In effect, Socialists appeared unpatriotic, while many of the farmers who had joined the party out of frustration over their debts found wheat and cotton in high demand during the later war years. Even after armistice and its accompanying drop in agricultural prices, the SP could not recover its former power base in Oklahoma. By the time Guthrie turned twelve in 1924, the party could not even get a candidate on the state ballot. Nevertheless, the ideas that propelled the SP in Oklahoma resonated with him by the late 1930s.

Another, more radical group active in Oklahoma during the early part of the twentieth century would also come to influence Guthrie's thinking. Members of the Industrial Workers of the World (IWW), known as "Wobblies," began organizing wage earners and striking for higher pay and better working conditions around the time of the SP's political ascendancy in Oklahoma. According to one historian, "Although the IWW recruited only a few thousand dues-paying members . . . in Oklahoma, the Wobblies would still have tremendous influence . . . [by] creating a sense of workers' solidarity and class consciousness."[15] We can see the IWW's core commitment to the working class and their opposition to the wealthy in the preamble to their 1905 constitution: "The working class and the employing class have nothing in common. There can be no peace so long as hunger and want are found among millions of working people and the few, who make up the employing class, have all the good things of life."[16] Yet the Wobblies limited their efficacy by eschewing the ballot box for the use of direct action, especially strikes and free-speech fights where songs by Joe Hill, Ralph Chaplin, and others played an important unifying role. Much like the situation with the SP, the effectiveness of the IWW dropped off after America entered the First World War, when the group's rebellious ways brought down the repression of both federal and state forces. Nevertheless, a small contingent of the IWW remained active in Oklahoma until the beginning of the Great Depression, leaving behind a legacy of almost thirty years of effort in the state.

Biographer Joe Klein speculates that Guthrie came into contact with members of the IWW during his early travels through Oklahoma, Texas, and other parts of the nation during the mid-1930s.[17] We know the singer became aware of the group's general philosophy by 1940 through the songs of the IWW, especially those of Joe Hill. Later in life, Guthrie even penned "Joe Hillstrom," a song tribute to the Wobbly bard.[18] Guthrie also had some awareness of the IWW that went beyond that expressed in their songs. In the introduction to the chapter "Some from the Old Wobblies" in the songbook *Hard Hitting Songs for Hard-Hit People*, he writes of the IWW, "They wanted to get control of all the farms and factories, mines, mills and railroads. They wanted to get good wages, short hours and better treatment all the way 'round." He also notes, "But they steered clear of politics," a criticism that later leads him to add, "you just can't outwit these people that's got the money unless you blast away in their faces with politics, votes, petitions, letters, unions, speeches and meeting halls running full blast. The rich folks got your money with politics. You can get it back with politics. Politics is how you vote. What Union you belong to."[19] Other influences on his personal philosophy during his youth in Oklahoma and Texas came from more traditional sources, such as the Democratic Party and Christianity, although Guthrie shaped them to his own satisfaction even as he absorbed them.

During the early years of Oklahoma, the politics of Guthrie's immediate family were far removed from those held by these radical groups, especially the SP. Guthrie's father, Charley, was an ardent Democrat who became a district court clerk under the party and who stiffly resisted Socialist influence in Oklahoma. In fact, he wrote the first of several editorials denouncing the principles of socialism for the Okemah *Ledger* in the fall of 1911. During the next year, he collected a number of these writings into the book *Kumrids: A Discussion of Scientific Socialism.* The foreword clearly states its goal: "The purpose of this little book is to give the reader an idea of the dangerous fangs of the tempting serpent which is lurking behind the advance claims of Socialism."[20] His condemnation of socialism does not surprise when we realize that his land holdings at this time, including farms, put him in the capitalist class firmly denounced by this ideology. Remembering his childhood, Guthrie writes, "Papa went to town and made real-estate deals with other people, and he brought their money home."[21] In time, Charley did try to give his political views to his son as a legacy, for Guthrie writes, "Papa taught me ... to curse the Republicans, to curse the Socialists, and to say good words for the Democrats."[22] But it seems that early on Guthrie did not follow his father's political leanings. His second wife, Marjorie, notes that her husband and his father often disagreed concerning politics, even when the singer was a young man.[23] Even so, Guthrie did have an interest in the Democratic Party throughout his life—although he would denounce its repressive side as much as he would praise its progressive one.

Also during Guthrie's early years, the religious leanings that would eventually inform his ideas of unionism started becoming pronounced. Although not raised in any particular church, Guthrie had been exposed to "hymns, spirituals, songs about how to save your lost and homeless soul and self" through his parents and his other family members when they lived in Okemah.[24] But only after moving to Pampa, Texas, in 1929 did he become particularly interested in religion; and he read "the bible and the life of Jesus almost day and night."[25] In the early 1930s, he also befriended a music-loving Church of Christ preacher who helped direct the singer's interest in Christianity and even baptized him.[26] Guthrie's attendance at this church did not last long; instead, he preferred to approach religion in his own individual and eclectic manner. This connection to Christianity but not to any particular church also finds itself played out in both the Populist and Socialist movements of the Great Plains, whose adherents often used biblical language and images to help get their points across about social and economic equality to their largely Protestant members. For example, well-known Populist editor and organizer Leo Vincent notes, "The law that labor recognizes is the law of the great Father above . . . [but] the law that capital works by is Mammon worship."[27] At this point in time, it does not appear that Guthrie had yet tied Christian principles to any of his political ideas—but that moment rapidly approached.

Taking some amalgam of these influences with him to Los Angeles in 1936, Guthrie eventually got a radio show on KFVD, where he began to perform songs of great sympathy for agricultural workers from the South and Southwest. In looking at this time in the singer's life, Joe Klein argues that Guthrie "simply didn't concern himself with specific issues or political figures; he seemed to have a philosophy, but no opinions."[28] Yet some evidence to refute this charge appears in his lyrics and other writing that appeared in his 1937 songbook. Here, Guthrie condemned the Los Angeles's police 1935 blockade against the Okies in the song "Do Re Mi" and denounced farm policies empowered by the first Agricultural Adjustment Act in an afterword to the song "My Pretty Snow-Deer." Nevertheless, Klein does correctly note that the singer's writings from this time do not express much in the way of a united political philosophy. In addition, not all of Guthrie's opinions expressed in the songbook seem very progressive—especially the racist-tinged song "The Chinese and the Japs." But we can see some of the underlying principles he had at this time that would blossom into his vision of a united world. For example, in the afternote to the song "Troubles of Mine," he writes, "Trouble is caused by two things. Fear is one. Greed is the other. It is removed by one thing, and that is Love." Then he adds, "That is the secret of secrets, and you will never educate yourself past it."[29] Soon he would begin getting his own education in leftist politics, especially concerning union activities, lessons that jibed with these sentiments and also gave them a particular direction.

That Guthrie began his lifelong support of the union movement during the late 1930s comes as no surprise considering the growing strength of organized labor at this time. Soon after the end of World War I, unions began losing power due to a combination of antilabor forces in industry and in government. Between 1919 and 1933, the American Federation of Labor (AFL) alone lost over two million members.[30] But with the signing of the Roosevelt administration's National Industrial Recovery Act (NIRA) on June 16, 1933, unions gained a powerful protective tool under Title I, Section 7(a). Pushed through the 1933 Congress by progressive Democrats, this provision granted all workers the right to organize themselves and to bargain collectively without any interference from employers. Almost immediately, union membership took a great leap upwards. This fact did not pass unnoticed by the leaders of industry, who often resisted the enforcement of the act. In the spring of 1935, a court case involving various code violations (although none involving union organizing) came before the Supreme Court, where the entirety of Title I of NIRA was overturned. That same year, daunted but not defeated by this decision, the Seventy-sixth Congress passed and the president signed the National Labor Relations Act (NLRA), better known as the Wagner Act due to its creation and support by New York Senator Robert Wagner. This law resurrected many of the provisions of the NIRA's Section 7(a) and even added enforcement power to them.

Just as the NIRA's regulations were assaulted in court, so were the NLRA's. Due to discrimination against members of a steel workers' union, the National Labor Relations Board (NLRB), which oversaw the enforcement of the act, ordered the powerful Jones and Laughlin Steel Corporation to comply with the pertinent laws. When the company did not follow this ruling, the NLRB eventually petitioned the Supreme Court to enforce the order. Unlike in the earlier NIRA case, the court did uphold the validity of this legislation in its 1937 decision, giving union organizers renewed hope.

During this expansive time period for unionism in general, a new organization sprang up in reaction to the conservatism of the AFL, which still clung to the outdated craft-unionism model. Just after the 1935 AFL convention, John L. Lewis's United Mine Workers (UMW) and seven other unions broke away to form the Committee for Industrial Organization, renamed the Congress of Industrial Organizations (CIO) in 1938. This group focused its efforts on industry-wide organization rather than by craft or individual jobs. The CIO also opened its membership up to women and African Americans as a means to gather strength. By the end of 1937, this approach garnered the group almost four million members, beating out the AFL as America's largest labor organization. Under the CIO's tutelage throughout the mid to late 1930s, unions sprang up in the mine, automobile, steel, textile, and garment industries—often in plants or facilities that the AFL had been unable to effectively organize. More important to Guthrie's story, around the same time the singer began crossing the country so did the new gospel of the CIO. Eventually, both he and the CIO encountered agricultural day workers in California's fields and worked to unify them.

One of the singer's first encounters with union activity occurred in the spring of 1938, when he traveled around the agricultural areas surrounding Los Angeles, through the San Joaquin Valley, and up to the Sacramento Valley. Frank Burke, owner of radio station KFVD, sent Guthrie out as a reporter for the little progressive paper *The Light* to look into various strikes involving Okies in these regions.[31] Although some of the labor unrest resulted from spontaneous responses to unfair conditions or wages, the newly created United Cannery, Agricultural, Packing and Allied Workers of America (UCAPAWA) came in and tried to organize these strikes. The previous year, the UCAPAWA chartered through the CIO and held to this umbrella organization's progressive strategies and policies rather that those followed by the AFL, which had sometimes undermined earlier strikes and organizing efforts of the state's agricultural field workers. Often the UCAPAWA received the tag of "communist union" from the Associated Farmers and other repressive California organizations in an attempt to focus resistance against any efforts to organize pickers.[32] During his trips through the state's agricultural areas during this time, Guthrie became familiar with this union and eventually even performed for its members in the San Joaquin Valley.[33] Reflecting back on this time, he notes, "I sung songs for the cotton pickers and cotton strikers, and for migratory workers, packers, canning house workers, fruit pickers."[34]

As a witness to the UCAPAWA's efforts in California, Guthrie could also find ample evidence that less than egalitarian attitudes often affected union activity. While there was a general upsurge in union activity in the state beginning in the last two years of the 1930s, a number of barriers to organizing the Okies appeared, including the group's stark poverty and fear of communism. Perhaps the single most important barrier to unionizing these workers came in the form of a long-established tradition: racism.

Many of the Okies brought a centuries-long tradition of racial prejudice with them when they came to California, just as Guthrie had. Well before these white migrants came to California, conflict between the races had been part of the history of labor disputes in the state. Since the late 1800s, one group after another—Chinese, Japanese, Indian, Filipino, and Mexican workers—had been brought in to displace another, creating a history of race-based labor tension in the agricultural areas of California.[35] But the Okies felt empowered by their whiteness and resisted any efforts to place them in the same category as past agricultural workers, most of whom had been dark-skinned.

When the Okies first started coming to California in the early 1930s, they particularly resisted integration with Mexican or African-American fieldworkers. After the deportation of over a hundred thousand Mexican laborers by California state and local authorities around the mid-1930s, the Okies became the dominant group among migrant fieldworkers in the state. By the mid to late 1930s, open conflict often broke out between the Okies and other, nonwhite migrant laborers during various strikes around California. For one, these southern and southwestern migrants would often work for lower wages than Mexican and Filipino laborers, resulting in tension, even as the Okies considered themselves socially superior to these groups.[36] These white migrant workers also seem to have strongly wanted to separate themselves from African Americans—just as they had done in the South and the Southwest—so as to retain their perceived superiority. Beginning in the early 1930s, cotton growers in California would segregate the migrants, creating "Negro" camps and "White-American camps."[37] Even those directly affiliated with unions working to organize all migrant laborers could express a desire for racial separation. The wife of the president of one UCAPAWA's local said, "You can't equalize me with no nigger—I don't care what."[38] Again and again, racism would appear to stymie union organizing, even with the CIO's clear mandate of inclusion. This type of struggle could not have escaped Guthrie's notice, and in less than two years, he would begin to express his thoughts on unionism, as he imagined it, overcoming any race separation among the working class.

After returning to Los Angeles from his wanderings in late 1938, Guthrie re-established his daily music show at KFVD. There he introduced himself to Ed Robbin, a leftist political commentator whose program immediately followed Guthrie's own. The two quickly became friends, partly because they shared a knowledge of the miseries of the agricultural workers in California.

Guthrie had just toured various agricultural areas outside Los Angeles and all the way up to Redding, while Robbin had investigated and written about the Salinas lettuce workers' 1936 strike. But Guthrie could turn to the other man for an education in industrial unions and contacts with their local membership. Robbin had begun his relationship with these groups during the sit-down strike at the Douglas Aircraft plant in Santa Monica in 1937, when he had helped with their organizing efforts. As a result of his connections, he booked some performances for Guthrie in 1939, including various union fund-raisers.[39] Perhaps most important, Robbin gave Guthrie access to union efforts and philosophy by introducing him to the newspaper *People's World*, the West Coast version of the *Daily Worker*. By 1939, Robbin was its Los Angeles editor, and his editorials often detailed and supported unionization efforts occurring around Los Angeles and the state as a whole. At Guthrie's request, Robbin later arranged for some of the singer's writings to be sent to Al Richmond, the paper's publisher. Soon after, Guthrie joined the staff with his column "Woody Sez," debuting on May 12, 1939.

Through this column, he met and sometimes befriended other writers who were also champions of union efforts. Of these people, writer Mike Quin stands out as an important early influence. Born into an Irish working-class family in San Francisco in 1906, Quin grew up with a strong sympathy for America's underclass. Later on, he witnessed strikes in the cotton fields of Imperial Valley and on the docks of San Francisco. These conflicts reinforced his belief in unionism, especially that encouraged by the CIO. He even worked as the group's California public relations director in the late 1930s and as a commentator on its radio program *Facts to Fight Fascism* in the mid-1940s.[40] Looking back on the writer's efforts, Harry Bridges, leader of the 1934 general strike in San Francisco, made this comment: "The ILWU [International Longshoremen's and Warehousemen's Union] and the whole CIO on the West Coast would not be the organizations they are today had it not been for the contributions of Mike Quin."[41] Much like Guthrie, Quin expressed himself through a variety of forms such as poems, songs, fables, essays, editorials, and novels. Much of this writing focused on labor issues, including a book-length work titled *The Big Strike*. Throughout his writing career, Quin spiritedly urged his readers to unite in their struggles against injustice and to imagine a better world for themselves. On August 17, 1947, just three days after Quin had died of cancer at the age of forty-one, Guthrie took up his notebook and wrote a moving tribute to him, praising his imagination and including these lines: "You handed our image making machinery back over to our work hands and you showed us that our biggest gun against our biggest owner rats is this thing we call our union vision hoping machine."[42]

These writers and the newspaper *People's World* itself also put Guthrie in direct contact with the Communist Party (CP). Like the union movement, the CP found increasing support during the 1930s. For over a decade before, it suffered under persecution from right-wing forces, especially those in the federal government. With the coming of the Russian Revolution of 1917, fears of communism grew in America, resulting in repressive countermeasures. In the first month of 1920, Attorney General A. Mitchell Palmer and the Justice Department made nationwide raids against the CP and affiliated groups and individuals, resulting in thousands of arrests. Afterward, many of the efforts of the CP were kept quiet by design so as to avoid this harassment. In addition, internecine struggles in the party also lessened its ability to gain membership and influence. Then came the Great Depression, and the environment for radicalism increased, raising the potential for party growth. Realizations about the need for unity against the forces of fascism in Europe pushed the CP in a new direction during the early and mid-1930s, bringing to life the Popular Front movement and starting a drive to promote communism as twentieth-century Americanism. As part of the effort, the CP strengthened its connection with other groups, such as the Democratic Party, the SP, and CIO-affiliated unions. Still, forces resistant to communism remained active even as Guthrie came in contact with the CP. Congress had recently created the Dies Committee, a group that would later become the House Un-American Activities Committee in the 1940s. So even as Guthrie began his connection to the CP, the federal anti-communist apparatus that would blossom in the cold war was already being put into place.

Sometime in early 1939, Robbin invited the singer to a CP rally in Los Angeles to celebrate the release of labor leader Tom Mooney, who had just spent twenty-two years in San Quentin for a crime he did not commit. Before taking Guthrie to the meeting, Robbin warned that the event was "sponsored by the Communist party, and it's a politically left-wing gathering." Supposedly, the singer retorted, "Left wing, right wing, chicken wing—it's the same thing to me. I sing my songs wherever I can sing 'em. So if you'll have me, I'll be glad to go."[43] Both the song "Mr. Tom Mooney Is Free" and its composer went over well with the crowd that night, resulting in further performances for CP gatherings and a number of other political groups and organizations. Guthrie writes of this time, "I sang at rallies and strikes, picket lines, marches, and all sorts of political meetings." But even as he got closer to the CP, he knew that there was a stigma attached to any connection to the party. Guthrie himself admits, "People called me Woody The Old Lone Wolf Communist" while he was on KFVD. In response, he adds provocatively, "Communist or no Communist, I like what I hear these Communists say."[44]

But the influence of Guthrie's experiences in the fields of California, his friendships with members of the left, his association with the *People's World*, and his new connections to the CP were not the only sources for the singer's interest in unionization efforts. Part of Guthrie's egalitarian vision continued to come out of his belief that a spiritual imperative urged all people to create harmony and fellowship with each other. We can see this impulse worked out in a couple of songs from this time period. In "No Disappointment in Heaven," based on the Carter Family's "No Depression in Heaven," his idea of equality manifests itself in his depiction of the Christian afterlife. In this vision, there are "No debts and no burdens . . . / No mortgage or loans to repay." Gone are all bankers and landlords. Instead, "we all will be equal in glory," and "You will work for each other in Heaven."[45] Containing a more inward exploration of Christian unity, the 1939 song "This Morning I Am Born Again" presents us with a narrator who does "not seek a heaven / In some deathly distant land," who "No longer desire[s] a pearly gate / Nor want[s] a street of gold." Reborn, he centers his life around helping others: "I give myself, my heart, my soul / To give some friend a hand." Through this selflessness, the narrator already finds himself "in the promised land."[46] But even at this point, Guthrie's thoughts on unity and unions remained removed from any particular religious viewpoint, just as they stood apart from any one political ideology.

Not long after, Guthrie began combining and equating many of his new influences with his earlier agrarian sympathies and his unique brand of Christianity. In an article he wrote later in life, he looks back in time to a night in California in the late 1930s when he came across a small rural church that was holding a service for striking cotton workers. In the course of the sermon, the preacher tells the assembled workers, "Jesus Christ of Nazareth, himself, was . . . a radical, a union organizer asking the rich to share their goods with you hungry and you poor, whose hand the rich has robbed." Even more interesting, Guthrie links this story to his first purchase of a piece of Communist literature, the Constitution of the Soviet Union, which he refers to as "my bible" at one point.[47] The story unfolded in this article, which very well may be partly fictionalized, nonetheless indicates that Guthrie has overlapped Christianity, unionism, and communism with little real differentiation being made between them. In his estimation, each becomes a force for justice and equality.

In the 1939 songbook *On a Slow Train through California*, Guthrie continues to equate and also defend various groups and politicians he admired. At one point, he pokes fun of a stereotypical depiction of CP members: "A Communist was seen walking down Main St., . . . without a bomb . . . without a piercing black eye, without a thought of war—without a job." Then he adds, "I am never overly attracted by anybody till every body else goes to jumpin' on 'em. Strikes me they framed up a Carpenter that same way, back over in Jerusalem." He goes on to point out how the term "Communist" had already been thrown about as fear tactic in an attempt to steer voters away from various progressive and populist Democrats: "Well every body is a callin' everybody elsa a communist. They called Roosevelt that. They called Upton Sinclair that. They called Hughey Long that." As a result of this fear, "They've got the govt. Inspectors out a huntin' the Communists and Red Activities, and Revolts—such a life! Accordion to all the neighbors, all of the other neighbors are Communists."[48] Although these various examples do not contain elaborate expressions of Guthrie's personal philosophy, we can see him defending and linking people and forces that he believed could help all Americans.

Beginning in the spring of 1939, Guthrie suggests in some of his songs that working-class unity could be a means to justice for all. We can see an uncertain but distinguishable union presence in his song "Indian Corn Song," written in August 1939. Here, a reflective narrator, after musing on how the "rich man," the "Big dictators," "Senators," "Finance-man," and others control the nation's wealth and its lands, decides that the "Workin' man got to / Get together, / Have a big meetin' down in town" where they will bring a more just world into being.[49] Also during this time, Guthrie writes his first explicit union song. In "Better Go Down and Join the Union," many different types of people form unions, although Guthrie does not approve of them all. Along with "Uncle Sam" and "Working Men," the narrator also notes that "the bankin' men," "Finance men," and "Landlords" have started unions, although those who join are described as "friskers" or "Lords."[50] In effect, the song advocates that the nation, especially the workers, should join together to counteract the collective efforts of the economic elite. A few years later, Guthrie would echo these ideas: "The Banking men has got their Big Union, and the Land Lords has got their Big Union, and the Merchants has got their Kiwanis and Lions Club, and the Finance Men has got their Big Union, and the Associated Farmers has got their Big Union." But he then notes that it is "a jail house offence for a few common everyday workers to form them a Union, and get together for higher wages and honest pay and fair treatment." Guthrie concludes, "It's damn funny how all of the big boys are in Big Unions, but they cuss and raise old billy hell when us poor damn working guys try to get together and make us a Working Man's Union."[51]

Even while seeing the promise of unions and related political movements on the West Coast at the end of the 1930s, Guthrie still felt that their efforts were not pronounced enough—both in their political power and in their ability to support those using art to advocate the cause. In a piece written in 1946, he looks back to this point in time and complains, "Labor in general, at that time, was in the nickel and the penny stages, very few strong and well run unions but lots of tear gas and guns being used by hired thugs and all kinds of vigilantes. The movement could not pay me enough money to keep up my eats, gas, oil, travel expenses, except five dollars here and three there, two and a quarter yonder, at places where I sung."[52] At the behest of his friend Will Geer, Guthrie left behind the people and organizations that had given him his first taste of unionism and traveled up to New York City in the very beginning of 1940. There, he would find greater opportunity for employment as a labor bard and other people who would expand his conception of "That Union Feeling."

In New York City, several of his early friendships with other performers reinforced his drive to express his thoughts on how unions could help give America's underclass access to legal and economic justice. In addition, many of these artists and the songs that they taught him did not come from an urban tradition but connected to his own brand of rural-flavored protest music. During the early months of 1940, as noted in chapter three, Guthrie met and performed with Aunt Molly Jackson, Jim Garland, and Sarah Ogan. He also learned their union songs: "I heard songs sung in the smoke of the fight that was the bloodiest county in the U.S.A. to bring union into."[53] All three had been active in the fierce and deadly labor struggles in Harlan County, Kentucky, in the late 1920s and early '30s. Although the songs that they wrote from this time and later sometimes include praise of the Communist-led National Miners Union and the CIO, these songs do not follow any set ideology. Instead, they note specific injustices and urge workers to come together to demand equal justice under the law, safe working conditions, and fair wages. These songs and performers gave Guthrie a glimpse into a rich tradition of union songs actually used on picket lines by workers, songs that had helped unify strikers facing armed company detectives and scabs, an enemy sometimes willing to kill to stop union drives.

Still, his encounters with these union songs and songwriters do not manifest themselves very directly in his recordings from this time. If we listen to his 1940 Library of Congress recordings with Alan Lomax, Guthrie utters not one word touching directly on union efforts, although there is much sympathy for farmers and other agricultural workers in these songs. That same year, his commercial release on Victor Records did contain a limited but recognizable commentary on the need for unions. In describing his album *Dust Bowl Ballads*, Guthrie brags of its progressive nature. He writes, "Most proud of anything, if anything, is the fact that I seem to have born a shade pink, and didn't have to read many books to be a proletariat, and you can guess that when you hear the records, as I'm sure Victor never done a more radical album."[54] Although the singer's assertion may be a little hyperbolic, the album does include several moments that jibe with his newfound ideas about unionism. Although taken from Steinbeck's book and John Ford's film based on it, Guthrie's narrative in "Tom Joad" does not slavishly follow either. Instead, it focuses solely on Tom Joad, his transformation from ex-criminal into labor leader. Just before he leaves his family to go out into the world alone, he tells his mother, "Everybody might be just one big soul." Before his murder, Preacher Casey tells Tom, "Us workin' folks has all got to organize, / Or we ain't got a chance anymore." In "Vigilante Man," Guthrie again appropriates the character Preacher Casey, who basically repeats himself by saying, "Unite the Working Man."[55] Although these two songs do not promote any particular labor organization, they clearly push for working-class unity.

Late in the spring of 1940, Guthrie would continue his encounters with union songs when he, Alan Lomax, and Pete Seeger joined forces in Washington, DC, to begin work on the book that would eventually become *Hard Hitting Songs for Hard-Hit People*. In his introduction to the book, Guthrie laments the abuses heaped upon those who try to band together for fair pay and safe working conditions: "This Book is full of songs that the working folks made up about the beatings and the sluggings and the cheatings and the killings that they got when they said they was a going to form them a Working Man's Union. It is a jail house crime for a poor damn working man to even hold a meeting with other working men. They call you a red or a radical or something, and throw you and your family off of the farm and let you starve to death." Although only referring to the plight of rural workers trying to join forces here, Guthrie encountered both urban and rural union songs while putting together the book, which documents the trials and tribulations of maids, longshoremen, cotton mill workers, auto workers, and several other types of people laboring in America. This collection also contains works by many of the nation's most important labor songsters: Maurice Sugar, John Handcox, Aunt Molly Jackson, Earl Robinson, Alfred Hayes, Joe Hill, Ralph Chaplin, Florence Reece, and Ella May Wiggins. Near the end of his introduction, Guthrie makes a prophecy concerning the book: "These songs will echo . . . till the world looks level—till the world is level—and there ain't no rich men, and there ain't no poor men, and every man on earth is at work and his family is living as human beings instead of like a nest of rats."[56]

Elsewhere in this songbook, we find Guthrie continuing to use his own vision of Christianity to comment on the injustices of the world, on its greed and lack of unity. In particular, he writes that "Preachers preach" the idea of "One Big Union." Then he adds, "You believe in it because the bible says You'll all be One in the Father. That is as High as Religion goes. Then on over there somewhere it says, God is Love. So you see that the Reason you got Religion is so's everybody can All be One in Love." He even uses Christianity to advocate against private ownership of land, a sentiment already expressed in "This Land": "Bible says God Owns Everything. That means that a Man is wrong when he jumps up and says, I own This Land, I own this House, I Own this Factory, YOU KEEP OUT!" Guthrie acknowledges that the "Rich Man" also thinks he follows God's way, for "They say they are 'religious,' say they're 'Christians,' say they're 'good.'" In the end, Guthrie's conclusions about Christianity conflict with the tenets of capitalism; he believes, "Th' very first thing you got to do to be a Christian is to sell all your goods and give it to the Poor." If you do, then and only then will you be deep within God's love: "That's Real Religion. Living, Loving and Giving."[57]

Guthrie's support for unions began to appear in some of his other writing from this time, especially in his column for the *Daily Worker*, which was a continuation of his earlier one for *People's World*. In one piece, he includes the lyrics to his first union song, "Better Go Down and Join the Union."[58] Later that month, in discussing the unionization efforts among the Okies, he concludes, "When they do take a notion to get going and get together, and organize and fight for what's right, they'll surprise the whole world, and in all probability strike at the right place stronger and faster than any of us can imagine at the present time."[59] In addition to these references, the idea of supporting organizing efforts in his songs becomes more pronounced. In "Been in Jail," written on March 4, 1940, Guthrie includes a verse about union activities. His narrator laments, "They got a union man in jail here / Just for fighting for higher pay." But he imagines a time in the future when a change will come and "I'll turn out this union man out, put that old police in some day."[60]

Several factors come together at this point to shape Guthrie's personal philosophy. All the injustice he had seen across America gave him a sympathy for others out on the road, for those looking for the promise of America but finding only more poverty and exclusion. Beginning in the early 1940s, he saw all injustices—past and present—through the lens of his free mixture of the various influences already mentioned, which also gave new focus and shape to his own experiences. In commenting on some of Guthrie's writing from this time period, music critic Dave Marsh notes that the singer's personal philosophy comes out of his thoughts about what he witnessed in late 1930s America rather than through an adherence to any particular political doctrine: "These thoughts and ideas were the ones that led him to socialism, not through ideology but as a way of explaining the poverty, neglect, and ignorance of the people he'd met on the road from Okemah to Los Angeles and back again to New York and Washington, DC, from the farm and oil territory to the lands of false promise."[61] But Marsh limits Guthrie's philosophy, describing it only as "socialism," while the sympathy the singer manifests at this time connects him to various political philosophies and organizations—some of which came out of a rural progressivism the same as his own, like populism and socialism, and others that he picked up in his travels throughout America, such as those taken from the CIO and the CP. Due primarily to these later influences, Guthrie moved beyond thinking of unions in a rural context, finally seeing them as a panacea for all the ills of the nation as a whole. This transformation first occurred in the summer of 1940, when he began to express his vision of a union world in song with a fervor even greater than before.

Woody Guthrie and Pete Seeger at the Highlander Folk School in Tennessee, 1940. Courtesy of the Harry Lasker Memorial Library and Resource Center.

During a trip from Washington, DC, to Pampa, Texas, with Pete Seeger in the summer of 1940, Guthrie became even more enamored with the idea of unionism, due in part to the groups and people the two met along the way. Drifting south, they decided to briefly visit Highlander Folk School in Monteagle, Tennessee. Founded in 1932, this institution trained rural union organizers and urged them to use songs to unite members. According to Joe Klein, the experience at the school left Guthrie "preoccupied with the idea of writing union songs."[62] One of the first results of this impulse was the song "66 Highway Blues," which ends with the narrator's admonition,

> I'm gonna start me a hungry man's union,
> Ainta gonna charge no dues,
> Gonna march down that road to the Wall Street Walls
> A singin' those 66 Highway Blues.[63]

Other encounters during this trip also led to Guthrie's continuing effort to express his thoughts and hopes concerning the good of unionization. After hitting his home state, Guthrie and Seeger stopped off in Oklahoma City, where they met and briefly assisted Bob and Ina Wood, who were state organizers for the CP. At this point during the trip, due to the education that these scattered groups and people had given him, Guthrie had an epiphany that would remain with him for the rest of his life. He writes, "I never did know that the human race was this big before." He also made a connection between poverty and institutional and covert abuse: "I never did really know that the fight had been going on so long and so bad. I never had been able to look out over and across the slum section nor a sharecropper farm and connect it up with the owner and the landlord and the guards and the police and the dicks and the bulls and the vigilante men with their black sedans and sawed off shot guns."[64] In effect, he attributes the time he spent with the Woods as the moment when he first realized the connectiveness between different peoples; and it was during this stay that he wrote his best-known union song, "Union Maid."

This song has two possible origins. Guthrie has indicated that at least one version was inspired by a female Sharecroppers Union member in Alabama who was assaulted due to her activities. In an afternote to this little-known version, which retells the events surrounding the woman's abduction and abuse, he writes, "[Anne May] Merriweather was the Union Sharecropper lady that [two antiunion thugs] stripped naked and beat up, then hung her for dead up to a rafter in the little shack."[65] Nonetheless, Joe Klein believes that Ina Wood actually inspired the original two-verse version of this song. Supposedly, she chastised Guthrie for never singing songs about the women in the labor movement.[66] He had encountered a similar criticism before. According to Guthrie, after he sang a version of "Curly-Headed Baby" to a group of migrant workers, one woman complained that he was "running' us women folks down" in the song. She then suggested, "You'd ought to sing another'n now to run the women up." In response, he sang a version of the folk song "John Henry" that included the following verse:

> Now John Henry had a little woman;
> And her name was little Polly Ann.
> When John Henry took sick and he had to go to bed,
> Polly Ann drove steel like a man, Lord God,
> Polly Ann drove steel like a man.[67]

Although not of Guthrie's own creation, these lines detail the strength of a woman, showing that he was aware of moments in well-worn songs that elevated women as labor heroes. So when Wood offered her criticism, he could have responded in a similar fashion by creating the pro-woman labor song "Union Maid," written to the tune of "Redwing."

The original version of this song certainly represents women workers as being as strong or stronger than their male counterparts. In the first verse, we meet "a union maid who never was afraid / Of goons and ginks and company finks / And the deputy sheriffs who made the raids." Instead of cowering before these unified antiunion forces, "She went to the union hall / When a meeting it was called." Then, in the face of the "company boys," she "always stood her ground" and belted out her views, which also stands as the song's chorus:

> Oh, you can't scare me,
> I'm stickin' to the union.
> I'm stickin' to the union,
> I'm stickin' to the union.
> Oh, you can't scare me,
> I'm stickin' to the union.
> I'm stickin' to the union
> Till the day I die.

Then in the second verse, we find that "This union maid was wise to the tricks of company spies." Instead, she remains steadfast, organizing the men and striking for "higher pay." Always defiant, she sticks her union card in the face of "the company guard" and launches into the rousing but simple chorus once again.[68]

Regardless of whether the example of Ina Wood or Anne May Merriweather pricked this song into being, Guthrie picked up on a trend in the union movement. Just as their male counterparts had, women had left the union movement in the 1920s, due in part to the AFL's continued refusal to require all affiliates to admit them. Then during the early years of the Great Depression and its accompanying tight job market, women found themselves discriminated against because business and labor leaders thought it better to employ males, who were considered the primary wage earners for their families. Still, women forcefully participated in strikes and labor-organizing efforts. In his nonfiction work *Puzzled America*, Sherwood

Anderson noticed and commented on the role women played in the unions he visited in the early 1930s: "The real leaders are seldom speech makers. In an amazing number of cases just now, they are rather small, sincere, determined women. Going about among union men and women in America gives you a curious respect for women. They have nerve."[69] By the late 1930s, more than eight hundred thousand women of nerve had joined labor unions, generally those affiliated with the CIO, and were active all over America.[70] Throughout the late 1930s and early '40s, the policies of the CIO, along with the equal rights stance of the CP, whose members had considerable influence in this organization, would contribute to the rise of women who carried union cards and stood on picket lines.

In addition, well before "Union Maid" came into being, some songs and songwriters that Guthrie knew had already pointed to women's efforts in labor disputes and unions. He certainly knew Joe Hill's "Rebel Girl," as did most people active in labor circles at the time. Instead of being one of the "blue-blooded queens and princesses, / Who have charms made of diamonds and pearl," the Rebel Girl has "hands . . . hardened from labor, / And her dress may not be very fine," but "She is true to her class and her kind." Much like the "Union Maid," when the Rebel Girl shows "her spite and defiance," those cheating the working class are left in "terror . . . trembling."[71] Guthrie also knew Aunt Molly Jackson's song "I Am a Union Woman." Here, we also find a defiant woman narrator. She proudly proclaims in the first verse, "I am a union woman, / Just as brave as I can be." Bravery is needed, for not only do the "bosses" call her a "Rooshian Red" and deny her husband work because of her union activities, but there is also the potential "To get killed out by gun-thugs, / And framed up by the law." Defiantly, she later adds, "We are many thousand strong" due to the organizing efforts of her union.[72]

No matter what swirl of influences brought "Union Maid" to life, the song's commanding protagonist does seem surprising coming from a man who has often been rightly criticized for a less than stellar history in his overall dealings with women—especially his three wives. One knowledgeable critic states, "A renowned womanizer, Guthrie largely ignored issues of gender politics."[73] A female folklorist goes even further in her criticism. She writes, "I . . . decry Guthrie's sexism, a recurrent motif in his writings and in his life."[74] True, the singer does not spend much time in his writing discussing the rights of women and sometimes objectifies them in his songs, poems, and prose. But there are moments in his work that make the appearance of the powerful woman in "Union Maid" seem less like lightning striking. For example, his song "She Came Along to Me" laments the status of women and then offers praise:

> They've not been any too well known
> For brains and planning and organized thinking
> But I'm sure the women are equal
> And they might be ahead of the men.[75]

Additionally, in his first letter to his newborn daughter Cathy Ann, he discusses women's plight by writing from her perspective: "Men have enjoyed an artificial superiority over women for several centuries. I have got to work and fight and do all I can to break the old slavery idea of the woman being chained to her house which, in many cases, certainly isn't a home."[76]

Unfortunately for the song's strong title character, soon an addition would be made that would recast the lyrics, making them less progressive than when first written. While preparing the Almanac Singers' second album *Talking Union* on Keynote Records in 1941, on which Guthrie did not appear, singer and writer Millard Lampell added a third verse that suggested a less than equal world for women in sympathy with the union:

> You gals who want to be free
> Take this little tip from me;
> Get you a man who's a union man
> And join the Ladies Auxiliary:
> Married life ain't hard
> When you got a union card,
> And a union man has a happy life
> When he's got a union wife.[77]

Thus, Lampell transformed the Union Maid from a primary to a secondary source of union power. These lyrics shift the song's general tenor and make it less of a shout for women's efforts in the labor movement. Nonetheless, the song's third verse has not remained fixed throughout the years; several other versions of the song exclude Lampell's verse and include other, more feminist expressions.[78]

When Guthrie eventually returned to New York City from his rambling trip down to Texas, the idea that unions should be promoted in song came to be one of his driving passions. In his "Woody Sez" column of June 24, 1940, he underhandedly brags about his new fascination. He writes, "Poor day today. Didn't write but 3 union songs."[79] But this push stands separate from his earlier political songs. In part, his work now became driven by the belief that songs could help bring people together and unite them in their striving for equality and justice. He had not only heard songs that came out of legendary labor conflicts in Harlan County but had performed alongside union organizers from the hills of Kentucky. We can find an example of him laying out his new beliefs in the pages of the *Daily Worker*. He writes, real "[F]olk Material . . . would help to do away with all of our silly little Clans and Herds and Legions and Cults—and it would be one of the best things that ever happened to the world—it would get all the folks in the world to knowing all of the other folks in the world and that's about as good as one world can get."[80] If this understanding brought about the unity of the underclass, then they could use democracy to end the nation's unfair economic system: "It takes big armies of working folks to make a jillionaire a jillionaire. There is one way for you to get out, that's the Union Way. To get together, stay together, and vote together."[81]

Even while denouncing the rich and urging the union of all workers, Guthrie was gaining success on nationwide radio, resulting in an exceptional salary during the waning of the Great Depression. In the span of nine months, he appeared on several radio programs, including *American School of the Air, We, the People, Back Where I Come From, Cavalcade of America*, and *Pursuit of Happiness*. Hundreds of dollars started rolling in, especially after November of 1940, when the producers of Model Tobacco's *Pipe-Smoking Time* brought him on as the show's new host. This influx of money and the restrictions that went with it irked him, however. By the turn of the year, his outspoken, iconoclastic behavior and politics resulted in his leaving the program. He explained the reason for the split: "I got disgusted with the whole sissified and nervous rules of censorship on all of my songs and ballads, and drove off down the road."[82] With his wife Mary and three children, he traveled through the South, dropping in unexpectedly on relatives on the way and eventually ending up out in California again.

While on the West Coast in the early months of 1941, Guthrie continued connecting his newer influences with his older beliefs: "When there shall be no want among you, because you'll own everything in common. When the Rich will give their goods unto the poor. I believe in this way. I just cant believe in any other way. This is the Christian way and it is already on a Big part of the earth and it will come. To own everything in Common. That's what the bible says. Common means all of us. This is pure old Commonism."[83] Unassuming and evoking a folksy Christianity, the language here makes the idea of communism less foreign, less threatening. By this time, Guthrie realized that many in America feared and hated the CP and any affiliated organizations, necessitating comparison with safer and more acceptable positions, much like the efforts advocated by the Popular Front movement. In fact, Guthrie's growing public sympathy and support for Communist organizations and ideas put him in line for criticism, no matter what type of folksy language he used. As early as 1939, he had been red-baited by a fellow KFVD member, cowboy singer Stuart Hamblen.[84] During this time out west, Guthrie had to come to grips with the fact that strong political associations and public sympathy with progressive forces, such as the CP, would greatly limit his potential for commercial success.

Even while continuing his allegiance to various progressive causes and groups, including Communist ones, Guthrie continued to dismiss the notion that any particular political affiliation controlled his personal beliefs. In a September 1940 letter to Alan Lomax, he complains, "They called me a communist and a wild man and everything you could think of but I dont care what they call me. I aint a member of any earthly organization my trouble is I really ought to go down in the morning and just join everything." Later in the same letter, Guthrie clearly stated his support for America and promised self-banishment if he ever harmed the nation in any way: "If I thought for two minutes that anything I do or say would hurt America and the people in it I would keep my face shut and catch the first freight out of the country."[85] But what was Guthrie's perception of America and its people at this time? What did he think would hurt his country?

In his extensive travels through the country during the late 1930s and early '40s, Guthrie met a nation heavily peopled by the working class. So when he advocated for their rights, for them to get an equal share of the nation's wealth—which they created through their labor—he saw himself pushing for the greater good of America. But for those forces pressing for the criminalization of political dissent, especially that of the CP, this support could be seen as revolutionary. In fact, Guthrie does advance strong measures in the song "The Final Call." Here, the narrator recognizes, "There's a world of Plenty here for one and all." As a result of this knowledge and the rightness of the working man's demands for equality, the narrator states, "I have seen the Vision, / I made my Decision." Then in the chorus he tells us what might be reality or part of his vision: "Look at the Workers Army marching through the Plentiful Valley, / The Working Man will win, and the Greedy Man will fall!" Finally, he warns, "Better get ready for the Final Call!" But what is this final call? Is it a summons for unity of the underclass or a cry for revolution? Perhaps the answer exists in Guthrie's afternote to the song:

> I aint in favor of a bloody revolution. You aint either. But I'm in favor of a Change in things that'll give you and me and all of our folks plenty of what they need to get along on, plenty of work, plenty of pay, plenty of rest, plenty of schooling, plenty of the pleasures of this life. I really hope to God that the Rich folks will give you these things as fast as you step up and throw out your chest and ask for them. They'd ought to be glad to. You build everything they got. You plant and raise everything they got. You make everything they got. There's a whole army of you, and just a little bunch of them. You need more things. They got more than they need. I hope to God that you don't have to hurt nobody in getting your fair and honest share. Nobody hates to have a tooth pulled or any blood shed and worse than me, but if she goes to giving you any trouble, fix it, yank it out and throw it away and forget about it. Dont poison your whole system just on account of one thing that's rotten. But in case anybody tries to step in and stop you from a changing things into a better world—use your strength. Got to use it.[86]

These comments emphasize group action rather than actual revolution as a means to gain the American Dream. But much like he does in some of his outlaw songs, Guthrie does seem to support violence, as the last resort, to gain justice and equality for all members of the nation's underclass.

Soon, Guthrie would swear that he was not a member of any group that advocated revolution. In the summer of 1941, through a recommendation from Alan Lomax, Guthrie briefly worked for the Bonneville Power Administration (BPA), a job consisting of writing songs for use in promotion programs for this federal dam project. Part of the employment process required his signing an oath that asked, "Do you have membership in any political party or organization which advocates the overthrow of our constitutional form of government in the United States?" He clearly responded,

"No."[87] Skeptics might suggest this denial was a simple lie to get work. With his New York money gone and little opportunity in Los Angeles, he desperately needed a job to support his wife and three children. By signing the form, though, he would not be lying. Throughout his life, Guthrie considered himself an American and a patriot. Never did he advocate an end to the democratic form of government; in fact, he often celebrated the peaceful shift of power through voting. In another letter to Lomax, Guthrie writes, "Most folks don't realize that your vote is about the best thing you got in the world because it the best thing you can use to change the world and make it better."[88] So when he signed an oath of loyalty to join the BPA, it is doubtful that he felt he was even bending the truth a little.

To the Federal Bureau of Investigation (FBI), the question asked Guthrie was an important one. In the summer of 1941, for the first time, members of the federal government began to track his movements, all because a "Confidential Informant" advised the San Francisco office of the FBI that he was a Communist. In fact, the bureau knew the singer was working for the BPA, which necessitated their initial investigation. Offices in New York City, Buffalo, Albany, and Portland also received notice of Guthrie's involvement with the CP. In a letter that summer, J. Edgar Hoover asked Assistant Attorney General Matthew McGuire if the FBI should look into the singer's political connection under "Public Law No. 135, . . . which directs this Bureau to undertake investigations of employees of the Federal Government who are members of subversive organizations or who advocate the overthrow of this government."[89] Luckily for Guthrie, by the time of Hoover's query, the contract with the BPA had ended, leaving the singer an ex-federal employee and out of the range of the bureau for a while.

If the FBI did look at the work that Guthrie produced for the BPA, it would have found little to criticize. During this time, he famously wrote twenty-six songs (perhaps more), work such as "Roll On Columbia" and "The Grand Coulee Dam," celebrating the wonder and the glory of the dam project and its resulting publicly controlled electricity. Promotion was necessary for the project, for some resisted it because it was government controlled and smacked of communism. In fact, Guthrie believed that those against the BPA thought "[t]he two big dams were communism because they would cause people to be able to work together faster, and when they worked together they would meet together and talk together and vote together and fight together and that was most certainly the worst possible and most deadly kind of communism you could get drunk and dream up."

In response to such misguided speculation, he simply responded, "Bull."[90] However, the songs he created in this brief but productive time contain little evidence of his ever more solidifying stance on unionization and certainly no mention of any particular political groups. In fact, there is only one direct reference to unions in this work, and it is used in a humorous vein. In the song "The Biggest Thing that Man Has Ever Done" ("The Great Historical Bum"), the mythical narrator who has lived since the beginning of time tells us that when he "worked in the Garden of Eden," he "join'd the apple pickers union" and "always paid my due."[91] Soon though, Guthrie's songs would be full of union references.

Late in the summer of 1941, Guthrie returned to New York City alone and immediately joined the Almanac Singers. Although newly formed, the group had already recorded the albums *Songs for John Doe* and *Talking Union*. The second of these included a version of Florence Reece's "Which Side Are You On?" and Guthrie's own "Union Maid." The Almanacs also included some of their own pro-labor songs, such as "Talking Union" and "Get Thee Behind Me Satan." The group's allegiance to union matters comes as no surprise considering the political leanings of the three original members. Lee Hays had only recently come to New York City from Mena, Arkansas, when he joined the group. Back home, he had been a student and then a teacher at Commonwealth Labor College, which offered classes in how to organize rural workers. In particular, both the school and Hays had often used their resources to help unionize sharecroppers in the region, especially through the Southern Tenant Farmers Union. Pete Seeger was also an original Almanac. He had grown up in the very liberal household of his father, folklorist and musician Charles Seeger. The younger Seeger also worked with Alan Lomax at the Library of Congress, where he encountered union songs from all over America. Certainly, his travels with Guthrie the previous year, visiting the Highlander Folk School and Communist organizers in the Southwest, would have also given Seeger a similar urge to praise the expanding union movement. Millard Lampell, the third original member, was the son of garment workers from Paterson, New Jersey. As such, he would have been aware of union activities in that industry, especially considering the union battle ground that Paterson had been for several decades. Pulling from varied sources, the Almanacs planned to support unionization efforts in New York City and throughout America.

Soon after Guthrie's arrival in the city, the Almanacs left for a cross-country tour of CIO union halls. Considering that over two million workers were out on strike at some point in 1941, these musicians had a large and avid audience awaiting them. The small group made stops from Philadelphia to San Francisco, singing selections from their second album for the various working men and women they met along the way. But the people they encountered also gave something back to the Almanacs, a sense of pride and power in unions. Lampell notes, "I think it was the first time that Woody—or any of us—saw organized labor with this kind of strength. There was such a sense of excitement and dedication to everything they were doing."[92] After a time on the West Coast, Lampell and Hayes returned to New York City; but Guthrie and Seeger continued on, "back up along the coast to Seattle and sang for the Commonwealth Federation of Washington, the Old Age Pensioners, the Unemployed Unions, the Farmers Unions, and the office and factory workers union." They also sang for "movements of every labor description," including "the gatherings of Communists everywhere we went."[93] The entire trip was a heady journey, with the songs and their singers finding appreciative audiences wherever they went.

Through his experiences with the Almanacs, Guthrie's interest in labor unions and organizing grew stronger and better developed. In a letter to Ed Robbin, he writes, "Being along with the Almanac Singers is some sort of a treat to me, as it is poking my head full of this stuff called Organization. Something that I still need a heap more of."[94] For the rest of his writing career, Guthrie would continuously learn more about unions and churn out songs supporting and celebrating their efforts. However, one historian mistakenly claims, "After 1941, Guthrie's devotion to the working class became so tempered with patriotism that he omitted from his repertory his anthems of union organizing, since strikes would hinder the American war effort and retard the opening of a second front against the invaders of Russia."[95] Actually, Guthrie became more enamored of union activity and wrote more songs supporting labor's efforts during the war years than at any other time of his life. By late 1941, he saw unionism as a means of deinvesting the economically powerful minority and empowering the underclass majority. For some time, he had broken the world into two factions—the rich and the poor. His fascination with unions simply added new groups to this separation: big business and scabs merging with the bankers and the landlords, union members joining ranks with tenant farmers and migrant workers. His songs from this time on reflect this new paradigm.

Sociologist R. Serge Denisoff argues, "Regardless of Guthrie's participation in union organizing, he was not an extoller of the labor movement but, rather, of the working class."[96] But the truth is that Guthrie supported both working people in general and the labor movement in particular. Especially after the Almanacs' 1941 tour, specific labor organizations begin appearing in a positive light in Guthrie's songs. For example, on December 13, 1942, he penned the tribute "Join That A. F. of L." Here, the narrator urges listeners to "Go join that A. F. of L." and gives them ample reasons for doing so. There is "better work and better pay," along with a "better house and a better world!"[97] Even with this litany of positives that the AFL could provide, this group did not find itself in the spotlight of many of Guthrie's union songs, perhaps due to its essentially conservative nature. Instead, the labor organization that found itself most in line for praise from the singer was the CIO.

As early as March 1939, Guthrie had noted the perseverance and power of the CIO in gaining equal rights for America's workers. In the afternote to the song "Chain of Broken Hearts," which details the loss of love, Guthrie adds an unexpected commentary on the activities of the group: "This was during the days when the CIO people were walking up and down the docks and the shipyards [of California] with signs that said: Quit Sending Scrap Iron to Japan." He goes on to explain, "The Japanese Imperialists took our good scrap iron and welded it into a long and heavy chain of blood and murder, and Hitler tried to use this chain to break down the trade unions. And the world marched out to show him that it would live union or die. And this war is doing more than all the other wars added up to chisel the chains of race hate and wage slavery off the legs of the human race."[98] Later, when putting together *Hard Hitting Songs for Hard-Hit People*, he made a strong pro-CIO statement in the introduction to his song "When You're Down and Out," written to the tune of Uncle Dave Macon's own protest song "All In Down and Out." After thinking about "a couple of big pearl handled 44s . . . and about the money in the banks, and about the hungry people," about his own desire to take up the outlaws' methods for the greater good, Guthrie tells us, "I never did get around to robbing or shooting. I found a better way to beat the rich men and the bankers at their own game, and that's the Union, the C.I.O., or any of it's Unions."[99] Here, the CIO becomes a positive channel for outlaw impulses. Around this same time, Guthrie first referred to this organization in one of his songs. During his trip with Pete Seeger to Texas in the summer of 1940, Guthrie revised his first union song "Better Go Down and Join the Union" so that it included the verse, "John L. Lewis started him a union. / Called it the CIO."[100]

During his trip with the Almanac Singers, Guthrie began a more pronounced connection with the CIO. As they swung through Pittsburgh to support a strike there, the group immortalized the town in song, and one version contains the lines "Allegheny to the Ohio, / They're joining up in the CIO."[101] Later during this trip, when Guthrie and Seeger found themselves in Duluth, Minnesota, they met up with a real-life union maid, Irene Paull. Writing under the pseudonym "Calamity Jane," Paull did a column for *Midwest Labor*, a lumber worker newspaper.[102] For her union efforts, she ends up celebrated, along with the CIO, in a Guthrie song titled after her own pen name. Here, Calamity Jane tells her beloved lumberjacks, "Your bunks and beds are flea bit, / And your wages they're too low." But there is hope through unity: "Come and join the union boys, they call the CIO."[103]

After the trip and throughout his time with the Almanacs, Guthrie's kind accolades for the CIO did not subside but became stronger. This support could come in surprising forms. For example, the CIO receives a positive mention in a Guthrie-penned square dance number, where the caller shouts out, "Promenade! And on you go! / I'm USA and CIO!"[104] Some of Guthrie's support was more pragmatic. In 1942, he wrote the songs "Boomtown Bill" and "Keep the Oil A-Rolling" as a commission from Edwin Smith, the organizing campaign director of the Oil Workers International Union (OWIU), a CIO-affiliated union.[105] Both songs emphasize the virtues of the CIO, although neither mentions the OWIU. In the first of these, Boomtown Bill brags, "I got my CIO card of which I'm mighty proud / Whatever I believe I like to holler loud."[106] Another of Guthrie's pragmatic approaches to supporting the CIO in the early 1940s comes through his songs written for specific strikes and other labor action. Also, some of his lyrics document the struggles of the United Automobile Workers (UAW) and the Transport Workers Union, both CIO-affiliated unions.[107]

Throughout the war years, Guthrie began expressing his belief in the power of all union effort, not only that of the CIO, as a means to overcome fascist aggression abroad and at home. As noted earlier, the singer generally separated the world into two factions, with all union members listed positively along with the working class as a whole. Then in 1941, he began adding Adolph Hitler and the Nazis to the side of big industry and scabs, the bad side in the struggle for justice and equality, a dichotomy that Guthrie lays out himself: "There aint but two sides, the working people's side and the big bosses side. The union side and the Hitler side."[108] This addition seems rather natural. His earlier work already linked union activity and true democracy. By the beginning of World War II, his belief in the positive spirit of unions expanded beyond an American context, with him eventually envisioning it defeating fascism throughout the world. In fact, his song "Roll On, My Union" explicitly links the struggle against big business at home with the fight against fascism in Europe. Here, the narrator not only states that the union has beaten "gun thugs," "finks," and "black market gangsters" in America but that it will also defeat "You Fascists! And Nazis!"[109]

Also during the early years of the war, some of Guthrie's lyrics began to promote unionism as a means to overcome racism. Years before, he had not only put aside his prejudices but also used some of his songs to denounce a litany of racially charged groups and actions such as the KKK and lynching. But only after 1941 did he come to see unions as the means to quashing the racism he had observed throughout America. Perhaps his thinking on this matter was influenced by the CIO and the CP since both groups had strong antiracist stances. As noted earlier, the CIO opened its membership to all races from the beginning. Eventually, this attitude created an environment where hesitant whites and blacks realized that only through a united effort would the working class have any real power. In his book *Twelve Million Black Voices*, Richard Wright noted that a change had occurred in many white union members' attitudes toward race:

> The general dislocation of life during the depression caused many white workers to learn through chronic privation that they could not protect their standards of living so long as we blacks were excluded from their unions. Many hundreds of thousands of them found that they could not fight successfully for increased wages and union recognition unless we stood shoulder to shoulder with them. As a consequence, many of us have recently become members of steel, auto, packing, and tobacco unions.[110]

In fact, hundreds of thousands of black workers had joined unions nationwide by this time. African Americans also began joining the ranks of the CP, which had long had a strong stance against prejudice based on race.

Regardless where this impulse came, during the early war years Guthrie definitely began to express his thoughts on the power of unions to quash racism. Some of these songs only offer flashes of his vision for racial equality through labor unity. In the song "You Fascists Bound to Lose," the narrator points out that the union forces allow "All colors of hands . . . [to] fight."[111]

Other songs are much more specific in their statements about how labor unions will allow people to extinguish race hate. In "Join that A. F. of L.," Guthrie's narrator notes that the "Poll tax [is] bad" and then says, "If you don't like that old Jim Crow" then "go down and join" the union.[112] Although it does not appear in every version of the song, a verse in "Boomtown Bill" actually points out the kinds of people who he believes push for racial unity:

> Across this rolling ocean,
> And this whole wide world around,
> My union brethren and sistren
> They're beatin' old race hate down.[113]

In fact, Guthrie links up these two positions in the song "Gotta Keep 'em Sailin'," which was written around this same time period. In the first verse, the narrator sets the scene by referring to the war: "'Round the whole wide world tonight / There's a great and bloody fight / In the wreckage the bombs and shrapnel rains." In part, the battle results from Hitler's attack on unions, which he threatens to "tear . . . down." However, the song's narrator adds, "The union will break those slavery chains." In the next verse, he makes this link even more explicit when he notes, "The dirty rotten lies / Spread around by fascist spies / To divide us and kill us one by one!" But the unionists will not be tricked, for they know "'Neath the color of our skin / . . . we all are kin."[114]

Also during this time, his idea of union expands well beyond the idea of trade association or even working-class unity. In a piece from March 1942, he writes,

> All of the laws of man working in nature and history and evolu-
> tion say for all human beings to come always closer and closer
> together—to know and understand all races, creeds, and colors
> better; and facism says for us to split ourselves up into the
> thousand cliques and klans and beat our own chains of slavery
> onto our ankles by wasting our strength fighting friend and
> neighbor—and allowing the facists to nip us off one by one,
> little by little, group by group.[115]

Other lyrics encourage the races to work together, and some even ask them to recognize their similarities rather than their differences. In one World

War II era rewrite of "So Long, It's Been Good to Know You," the narrator speaks of his new realization:

> I went to my neighbor and got to be friends,
> We talked about things we are fighting to win;
> We're both different colors, but feel sort of kin,
> We're both the same color just under our skin.[116]

In effect, Guthrie believed that personal interaction between ordinary Americans, brought about by the war, could create positive race relations. In 1942, he wrote "She Came Along to Me," which contains the following verse:

> And all creeds and kinds and colors
> Of us are blending
> Till I suppose ten million years from now
> We'll all be just alike
> Same color, same size, working together.[117]

Here, Guthrie theorizes that through interracial relationships, the union of all people would be achieved so thoroughly that no separation concerning race could be made.

In his 1943 autobiographical novel *Bound for Glory*, Guthrie takes on a number of the issues that had been on his mind touching on race and class unity. The majority of the poor black, white, and brown characters who appear in the book unite in their misery and in their hope. But this connection that Guthrie manifests throughout the narrative does not seem to follow any particular political tract. In fact, one critic aptly notes, "The book . . . without lapsing into the rhetoric of ideology, slowly builds for the artist an ideological orientation, and a currency of value the foundation of which arises from the living contact with poverty, hate, danger, and struggle he encounters on the road and on the rails rather than being imposed by the politically correct authority of party or tract."[118] Indeed, the harmony of peoples that Guthrie advocates in this novel does not come through any organized drive from any political viewpoint. Even union activity only makes a marginal appearance here when a local officer in a small town stops Guthrie for being a vagrant and asks him if he is "One of them labor boys." A moment later, the policeman also adds, "Maybe, you're one of them trouble causers." Although they do not assault Guthrie, the police chase him out of town.[119] So even the hint of labor organization in the novel points to repressive countermeasures, the same sort found in the song "Vigilante Man."

Other moments in this novel much more explicitly comment on the selfishness of churches and the necessity of prayer. Perhaps this mix seems strange, but it comes across quite naturally here. While traveling from Texas to California by hoboing, Guthrie makes a stop in Tucson, Arizona. Although warned to stay on "the working folks' end of town," he ends up wandering through the "rich part" of the city. Hungry, he stops at several churches to see if he could "do a job of work . . . [to] earn a bite to eat." But whether Protestant or Catholic, no one will help him with a meal; he even gets a lecture on charity from a priest, including the comment, "Charity here is like charity everywhere; it helps for a moment, and then it helps no more." Then the singer walks "down to the shacks of the railroad workers, the Mexicanos, the Negroes, the whites," where food is given freely, even though the generous have few worldly goods themselves. Later on in California, Guthrie meets up with several other men who have been riding the rails. Noticing a sign reading, "Free Meal & Nights Lodging. Rescue Mission," the men start joking around about prayer. Suddenly, the conversation turns serious, with a cast of rough characters opening up about the power of prayer and religion in their own lives. But the concluding comment comes from "an old white-headed man" who tells the assembled men, "All of this talking about what's up in the sky, or down in hell, for that matter, isn't half as important as what's right here, right now, right in front of your eyes. Things are tough. Folks broke. Kids hungry. Sick. Everything. And people has just got to have more faith in one another, believe in each other. There's a spirit of some kind we've all got. That's got to draw us together." After the old man speaks, the rest nod their heads in agreement.[120] So we find these men of the road, these bums, all subscribing to the idea that a unifying spirit resides in the people of America. Here, Guthrie's own ideas come out of the mouths of several characters concerning his own ideas about Christian unity in this world rather than the next.

Throughout the early war years, Guthrie continued to perform his songs, especially those about union forces defeating the Nazis, at various public gatherings and even on radio broadcasts in New York City. Many of these performances were with the Almanac Singers, and their connection with the CP often caused them trouble even though the Soviet Union was America's ostensible ally at the time. As result, the group's opportunities were limited. Also, several members of the group were drafted or joined the armed forces, and other members left the East Coast for Detroit, where they continued as the Almanac Singers until the spring of 1943. Yet Guthrie stayed and continued to perform during this time, especially after his book *Bound for Glory* came out, giving him renewed publicity. In time, through the urging of his friend Cisco Houston, Guthrie joined the war effort by becoming a member of the merchant marines. He shipped out for the first time in late June 1943 on the Liberty ship *William B. Travis*, then went on two other voyages in 1944, carrying men and supplies across the dangerous Atlantic to aid the war effort.

While in the merchant marines, Guthrie wrote a number of songs that combined the religious fixations that he had long entertained and his passion for uniting all the members of the working class. Mistakenly, biographer Joe Klein points to the singer's voyages with this group as the moment when "he developed a coherent philosophy that managed to encompass both his earlier spirituality and his current Marxism."[121] As noted earlier, the singer started making this connection as early as 1939, although some of his writing from this time, such as "Union Spirit" and "Union's My Religion," does connect religious feeling with union efforts more explicitly than before.[122] One of the most interesting union pieces he wrote during this time at sea is "Good Old Union Feeling," which emphasizes the Christian spirit inherent in the unity that Guthrie craved.

In looking at this song, we find that "Jesus of Nazareth told his people one and all; / You must join the Union Army / When you hear that Spirit call!" Guthrie expands the Christian influence in this song by connecting to an image often found in the spirituals created during slavery in America: "Abraham led the slaves of Egypt through the sea! / We'll be slaves to greed and fear / Until our Union set us free!" Unionization as a means to overcoming slavery makes another appearance in verse four, where the narrator reveals that "Old Abe Lincoln" said, "Not a white man can be free / While the dark man is a slave." Stealing lines from the earlier song "Union Spirit," the last verse offers us a vision of golden unity: "The Union shining like the sun / . . . draws us all together! / And melts us into one!"[123] Here, the Christian spirit, tied briefly with the Old Testament vision of exodus and the Republican ideas of Lincoln, unites all workers—black and white—into one force, one union body.

In looking through the songs that Guthrie wrote during this time period, one critic claims that "these later songs possessed many of the characteristics of organizing songs" but that "they were now becoming utopian in spirit in that they had lost their class-based activist referent and had become increasingly mystical and escapist."[124] But during the same time that he whipped up such Christian-based union songs as "Good Old Union Feeling," Guthrie also penned a number of songs about particular union issues and struggles that can in no way be considered "utopian," "mystical," or "escapist." A main example of the type of work he did at this time concerns the National Maritime Union (NMU), the East Coast merchant seaman's union of which he was a member. In fact, at this point in his life, he probably came the closest to understanding the true necessity of having strong labor unions to represent the day to day struggles of their members.

In 1943, the NMU was only six years old, having been formed in May 1937 as an alternative to the International Seamen's Union (ISU), which had long been affiliated with the AFL. Throughout much of the Great Depression, many of the ISU rank and file felt the organization was ineffectual and corrupt due to its coziness with shipping interests and its inability to garner higher wages and better working conditions. Out of this frustration and under the leadership of Joe Curran, a longtime merchant seaman, the NMU was born and soon became affiliated with the CIO. This new organization created a charter emphasizing equality and democracy for all merchant seamen. Although the NMU soon came under attack for being Communist-controlled, the group became more effectual than the ISU throughout the late 1930s. With the advent of WWII, merchant marines became indispensable, sailing the Liberty ships that brought much-needed supplies and armaments to American troops fighting in Europe and Africa. So important was their mission, in fact, that the selective service granted this group an exemption from the military draft in the spring of 1943, just months before Guthrie joined them and the NMU.

Long before he became a member of the NMU, Guthrie had supported this group through his artistic efforts. Soon after coming to New York City in 1940, he spent time playing and getting to know merchant seamen. Then when the Almanacs made their landmark tour of the nation in 1941, they sang for the NMU National Convention in Cleveland and even helped the group's organizing efforts in San Francisco. After the Almanacs returned to New York City, Guthrie continued to play for them, including a performance for the NMU's Women's Auxiliary in December 1941.[125]

Cisco Houston, Woody Guthrie, and Jim Longhi performing at the National Maritime Union Hall, New York, 1943. Courtesy of Longview Publishing Company.

After joining the merchant marines, Guthrie had a stronger commitment to the NMU than at any other point before. On all three ships that he sailed, his friends and fellow shipmates Cisco Houston and Jimmy Longhi both became union leaders, which helped educate him on the nuts and bolts of the group's activities.[126] Through his direct contact with the NMU, Guthrie also came to understand union members' hardships in an up close and personal manner. For one, he learned exactly how unions could directly improve the lives of workers. In a union meeting during his first voyage, the ship's bosun told of his experiences before the NMU came to power: "Before the union, we had to live in small cabins with twelve men piled three high, on bare mattresses. Once I had a top bunk under a dripping steam pipe, and I had to curl up like a pretzel so the scalding water wouldn't drip on me while I slept." Later, Guthrie experienced less than pleasant conditions himself when he sailed home aboard a ship not under an NMU contact.[127]

Later, he also came to realize that even with a union, conditions onboard needed improvement, especially concerning the treatment of the navy gunners who helped defend the ship during the constant attacks from Nazi submarines and planes. In a letter sent to *Pilot*, the NMU's weekly newspaper, Guthrie complained of conditions on the *Sea Porpoise*, his third ship. In particular, he argued that as a messman, he had to serve too many of the gunners to give them adequate attention, while the officers had a much larger staff although there were fewer people being served. Guthrie felt that the navy men deserved better service since they risked their lives for the good of the nation.[128]

During his voyages, Guthrie became well aware of the dangers faced by those aboard the supply ships traveling through the North Atlantic, for he had two of his ships sunk under him—one from a torpedo and another from an underwater mine. But even in the midst of this destruction, he could find good. After his ship was torpedoed in the Mediterranean in the summer of 1943, he writes that the incident "caused all of the men of our crew to become more closely united, better union brothers."[129] So even as he created some union songs that focus more on spiritual topics than on bread and butter union issues, he daily faced a work situation where he desired strong labor representation.

This support for the NMU spilled over into several songs Guthrie wrote during his voyages. In some of these lyrics, the union only makes a brief appearance, such as in "Talking Merchant Marine," where the narrator brags,

> I'm just one of the merchant crew,
> Belong to the union called the NMU.
> I'm a union man from head to toe,
> I'm USA—and CIO!

But the obvious excitement here has a practical and necessary purpose, for this union man is also "Fighting out here on the water, / Gonna win us some freedom / On good dry land" against the Nazis.[130] Understandably, many of Guthrie's lyrics written during his time as a merchant seaman focused on how the allies, aided by the power of unions, would help defeat the Nazis. In "S.S. NMU," Guthrie transforms the union into a Liberty ship, one that "can't be sunk by bullets, / Torpedoes, bombs, nor mines" as "she's winning our freedom fast."[131] Overall, Guthrie did believe that all unions, but especially the NMU, were going to defeat the Axis powers, no matter how difficult the struggle. In a piece more poem than song, he describes a union hall where "I can see the war on everybody's face." But the assembled union men already "had to fight a long, hard, bloody old battle / Before they even won the right to get together in this hall," so it seems doubtful that they will fail to win against the Nazis or any other group that stands against them.[132]

After returning to New York City from the merchant marines in late 1944, Guthrie continued supporting union efforts though his writing and performances. In December, he began a radio show on station WNEW, playing a variety of songs including those in strong support of labor. In the opening night announcement, along with various other pro-union comments, he said, "The folks around the world have been fighting now for a hundred centuries to be all union and to all be free and I sing the songs that tell you about that."[133] Yet the songbook he hawked on the program, *Ten of Woody Guthrie's Twenty-Five Cent Songs*, did not contain any lyrics directly pushing unionization, although some of the prose pieces he included do emphasize the need for unity, especially in the continuing face of fascism abroad. As noted in chapter one, in an endnote to the version of "This Land Is Your Land," he links his most famous composition to the idea of unionization: "The main idea about this song is, you think about these . . . words all the rest of your life and they'll come a bubbling up into Eighty Jillion all Union. Try it and see." In fact, at this point in his life, his thoughts about unions had expanded well beyond a limited conception of that involved with labor organizations; for he believed that all the songs here could help create unity between all people: "No matter who you are or where you're from, no matter what your color or your language, you will taste, hear, see and feel an old spark of your whole life somewhere in these songs." Throughout this songbook and in much of his writing of this time, Guthrie continues to look forward to a future when the unity of all people is achieved, a time he describes as "our new union world."[134]

The idea that understanding between different peoples could be created through song continued to appear in Guthrie's work throughout the mid-1940s. This impulse also manifests itself through his songs that posit unionism as a religion, especially his own particular brand of Christianity. In January 1945, he revised his song "This Morning I Am Born Again," changing a few lines and adding a whole new verse, which contains these lines:

> I see just one big family
> In this whole big human race
> When the sun looks down tomorrow
> I will be in a union place.[135]

Although the song still reflects the narrator's newfound realization that this world, not the next, can be heavenly, the added verse gives this vision a new focus. For if the world embraces the idea of union, then others may be able to share in the rebirth described here. Unionism even becomes a religion in itself, one offering the promise that anyone joining it can be born again. A year later, Guthrie again takes up this idea, just as he had done earlier in "Union's My Religion" and other writing. In his notebook, he writes, "The best religion I ever felt or ever seen is world union. The highest step in any religion is your joining up with the union of every mind and hand in the world."[136]

Along with this type of visionary writing, Guthrie also continued to create pieces where he links the drive for unity with particular people he respected, especially Franklin Roosevelt. In March 1945, Guthrie revised the Almanac Singers' song "Union Train" to incorporate his current views on the war effort. In this new version, the Allied forces unite against the Axis and other organizations or people whom Guthrie saw as antiunion, including those he had celebrated in the past. Aboard this train, we find Roosevelt, Churchill, and Stalin racing towards victory against Hitler and the "Imperial Japs." But the Axis forces are joined by some American confederates who try to derail the train: Isolationist and Nazi apologist Charles Lindbergh along with racist and red-baiting Texas Senator Martin Dies make appearances here. However, we also find John L. Lewis trying to stop this union train. Here, "Johnny Lewis jumped up on the coal car" and attempts to steal its contents, saying, "'I'll steal the fire out of the boiler / So this union train can't roll!' "[137] Indeed, Lewis did lead the coal miners of the UMW out on several strikes in 1943–44, which slowed shipments of supplies to the Allied war effort, making him one of the most unpopular men in the nation. So Guthrie's song reflects the attitude of many people who thought that Lewis's actions were hurting the war effort and even costing the lives of American servicemen abroad.

After Roosevelt died on April 12, 1945, Guthrie composed a song of condolence addressed to the president's wife, emphasizing Roosevelt's past pro-union stance. In "Dear Mrs. Roosevelt," the narrator exclaims in the chorus, "This world was lucky to see him born." But the song also specifically links the president to labor support with lines such as "He helped to build my union hall" and "He fought my war the union way and the hate gang all got beat."[138] Nevertheless, Guthrie's support for Roosevelt and the New Deal in general was always tempered by an unyielding faith in unions. We can see this impulse in his introduction to his earlier song "I'm a-Lookin' for That New Deal Now," when he writes, "The only New Deal that will ever amount to a dam thing will come from Trade Unions."[139] With Roosevelt's passing, much of the rank and file of the labor movement believed they had lost a supporter of labor and a defender of the working class.

Even with the loss of Roosevelt, the beginning of 1946 must have looked promising to Guthrie and other progressives who supported the labor movement; for the war years had brought much power to union forces throughout America. Around fifteen million Americans were enrolled in unions, including a substantial number of women and African Americans. In addition, collective bargaining agreements covered the majority of these workers, guaranteeing them set wages and job protection. When industry refused to share wartime profits with the unions in the aftermath of the war, almost two million steel, automobile, oil, electrical, and other work-ers went out on strikes, the largest showing of union power in America's history.

Realizing the opportunities of this exploding union activity, Guthrie joined with a number of other progressive folksingers such as Pete Seeger and Lead Belly to create the organization People's Songs in December 1945. Guthrie describes the purpose of this group succinctly: "The reason for Peoples Songs is to shoot your union the kind of a song or songs when you want it and fast. To help you to make a songbook, a program, a throwaway songsheet, a whole evening, or just some historical material about some of the people that have made the history of our trade union movement."[140] The organization also offered to send its various members out into America to help with strikes and union organizing, going wherever they were needed; the group even formed People's Artists as a booking agency. In March 1946, Guthrie, along with Pete Seeger and Lee Hays, returned to Pittsburgh under the auspices of People's Artists, this time to help support the strike against Westinghouse Electric by the United Electrical Workers. While there, the assembled strikers "roared like the ocean in a rock cavern" when the three played, including two songs made up especially for the occasion.[141] Afterwards, Guthrie buoyantly looked forward to further collaborations between the artists of People's Songs and the labor movement.

Unfortunately for this hope, much change occurred within the Demo-cratic Party, the CIO, and the CP early on in the postwar era. These inter-nal shifts upset the sometimes tenuous unity that had existed among these groups since the early 1940s. Although he initially continued to follow the past administration's sympathetic attitude toward labor, Harry Truman directly antagonized both the CIO and the AFL in May 1946 when he threatened to seize control of America's railroads so as to stop a nationwide strike by Locomotive Engineers and the Railroad Trainmen unions. He even went before Congress to ask for repressive special powers to put down strikes in case of national emergency. Although not granted this authority, he soon found himself vilified by a majority of the American labor movement. Afterwards, Truman began to support other legislation being proposed by the growing antilabor contingency in Congress.

With the ascendancy of the Republican Party in the House and Senate races in 1946, efforts were taken to limit the power of unions, such as the Portal-To-Portal Act. Then in June 1947, Congress passed the Taft-Hartley Act, which severely curtailed the rights given to labor by the earlier Wagner Act. Among other changes to federal labor law, the act banned the closed shop and prohibited union contributions to national political campaigns. A provision of Taft-Hartley also pricked at the CP's influence in unions by requiring all officers to sign affidavits stating that they were not Communists. Although Truman vetoed the act, only to have it ratified by Congress anyway, he issued that same year an executive order compelling all federal employees to sign loyalty oaths. Efforts to rid CP influence in America were not limited to the federal government, however.

Even without the heavy-handed provisions of the Taft-Hartley Act, the CIO leadership had already decided to rid itself of members involved in the CP. For example, in 1947, the UAW and the NMU, both of which had long had strong ties to the CP, began to purge themselves of those in the party. Thus, the CIO joined its repressive brother, the AFL, in the red-baiting that would drive out much of the progressive element that had brought it to so much power in the late 1930s and the early 1940s. These dismissals had repercussions affecting other elements in the unions' membership; as one historian notes: "[This anti-CP action] had particularly adverse effect on black workers because the unions usually expelled those black and white leaders who had done most to recruit blacks in the first place."[142] In all, the postwar era would become particularly harsh for the CP and for progressive forces in both the Democratic Party and the CIO.

Guthrie recognized these political shifts early on and denounced them— and all those he believed were doing little or nothing to stop what he saw as a drift towards divisiveness in the forces that had once championed the unity of America's underclass. In his journal on January 23, 1946, Guthrie included these comments about the president's attitude towards those groups that he respected the most: "Truman has proved to me that he doesn't like my trade unions, don't like organized labor, don't like the Communist Party, don't like the human race."[143] However, much more of the singer's ire went against the much hated Taft-Hartley Act and the forces in the labor movement who he felt had capitulated too much to the federal government and American industry. In a notebook entry dated July 2, 1947, he denounced both John Lewis and the AFL for their lack of direct defiance to Taft-Hartley: "I see that you [Lewis] . . . and the mine owners vote no on pulling off a strike to fight this awful law called the Taft & Hartley bill. I see that the bigbosses of the AF of L voted no strike, too. How are you going to fight a fight against our lordly owners as long as you let them make up all of the rules of the battle? This is the saddest and funniest joke of human life and human death I've ever heard so far since I've been born."[144] In these pronouncements, Guthrie is more than a bit unfair to Lewis, who did lead a strike in 1946, only to end it after a court ruling against him and the UMW. Later, after the removal of restrictions against him, Lewis did win a new and favorable contract with mine operators in the summer of 1947, soon after Guthrie wrote his harangue.

Other promises of unionism also seemed lost after World War II, especially racial harmony. In the aftermath of Taft-Hartley, unions began an intensive organizational drive in the South, during which an old specter raised its head and helped curtail the efficacy of these efforts: racism. Guthrie himself became aware of this situation in late 1947. Through People's Artists, the performance branch of People's Songs, he went to Winston-Salem, North Carolina, to support a strike by the Food, Tobacco, and Allied Workers (FTA). While there, he added a new verse encouraging racial unity to his old union song "You Gotta Go Down and Join the Union":

> All colors of hands gonna work together
> All colors of eyes gonna laugh and shine
> All colors of feet gonna dance together
> When I bring my CIO to Caroline, Caroline

Unfortunately, local FTA organizers demanded that he cut these lyrics from the song because the event that he was to sing at was segregated. That same night, Guthrie saw the situation firsthand when he played for "a handful of Negro workers, about 20 in a hall that would hold 125." In writing about this moment, he notes, "It cut me to my bones to have to play and sing for those negroes with no other colors mixing in." Nevertheless, Guthrie's own optimism did not falter during this time. He still believed that the "union feeling" that he had thought about so much and that he had expressed time and time again in his writing would win out in the end.[145]

The disappointment Guthrie felt towards the Democratic Party and the CIO manifested itself during the 1948 presidential election season when he joined in with several other progressive musicians in creating songs supporting the candidacy of Henry Wallace. These efforts had much to counter since both the Democratic Party and the majority of the trade unions were firmly behind Truman, the latter not so much in their faith in the president but because of their fear of John Dewey, the antiunion Republican candidate. Guthrie expressed his displeasure with all these groups in his song "Go Down and See," written expressly for the Wallace campaign. Here, the Democrats, the Republicans, Truman, and "old race hate" all come in for criticism. We can see what these forces have done if we "go down" to the "bowry," "the slums," "the jail," and "the lynch-rope country." In the song "The Farmer-Labor Train," set to the tune of "The Wabash Cannonball," Guthrie imagines a victorious Wallace "pulling into Washington one bright and happy day," where the assembled crowd will shout at his train, "she's full of union men."[146] Unfortunately, Guthrie's songs did little to help Wallace. The former vice president pulled fewer votes than even Strom Thurmond, the racist Dixiecrat candidate.

With the defeat of Wallace and the growing anti-Communist spirit in America, Guthrie found less and less opportunity to perform for the unions that he so clearly loved. In addition, Huntington's chorea began to make it hard for him to concentrate for extended periods of time, and his wandering nature made his home life uncertain at best. But even though he did not put himself into any other campaign for change and became more distanced from direct union activities, he did not give up writing about his belief in the power and strength that unions could offer to all members of the underclass, although his belief in the labor organizations he had once championed decreased greatly in the early 1950s. In the song "Where Are You Going My CIO?" he denounced the CIO's move to connect with the money interests rather than return to their radical stance of the late 1930s. Here, the group denounces itself in its reply to the title question: "I'm going over yonder where that big money grows" and where "no working stiff can follow."[147] Then in the song "Uncle Stud," when asked by an unnamed narrator, "Do you like a trade union," the title character has some harsh words: "Hell no dammed if I do / If it fights no more than my CIO / And my dam'd old AFL." Regardless, his beliefs in the idea of unions in general was as strong as ever. In answer to the question of whether he needs "a good union," Uncle Stud replies, "Hell yes, I dam shore do / 'Cause I couldn't live a day / If I didn't have a union fulla folks like you."[148]

By the mid-1950s, the effects of Guthrie's disease had become quite pronounced and severely decreased the singer's creative output, except in his letters and diaries. Even during this difficult time, Guthrie continued to believe in unionism in its many manifestations and sometimes found the will to express this position in song, although his spelling became even more idiosyncratic than it normally was. He fooled around with others' union songs, revising the lyrics to Ralph Chaplin's "Solidarity Forever" and Aunt Molly Jackson's "I Am a Union Woman."[149] But he also created new songs of his own that supported union efforts, including "My Sweetyold CIO," where he found forgiveness for this organization, although he still strongly denounced the "damn foole AFL."[150] Perhaps his most touching comments about unions from this time comes in a June 1955 letter he wrote to a friend: "If my damd damd old chorea stuff has already knocked me down too damd dizzery in my body to pace along any more good fine laborey daye parades with alla my best best bestest union men and my union maides, well, my heart and my mind and my spirit and my strength and my everliving love will go on stepping it on down along past by here . . . with alla my only people that love on this earth, my union hearted army."[151] Within two years' time, the progressing deterioration caused by his disease completely stilled Guthrie's pen. Nevertheless, some of his last written commentary continued to express his vision of all people coming together in one big union.

As we have seen, Guthrie began his relationship with unions slowly, letting various influences direct his own thoughts about equality and justice in America. This faith did have its moments of ebb and flow, especially concerning particular groups and people such as the CIO and John L. Lewis. As Dave Marsh notes, he "had to struggle for personal and political responsibility and felt troubled and sometimes even defeated when he couldn't get a handle on it; a man who doubted in the dead of night; a man who matched unquenchable faith and optimism with an intimate knowledge of the near impossibility of living up to expectations."[152] Yet even in his doubts, Guthrie believed that those who wanted to could replenish themselves by realizing the need for unity, by seeing possibilities in joining with others. He firmly believed that only selfishness could destroy the soul of man. In an oft-cited comment, he writes, "There is just one thing that can cut you to drifting from the people, and that's any brand of style of greed. There is just one way to save yourself and that's to get together and work and fight for everybody."[153]

Perhaps the philosophy that we can gather together from Guthrie's comments about unions does still seem simplistic. He was no theorist, no policy maker. But his vision of a union world is still a worthwhile one. His friend Ed Robbin defines the singer's position well: "Woody traveled the land seeking to organize, to get people together to fight for a better world, to wipe our discrimination against minorities and recognize the common enemy, the tyranny of a system that made a few rich and the many poor."[154] Neither the Communists, the Socialists, the Democrats, the Populists, nor any other group has a lock on these desires—no one person or group can solely claim the hunger for justice. Although drawing from all of these groups and others in varying degrees, Guthrie formulated his own vision of a just world; and even as he often failed to live up to his own ideals at many points, these missteps do not undermine the validity of his vision of union, of solidarity, and of a world where social and economic equality for all people is the standard.

During the roughly fifteen-year period that Guthrie wrote union songs, he did not create many focusing on particular labor concerns or conflicts. Most of his songs would fit any union, whether AFL or CIO affiliated. In fact, he generally avoided applying the terms such as Christian, Democrat, Communist, CIO, or Socialist in his support for unionization. He took from the groups encountered whatever he found useful. His emphasis was on the idea of people coming together for the greater good of all. In effect, he took Whitman's admonition to "re-examine all you have been told at school or church or in any book, dismiss whatever insults your own soul, and your very flesh shall be a great poem."[155] What he did take from all these varied, and sometimes conflicting, influences was the central idea that the majority of the people, most often those who labored day to day for their pay, should unite so as to have a voice with which to protest the wrongs they saw or experienced. As Moses Asch has noted, "There was a deep philosophy in each song—of the rights of man, of brotherhood."[156] In his songs, Guthrie denounced fascism, race hate, and greed—and celebrated the promise of the unity of men and women in various forms. He wanted all Americans to join together to demand justice for themselves, so they could have shelter and food, dignity and joy—all gained through the people's "union feeling." This was Woody Guthrie's vision; this was his prophecy.

Epilogue

THIS SCRIBBLING MIGHT STAY

Resurrected by the music of Billy Bragg and the voice of Jeff Tweedy, Woody Guthrie's song "Another Man's Done Gone" on the 1998 *Mermaid Avenue* album finds the songwriter reflecting on the potential of his own work: "I don't know, I may go down or up or anywhere / But I feel like this scribbling might stay."[1] Here, Guthrie speculates on his own future, on the staying power of his words. It is a statement of fragile hope. Throughout his life, he documented the stories and experiences of many groups of marginalized Americans, using his artistry to illustrate their misery and then to offer them hope of a better future. He also hungered for his work to last so that it would touch future generations. Today, we know that his "scribbling" has lingered on, living on well beyond the life of its creator. His songs, especially "This Land Is Your Land," have become part of American culture, perhaps even a national treasure. But we lose much of their power if we only appreciate them as beautiful relics. For even though Guthrie's words of protest and prophecy come from our nation's past, they still have much to say to our present and our future.

Certainly, some of his work only remains significant primarily as a historical document. America has thankfully dismantled the sharecropper system and abolished the poll tax. Unfortunately, many of the other injustices that Guthrie railed against in his own time continue to exist today, making his songs relevant to those willing to listen. We can still find instances where some Americans fear migrant laborers for the same reasons that Guthrie discussed in his songs. In the early 1990s, California authorities mandated that for their first year, newly arrived families who were eligible for welfare could only receive assistance at the same level permitted in their home state, just as long as the rate was lower than that offered by the Golden State. Just as Kenneth Crist asserted in the *Los Angeles Times* in 1939, some contemporary Californians believed that the poor were flocking to their state to soak up welfare, an attitude attacked by Guthrie with great vigor in the 1930s, as noted in the end of chapter two.[2] Other Americans still fear Mexican and other migrants, even as they come to this country to take up essential jobs in construction, agriculture, and cleaning services that our own people appear unwilling to do. We can see this fear in a speech given by conservative politician Pat Buchanan when he offered his own right-wing insight into immigration: "America is not some polyglot boarding house for the world; this land is our land, this home is our home."[3] Here, Buchanan perverts the original intention of "This Land" and exhibits a desperate need for some of the compassion that Guthrie so eloquently expressed in "Deportee." Other of Guthrie's songs are still needed, for lynchings have not disappeared from America. Who could forget the infamous example of James Byrd, Jr., the African-American man who was dragged to death by white assailants behind a pickup truck in Jasper, Texas, in 1998? So we can still sing "Slipknot" and share in Guthrie's hope for "a day when such will be no more."[4] There are many other examples of Guthrie's work that still resonate, too many wrongs from the 1930s and '40s that linger on today.

Part of the reason that many of Guthrie's songs can still be sung on picket lines or at protests today with no or little change is due to his effort to make his work touch some sustained note, some eternal essence of the human condition. In a 1941 letter to the Almanac Singers, he explains his desire to achieve a lasting significance while documenting the events of the day: "Our job is the Here & Now. Today. This week. This month. This year. But we've got to try and include a Timeless Element in our songs. Something that tomorrow will be as true as it is today. The secret of a lasting song is not the record current event, but this timeless element which may be contained in their chorus or last line or elsewhere."[5] Perhaps this "Timeless Element" can be described as art. Or it could also be an acknowledgment of certain issues that have haunted the human race, a recognition of our own long-lasting but not necessarily eternal shortcomings.

Beyond the relevance of his songs from the past and how they speak to our present, the influence of Guthrie's drive to document his time and his thoughts, his crystal-clear vision of a future speaks to new artists, singers, and writers from our own time who have the same hope. They want to put today's stories into song; they want to speak out against injustice and hate they see in contemporary America. These singers want to wail out the miseries of our time and to offer up dreams and visions of a better world just beyond the horizon. Many current songwriters look to Guthrie for inspiration and guidance; we can hear the echo of his words and ideas in their work. Certainly, Bob Dylan has been pointed to again and again as the inheritor of many of Guthrie's passions as expressed in song. Others have also been moved by Guthrie's songs, the torch being handed from generation to generation, which is Guthrie's greatest legacy.

Hundreds of America's best-known performers have paid homage to Guthrie by covering his songs, people and groups such as Ry Cooder, the Byrds, Country Joe and the Fish, Nazareth, Joan Baez, John Mellencamp, Odetta, Judy Collins, the Kingston Trio, Bruce Springsteen, Pete Seeger, X, Nanci Griffith, Corey Harris, the Grateful Dead, Frank Sinatra, Lester Scruggs, and Peter, Paul, and Mary. This group of artists includes a wide range of traditions—rock, punk, folk, jazz, bluegrass—and comes from divergent political views. But all are linked by an appreciation for Guthrie's songs. As music critic Greil Marcus has noted, "The best popular artists create immediate links between people who might have nothing in common but a response to their work."[6] These artists are united by their appreciation of Guthrie's songs, their honesty and message.

Other of this country's best-known protest songwriters paid tribute to Guthrie in a creation of their own. Bob Dylan's "Song to Woody," Phil Ochs's "Bound for Glory," and Tom Paxton's "Fare Thee Well, Cisco" all contain bowed heads and heartfelt thanks to their musical mentor. We can find a similar nod to Guthrie's influence from more contemporary work. In it, Guthrie's influence does not necessarily manifest itself in a direct invocation of the man but more often of his lyrics or even his attitude toward injustice. In the song "Ghost of Tom Joad," we can find links to the past; for its creator—Bruce Springsteen—read John Steinbeck's novel, watched John Ford's film, and listened to Woody Guthrie's song.[7] In effect, the same blood runs in both Guthrie's and Springsteen's songs. Later, when the politically charged band Rage Against the Machine covered Springsteen's song, this particular bloodline continued on.

Others connect to Guthrie as well, in style as well as purpose. We can see a link in this chain in Steve Earle's song "Christmas in Washington."

Musing on the state of America in the postelection season of 1996, the narrator throws up a prayer, saying,

Come back Woody Guthrie,
Come back to us now.
Tear your eyes from Paradise
And rise again somehow.
If you run into Jesus
Maybe he can help you out
Come back Woody Guthrie to us now.

Why is Guthrie needed? In answer, the narrator adds, "To listen to the radio you'd think that all was well. / But you and me and Cisco know that it's goin' straight to hell."[8] Here, Earle echoes Guthrie in many ways; both tell us that the radio—the mass media—offers up sounds and images that pacify, that give voice to the lie that America is fine, no adjustments necessary. But just as Guthrie did in his time, Earle uses his songs to offer up a vision of the nation as he sees it—both its glory and its injustices. This impulse is Guthrie's greatest bequest—an encouragement to others to continue on the path he chose, to offer us new "living songs."

Yet it does not take a star to become part of this link, this chain. It is easy to touch this strength, for even the most rudimentary performers can usually find chords on which to ride their own thoughts. Or they can do as Guthrie did, take a folk song and remake it. When these changes are made, the new creations can still have strength enough to be altered. Elastic, they can be pulled at and stretched in new ways. Repeated and repeated, some songs become chants, rituals, habits. The nation becomes their singer and audience. Guthrie urges us to capture our own stories, our own history and ideas for future generations:

I am no more of a poet than you are. I am no more of a writer of songs than you are, no better a singer. The only story that I have tried to write has been you. I never wrote a ballad nor a story neither one that told all there is to tell about you. You are the poet and your everyday talk is our best poem by our best poet. All I am is just sort of a clerk and climate tester, and my workshop is the sidewalk, your street, and your field, your highway, and your buildings. So let me call you the poet and you the singer, because you will read this with more song in your voice than I will.[9]

Not all who try to follow Guthrie's suggestion will make the same impact he did, but the desire for others to try to reshape their experiences, their joys and pains into song for those to sing in years to come is an essential part of what makes Guthrie an important figure in American culture, worthy of study.

In the foreword to *Hard Hitting Songs for Hard-Hit People*, John Steinbeck notes, "The songs of the working people have always been their sharpest statement and the one statement which cannot be destroyed. You can burn books, buy newspapers, you can guard against handbills and pamphlets, but you cannot prevent singing."[10] Certainly, much of Guthrie's work has continued to be sung, even when the sentiments that he expressed in song chaffed against current societal standards. His lyrics and other writing have endured, a sign of their appeal. But some of the ideas embedded in his songs must also be eternal. There is a need to denounce racial prejudice and economic injustice; and although the historical landscape has shifted much since Guthrie wrote the lyrics quoted throughout this book, the issues raised in them continue to haunt our nation. Guthrie's ability to see lasting problems came in addition to his optimism that one day there will be a solution to them. His belief in the coming together of all peoples—regardless of race, religion, sex, politics, and class—stemmed out of his faith in the giving impulse he saw around him, even as he noted many instances of greed, fear, and hate. But it is his hope for unity that is his most lasting vision and that he expressed with his words, his voice. Although not his only one, this impulse to see the wrongs of society and yet look forward to a better world surely must be one of his most important legacies to the American people.

Notes

Abbreviations:

WGA   Woody Guthrie Archives. 250 West 57th, Suite 1218. New York City, New York.

WGP   Woody Guthrie Papers, Moses and Frances Asch Collection. Ralph Rinzler Archives, Center for Folklife and Cultural Heritage. 750 9th Street, NW, Washington, District of Columbia.

WGMC   Woody Guthrie Manuscript Collection. American Folklife Center, Library of Congress. 101 Independence Avenue, SE, Washington, District of Columbia.

Prologue

1. Quoted in Jim Longhi's *Woody, Cisco & Me: Seamen Three in the Merchant Marine.* Urbana: University of Illinois Press, 1997: 58. Also see "Living & Dying & Singing." *The Woody Guthrie Songbook.* Ed. Harold Leventhal and Marjorie Guthrie. New York: Grossett & Dunlap, 1976: 30–31. In this quote and in all others used throughout this book, Guthrie's idiosyncratic prose style and spellings have been retained.

2. Woody Guthrie. *Ten of Woody Guthrie's Twenty-Five Cent Songs.* (c. 1945): 1. A copy of this mimeographed songbook is held in the WGP Box 2, Folder 1.

3. Woody Guthrie. *Pastures of Plenty: A Self-Portrait.* Ed. Dave Marsh and Harold Leventhal. New York: HarperCollins, 1992: 83.

4. Woody Guthrie. *Woody Sez.* New York: Grosset & Dunlap, 1975: 140–41.

5. Guthrie, *Ten of Woody Guthrie's Twenty-Five Cent Songs* 1.

6. Woody Guthrie. "History Singing." *The Woody Guthrie Songbook.* New York: Grosset & Dunlap, 1976: 34.

7. Guy Logsdon. "Woody Guthrie: Poet of the People." *University of Tulsa Magazine.* 9:2, 1970: 3.

8. Frederick Turner. "'Just What the Hell Has Gone Wrong Here Anyhow?' Woody Guthrie and the American Dream." *American Heritage.* 28:6 (October), 1977: 39.

9. Woody Guthrie. *Alonzo M. Zilch's Own Collection of Original Songs and Ballads*. (c. 1935): 1. A copy of this mimeographed songbook is held in the WGMC Box 1, Folder 1.

10. Quoted by Pete Seeger in the acknowledgments of *Incompleat Folksinger*. Lincoln: University of Nebraska Press, 1992.

11. Joe Klein. *Woody Guthrie: A Life*. New York: Delta Book, 1999: 97.

12. Richard A. Reuss. "Woody Guthrie and His Folk Tradition." *Journal of American Folklore*. 83:329 (July–September), 1970: 289. 34.

13. Studs Terkel. "Woody Guthrie: Last of the Great Balladeers." *Climax*. 9:3 (December), 1961: 60. In addition, Jerome Rodnitzky argues, "Guthrie's songs do not lend themselves to simple verbal analysis, since his style was always more important than his message," as noted in *Minstrels of the Dawn: The Folk-Protest Singer as a Cultural Hero*. Chicago: Nelson-Hall, 1976: 55.

14. Guthrie, *Woody Sez* 139.

15. Olin Downes and Elie Siegmeister. *A Treasury of American Song*. New York: Howell, Soskin & Co., 1940: 2.

16. Louis Adamic. "Twentieth-Century Troubadour." *The Saturday Review*. April 17, 1943: 14.

17. John Greenway. *American Folksongs of Protest*. Philadelphia: University of Pennsylvania Press, 1953: 275–302.

18. Woody Guthrie, *Woody Guthrie Folk Songs*. Ed. Pete Seeger. New York: Ludlow Music, 1963.

19. Woody Guthrie. *Born to Win*. Ed. Robert Shelton. New York: MacMillan, 1965.

20. *Hard Hitting Songs for Hard-Hit People*. Ed. Alan Lomax, Woody Guthrie, and Pete Seeger. New York: Oak Publications, 1967.

21. Woody Guthrie. *Bound for Glory*. New York: E. P. Dutton, 1967.

22. Reuss, "Woody Guthrie and His Folk Tradition" 274.

23. John Greenway. "Woody Guthrie: The Man, The Land, and The Understanding." *The American West* 3:4 (Fall), 1966: 28.

24. Robert Shelton. Introduction. *Born to Win*. Ed. Robert Shelton. New York: MacMillan Company, 1965: 14.

25. D. K. Wilgus. *Journal of American Folklore*. 8:316 (April–June), 1967: 204.

26. Ellen J. Stekert. *Western Folklore* 25:4 (October), 1966: 275.

27. See R. Serge Denisoff's *Great Day Coming: Folk Music and the American Left*. Urbana: University of Illinois Press, 1971; Richard Reuss's "American Folklore and Left-Wing Politics, 1927–1957." Doctoral dissertation. Indiana University, 1971 (finally published by Scarecrow Press in 2000); and David Noebel's *The Marxist Minstrels: A Handbook on Communist Subversion of Music*. Tulsa: American Christian College Press, 1974.

28. Woody Guthrie. *Woody Sez*. New York: Grosset and Dunlap, 1975.

29. Henrietta Yurchenco. *A Mighty Hard Road: The Woody Guthrie Story*. New York: McGraw-Hill, 1970.

30. Edward Robbin. *Woody Guthrie and Me: An Intimate Reminiscence*. Berkeley: Lancaster-Miller Publishers, 1979.

31. Joe Klein. *Woody Guthrie: A Life*. New York: Alfred Knopf, 1980.

32. Robbie Lieberman. *"My Song Is My Weapon": People's Songs, American Communism, and the Politics of Culture, 1930–1950*. Urbana: University of Illinois Press, 1989.

33. Wayne Hampton. *Guerrilla Minstrels: John Lennon, Joe Hill, Woody Guthrie, and Bob Dylan*. Knoxville: University of Tennessee Press, 1987: 93–148.

34. Woody Guthrie. *Pastures of Plenty: A Self-Portrait*. Ed. Dave Marsh and Harold Leventhal. New York: HarperCollins Publishers, 1990.

35. Ed Cray. *Ramblin' Man: The Life and Times of Woody Guthrie*. New York: W. W. Norton, 2004.

36. *Hard Travelin': The Life and Legacy of Woody Guthrie*. Ed. Robert Santelli and Emily Davidson. Hanover: Wesleyan University Press, 1999; and Bryan Garman. *A Race of Singers: Whitman's Working-Class Hero from Guthrie to Springsteen*. Chapel Hill: University of North Carolina Press, 2000.

37. John Steinbeck. Foreword. *Hard Hitting Songs for Hard-Hit People*. Ed. Alan Lomax, Woody Guthrie, and Pete Seeger. Lincoln: University of Nebraska, 1999: 9.

38. Woody Guthrie, letter to Alan Lomax. September 19, 1940. WGMC Box 1, Correspondence folder.

39. William Stott. *Documentary Expression and Thirties America*. New York: Oxford University Press, 1973: 14, 18.

40. Guthrie, *Born to Win* 28.

Chapter One

1. Original in WGA Songs 1, Box 3, Folder 27. Pete Seeger states he first heard the song from a recording rather than from Guthrie firsthand. Pete Seeger. "A Tribute to Woody Guthrie." *This Land Is Your Land*. Woody Guthrie and Kathy Jakobsen. New York: Little, Brown and Company, 1998: 30. Additionally, when working with him in labor reform circles in California, Seema Weatherwax assumed Guthrie had not written "This Land" when they visited the migrant camps around Los Angeles in early 1940 because he never performed it for the laborers or their families. Seema Weatherwax, interview by Jane Yett. "In Touch with the Human Spirit: On the Road with Woody Guthrie." *Californians* 10:4, 1993: 33.

2. Clifton Fadiman. "Minstrel Boy." *The New Yorker*. 19:5 (March), 1943: 68.

3. WGA Songs 1, Box 3, Folder 27.

4. Generally, the popular version consists of the following chorus and three verses:

> (Chorus)
> This land is your land, this land is my land,
> From California to the New York island;
> From the redwood forest to the Gulf Stream waters,
> This land was made for you and me.

As I was walking that ribbon of highway,
I saw above me that endless skyway.
I saw below me that golden valley.
This land was made for you and me.

I've roamed and rambled, and I followed my footsteps
To the sparkling sands of her diamond deserts;
And all around me a voice was sounding:
"This land was made for you and me."

When the sun came shining and I was strolling
As the wheat fields waving and the dust clouds rolling.
As the fog was lifting, a voice was chanting,
"This land was made for you and me."

5. Laurence Bergreen. *As Thousands Cheer: The Life of Irving Berlin*. New York: Viking Press, 1990: 155.

6. "What Makes a Song: A Talk with Irving Berlin." *New York Times Magazine*. July 28, 1940: 7.

7. Charles Braun. "Let's Waive 'The Star-Spangled Banner.'" *Fact*. 2:1 (January/February), 1965: 8.

8. Quoted in Bergreen 370.

9. Irving Berlin. *Songs of Irving Berlin*. Milwaukee: Hal Leonard Corporation, 1998: 16.

10. David Ewen. *The Story of Irving Berlin*. New York: Henry Holt and Company, 1950: 124; and Michael Freedland. *A Salute to Irving Berlin*. London: W. H. Allen, 1986: 178.

11. The sheet music sales figures from this time period appear in the following issues of *Variety* magazine in 1939: February 15, no. 12; February 22, no. 13; March 1, no. 9; March 8, no. 10; March 15, no. 9; March 22, no. 5; March 29, no. 6; April 5, no. 11; April 19, no. 6; April 26, no. 7; May 3, no. 10; May 10, no. 10; May 17, no. 13; May 24, no. 8; May 31, no. 12; June 7, no. 13; June 28, no. 13; July 12, no. 13.

12. "Footnotes on Headliners." *New York Times*. July 14, 1940: 4.

13. Joe Klein. *Woody Guthrie: A Life*. New York: Delta, 1999: 140–41.

14. Woody Guthrie. *Sing Out!* 17:6 (December/January), 1967/68: 4.

15. Woody Guthrie. *American Folksong*. New York: Oak Publications, 1961: 4.

16. Klein 142.

17. WGP Box 2, Folder 3.

18. Woody Guthrie. *Born to Win*. New York: MacMillan Company, 1965: 146; and "Irving Berlin Tells Adela Rogers St. Johns: 'I'd Like to Write a Great Peace Song.'" *New York Journal American*. September 4, 1938: E:3.

19. Woody Guthrie, letter to Alan Lomax. September 19, 1940, WGMC Box 1, Correspondence folder.

20. Ed Cray. *Ramblin' Man: The Life and Times of Woody Guthrie*. New York: W. W. Norton: 165; Guy Logsdon. "Notes on the Songs." *This Land Is Your Land: The Asch Recordings, Vol. 1*. Smithsonian Folkways Records, 1997: 10; and Guy Logsdon. "Woody's Roots." *The Music Journal*. December, 1976: 21.

21. Woody Guthrie. "Mario Russo." WGP Box 4, Folder 2.

22. WGA Songs 1, Box 3, Folder 27.

23. Ernie Marrs. "The Rest of the Song." *Broadside*. No. 8 (January), 1968: 8.

24. Woody Guthrie, letter to Marjorie Mazia. December 17, 1942: 4–6. WGA Songs 2, Notebook 11.

25. "Army, Navy Back Bill to Hit Aliens." *New York Times*. April 13, 1939: 92.

26. *This Land Is Your Land: The Asch Recordings, Vol. 1*. Smithsonian Folkways Records, 1997: Track 14.

27. Woody Guthrie. *Ten of Woody Guthrie's Twenty-Five Cent Songs*. (c. 1945): 7. A copy of this mimeographed songbook is held in the WGP Box 2, Folder 1.

28. Gordon Friesen. "Woody Guthrie: Hard Travellin'." *Mainstream*. 16:8, 1963: 5.

29. Guthrie, *Ten of Woody Guthrie's Twenty-Five Cent Songs* 3.

30. Jeff Place, interview with author. March 31, 1999.

31. *This Land Is Your Land*. Folkways Records, 1951: Side 1, Track 1; and Pete Seeger. "A Tribute to Woody Guthrie." *This Land Is Your Land*. Woody Guthrie and Kathy Jakobsen. New York: Little, Brown and Company, 1998: 30. In this article, Seeger mistakenly writes that he heard this recording in 1949, rather than in 1951 when Folkways first released it.

32. *Bound for Glory. The Songs and Story of Woody Guthrie*. Folkways Records, 1956: Side 2, Track 1; *Songs to Grow On: American Work Songs, Vol. 3*. Folkways Records, 1961: Side 1, Track 1; *The Folk Box*. Elektra Records, 1964: Side 7, Track 10; *The Greatest Songs of Woody Guthrie*. Vanguard, 1972: Side 1, Track 1; *Bonneville Dam and Other Columbia River Songs*. Verve/Folkways, 1966: Side 2, Track 1; *This Land Is Your Land*. Folkways Records, 1967: Side 2, Track 1; *World of Popular Music: Folk and Country*. Follett Publishing Company, 1975: Side 5, Track 10; *Original Recordings Made by Woody Guthrie*. Warner Brothers, 1977: Side 2, Track 5; *Folkways: The Original Vision*. Smithsonian Folkways Records, 1988: Side 2, Track 7; *Troubadours of the Folk Era, Vol. 1*. Rhino Records, 1992: Track 1; *Folk Hits Around the Campfire*. K-Tel, 1995: Track 2; *American Roots Collection*. Smithsonian Folkways Records, 1996: Track 15; *This Land Is Your Land: The Asch Recordings, Vol. 1*. Smithsonian Folkways Records, 1997: Track 1.

33. Woody Guthrie. "This Land Is Your Land." Decca Records, January 1952. A recording of this track is held by the Ralph Rinzler Archives. Guthrie wrote another version similar to this one. It is held by the Woody Guthrie Archives, Songs 1, Box 3, Folder 27.

34. *Songs for Political Action: Folkmusic, Topical Songs, and the American Left 1926–1953*. Comp. and ed. by Ronald Cohen and Dave Samuelson. Bear Family Records, 1996: Disc 10, Track 31.

35. Moses Asch, interview by Israel Young. "Moses Asch: Twentieth Century Man, Part II." *Sing Out!* 26:2, 1977: 26.

36. Klein 286.

37. Klein xii.

38. Klein 458.

39. Pete Seeger. *Where Have All the Flowers Gone.* Bethlehem: Sing Out Publications, 1993: 142.

40. Harold Leventhal, interview with author. October 16, 1998.

41. Judy Bell, interview with author. November 28, 2001; and Klein 375.

42. Examples of these publishers are Birchard, Silver Berdett, and Ginn, as noted by Judy Bell in an interview with author. November 3, 2000.

43. Klein 375.

44. John Cashman. "Folk Hero." *New York Post.* April 19, 1966: 27:1.

45. Hendrick Hertzberg. "Star-Spangled Banter." *The New Yorker.* 73:20 (July 21), 1997: 5.

46. *Sing Out!* 4:7, 1954: 3; *Reprints from Sing Out! Vol.* 1. Ed. Irwin Silber. New York: Oak Publication, 1959: 1; and *The Collected Reprints from Sing Out!* (1959–64) Vol. 1–6. Ed. Irwin Silber, Paul Nelson, Ethel Raim, Pete Seeger, and Jerry Silverman. Bethlehem: Sing Out Publications, 1990: 4.

47. Woody Guthrie. *California to the New York Island: Being a Pocketful of Brags, Blues, Bad-Men, Ballads, Love Songs, Okie Laments and Children's Catcalls by Woody Guthrie.* Ed. Millard Lampell. New York: The Guthrie Children's Trust Fund, 1958: 45.

48. Woody Guthrie. *Woody Guthrie Folk Songs: A Collection of Songs by America's Foremost Balladeer.* Ed. Pete Seeger. New York: Ludlow Music, 1963: 7.

49. *Variety.* May 1, 1963: 75.

50. Seeger, *Where Have All the Flowers Gone* 143.

51. The better known of these artists include Paul Anka, Harry Belafonte, the Brothers Four, Glen Campbell, David Carradine, the Mike Curb Congregation, Jim Croce, Bing Crosby, Jack Elliott, Lester Flatt and Earl Scruggs, Connie Francis, Arlo Guthrie, the Harvesters, Ella Jenkins, the Kingston Trio, the Limeliters, Loretta Lynn, Jay and the Americans, Country Joe McDonald, the Mormon Tabernacle Choir, the New Christy Minstrels, Odetta, Peter, Paul, and Mary, Tex Ritter, Earl Robinson, Pete Seeger, the Staple Singers, Bruce Springsteen, the Tarriers, the Wayfarers, the Weavers, and Glen Yarbrough.

52. *The Bosses' Songbook: Songs to Stifle the Flames of Discontent.* 2nd ed. Collected and edited by Dave Van Ronk and Richard Ellington. New York: R. Ellington, 1959: 3, 8, 14.

53. *The Bosses' Songbook* 22.

54. *The Bosses' Songbook* 22.

55. Marrs 8, 9.

56. *American Favorite Ballads: Tunes and Songs as Sung by Pete Seeger.* New York: Oak Publications, 1961: 30. This songbook primarily draws upon the selections Seeger included in the Folkways five-volume series *American Favorite Ballads*, although "This Land Is Your Land" does not appear on any of these albums.

57. "Woody Guthrie/Another Image." *Sing Out!* 18:4 (October/November), 1968: 34.

58. *A Tribute to Woody Guthrie*. Warner Brothers Records, 1972: Track 27.

59. *A Tribute to Woody Guthrie* Track 27.

60. *A Tribute to Woody Guthrie*. New York: Ludlow Music, 1972: 65.

61. Pete Seeger. "Portrait of a Song as a Bird in Flight." *Village Voice*. July 1, 1971: 5.

62. *The Vietnam Songbook*. Ed. Barbara Dane and Irwin Silber. New York: The Guardian, 1969: 128.

63. Seeger, "Portrait of a Song as a Bird in Flight" 5.

64. Woody Guthrie, letter to Columbia Recording Company. (c. June 1942.) WGMC Box 1, Correspondence folder.

65. Seeger, "Portrait of a Song as a Bird in Flight" 5. However, it was only in a version of this article in his 1993 book *Where Have All the Flowers Gone* (p. 145) that Seeger actually attributed the first of these verses to McDonald.

66. Judy Bell, interview with author. February 1, 1999.

67. Woody Guthrie. *101 Woody Guthrie Songs, Including All the Songs from "Bound for Glory."* Ludlow Music, 1977: 86–88.

68. *Bound for Glory*. Directed by Hal Ashby. United Artists, 1976. Re-released by MGM/UA Home Video, 1991.

69. *Woody Guthrie: Hard Travelin'.* Directed by Jim Brown. Ginger Group and Harold Leventhal Management, 1984. Re-released on MGM/UA Home Video, 1986.

70. *A Vision Shared: A Tribute to Woody Guthrie and Lead Belly*. CBS Records, 1988: Track 14.

71. Seeger, *Where Have All the Flowers Gone* 143.

72. Tom Burton, interview with author. March 2, 1999.

73. Jerome L. Rodnitzky. *Minstrels of the Dawn: The Folk-Protest Singer as a Cultural Hero.* Chicago: Nelson Hall, 1976: 146.

74. Howard Zinn. *Postwar America: 1945–1971.* Indianapolis: Bobbs-Merrill Company, 1973: 179.

75. Peter D. Goldsmith. *Making People's Music: Moe Asch and Folkways Records.* Washington: Smithsonian Press, 1998: 360.

76. Wayne Hampton. *Guerrilla Minstrels: John Lennon, Joe Hill, Woody Guthrie, Bob Dylan.* Knoxville: University of Tennessee Press, 1986: 243.

77. Kristi Witker. *How to Lose Everything in Politics Except Massachusetts.* New York: Manson and Lipscomb, 1974: 135.

78. Seeger, *Where Have All the Flowers Gone* 144.

79. David Dunaway. *How Can I Keep from Singing: Pete Seeger.* New York: McGraw-Hill, 1981: 276.

80. Seeger, "Portrait of a Song as a Bird in Flight" 5. However, it was only in his 1993 book *Where Have All the Flowers Gone* (p. 145) that Seeger actually attributed this verse to Cappy Israel.

81. Greil Marcus. *Mystery Train: Images of America in Rock 'n' Roll Music.* New York: E. P. Dutton, 1976: 125.

82. For particulars concerning this issue, see Dave Marsh's *Glory Days: Bruce Springsteen in the 1980s*. New York: Pantheon Books, 1987: 255, 260–64, 266; and Jon Wiener's *Professors, Politics and Pop*. London: Verso, 1991: 309.

83. Quoted by Mark Rowland. "Notebooks of Plenty." *Musician*. No. 236 (July), 1998: 23.

Chapter Two

1. WGA Songs 1, Box 3, Folder 27.

2. Woody Guthrie. *Bound for Glory*. New York: Plume, 1983: 295.

3. Nicholas Dawidoff. *In the Country of Country: People and Places in American Music*. New York: Pantheon Books 1997: 7.

4. Quoted in Pete Seeger's *The Incompleat Folksinger*. Lincoln, Nebraska: University of Nebraska, 1992: 59.

5. Woody Guthrie, letter to Alan Lomax. September 19, 1940. WGMC Box 1, Correspondence folder.

6. In discussing Steinbeck's *Grapes of Wrath*, Guthrie states that the novel "is about us pullin' out of Oklahoma and Arkansas and down south and driftin' around over the state of California, busted, disgusted, down and out and lookin' for work. Shows you how come us got to be that way. Shows the damn bankers, men that broke us and the dust that choked us, and it comes right out in plain English and says what to do about it." Quoted in Ed Robbin's *Woody Guthrie and Me: An Intimate Reminiscence*. Berkeley, California: Lancaster-Miller Publishers, 1979: 31.

7. He not only published this piece in his first professionally produced songbook but also recorded it on April 25, 1944, although it was not released until 1964. Woody Guthrie. *Woody and Lefty Lou's Favorite Collection: Old Time Hill Country Songs, Being Sung for Ages Still Going Strong*. Gardena, California: Spanish American Institute Press, 1937. N. pag.; *Woody Guthrie Sings Folk Songs, Vol II*. Folkways Records, 1964: Side 1, Track 4.

8. Woody Guthrie. *Alonzo M. Zilch's Own Collection of Original Songs and Ballads*. (c. 1935): 5, 8, 10. A copy of this mimeographed songbook is held in the WGMC Box 1, Folder 1.

9. *Woody Guthrie: Dust Bowl Ballads*. Rounder Records, 1988: Track 3.

10. Guthrie, *Bound for Glory* 178.

11. Guy Logsdon. Liner Notes. *Dust Bowl Ballads*. Rounder Records, 1988.

12. *Woody Guthrie: Hard Travelin'*. Directed by Jim Brown. Ginger Group/Harold Leventhal Management, Inc. Film, 1984. Re-released on MGM/UA Home Video, 1986.

13. Woody Guthrie. *Library of Congress Recordings*. Rounder Records, 1988: Disc 1, Track 8.

14. Joe Klein. *Woody Guthrie: A Life*. New York: Delta, 1999: 71; Ed Cray. *Ramblin' Man: The Life and Times of Woody Guthrie*. New York: W.W. Norton: 69.

15. Guthrie, *Dust Bowl Ballads* Track 14.

16. Guthrie, *Dust Bowl Ballads* Track 14.

17. Guthrie, *Library of Congress Recordings* Disc 1, Track 8.

18. *Surviving the Dust Bowl*. Directed by Ghana Gazit and David Steward. WGBH Boston Educational Foundation, 1998.

19. Guthrie, *Dust Bowl Ballads* Track 14.

20. Thomas Alfred Tripp. "Dust Bowl Tragedy." *Christian Century* 57:4, 1940: 109.

21. Klein 371.

22. Guthrie, *Dust Bowl Ballads* Track 14.

23. Guthrie, *Library of Congress Recordings* Disc 1, Track 9.

24. Donald Worster. *Dust Bowl: The Southern Plains in the* 1930s. New York: Oxford University Press, 1979: 170.

25. Caroline Henderson. "Letters from the Dust Bowl." *The Atlantic* 157:5, 1936: 550.

26. Guthrie, *Dust Bowl Ballads* Track 14.

27. *Grant County Republican* August 27, 1936: 1.

28. James N. Gregory. *American Exodus: The Dust Bowl Migration and Okie Culture in California*. New York: Oxford University Press, 1989: 201.

29. WGP Box 1, Folder 2.

30. Woody Guthrie. *Songs of Woody Guthrie*. (c. 1941): 7. Copy held by WGMC Box 2.

31. Guthrie, *Dust Bowl Ballads* Track 1.

32. Guthrie, *Dust Bowl Ballads* Track 1.

33. Guthrie, *Dust Bowl Ballads* Track 1.

34. Guthrie, *Dust Bowl Ballads* Track 1.

35. Guthrie, *Dust Bowl Ballads* Track 1.

36. Guthrie, *Songs of Woody Guthrie* 7.

37. Worster 20–21.

38. Klein 70.

39. Guthrie, *Dust Bowl Ballads* Track 6.

40. Guthrie, *Dust Bowl Ballads* Track 6.

41. Guthrie, *Songs of Woody Guthrie* 8.

42. Guthrie, *Dust Bowl Ballads* Track 5.

43. Gregory 11.

44. Carey McWilliams. *Factories in the Field: The Story of Migratory Farm Labor in California*. Boston: Little, Brown, and Company, 1939: 306.

45. Guthrie, *Dust Bowl Ballads* Track 11.

46. *Songs of Work and Protest*. Ed. Edith Fowke and Joe Glazer. New York: Dover Publications, 1973: 104–105. Guthrie sings a fragment of Miller's song, which the singer calls "Seven Cent Cotton" in the unedited interview with Alan Lomax. March 22, 1941. Copy held by American Folklife Center at the Library of Congress.

47. Paul Taylor and Dorothea Lange. *An American Exodus*. New York: Reynal & Hitchcock, 1939: 14.

48. US Bureau of the Census. *Fifteenth Census of the United States: 1930 Agriculture*. Vol. II, Part I. Washington: Government Printing Office, 1932: 30–31.

49. Taylor and Lange 50.

50. David Eugene Conrad. *The Forgotten Farmers: The Story of Sharecroppers in the New Deal*. Urbana: University of Illinois, 1965: 1–2.

51. Anna Rochester. *Why Farmers Are Poor: The Agricultural Crisis in the United States*. New York: International Publishers, 1940: 60.

52. Lorena Hickok. *One Third of a Nation: Lorena Hickok Reports on the Great Depression*. Urbana, Illinois: University of Illinois Press, 1981: 186, 158.

53. Guthrie, *Bound for Glory* 41.

54. Woody Guthrie. *Pastures of Plenty: A Self-Portrait*. Ed. Dave Marsh and Harold Leventhal. New York: Harper Perennial, 1992: 23.

55. John Handcox. *John Handcox: Songs, Poems, and Stories of the Southern Tenant Farmers Union*. Morgantown: West Virginia University Press, 2004: Track 1.

56. H. L. Mitchell. *Mean Things Happening in This Land: The Life and Times of H. L. Mitchell, Co-Founder of the Southern Tenant Farmers Union*. Montclair: Allanheld Osmun & Company, 1979: 77.

57. Woody Guthrie. *Hard Hitting Songs for Hard-Hit People*. Lincoln: University of Nebraska Press, 1999: 266–73, 276–77.

58. Woody Guthrie. *101 Woody Guthrie Songs Including All the Songs from "Bound of Glory."* New York: Ludlow Music, 1977: 107.

59. Guthrie, *Songs of Woody Guthrie* 128.

60. Woody Guthrie. *American Folksong*. New York: Oak Publications, 1961: 37.

61. WGP Box 1, Folder 1.

62. Guthrie, *Dust Bowl Ballads* Track 2.

63. Guthrie, *American Folksong* 19.

64. Taylor and Lange 82.

65. Paul Taylor. "Power Farming and Labor Displacement." *Monthly Labor Review*. 46:4, 1938: 852–53, 55, 65.

66. Guthrie, *Songs of Woody Guthrie* 93.

67. Guthrie, *Dust Bowl Ballads* Track 5, 9, and 10. The term "Cats" in this last quote refers to Caterpillar tractors, which became quite prevalent in American agriculture by the early 1940s.

68. Studs Terkel. "Woody Guthrie: The Last of the Great Balladeers." *Climax* 9:3, 1961: 61.

69. *The Songs of the Gold Rush*. Ed. Richard A. Dwyer and Richard E. Lingenfelter. Berkeley: University of California Press, 1964: 15.

70. William Stott. *Documentary Expression and Thirties America*. New York: Oxford University Press, 1973: 186. Ironically, though, the pamphlet's author, James Rorty, later wrote a sarcastically titled travelogue book also called *Where Life Is Better*, in which the ills of America that he found are documented in great and unrelenting detail.

71. Gerald Haslam, Stephen Johnson, and Robert Dawson. *The Great Central Valley: California's Heartland*. Berkeley: University of California Press, 1993: x, 107.

72. Todd-Sonkin Recordings. September 29, 1939; August 1, 1940; and August 9, 1940. Copies held by the American Folklife Center at the Library of Congress.

73. McWilliams 193–96.

74. Guthrie, *Library of Congress Recordings* Disc 3, Track 5.

75. Guthrie, *Library of Congress Recordings* Disc 3, Track 5.

76. Jimmie Rodgers. *Jimmie Rodgers, 1928–1929: The Early Years*. Rounder Records, 1990: Track 2.

77. Guthrie, *Woody and Lefty Lou's Favorite Collection*. N. pag.

78. Gregory 31–34.

79. Guthrie, *Dust Bowl Ballads* Track 3.

80. Charles Todd and Robert Sonkin. "Ballad of the Okies." *New York Times Magazine* November 17, 1940: 6.

81. *The Grapes of Wrath*. Directed by John Ford. Warner Brothers, 1940.

82. Guthrie, *Hard Hitting Songs for Hard-Hit People* 215.

83. Greenway 206–207.

84. Guthrie, *Library of Congress Recordings* Disc 3, Track 5.

85. Guthrie, *Bound for Glory* 255.

86. Guthrie, *Hard Hitting Songs for Hard-Hit People* 217.

87. Michael Wallis. *Route 66: The Mother Road*. New York: St. Martin's Press, 1990: 9.

88. John Steinbeck. *The Grapes of Wrath*. New York: Penguin Books, 1981: 127–28.

89. Seymour J. Janow and William Gilmartin. "Labor and Agricultural Migration to California, 1935–40." *Monthly Labor Review* 53:1, 1941: 18, 20, 23, 24.

90. Woody Guthrie. *Ten of Woody Guthrie's Twenty-Five Cent Songs*. (c. 1945): 3 and 8. A copy of this mimeographed songbook is held by the WGP Box 2, Folder 1.

91. Guthrie, *Hard Hitting Songs for Hard-Hit People* 62–63.

92. Guthrie, *Library of Congress Recordings* Disc 3, Track 7.

93. Guthrie, *Library of Congress Recordings* Disc 3, Track 7.

94. Kevin Starr. *Endangered Dreams: The Great Depression in California*. New York: Oxford University Press, 1996: 177–79.

95. Guthrie, *Woody and Lefty Lou's Favorite Collection*. N. pag.

96. Guthrie, *Dust Bowl Ballads* Track 12.

97. Guthrie, *Dust Bowl Ballads* Track 12.

98. Guthrie, *Library of Congress Recordings* Disc 1, Track 11. Throughout his tenure (1934–39), stalwart pro-business Republican Governor Frank Merriam had no sympathy for the poor who streamed to his state looking for new opportunities.

99. Guthrie, *Woody and Lefty Lou's Favorite Collection*. N. pag.

100. Guthrie, *Dust Bowl Ballads* Track 9.

101. McWilliams 5.

102. Steinbeck 225.

103. Guthrie, *Library of Congress Recordings* Disc 3, Track 5.

104. Guthrie, *Dust Bowl Ballads* Track 11.

105. Quoted in Bill Ganzel's *Dust Bowl Descent*. Lincoln: University of Nebraska Press, 1984: 30.

106. Quoted in McWilliams 225.

107. Quoted in Paul Hemphill's "Merle Haggard." *Atlantic Monthly* 228:3, 1971: 100.

108. Guthrie, *Library of Congress Recordings* Disc 3, Track 5.

109. Guthrie, *American Folksong* 39.

110. Quoted in McWilliams 319.

111. Guthrie, *American Folksong* 39.

112. Quoted in Gregory 9.

113. McWilliams 193–94; and Starr 227.

114. Quoted in Leon Harris's *Upton Sinclair: American Rebel*. New York: Crowell, 1975: 306.

115. Woody Guthrie. "Migratious Workers Take Lots of Abuse." *People's World*. May 23, 1939: 4.

116. Kenneth Crist. "Career Men—in Relief." *Los Angeles Times Sunday Magazine*. May 14, 1939: 4–5, 8. My thanks to Pete LaChapelle for sharing this article from his own research on Guthrie.

117. Guthrie, "Migratious Workers" 4.

118. Guthrie, *Pastures of Plenty* 38.

119. Dave Marsh. Introduction to "The Govt Road." *Pastures of Plenty* 37.

120. Woody Guthrie. *Columbia River Collection*. Rounder Records, 1987: Track 16.

121. Guthrie, *Columbia River Collection* Track 16.

122. Lionel Trilling. "Greatness with One Fault in It." *Kenyon Review*. 4:1 (Winter), 1942: 102.

123. Klein 100.

124. Guthrie, *Born to Win* 223–24.

Chapter Three

1. James R. Curtis. "Woody Guthrie and the Dust Bowl." *The Sounds of People and Places: Readings in the Geography of American Folk and Popular Music*. Ed. George Carney. Lanham: University Press of America, 1987: 276.

2. WGMC Box 1, Folder 2.

3. WGP Box 1, Folder 1.

4. Woody Guthrie. *Songs of Woody Guthrie*. (c. 1941): 56. Copy held by WGMC Box 2.

5. U.S. Department of Commerce, Bureau of the Census. *Historical Statistics of the United States, Colonial Times to 1970*, Series G-319-336. Washington: Government Printing Office, 1975: 301.

6. Ed Cray. *Ramblin' Man: The Life and Times of Woody Guthrie*. New York: W. W. Norton: 5.

7. Joe Klein. *Woody Guthrie: A Life*. New York: Delta, 1999: 126.

8. Woody Guthrie. *American Folksong*. New York: Oak Publications, 1961: 5.

9. Guthrie, *Songs of Woody Guthrie* 22, 37.

10. Woody Guthrie. *Dust Bowl Ballads*. Rounder Records, 1988: Track 2.

11. Guthrie, *Songs of Woody Guthrie* 87.

12. Guthrie, *Songs of Woody Guthrie* 93.

13. Guthrie, *Songs of Woody Guthrie* 93.

14. Lorena Hickok. *One Third of a Nation: Lorena Hickok Reports on the Great Depression.* Ed. Richard Lowitt and Maurine Beasley. Urbana: University of Illinois Press, 1981: 106.

15. Quoted in Hickok 345.

16. Ronald D. Eller. *Miners, Millhands, and Mountaineers: Industrialization of the Appalachian South, 1880–1930*. Knoxville: University of Tennessee, 1982: 159.

17. Hickok 130, 133; George Korson. *Songs and Ballads of the Anthracite Miner*. New York: Grafton Press, 1926: xviii; and Eller 174–75.

18. For example, he generally refers to workers in "The Final Call" (WGMC Box 1, Folder 1), "Ramblin' Blues" (WGP Box 1, Folder 6), and "Baking for Wallace" (WGP Box 1, Folder 1).

19. Woody Guthrie. *Bound for Glory*. New York: Plume, 1983: 249.

20. Woody Guthrie. *Alonzo M. Zilch's Own Collection of Original Songs and Ballads.* (c. 1935): 16. A copy of this mimeographed songbook is held in the WGMC Box 1, Folder 1.

21. Guy Logsdon. "Notes On the Songs." *Buffalo Skinners: The Asch Recordings, Vol. 4.* Smithsonian Folkways Records, 1999: 16.

22. Woody Guthrie. *Struggle*. Smithsonian Folkways Records, 1990: Track 3.

23. Guthrie, *Struggle* Track 9.

24. Logsdon, "Notes On the Songs." *Buffalo Skinners*, 13.

25. Guthrie, *Bound for Glory* 40.

26. Quoted in Woody Guthrie's *Roll On Columbia: The Columbia River Collection*. Ed. Bill Murlin. Bethlehem: Sing Out Publications, 1991: 89.

27. Pete Seeger and Robert Santelli. "Hobo's Lullaby." *Hard Travelin': The Life and Legacy of Woody Guthrie*. Ed. Robert Santelli and Emily Davidson. Hanover: Wesleyan University Press, 1999:29.

28. WGP Box 2, Folder 3.

29. Woody Guthrie. *My New Found Land*. (c. 1946): 78. Microfilmed copy held by the Performing Arts Reading Room, Library of Congress.

30. Guthrie, *Roll on Columbia* 74.

31. Guthrie, *My New Found Land* 81.

32. Guthrie, *Roll On Columbia* 75.

33. Guthrie, *Roll On Columbia* 75.

34. Hickok 352.

35. Vernon H. Jensen. *Lumber and Labor*. New York: Arno and The New York Times, 1971: 11; and Hickok 352.

36. Guthrie, *Roll On Columbia* 61, 75–76.

37. Guthrie, *Roll On Columbia* 75–76.

38. Woody Guthrie. *The Woody Guthrie Songbook*. Ed. Harold Leventhal and Marjorie Guthrie. New York: Grosset and Dunlap, 1976: 61.

39. Guthrie, *My New Found Land* 81–82.

40. Guthrie, *Roll On Columbia* 46–47.

41. WGMC Box 1, Folder 7.

42. Guthrie, *My New Found Land* 78.

43. Guthrie, *Roll On Columbia* 48–49, 52–53.

44. Quoted in Klein 222.

45. Guthrie, *Roll On Columbia* 28–29.

46. Klein 206.

47. WGP Box 3, Folder 6.

48. *The Collected Reprints from Sing Out! The Folk Song Magazine*. Vols. 1–6, 1959–1964. Ed. Irwin Silber, Paul Nelson, Ethel Raim, Pete Seeger, and Jerry Silverman. Bethlehem: Sing Out Publications, 1990: 47.

49. Hickok 352–53.

50. WGP Box 3, Folder 6; and Woody Guthrie. *California to the New York Island: Being a Pocketful of Brags, Blues, Bad-Men Ballads, Love Songs, Okie Laments and Children's Catcalls*. Ed. Millard Lampell. New York: The Guthrie Children's Trust Fund, 1958: 28.

51. Guthrie, *My New Found Land* 79.

52. Guthrie, *American Folksong* 2.

53. Archie Green. "Woody's Oil Songs." *Songs about Work: Essays in Occupational Culture*. Bloomington: Folklore Institute, 1993: 210.

54. Guthrie, *American Folksong* 23–24.

55. WGA Songs 3, Notebook 2.

56. *Thirteenth Convention Proceedings*. Fort Worth: Oil Workers International Union, 1942: 33. Quoted in Green 211.

57. "Arbitration Urged on T.W.U. by Quill." *New York Times*. January 7, 1943: 40.

58. WGP Box 1, Folder 4.

59. Rhoda Epstein. "Overcrowded Subway Trains." *New York Times*. February 20, 1943: 12.

60. WGP Box 1, Folder 4.

61. "Transit Safety Held Unimpaired." *New York Times*. February 11, 1943: 21.

62. "Mayor Prescribes Rest by Trainmen." *New York Times*. June 6, 1944: 19.

63. WGP Box 1, Folder 4.

64. Guthrie, *American Folksong* 2.

65. John Greenway. *American Folksongs of Protest*. Philadelphia: University of Pennsylvania Press, 1953: 295.

66. George Korson. *Coal Dust on the Fiddle: Songs and Stories of the Bituminous Industry*. Philadelphia: University of Pennsylvania Press, 1943: 4, 14–5; and Hickok 22–3, 26, 31.

67. Guthrie, *Bound for Glory* 40; and Guthrie, *American Folksong* 2.

68. WGP Box 3, Folder 6.

69. Guthrie, *American Folksong* 2.

70. Guthrie, *Songs of Woody Guthrie* 154.

71. Woody Guthrie, letter to Alan Lomax. (c. July 1940.) WGMC Box 1, Correspondence folder.

72. Guthrie, *American Folksong* 10–11.

73. Guthrie, *Alonzo M. Zilch's* 3.

74. Guthrie, *California to the New York Island* 28.

75. Guthrie, *My New Found Land* 78.

76. Guy Logsdon. "Notes on the Songs." *Hard Travelin': The Asch Recordings, Vol. 3.* Smithsonian Folkways Records, 1998: 29.

77. Guthrie, *Hard Travelin'* Track 22.

78. Mother Bloor. *We Are Many.* New York: International Publishers, 1940: 118–38.

79. Woodbridge N. Ferris, Records Relating to Labor Strike in Copper Mining Industry, 1913–14, Michigan State Archives, RG-46, B1, F1.

80. Arthur Thurner. *Rebels on the Range: The Michigan Copper Miners' Strike of 1913–1914.* Lake Kinden, Michigan: John H. Forster Press, 1984: 48, 69–74, 115, 134.

81. Thurner 141–42.

82. Bloor 122–24.

83. Thurner 151.

84. Guthrie, *Struggle* Track 12.

85. Guthrie, *Struggle* Track 12.

86. Thurner 167–71.

87. For example, Guy Logsdon repeats the errors in his notes for "1913 Massacre" in *Hard Travelin'*, 24.

88. George McGovern and Leonard F. Guttridge. *The Great Coalfield War.* Niwot: University Press of Colorado, 1996: 186; and Mother Jones. *The Autobiography of Mother Jones.* Chicago: Charles H. Kerr and Company, 1925: 183.

89. McGovern and Guttridge 219, 221, 223, 230.

90. Guthrie, *Struggle* Track 11.

91. Guthrie, *Struggle* Track 11.

92. Earl Robinson and Alfred Hayes. *Hard Hitting Songs for Hard-Hit People.* Ed. Alan Lomax, Woody Guthrie, and Pete Seeger. Lincoln: University of Nebraska, 1999: 332–33; and Archie Green. "Woody's Oil Songs." *Songs about Work: Essays in Occupational Culture.* Bloomington: Folklore Institute, 1993: 210–11.

93. For details concerning the whole of this conflict, see George McGovern and Leonard F. Guttridge. *The Great Coalfield War.* Niwot: University Press of Colorado, 1996; *Massacre at Ludlow.* Ed. Leon Stein and Philip Taft. New York: Arno, 1971; and Howard Zinn. "The Colorado Coal Strike, 1913–14." *Three Strikes.* Boston: Beacon Press, 2001: 7–55.

94. "Krug Report Submitted." *New York Times.* April 4, 1947, 3:1.

95. H. B. Humphrey. *Historical Summary of Coal-Mine Explosions in the United States.* Washington: US Printing Office, 1959: 168–74.

96. "Mine Conditions Criticized." *New York Times.* March 27, 1947, 5; and Joseph Loftus. "U.S. Chief Explains Centralia Inquiry." *New York Times.* April 12, 1947: 2.

97. "Medill Is Accused in Mine Disaster." *New York Times.* April 1, 1947, 22.

98. Quoted in "Inquiries Finished at Centralia Mine." *New York Times.* April 6, 1947, 5.

99. Woody Guthrie. "Three Songs for Centralia." *People's Songs.* 2:4 (May), 1947: 6–7.

100. WGP Box 1, Folder 5.

101. Woody Guthrie. *Long Ways to Travel: The Unreleased Folkways Masters, 1944–1949.* Smithsonian Folkways Records, 1994: Track 2.

102. Guthrie, *Long Ways to Travel* Track 2.

103. Guthrie, *Long Ways to Travel* Track 2.

104. WGP Box 1, Folder 3.

105. "Super-Blast Held Mine Death Cause." *New York Times.* April 5, 1947, 3:1.

106. "Dying Miners Wrote Notes to Their Families as Deadly Gas Swept on Them in Illinois Pit." *New York Times.* March 31, 1947, 8:3.

107. Guthrie, "Three Songs for Centralia" 7.

108. Guthrie, *Struggle* Track 6.

109. Guthrie, *Struggle* Track 6.

110. Guthrie, *Struggle* Track 5.

111. Guthrie, *Struggle* Track 5.

112. Korson 31.

113. Hickok 20.

114. Greenway 295.

115. Pinewood Tom. "Silicosis is Killing Me." *Hard Hitting Songs for Hard-Hit People* 134.

116. Woody Guthrie. "State Line to Skid Row." *Common Ground.* 3:1 (Autumn), 1942: 42.

117. Guthrie, *Hard Hitting Songs for Hard-Hit People* 154.

118. Quoted in Greenway's *American Folksongs of Protest* 295–96.

119. John Steinbeck. Foreword. *Hard Hitting Songs for Hard-Hit People* 8.

120. Walt Whitman. "1855 Preface to *Leaves of Grass.*" *Leaves of Grass.* Oxford: Oxford University Press, 1990: 452.

Chapter Four

1. Woody Guthrie. *Bound for* Glory. New York: Plume, 1983: 221–22.

2. Woody Guthrie, unedited interview with Alan Lomax for the Library of Congress. March 21, 1941. Copy held by American Folklife Center at the Library of Congress.

3. Woody Guthrie. *Woody Guthrie: Hard Travelin': Asch Recordings, Vol. 3.* Smithsonian Folkways Records, 1998: Track 6.

4. Music critic Dave Marsh refers to comments made by Jimmy Longhi and Joe Klein at a Woody Guthrie conference as evidence that some informed commentators see the singer as

"color-blind, not only free of race hatred but of the patronizing liberal condescension." Dave Marsh. "Deportees: Woody Guthrie's Unfinished Business." *Hard Travelin': The Life and Legacy of Woody Guthrie*. Ed. Robert Santelli and Emily Davidson. Hanover: University Press of New England, 1999: 171.

5. Marsh 174. The other essay in *Hard Travelin'* that discusses Guthrie's attitude towards race is Craig Werner's "Democratic Visions, Democratic Voices," 69–82.

6. *Woody and Lefty Lou's Favorite Collection: Old Time Hill Country Songs, Being Sung for Ages, Still Going Strong*. Gardena: Spanish American Institute Press, 1937. N. pag.

7. WGA Songs 1 Box 1, Folder 5.

8. Guthrie, *Bound for Glory* 266.

9. Joe Klein. *Woody Guthrie: A Life*. New York: Delta, 1999: 106.

10. Quoted in Ed Robbin's *Woody and Me: An Intimate Reminiscence*. Berkeley: Lancaster-Miller Publishers, 1979: 90.

11. WGP Box 4, Folder 1.

12. Cary McWilliams. *Factories in the Field: The Story of the Migratory Farm Labor in California*. Boston: Little, Brown, and Company, 1939: 129; and Cary McWilliams. "Getting Rid of the Mexican." *American Mercury* 28:11 (March), 1933: 323.

13. Walter J. Stein. *California and the Dust Bowl Migration*. Westport: Greenwood Press, Inc., 1973: 62.

14. Stein 215.

15. Klein 185.

16. John Greenway. *American Folksongs of Protest*. Philadelphia: University of Pennsylvania Press, 1953: 294.

17. Although Guthrie wrote the words, Martin Hoffman wrote the tune that now accompanies the song.

18. Woody Guthrie. *Woody Guthrie Sings Folk Songs: A Collection of Songs by America's Foremost Balladeer*. Ed. Pete Seeger. New York: Ludlow Music, 1963: 24–25.

19. Quoted in Ernesto Galarza's *Strangers in Our Fields* 2nd ed. Washington: Joint United States–Mexico Trade Union Committee, 1956: 1.

20. Guthrie, *Woody Guthrie Sings Folk Songs* 25.

21. Guthrie, *Woody Guthrie Sings Folk Songs* 25.

22. Guthrie, *Woody Guthrie Sings Folk Songs* 25.

23. Nanci Griffith and Joe Jackson. *Nanci Griffith's Other Voices: A Personal History of Folk Music*. New York: Three Rivers Press, 1998: 211.

24. Jimmie Lewis Franklin. *The Blacks in Oklahoma*. Norman: University of Oklahoma Press, 1980: vi.

25. Guthrie, unedited interview with Alan Lomax. March 21, 1941. Copy held by American Folklife Center at the Library of Congress.

26. Franklin vi, 17, 21–24, 29–31.

27. C. Vann Woodward. *The Strange Career of Jim Crow*. New York: Oxford University Press, 1957: 102.

28. Concerning the death toll of the Tulsa riot, various writers and scholars still do not agree on exact figures. See Scott Ellsworth. *Death in a Promised Land: Tulsa Race Riot of* 1921. Baton Rouge: Louisiana State Press, 1982: 66; James S. Hirsch. *Riot and Remembrance: The Tulsa Race War and Its Legacy.* Boston: Houghton Mifflin, 2002: 6, 249, 308; Tim Madigan. *The Burning: Massacre, Destruction, and the Tulsa Race Riot of* 1921. New York: St. Martin's Press, 2001: 222–24; and Alfred L. Brophy. *Reconstructing the Dreamland: The Tulsa Riot of* 1921. Oxford: Oxford University Press, 2002: 59–60.

29. The details of the Nelsons' end have been drawn from the following sources: Leon F. Litwack. "Hellhounds." *Without Sanctuary: Lynching Photography in* America. Twin Palm, 2000: 16; "Crime." *Crisis.* 2:3 (July 1911): 99–100; Notes to the Photographs. *Without Sanctuary: Lynching Photography in* America. Twin Palm, 2000: 178–80; and Klein 10.

30. Klein 10, 23.

31. Ed Cray. *Ramblin' Man: The Life and Times of Woody Guthrie.* New York: W. W. Norton, 2004: 5.

32. Richard Reuss. "Woody Guthrie's Okemah Revisited." *Broadside.* No. 80, 1967: 15.

33. The following examples come from song books that Guthrie was known to have used on his radio programs at KFVD. Endnote to "Little Liza Jane." KFVD Songbook (c. 1937): 175. Microfilmed copy held by WGA; Woody Guthrie. "Kitty Wells." *Songs of Woody Guthrie.* (c. 1941): 175. Copy held by WGMC Box 2; Klein 96–97.

34. Woody Guthrie. *Santa Monica Social Register Examine 'Er.* (c. 1936.) Microfilm copy held by WGA.

35. Stein 60.

36. Cary McWilliams. "California Pastoral." *Antioch Review.* 2:1, 1942: 116.

37. Howell Terrence, letter to Woody Guthrie. October 20, 1937. Microfilm copy held by WGA.

38. Klein 95.

39. WGA Songs 1, Box 3, Introductions folder.

40. WGP Box 3, Folder 6.

41. Nora Guthrie, interview with author. December 12, 2000.

42. See Mark Solomon's *The Cry Was Unity: Communists and African-Americans, 1917–1936.* Jackson: University Press of Mississippi, 1998; Mark Naison's *Communists in Harlem During the Depression.* Urbana: University of Illinois Press, 1983; and Wilson Record's *Race and Radicalism: The NAACP and the Communist Party in Conflict.* Ithaca: Cornell University Press, 1964 for in-depth discussions of the issues and history concerning the Communist Party's efforts to reach out to the black community during the first half of the twentieth century.

43. Quoted in Charles Wolfe and Kip Lornell's *The Life and Legacy of Leadbelly.* New York: DaCapo Press, 1999: 217.

44. Nora Guthrie, interview with author. December 12, 2000.

45. Klein 214.

46. Woody Guthrie. *American Folksong.* New York: Oak Publications, 1961: 7.

47. As told by Sonny Terry in *Woody Guthrie: Hard Travelin'.* Directed by Jim Brown. Ginger Group and Harold Leventhal Management, 1984. Re-released on MGM/UA Home Video, 1986.

48. Woody Guthrie, letter to Moses Asch. August 15, 1946. WGP Box 4, Folder 1.

49. Woody Guthrie. *My New Found Land.* (c. 1946): 28. Microfilmed copy held by Performing Arts Reading Room, Library of Congress.

50. WGP Box 1, Folder 1; This verse was never recorded although the song was in April 19, 1944.

51. Guthrie, *My New Found Land* 1.

52. Woodward 35.

53. *The Poll Tax Repeal Handbook.* Washington: National Committee to Abolish the Poll Tax, 1943: 56.

54. Woodward 68.

55. Barry Bingham. "Americans Without Votes." *The Poll Tax.* Washington: American Council on Public Affairs, 1940: 6.

56. Woody Guthrie, letter to Alan Lomax. September 1940. WGMC Box 3, Folder 8.

57. Harvard Sitkoff. *A New Deal for Blacks: The Emergence of Civil Rights as a National Issue, Volume I.* New York: Oxford University Press, 1978: 116–36.

58. Woody Guthrie. "Poll Tax Chain." *People's Songs.* Vol. 6, July 1946: 3.

59. Guthrie, "Poll Tax Chain" 3.

60. For example, see "Revolutionary Mind." WGP Box 1, Folder 7; and "This Train Is a Union Flyer." WGP Box 1, Folder 8.

61. WGMC Box 1, Folder 7.

62. Guthrie, "Poll Tax Chain" 3.

63. James H. Dormon. "The Strange Career of Jim Crow Rice." *Journal of Social History.* 3:2 (Winter), 1969–70: 110.

64. Woodward xiii.

65. Woody Guthrie. *Ten of Woody Guthrie's Twenty-Five Cent Songs.* (c. 1945): 4. A copy of this mimeographed songbook is held by WGP Box 2, Folder 1.

66. Woody Guthrie. "Big Guns." *Pastures of Plenty: A Self-Portrait.* Ed. Dave Marsh and Harold Leventhal. New York: Harper Perennial, 1992: 78.

67. Almanacs. "Jim Crow." *People's Songs.* 2:10 (November), 1947: 8.

68. WGP Box 1, Folder 5 and Box 2, Folder 2.

69. *The Collected Reprints from Sing Out! The Folk Song Magazine.* Vols. 1–6, 1959–1964. Ed. Irwin Silber, Paul Nelson, Ethel Raim, Pete Seeger, and Jerry Silverman. Bethlehem: Sing Out, 1990: 155.

70. WGP Box 1, Folder 1. Thomas Dewey was a Republican candidate for president in 1944 and 1948, Robert Taft was a Republican party leader, and Fred Hartley was the chairman of the House Labor Committee and a Republican from New Jersey; together, Taft and Hartley created the infamous Taft-Hartley act, which restricted labor rights in America.

71. "Study Is Ordered of Negro Deaths." *New York Times*. July 6, 1946: 1, 16; "Brothers Describe Freeport Killing." *New York Times*. July 18, 1946: 27, 41; and "Freeport Inquiry Closed by Dewey." *New York Times*. August 4, 1946: 1, 39.

72. WGP Box 1, Folder 3.

73. WGP Box 1, Folder 3. Guthrie mistakenly uses "Alonzo" rather than "Alfonso" in referencing the second Ferguson brother who was shot and killed.

74. WGP Box 1, Folder 3.

75. "Study Is Ordered of Negro Deaths" 1, 16; "Brothers Describe Freeport Killing" 27; and memo from Franklin H. Williams to Thurgood Marshall. March 19, 1946: 7. NAACP files, Part II. Box B32, Folder 8. Copy held by Manuscript Reading Room in the Library of Congress.

76. "Eyes Gouged Out by Carolina Cop." *Daily Worker*. July 13, 1946: 4; "Negro Vet's Blinding by Carolina Cops." *New York Post*. July 17, 1946, 24; "Acquit Cop Who Blinded Negro Vet." *Daily Worker*. November 6, 1946: 9; and "Police Chief Freed in Negro Beating." *New York Times*. November 6, 1946: 48.

77. WGP Box 1, Folder 1.

78. Woody Guthrie. "The Blinding of Isaac Woodard." *Born to Win*. Ed. Robert Shelton. New York: MacMillan Company, 1965: 229–30.

79. Guthrie, "The Blinding of Isaac Woodard" 230.

80. Guthrie, "The Blinding of Isaac Woodard" 230–31.

81. Greenway 281–82; and Klein 329.

82. Quoted in the liner notes to Woody Guthrie's *Struggle*. Smithsonian/Folkways, 1990.

83. Woody Guthrie. *Alonzo M. Zilch's Own Collection of Original Songs and Ballads*. (c. 1935): 1. A copy of this mimeographed songbook is held in the WGMC Box 1, Folder 1.

84. Guthrie, *Alonzo M. Zilch's Own Collection of Original Songs and Ballads* 17.

85. Woody Guthrie. *Library of Congress Recordings*. Rounder Records, 1988: Disc 2, Track 7.

86. Woody Guthrie. *Struggle*. Smithsonian Folkways Records, 1990: Track 8.

87. Guthrie, *My New Found Land* 38–39.

88. John W. Roberts. *From Trickster to Badman: The Black Folk Hero in Slavery and Freedom*. Philadelphia: University of Pennsylvania Press, 1989: 189.

89. Guthrie, *My New Found Land* 38–39.

90. Guthrie, *My New Found Land* 70.

91. Raymond Grann Lloyd. *White Supremacy in the United States: An Analysis of Its Historical Background, with Especial Reference to the Poll Tax*. Washington: Public Affairs Press, 1952: 6–8; and E. M. Beck and Steward E. Tolnay. "When Race Didn't Matter: Black and White Mob Violence against Their Own Color." *Under Sentence of Death: Lynchings in the South*. Ed. W. Fitzhugh Brundage. Chapell Hill: University of North Carolina, 1997: 133–34.

92. Quoted in David Margolick's *Strange Fruit: Billie Holiday, Café Society, and an Early Cry for Civil Rights*. Philadelphia: Running Press, 2000: 34–35.

93. Quoted in Charles Wolfe and Kip Lornell's *The Life and Legend of Leadbelly*. New York: DeCapo Press, 1999: 97–8.

94. Quoted in Robert Shelton's *The Josh White Song Book*. Chicago: Quadrangle Books, 1963: 17.

95. Woody Guthrie. "Woody's Artist Friend Paints Lynch Scene." *Daily Worker*. April 22, 1940: 7.

96. Guthrie, "Woody's Artist Friend Paints Lynch Scene" 7.

97. Guthrie, *My New Found Land* 78.

98. Guthrie, "Poll Tax Chain" 3.

99. Guthrie, *Pastures of Plenty* 36–37.

100. Guy Logsdon. "Notes on the Songs." *Buffalo Skinners: Asch Recordings, Vol. 4*. Smithsonian/Folkways, 1999: 17.

101. Guthrie, *Pastures of Plenty* 37.

102. Guthrie, *Pastures of Plenty* 37, 25.

103. Guthrie, *My New Found Land* 4.

104. Greenway 71; and Patricia Smith. *Africans in America: American's Journey though Slavery*. New York: Harcourt Brace & Company, 1998: 92.

105. Guthrie, *Buffalo Skinners*, Track 23.

106. Guthrie, *Woody Guthrie Folk Songs* 183.

107. Stephen B. Bright. "Discrimination, Death and Denial: The Tolerance of Racial Discrimination in Infliction of the Death Penalty." *Santa Clara Law Review*. 35:5, 1995: 440.

108. Quoted in Allison Davis, Burleigh B. Gardner, and Mary R. Gardner's *Deep South: A Social Anthropological Study of Caste and Class*. Chicago: University of Chicago Press, 1941: 26–27.

109. Arthur Raper. *The Tragedy of Lynching*. New York: Dover, 1970: 47.

110. William Bowers. *Legal Homicide: Death as Punishment in America, 1864–1982*. Boston: Northeastern University Press, 1984: 36–37, 59.

111. Guthrie, *Woody Guthrie Folk Songs* 235.

112. "Benefit to Aid Negroes' Defense." *New York Times*. May 31, 1949: 18.

113. Woody Guthrie. "Buoy Bells for Trenton." *American Folksongs of Protest* 119.

114. WGP Box 1, Folder 8.

115. Guthrie, *Woody Guthrie Folk Songs* 235.

116. Guthrie, *Woody Guthrie Folk Songs* 138–39.

117. Guthrie, *Bound for Glory* 232, 63.

118. Woody Guthrie. *Seeds of Man: An Experience Lived and Dreamed*. New York: E. P. Dutton, 1976: 134.

119. Craig Werner. "Democratic Visions, Democratic Voices." *Hard Travelin': The Life and Legacy of Woody Guthrie*. Ed. Robert Santelli and Emily Davidson. Hanover: University Press of New England, 1999: 70.

120. Guthrie, *American Folksong* 46.

121. Quoted in Klein 434.

Chapter Five

1. Charles Todd and Robert Sonkin. "Ballads of the Okies." *New York Times Magazine*. November 17, 1940: 7.

2. For example, see Walter J. Stein. *California and the Dust Bowl Migration*. Westport, Connecticut: Greenwood Press, 1973: 264–71. Also see James N. Gregory. *American Exodus: The Dust Bowl Migration and Okie Culture in California*. New York: Oxford University Press, 1989: 154–69. However, Gregory does temper his discussion of the individual identity of many Okies, especially former small farmers, with an exploration of this same group's experiences with collective action through various leftist organizations that had been active in Oklahoma and the surrounding states from the late 1800s to the mid-1930s.

3. Woody Guthrie. *Pastures of Plenty: A Self-Portrait*. Ed. Dave Marsh and Harold Leventhal. New York: HarperPerennial, 1992: 79; Woody Guthrie. *Dust Bowl Ballads*. Rounder Records, 1988: Track 7; and Woody Guthrie. "Ear Players" *Common Ground*. 2:3 (Spring)1942: 38

4. E. J. Hobsbawm. *Bandits*. New York: Pantheon Books, 1981: 17.

5. William Stott. *Documentary Expression and Thirties America*. New York: Oxford University Press, 1973: 20.

6. Guthrie, *Pastures of Plenty* 70.

7. Woody Guthrie. *Born to Win*. Ed. Robert Shelton. New York: MacMillan Company, 1965: 224.

8. Woody Guthrie, *Library of Congress Recordings*. Rounder Records, 1988: Disc 2, Track 2.

9. John Greenway. "Woody Guthrie: The Man, the Land, the Understanding." *The American West*. 3:4(Fall)1966: 28.

10. Woody Guthrie. *American Folksong*. New York: Oak Publications, 1961: 1; and Joe Klein. *Woody Guthrie: A Life*. New York: Delta Book, 1999: 2.

11. Woody Guthrie. *Songs of Woody Guthrie*. (c. 1941): 72. Copy held by WGMC Box 2. Other versions of the song "The Unwelcome Guest" appear in WGP Box 2, Folder 2 and on the album *Mermaid Avenue* Elektra 1998: Track 15 as performed by Billy Bragg and Wilco.

12. Billy Bragg, interview with Jeff Place. Ralph Rinzler Archives.

13. Graham Seal. *The Outlaw Legend: A Cultural Tradition in Britain, America, and Australia*. Cambridge: Cambridge University Press, 1996: 60–61, 81–82, 212–13, 216.

14. Guthrie, *Songs of Woody Guthrie* 72.

15. Woody Guthrie. *Buffalo Skinners: The Asch Recordings, Vol. 4*. Smithsonian Folkways: Track 2.

16. Guthrie, "Ear Players" 32.

17. Grant Foreman. *A History of Oklahoma*. Norman: University of Oklahoma Press, 1942: 240–41, 278–86.

18. Klein 3; and Guthrie, *American Folksong* 2.

19. Richard White. "Outlaw Gangs of the Middle Border: American Social Bandits." *Western Historical Quarterly*. 12:4 (October), 1981: 390–92; and Glenn Shirley. *Six-Gun and Silver Star*. Albuquerque: University of New Mexico, 1955: 27.

20. WGA Songs 2, Notebook 4.

21. Emmett Dalton. *When the Daltons Rode.* Garden City, New York: Doubleday, Doran & Co., 1931: 1–8.

22. WGA Songs 2, Notebook 4.

23. Ruthe Winegarten. "Belle Starr: The Bandit Queen of Dallas." *Legendary Ladies of Texas.* Dallas: E-Heart Press, 1981: 43–47; and Glenn Shirley. *Law West of Fort Smith: A History of Frontier Justice in the Indian Territory, 1834–1896.* Lincoln: University of Nebraska Press, 1968: 88–93.

24. Guthrie clearly acknowledges his use of the article "More Deadly Than the Male," which appeared in the *Sunday News* on December 2, 1945, in that he writes the following note at the top of a copy held by the WGP: "I got Belle Starr ballad here." WGP Flat Files, Drawer 2–Right Side (To Be Sorted File).

25. Guthrie, *American Folksong* 289.

26. Guthrie, *Library of Congress Recordings* Disc Two, Track 2.

27. William A. Settle, Jr. *Jesse James Was His Name.* Columbia: University of Missouri Press, 1966: 172.

28. Woody Guthrie. *Woody and Lefty Lou's One 1000 Laffs and Your Free Gift of 100 Songs.* (c. 1938): 88. Copy held in WGA Songs 2, Notebook 91; Woody Guthrie. *On a Slow Train Through California.* (c. 1939): 17. Copy held in WGA Song 2, Notebook 89; Guthrie *Songs of Woody Guthrie,* 3, 200; and "Jesse James and His Boys" WGP Box 2, Folder 2.

29. For varying examples of the best-known folk song about Jesse James, see *American Ballads and Songs.* Ed. Louise Pound. New York: Charles Scribner's Sons, 1922: 145–46; *Cowboy Songs and Other Frontier Ballads.* Ed. John and Alan Lomax. New York: MacMillan Co., 1938: 152–58; and *Cowboy and Western Songs.* Ed. Austin and Alta Fife. New York: Clarkson N. Potter, Inc., 1969: 253–60.

30. Woody Guthrie. *Cowboy Songs on Folkways.* Smithsonian Folkways Records, 1991: Track 18.

31. See pages 257–60 in *Cowboy and Western Songs* for two examples of folk songs that use James's life to warn of the dangers of criminal behavior.

32. Bill Malone. *Country Music USA.* Austin: University of Texas Press, 1993: 49.

33. Andrew Jenkins. "Billy the Kid." *He Was Singin' This Song.* Ed. Jim Bob Tinsley. Orlando: University Press of Florida, 1981: 180.

34. Woody Guthrie, interview with Alan Lomax. March 22, 1941. Copy held by American Folklife Center at the Library of Congress.

35. Song notes. *The Life Treasury of American Folk Music.* Time Records, 1961: 5.

36. Guthrie, *Buffalo Skinners* Track 3; and Jenkins, "Billy the Kid" 180.

37. Ralph Ellison. "Richard Wright's Blues." *Antioch Review.* 5:2 (Summer), 1945: 202–203.

38. Greil Marcus. *Mystery Train: Images of America in Rock 'n' Roll Music.* New York: E. P. Dutton, 1976: 76. Also see pages 76–79 and 229–34 for further information and a listing of other Stagger Lee sources.

39. John W. Roberts. *From Trickster to Badman: The Black Folk Hero in Slavery and Freedom.* Philadelphia: University of Pennsylvania Press, 1989: 171–215.

40. First, he did a version of "Stagolee" for Alan Lomax on January 4, 1941. Guthrie recorded it again in 1944 when he visited the BBC offices in London during a brief stay in England on one of his tours in the merchant marine. Later that same year on April 19, he recorded it for Moses Asch. Near the end of his recording career in the early 1950s, Guthrie returned to the song again in a session for Stinson Records, which then appeared on the album *Chain Gang, Vol.* 1.

41. Rick Mattix and William J. Helmer. "Evolution of an Outlaw Band: The Making of the Barker-Karpis Gang." www.oklahombres.org, 1995: 4–5; Dee Cordy. "The Outlaw and Lawman Map of Oklahoma." www.oklahombres.org, 1995: 2; and Dee Cordy. "John E. Johnston: Sequoyah County Lawman." www.oklahombres.org, 1998: 1.

42. Woody Guthrie. *Hard Hitting Songs for Hard-Hit People.* Lincoln: University of Nebraska Press, 1999: 116–17.

43. Guthrie, *Hard Hitting Songs for Hard-Hit People* 116.

44. Guthrie, *Songs of Woody Guthrie* 97.

45. Quoted in Jeffrey S. King's *The Life and Death of Pretty Boy Floyd.* Kent: The Kent State University Press, 1998: 1, 186.

46. "Dubbed 'Pretty Boy' by Hill Folk." *New York Times.* October 23,1934: 2.

47. Jay Nash. *Bloodletters and Badmen.* New York: Warner Books, 1975: 180.

48. Studs Terkel. "Woody Guthrie: Last of the Great Balladeers." *Climax.* 9:3, 1961: 67.

49. Kent L. Steckmesser's "The Oklahoma Robin Hood." *The American West,* 7:1, 1970; Michael Owen Jones's "(PC + CB) × SD (R + I + E) = HERO." *New York Folklore Quarterly.* 27:3, 1971; Richard E. Meyer's "The Outlaw: A Distinctive American Folktype." *Journal of the Folklore Institute* 17:2/3, 1980; Paul Kooistra's *Criminals As Heroes: Structure, Power, & Identity.* Bowling Green: Bowling Green State University Popular Press, 1989; and Roger A. Bruns's *The Bandit Kings: From Jesse James to Pretty Boy Floyd.* New York: Crown Publishers, 1995.

50. Woody Guthrie. *Dust Bowl Ballads.* Rounder Records, 1988: Track 7.

51. Guthrie, *Dust Bowl Ballads* Track 7.

52. Guthrie, *Library of Congress Recordings* Disc 2, Track 1; and Guthrie, *Dust Bowl Ballads* Track 7.

53. Guthrie, *Dust Bowl Ballads* Track 7.

54. Guthrie, *Dust Bowl Ballads* Track 7.

55. Quoted in Michael Wallis's *Pretty Boy: The Life and Times of Charles Arthur Floyd.* New York: St. Martin's Press, 1992: 227.

56. Quoted in *American Murder Ballads and Their Stories.* Collected and edited by Olive Woolley Burt. New York: Oxford University Press, 1958: 213–14.

57. Guthrie, *Dust Bowl Ballads* Track 7.

58. Quoted in Wallis 270.

59. Guthrie, *Dust Bowl Ballads* Track 7.

60. Quoted in Wallis 296.

61. Lomax and Guthrie, *Library of Congress Recordings* Disc 2, Track 1.

62. Guthrie, *Dust Bowl Ballads* Track 7.

63. Tristram P. Coffin. "The Folk Ballad and the Literary Ballad: An Essay in Classification." *Midwest Folklore.* 9:1, 1959: 8.

64. Edward Anderson. *Hungry Men.* Garden City: Doubleday, Doran, & Co., Inc., 1935: 135.

65. Guthrie, *Hard Hitting Songs for Hard-Hit People* 18.

66. Guthrie, *Hard Hitting Songs for Hard-Hit People* 232.

67. Guthrie, *Library of Congress Recordings* Disc 2, Track 1.

68. Woody Guthrie. *Alonzo M. Zilch's Own Collection of Original Songs and Ballads.* (c. 1935): 11. A copy of this mimeographed songbook is held in the WGMC Box 1, Folder 1.

69. Guthrie, *Library of Congress Recordings* Disc 2, Track 4.

70. Woody Guthrie. "Woody Sez." *People's World.* June 1, 1939: 4.

71. Guthrie, *Dust Bowl Ballads* Track 4.

72. Woody Guthrie. "Woody Sez." *People's World.* August 11, 1939: 4.

73. Woody Guthrie. "Woody Sez." *Daily Worker.* March 30, 1940: 7.

74. Guthrie, *Dust Bowl Ballads* Tracks 9 and 10.

75. Guthrie, *Dust Bowl Ballads* Tracks 9 and 10.

76. John Steinbeck. *Grapes of Wrath.* New York: Penguin Books, 1981: 26; and *Grapes of Wrath.* Directed by John Ford. 20th Century Fox, 1940.

77. Guthrie, *Dust Bowl Ballads* Tracks 9 and 10.

78. Ed Cray. *Ramblin' Man: The Life and Times of Woody Guthrie.* New York: W. W. Norton, 2004: 174.

79. For a very enlightening discussion of Guthrie's version versus the Carter Family's, see Bryan Garman's "The Ghost of History: Bruce Springsteen, Woody Guthrie, and the Hurt Song." *Popular Music and Society.* 20 (Summer), 1997: 69–120.

80. Woody Guthrie. *Mule Skinner Blues: The Asch Recordings, Vol. 2.* Smithsonian Folkways Records, 1997: Track 17.

81. Earl Conrad. *Harriet Tubman: Negro Soldier and Abolitionist.* New York: International Publishers, 1942: 20.

82. Earl Conrad. *Harriet Tubman: Negro Soldier and Abolitionist.* New York: International Publishers, 1942.

83. Sarah H. Bradford. *Scenes in the Life of Harriet Tubman.* Freeport: Books for Libraries Press, 1869: 3.

84. John Greenway. *American Folksongs of Protest.* Philadelphia: University of Pennsylvania Press, 1953: 90–92.

85. Woody Guthrie. *Long Ways to Travel, the Unreleased Folkways Masters, 1944–1949.* Smithsonian Folkways Records, 1994: Track 4.

86. Guthrie, *Long Ways to Travel* Track 4.

87. Conrad 5–7.

88. Guthrie, *Long Ways to Travel* Track 4.

89. Bradford, *Scenes from the Life of Harriet Tubman* 15.

90. Guthrie, *Long Ways to Travel* Track 4.

91. Guthrie, *Long Ways to Travel* Track 4.

92. Quoted in Sarah Bradford's *Harriet, the Moses of Her People*. New York: G. R. Lockwood and Son, 1886: 29.

93. Guthrie, *Long Ways to Travel* Track 4.

94. Quoted in Bradford, *Scenes in the Life of Harriet Tubman* 19.

95. Quoted in Bradford, *Harriet, the Moses of Her People* 32.

96. Guthrie, *Long Ways to Travel* Track 4.

97. Conrad 14. For a more detailed discussion of this incident see Conrad's book-length work *Harriet Tubman*. Washington, DC: Associated Publishers, 1943: 63.

98. Guthrie, *Long Ways to Travel* Track 4.

99. Guthrie, *Long Ways to Travel* Track 4.

100. Quoted in George Metcalf's *Black Profiles*. New York: McGraw-Hill, 1968: 184.

101. Guthrie, *Long Ways to Travel* Track 4.

102. Quoted in Lydia Maria Child's *Letters of Lydia Maria Child*. New York: Ams Press, 1971: 161.

103. Guthrie, *Long Ways to Travel* Track 4.

104. Guthrie, *Long Ways to Travel* Track 4.

105. Albert Bushnell Hart. *Slavery and Abolition*. New York: Negro Universities Press, 1968: 209.

106. Guthrie, *Long Ways to Travel* Track 4.

107. Conrad 13.

108. Barbara Dianne Savage. *Broadcasting Freedom: Radio, War, and the Politics of Race, 1938–1948*. Chapel Hill: University of North Carolina, 1999: 169–77.

109. Judith Nies. *Seven Women: Portraits from the American Radical Tradition*. New York: Viking Press, 1977: 35, 58.

110. Cray 85–86; and Guthrie, *Hard Hitting Songs for Hard-Hit People* 22.

111. Quoted in Ed Robbin's *Woody Guthrie and Me: An Intimate Reminiscence*. Berkeley: Lancaster-Miller Publishers, 1979: 121.

112. Guthrie, *Bound for Glory* 177.

113. Klein 163.

114. Woody Guthrie. *This Land Is Your Land: The Asch Recordings, Vol. 1*. Smithsonian Folkways Records, 1997: Track 13.

115. Guthrie, *Hard Hitting Songs for Hard-Hit People* 336.

116. Guthrie, *This Land Is Your Land* Track 13.

117. Wayne Hampton. *Guerrilla Minstrels: John Lennon, Joe Hill, Woody Guthrie, and Bob Dylan*. Knoxville: University of Tennessee Press, 1986: 130.

118. Guthrie, *Bound for Glory* 251.

119. Guthrie, *Pastures of Plenty* 43. Although Guthrie never recorded the song himself, it was included on the first *Mermaid Avenue* album. Elektra, 1998: Track 9.

Chapter Six

1. Woody Guthrie. *Born to Win*. Ed. Robert Shelton. New York: MacMillan Company, 1965: 224.

2. Woody Guthrie. *Pastures of Plenty: A Self-Portrait*. Ed. Dave Marsh and Harold Leventhal. New York: HarperPerennial, 1992: 79–80.

3. Stephen J. Whitfield. *The Culture of the Cold War*. Baltimore: Johns Hopkins University Press, 1991: 201.

4. Quoted in Ed Robbin's *Woody Guthrie and Me: An Intimate Reminiscence*. Berkeley: Lancaster-Miller Publishers, 1979: 133.

5. Quoted in Mark Rowland's "Notebooks of Plenty." *Musician*. 236 (July), 1998: 23.

6. Quoted by S. J. Woolf. "Lewis Charts His Course for American Labor." *New York Times Magazine*. March 21, 1937: 3.

7. Joe Klein. *Woody Guthrie: A Life*. New York: Delta, 1999: 280; and Dave Marsh. Introduction. *Pastures of Plenty* xxi.

8. Robert S. McElvaine. *Down and Out in the Great Depression: Letters from the "Forgotten Man."* Chapel Hill: University of North Carolina Press, 1983: 16.

9. Robbin 41.

10. Worth Robert Miller. *Oklahoma Populism: A History of the People's Party in the Oklahoma Territory*. Norman: University of Oklahoma Press, 1987: 71–73, 87–88, 117, 157–65.

11. John Anthony Scott. *The Ballad of America: The History of the United States in Song and Story*. New York: Bantam Books, Inc., 1966: 267; and Carl Sandburg. *The American Songbag*. New York: Harcourt Brace Jovanovich, Inc., 1927: 282.

12. Woody Guthrie. *Hard Hitting Songs for Hard-Hit People*. Lincoln: University of Nebraska Press, 1999: 32.

13. Miller 177–78.

14. Garin Burbank. *When Farmers Voted Red: The Gospel of Socialism in the Oklahoma Countryside, 1910–1924*. Westport: Greenwood Press, 1976: 5–7, 9, 203.

15. Nigel Anthony Sellars. *Oil, Wheat, & Wobblies*. Norman: University of Oklahoma Press, 1998: 11.

16. *Proceedings of the First Convention of the Industrial Workers of the World*. New York: Labor News Company, 1905: 247.

17. Klein 82.

18. Woody Guthrie. *American Folksong*. New York: Oak Publications, 1961: 22.

19. Guthrie, *Hard Hitting Songs for Hard-Hit People* 87.

20. C. E. Guthrie. *Kumrids: A Discussion of Scientific Socialism*. Okemah: Ledger Printing, 1912: 5.

21. Woody Guthrie. *Bound for Glory*. New York: Plume, 1983: 39.

22. WGP Box 3, Folder 6.

23. Quoted in Robbin 133.

24. Guthrie, *American Folksong* 2.

25. Guthrie, *Hard Hitting Songs for Hard-Hit People* 22.

26. Ed Cray. *Ramblin' Man: The Life and Times of Woody Guthrie*. New York: W. W. Norton, 2004: 85–86.

27. Quoted in Miller 113. Also look at Garin Burbank's chapter "The Gospel According to Local Socialists" (pp. 14–43) in *When Farmers Voted Red: The Gospel of Socialism in the Oklahoma Countryside, 1910–1924* for a detailed discussion of Oklahoma Socialists' use of Christianity.

28. Klein 112.

29. *Woody and Lefty Lou's Favorite Collection of Old Time Hill Country Songs: Being Sung for Ages Still Going Strong*. Gardena, CA: Institute Press, 1937. N. pag.

30. James Green. *The World of the Worker: Labor in Twentieth-Century America*. New York: Hill and Wang, 1980: 101.

31. Klein 114 and Cray 127–29.

32. Carey McWilliams. *Factories in the Field: The Story of Migratory Farm Labor in California*. Boston: Little, Brown, and Company, 1939: 212, 258, 270–71; and Walter J. Stein *California and the Dust Bowl Migration*. Westport: Greenwood Press, Inc., 1973: 233–36.

33. Klein 119.

34. Guthrie, *American Folksong* 4.

35. Cletis Daniel. *Bitter Harvest: A History of California Farmworkers, 1870–1941*. Ithaca: Cornell University Press, 1981: 15–70.

36. Stein 41–42, 51, 271–72.

37. Carey McWilliams. "California Pastoral." *Antioch Review*. 2:1 (Spring), 1942: 114.

38. Quoted in James N. Gregory's *American Exodus: The Dust Bowl Migration and Okie Culture in California*. New York: Oxford University Press, 1989: 162.

39. Robbin 19–22, 23–24, 35.

40. Harry Carisle. "Mike Quin." *On the Drumhead: A Selection from the Writings of Mike Quin*. San Francisco: Pacific Publishing Foundation, 1948: xx, xxvii, xxx, xxxiii.

41. Harry Bridges. Foreword. *The Big Strike*. New York: International Publishers, 1979: xii.

42. WGA Songs 2, Notebook 57.

43. Quoted in Robbin 32.

44. WGP Box 3, Folder 6.

45. Woody Guthrie. *Songs of Woody Guthrie*. (c. 1941): 178. Copy held by WGMC Box 2.

46. Guthrie, *Pastures of Plenty* 27.

47. Woody Guthrie. "My Constitution and Me." *Daily Worker Magazine*. June 19, 1949: 3, 12.

48. Woody Guthrie. *On a Slow Train Through California*. (c. 1939): 2, 23. Copy held in WGA Song 2, Notebook 89.

49. Guthrie, *Songs of Woody Guthrie* 22.

50. Woody Guthrie. "Songs of the Migratory Trails." *Daily Worker*. April 16, 1940: 7.

51. Guthrie, *Hard Hitting Songs for Hard-Hit People* 17.

52. Guthrie, *American Folksong* 4.

53. WGP Box 3, Folder 6.

54. Woody Guthrie. "Tom Joad in American Ballad." *Daily Worker*. May 3, 1940: 7.

55. Woody Guthrie. *Dust Bowl Ballads*. Rounder Records, 1988: Tracks 4 and 9–10.

56. Guthrie, *Hard Hitting Songs for Hard-Hit People* 17.

57. Guthrie, *Hard Hitting Songs for Hard-Hit People* 281.

58. Guthrie, "Songs of the Migratory Trails" 7.

59. Woody Guthrie. "Woody Sez That Okies Haven't Given Up Fight." *Daily Worker*.
April 23, 1940: 7.

60. Guthrie, *American Folksong* 19.

61. Dave Marsh. Introduction to a letter to Mary Jo Guthrie. *Pastures of Plenty* 25.

62. Klein 167.

63. Guthrie, *Hard Hitting Songs for Hard-Hit People* 63.

64. Guthrie, *American Folksong* 5.

65. WGA Songs 1, Box 3, Folder 28.

66. Klein 168.

67. Woody Guthrie. "State Line to Skid Row." *Common Ground*. 3:1 (Autumn), 1942: 36.

68. Woody Guthrie. *Woody Guthrie Songs*. Ed. Judy Bell and Nora Guthrie. New York:
Ludlow Music, 1994: 20.

69. Sherwood Anderson. *Puzzled America*. New York: Scribner, 1935: 113.

70. Philip Foner. *Women and the American Labor Movement: From the First Trade Unions to
the Present*. New York: The Free Press, 1979: 330–37.

71. Joe Hill. *The Songs of Joe Hill*. Ed. Barrie Stavis and Frank Harmon. New York:
People's Artists, 1955: 7.

72. Aunt Molly Jackson. "I Am a Union Woman." *Hard Hitting Songs for Hard-Hit People*,
142–43.

73. Bryan Garman. "The Ghost of History: Bruce Springsteen, Woody Guthrie, and the
Hurt Song." *Popular Music and Society*. 20 (Summer), 1997: 106.

74. Ellen J. Stekert. Author's introduction to "Cents and Nonsense in the Urban Folksong
Movement: 1930–66." *Transforming Tradition: Folk Music Revivals Examined*. Ed. Neil V
Rosenberg. Urbana: University of Illinois Press, 1993: 90.

75. Lyrics by Woody Guthrie. Billy Bragg and Wilco. *Mermaid Avenue*. Elektra Records,
1998: Track 6.

76. Quoted in Klein 263.

77. Almanac Singers. *Talking Union*. Keynote, 1941: Track 2.

78. For examples of various feminist-tinged verses, see Nancy Katz's verse in *I.W.W.
Songs*, 34th ed. Chicago: Industrial Workers of the World, 1973: 46; also see several verses
noted by Pete Seeger in the songbook *Carry It On!* New York: Simon and Schuster,
1985: 154.

79. Woody Guthrie. "Woody Advises Folks to Write Union Songs." *Daily Worker*. June 24, 1940: 7.

80. Woody Guthrie. "Real Folk Songs Are Pretty Rare, Asserts Woody." *Daily Worker*. September 26, 1940: 7.

81. Woody Guthrie. "Takes Big Army of Slaves to Make One King." *Daily Worker*. August 20, 1940: 7.

82. Guthrie, *American Folksong* 5.

83. Handwritten note on an original copy of *Alonzo M. Zilch's Own Collection of Original Songs and Ballads* held by the WGA.

84. Klein 138.

85. Woody Guthrie, letter to Alan Lomax. September 19, 1940. WGMC Box 1, Correspondence folder.

86. WGMC Box 1, Folder 3.

87. A copy of this document appears on page 26 of *Pastures of Plenty*.

88. WGP Box 3, Folder 11.

89. John Edgar Hoover, memo to Matthew F. McGuire. July 18, 1941. Woodrow Wilson Guthrie file, No. FBIHQ 100-29988. FBI Headquarters, Washington, DC.

90. WGP Box 3, Folder 6.

91. Woody Guthrie. *Roll on Columbia, The Columbia River Collection*. Ed. Bill Murlin. Bethlehem: Sing Out Publications, 1991: 42.

92. Quoted in Klein 210.

93. Guthrie, *American Folksong* 6; and WGP Box 3, Folder 6.

94. Quoted in Robbin 149.

95. Whitfield 201.

96. R. Serge Denisoff. *Great Day Coming: Folk Music and the American Left*. Urbana: University of Illinois Press, 1971: 65.

97. WGP Box 1, Folder 5.

98. WGP Box 2, Folder 3.

99. Guthrie, *Hard Hitting Songs for Hard-Hit People* 232.

100. WGA Songs 2, Notebook 7.

101. *The Collected Reprints from Sing Out! The Folk Song Magazine*. Vols. 1–6, 1959–64. Ed. Irwin Silber, Paul Nelson, Ethel Raim, Pete Seeger, and Jerry Silverman. Bethlehem: Sing Out Publications, 1990: 47.

102. Pete Seeger and Robert Santelli. "Hobo's Lullaby." *Hard Travelin': The Life and Legacy of Woody Guthrie*. Ed. Robert Santelli and Emily Davidson. Hanover: Wesleyan University Press, 1999: 29.

103. WGP Box 2, Folder 3.

104. WGA Songs 2, Notebook 9.

105. Archie Green. "Woody's Oil Songs." *Songs about Work: Essays in Occupational Culture*. Bloomington: Folklore Institute, 1993: 210.

106. Guthrie, *American Folksong* 23–24.

107. WGA Songs 1, Box 2, Folder 18; and WGA Songs 1, Box 1, Folder 11.

108. Guthrie, *Pastures of Plenty* 80, 82.

109. Woody Guthrie. *My New Found Land.* (c. 1946): 89. Microfilmed copy held by Performing Arts Reading Room, Library of Congress.

110. Richard Wright. *12 Million Black Voices: A Folk History of the Negro in the United States.* New York: Viking Press, 1941: 143–44.

111. Guthrie, *My New Found Land* 89.

112. WGP Box 1, Folder 5.

113. Woody Guthrie. *Woody Guthrie Folk Songs: A Collection of Songs by America's Foremost Balladeer.* Ed. Pete Seeger. New York: Ludlow Music, 1963: 19.

114. WGMC Box 1, Folder 7.

115. Guthrie, *Pastures of Plenty* 104–105.

116. WGA Box 1, Folder 7.

117. Lyrics by Woody Guthrie. Billy Bragg and Wilco. *Mermaid Avenue.* New York: Elektra Records, 1998: Track 6.

118. James C. McKelly. "The Artist as Busker: Woody Guthrie's *Bound for Glory.*" *Heritage of the Great Plains.* 23:4, 1990: 15.

119. Guthrie, *Bound for Glory* 237–38.

120. Guthrie, *Bound for Glory* 203–204, 208–12, and 229–30.

121. Klein 280.

122. WGA Songs 1, Box 3, Folder 28; and WGA Songs 1, Box 3, Folder 28.

123. Guthrie, *American Folksong* 33.

124. Wayne Hampton. *Guerrilla Minstrels: John Lennon, Joe Hill, Woody Guthrie, and Bob Dylan.* Knoxville: University of Tennessee Press, 1986: 130.

125. Klein 142, 207, 225.

126. Jim Longhi. *Woody, Cisco, & Me: Seamen Three in the Merchant Marine.* Urbana: University of Illinois Press, 1997: 52–54.

127. Longhi 53, 113.

128. Guthrie, *Pastures of Plenty* 131–33.

129. Guthrie, *Pastures of Plenty* 137.

130. Guthrie, *Woody Guthrie Folk Songs* 79.

131. WGA Songs 2, Notebook 33.

132. "In This Hall Here." WGA Songs 3, Notebook 10.

133. Guthrie, *Born to Win* 225.

134. Woody Guthrie. *Ten of Woody Guthrie's Twenty-Five Cent Songs.* (c. 1945): 4. A copy of this mimeographed songbook is held by WGP Box 2, Folder 1.

135. *The Woody Guthrie Newsletter.* January 1968: 6. A copy of this newsletter is held by the Performing Arts Reading Room in the Library of Congress.

136. Guthrie, *Pastures of Plenty* 172.

137. WGA Songs 1, Box 3, Folder 28.

138. Woody Guthrie. *The Woody Guthrie Songbook*. Ed. Harold Leventhal and Marjorie Guthrie. New York: Grosset and Dunlap, 1976: 71.

139. Guthrie, *Hard Hitting Songs for Hard-Hit People* 206–207.

140. WGP Box 3, Folder 6.

141. Guthrie, *Pastures of Plenty* 173–75.

142. William H. Harris. *The Harder We Run: Black Workers Since the Civil War*. New York: Oxford University Press, 1982: 124.

143. Guthrie, *Pastures of Plenty* 173.

144. WGA Songs 2, Notebook 63.

145. Woody Guthrie. "A Minstrel in Tobacco Land." *Workers Magazine*. January 18, 1948: 2. In a response to this article, John Tisa, who was the international organizational director of the FTA, attempted to rebut Guthrie's claims that the union's events were segregated. John Tisa. "Unionist Condemns Guthrie's Article." *The Worker*. February 1, 1948: 8.

146. Woody Guthrie. *Songs for Wallace*. New York: People's Songs, 1948: 11, 10.

147. WGA Songs 1, Box 3, Folder 30.

148. Guthrie, *Pastures of Plenty* 242.

149. WGA Box 3, Folder 24; WGA Songs 1, Box 3, Folder 28.

150. WGA Songs 1, Box 2, Folder 18.

151. Woody Guthrie, letter to Jolly Robinson (Smolen). Quoted in Gordon Friesen's "The Man Woody Guthrie." *Broadside*. No. 57 (April 10), 1965: 11.

152. Dave Marsh. Introduction. *Pastures of Plenty* xix.

153. Quoted in Pete Seeger's *The Incompleat Folksinger*. Lincoln: University of Nebraska Press, 1992: 59.

154. Robbin 157.

155. Walt Whitman. "1855 Preface to *Leaves of Grass*." *Leaves of Grass*. Oxford: Oxford University Press, 1990: 446.

156. Moses Asch. "The Ballad of Chanukah." *Sing Out!* 17:6 (December–January), 1967/68: 12.

Epilogue

1. Billy Bragg and Wilco. *Mermaid Avenue*. Elecktra Records, 1998: Track 14.

2. Kenneth Crist. "Career Men—In Relief." *Los Angeles Times Magazine*. May 14, 1939: 4.

3. Quoted in Arianna Huffington's "Demagogue, thy name is Pat Buchanan." *San Diego Union-Tribune*. March 10, 1999: B-8.

4. Woody Guthrie. *Pastures of Plenty: A Self-Portrait*. Ed. Dave Marsh and Harold Leventhal. New York: HarperPerennial, 1992: 336–37.

5. Guthrie, *Pastures of Plenty* 55.

6. Greil Marcus. *Mystery Train: Images of America in Rock 'n' Roll Music*. New York: E. P. Dutton, 1976:7.

7. Bruce Springsteen. *The Ghost of Tom Joad*. Columbia, 1995: Track 1; and Dave Marsh. *Glory Days: Bruce Springsteen in the* 1980s. New York: Pantheon Books, 1987: 34, 66, 101, 112.

8. Steve Earle. *El Corazon*. Warner Brothers, 1997: Track 1.

9. Woody Guthrie. *Sing Out!* 17:6 (December–January), 1967/68: 4.

10. John Steinbeck. Foreword. *Hard Hitting Songs for Hard-Hit People*. Ed. Alan Lomax, Woody Guthrie, and Pete Seeger. Lincoln: University of Nebraska, 1999: 8.

Index

Adamic, Louis, 8–9
Agee, James, 90
"All In Down and Out," 234
Almanac Singers, 101, 106–7, 139, 232–33, 235, 239, 241, 254
Alonzo M. Zilch's Own Collection of Original Songs and Ballads, 7, 49
Anti-Communism, 9, 28, 30, 40, 216, 247, 249
American Civil Liberties Union, 78, 148
American Exodus (Gregory), 72
American Exodus, An (Taylor and Lange), 132
American Favorite Ballads, 38
American Federation of Labor (AFL), 212–13, 234, 241, 247, 250, 251
American Folksong, 106, 111, 138
American Folksongs of Protest, 9
American Jewish Congress, 148
American School of the Air, 228
"America the Beautiful," 20, 43
Ammons, Elias, 116
Anderson, "Bloody" Bill, 174
Anderson, Sherwood, 225–26
"Angola Blues," 154
Angola prison, 153, 154

"Another Man's Done Gone," 253
Asch, Moses, 32, 33, 140, 141, 154, 176, 251–52, 282n
Asch Records, 31
Association of Southern Women for the Prevention of Lynching, 155
"At the End of Every Row" ("End of Every Row"), 141, 154–55
"Avondale Mine Disaster," 118

Back Where I Come From, 228
Baez, Joan, 10, 41, 42, 181, 255
Bailey, Pearl, 151
"Barbara Allen," 169
Barker, Herman, 178
Barker gang, 178
Basie, Count, 151
Bates, Ruby, 162
"Been in Jail," 94, 222
"Belle Starr," 173
Benton, Thomas Hart, 156
Berlin, Irving, 21, 22–23, 25
"Bet on Wallace," 146
"Better Go Down and Join the Union," 218, 222, 234
"Better World a Coming," 141

"Biggest Thing Man Has Ever Done,
The" ("The Great Historical Bum"), 103,
142, 232
Big Strike, The, 215
Bilbo, Theodore, 143
Billboard, 19
"Billy the Kid" (Guthrie), 176–77
"Billy the Kid" (Jenkins), 53, 175–77
"Birmingham Jail," 153
Black Boy, 177
"Black Lung," 126
"Blinding of Isaac Woodward," 141,
151–52, 192
Bloor, Ella May "Mother," 113, 114
"Blowin' Down This Road," 73
"Blue Yodel #4" ("California Blues"), 70–71
Board of Transportation (BT), 108, 109
"Bold Jack Donahue," 166
Bonneville Power Administration (BPA),
89, 101, 102, 104, 105, 106, 230–31
Bonnie and Clyde, 178, 184
"Bonnie Black Bess" ("The Unwelcome
Guest"), 169, 170–71
"Boomtown Bill," 107–8, 235, 237
"Born in the USA," 46
Born to Win, 10, 11
Bosses' Songbook, The, 36
Bound for Glory, 8, 10, 13, 42, 73, 99, 127, 130,
164, 199, 200, 238–39, 240
"Bound for Glory," 255
Bracero program, 132, 134
Bradford, Sarah, 192
Bragg, Billy, 46, 170, 205, 253
Bridges, Harry, 215
Broadside, 37
Broadwell, Dick, 172
Brodas, Edward, 192
Brown, John, 196
Bryant, Jack, 69
Buchanan, Pat, 254
"Buffalo Skinners," 100, 171

"Buoy Bells for Trenton," 163
Burke, Frank, 213
Burleson, Hugh, 163
Byrd, James, Jr., 254
Byrds, 181, 255

"Calamity Jane," 101, 235
"California! California!," 71
"Californy Gold," 112
Calloway, Cab, 151
"Canaday IO," 100
"Can't Do What I Want To," 50
Carawan, Guy, 43
Carter Family, 26, 64, 191
Cavalcade of America, 228
"Chain Around My Leg," 153
"Chain Gang Special," 154
"Chain of Broken Hearts," 234
Chapin, Imogene, 69
Chaplin, Ralph, 209, 221
Child, Lydia Maria, 196
"Chinese and the Japs, The," 129–30, 211
"Chisholm Trail," 5, 100
"Christ for President," 201
Christian Century, 55
"Christmas in Washington," 255
Churchill, Winston, 245
Civil Rights Congress, 163
"Clay Country Miner," 126
"Clippings from the personal diary of a
Full-Fledged son of the beach," 137
"Colley's Run IO," 100
Collier, Jimmy, 44, 45
Collins, Judy, 255
Colorado Fuel and Iron Company
(CFIC), 116
"Columbia Waters," 105
"Columbus Stockade," 36
"Come All You Coal Miners," 112
Commonwealth Federation of
Washington, 233

Commonwealth Labor College, 139, 232

Communist Party (CP), 139, 148, 156, 205,
 216–17, 218, 222, 224, 229, 236, 240, 246,
 247, 248

Congress of Industrial Organizations
 (CIO), 212–13, 215, 216, 220, 222, 226, 232,
 234, 235, 241, 246, 247, 248, 249, 250, 251

Conrad, Earl, 192, 194, 198

Cooder, Ry, 255

"Cowboy's Philosophy," 99

Cradle Will Rock, The, 96

"Crawdad Hole," 106

Cray, Ed, 12, 137

Crist, Kenneth, 87, 254

Crowdog, Henry, 44, 45

"Curly-Headed Baby," 224

Curran, Joe, 241

Curtis, James, 94

Daily Worker, 96, 139, 143, 152, 156, 215,
 221, 228

Dalhart, Vernon, 175

Dalton, Bob, 172

Dalton, Emmett, 172

Dalton, Grant, 172

"Dalton Boys, The," 172, 173

Dalton gang, 171, 172

Dane, Barbara, 39

Davis, James Edgar, 76, 78

Dawidoff, Nicholas, 48–49

"Dead from the Dust," 125–26

"Dear Mrs. Roosevelt," 245

"Death Row," 162, 163

Debs, Eugene V., 208

Decca Records, 32

DeCormier, Robert, 35

Delaney, John, 108, 109

Democratic Party, 210, 216, 246, 247, 249

Denisoff, R. Serge, 233–34

"Deportee" ("Plane Wreck at Los Gatos"),
 15, 133–35, 152, 254

Dermer, Emma, 61

Dewey, Thomas, 146, 148, 249

Dickens, Hazel, 126

Dies, Martin, 143, 245

*Documentary Expression and Thirties
 America*, 14

Donnelly, Robert, 111

"Don't Go Down in the Mine," 111

"Don't Kill My Baby" ("Old Dark Town"
 and "Old Rock Jail"), 141, 159–60

"Do Re Mi," 25, 78–79, 211

Douglass, Frederick, 196

"Down in Oklayhoma," 63

"Dream of a Miner's Child," 111, 122

Dust Bowl, 50–60

Dust Bowl Ballads, 52, 93, 220

"Dust Bowl Refugee," 25, 60, 81

"Dust Can't Kill Me," 60, 66, 97

"Dust Pneumonia Blues," 25, 59–60, 71, 125

"Dust Storm Disaster" ("The Great Dust
 Storm"), 25, 56–59, 151

"Dying Miner, The" ("Goodbye Centralia"),
 121–22

Dylan, Bob, 10, 41, 181, 255

Earle, Steve, 255–56

Eisler, Hans, 30

"Eleven-Cent Cotton and Forty-Cent
 Meat," 61

Ellington, Richard, 36

Elliott, Ramblin' Jack, 36, 181

Ellison, Ralph, 177

Factory in the Fields, 89, 132

Facts to Fight Fascism, 215

Fadiman, Clifton, 19

"Fare Thee Well, Cisco," 255

"Fare Ye Well Old Ely Branch," 112

"Farmer Is the Man, The," 49, 208

"Farmer-Labor Train, The," 249

Farmers Unions, 233

Farm Security Administration (FSA), 67

"Farther Along," 94

"Fascists Bound to Lose," 141

Federal Bureau of Investigation (FBI), 231

Ferguson, Alfonso, 146, 148

Ferguson, Charles, 146, 148, 150

Ferguson, Joseph, 148, 150

Ferguson, Richard, 148

"Ferguson Brothers Killing, The" ("The
    Killing of the Ferguson Brothers"), 141,
    148–50, 152

Ferris, Woodbridge, 113

"Final Call, The," 229–30

Floyd, Charles "Pretty Boy," 16, 180–81, 183,
    184, 185, 187, 188

Floyd, Dempsey, 183

Folkways Records, 31, 32, 33, 35

Food, Tobacco, and Allied Workers (FTA),
    248–49, 290n

Ford, John, 73

Ford, Robert, 174

Franklin, Jimmie Lewis, 135

"Free and Equal Blues," 139

Friedman, Kinky, 181

Friesen, Gordon, 31, 105

Fugitive Slave Law, 198

Garland, Jim, 111–12, 219

Garman, Bryan, 12

Garrett, Pat, 175, 176–77

Garrison, William Lloyd, 196

Geddes, Will, 111

Geer, Will, 38, 96, 139, 180, 199, 219

"Get Thee Behind Me Satan," 232

"Get Your Kicks on Route 66," 74

"Ghost of Tom Joad," 255

"Girl in the Red, White, and Blue,
    The," 104

"Give Me Three Grains of Corn,
    Mother," 121

"God Bless America," 20, 21, 22–23, 25, 43

"Go Down and See," 249

Gold, Mike, 139

"Good Old Union Feeling," 240, 241

"Gotta Keep 'em Sailin'," 237

"Govt Road," 89

"Grand Coulee Dam, The," 101, 231

"Grand Coulee Powder Monkeys," 104

Grapes of Wrath (book), 56, 67, 73, 80, 82, 89,
    132, 190, 266n

Grapes of Wrath (film), 67, 73, 80, 82, 89, 132,
    190, 220

Grateful Dead, 255

Green, Harriet, 192

Greenway, John, 9, 10, 73, 110, 152, 168

Gregory, James N., 72, 280n

Griffith, Nanci, 135, 255

Guerrilla Minstrels, 12

Guthrie, Arlo, 33, 38, 39, 42, 181

Guthrie, Cathy Ann, 227

Guthrie, Charley, 95, 136, 169, 210

Guthrie, Marjorie, 28, 205, 210

Guthrie, Mary, 130, 228

Guthrie, Mary Jo, 59

Guthrie, Nora (daughter), 139, 140

Guthrie, Nora (mother), 95, 169, 171

Guthrie, Woody: attitude toward
    Hoovervilles, 84, 87–89; attitude toward
    IWW, 209–10; Christian views, 211, 217–
    18, 221, 228–29; connection to Communist
    Party, 205, 217–18; comments on Aunt
    Molly Jackson, 111; comments on Harry
    Truman, 248; comments on Jim Garland,
    111–12; comments on Mike Quin, 215–16;
    comments on "Pretty Boy" Floyd, 182,
    185–86; comments on Sarah Ogan, 112;
    documentary attitude, 49, 51–52; eco-
    nomic history of, 4, 16, 25, 48, 95; experi-
    ences in California, 4, 23, 24, 48, 49, 79,
    81, 84, 87–89; experiences in Dust Bowl,
    4, 48, 51, 52, 54, 56; on Mary Guthrie's
    racial attitude, 130; on mechanization,

66–67, 97–98, 103; opinion of media, 3–4; on outlaws, 204; racial attitude, 127–29, 130, 137, 139, 140, 146, 237–38; reaction to chain gangs, 153–54; on reasons for Okie migration, 70–71; on revolution, 230; songwriting methodology, 7, 26; status as artist, 7–9, 10–11; on tenant farming, 62–65

"Gypsy Davy," 169

Haggard, Merle, 82–84
Hamblen, Stuart, 229
Hampton, Wayne, 12
Handcox, John, 63, 221
"Hang Out Your Front Door Key," 78
Hard Hitting Songs for Hard-Hit People, 10, 14, 63, 126, 187, 209, 220, 234, 257
"Hard Times on the Subway," 108–10
Hard Travelin', 12, 129
"Hard Travelin'," 74–75, 105–6, 107, 112
Harriet Tubman, 192
"Harriet Tubman," 192–98
Harris, Corey, 255
Hart, Albert Bushnell, 197
Hartley, Fred, 146, 277n
Hayes, Alfred, 221
Hays, Lee, 139, 146, 232, 233, 246
Hearst, William Randolph, 86, 94
Henderson, Caroline, 55
Hickok, Lorena, 62, 98, 102, 125
"High Balladree," 62–63, 159
Highlander Folk School, 223, 232
Hill, Joe, 64, 155, 209, 221
Hitler, Adolf, 235, 245
Hobsbawn, Eric, 167
Hoffman, Martin, 275n
"Ho! For California," 68
Hogue, Alexander, 51
Holiday, Billie, 151, 155
Hoover, Herbert, 50
Hoover, J. Edgar, 180, 186, 231

"Hooversville," 84–85
Hoovervilles, 82
House Un-American Activities Committee (HUAC), 9, 28, 216
Houston, Cisco, 31, 130, 240, 242
"Hungry Eyes," 84
Hungry Men, 187
Huntington's chorea, 5, 9, 34, 95, 165, 206, 249, 250
Hutchinson Family Singers, 68

"I Ain't Got No Home in This World Anymore," 24, 64–65, 94, 97, 188
"I Am a Girl of Constant Sorrow," 112
"I Am a Union Woman," 226, 250
"I Can't Feel at Home in This World Anymore," 64
"I Don't Feel at Home on the Bowery No More," 24, 94
"I Feel Like I'm Fixin' to Die Rag," 41
"If I Was Everything on Earth," 50, 188
"I'll Say It's Hard Times," 63
"I Looked at the World," 97
"I'm a-Lookin' for That New Deal Now," 94, 246
"I'm a Rounder's Name," 101, 104–5, 107, 112
"Indian Corn Song," 97, 218
Industrial Workers of the World (IWW), 209–10
International Labor Defense, 162
International Longshoremen's and Warehousemen's Union (ILWU), 215
International Seamen's Union (ISU), 241
"I Ride an Old Paint," 100
"Isle of Capri," 153
Israel, Crappy, 45
"It Takes a Chain Gang Man," 154

"Jackhammer John" ("Jackhammer Blues"), 104, 105
Jackson, Aunt Molly, 111, 219, 221

James, Frank, 174

James, Jesse, 16, 168, 173–74, 175, 178

Jenkins, Andrew, 53, 175

Jennings, Matt, 52

"Jesse James" (folksong), 5, 168

"Jesse James" (Guthrie), 175, 199

"Jesse James and His Boys," 174–75

"Jesus Christ," 199–200

Jewish Young People's Folksingers Chorus, 35

Jim Crow, 145–46

"Jim Crow" (Almanac Singers), 146

"Jim Crow" (Rice), 145

"Jim Crow Blues," 146

"Job's Just Around the Corner, The," 69

"Joe Hillstrom," 209

"John Dillinger," 166

"John Hardy," 166, 191

"John Henry," 224

"Johnny Harty," 191

"Join That A.F. of L.," 146, 234, 237

"Jolly Banker," 188

Jones, Mother, 113, 116

Jordan, Louis, 151

"Kansas Boys," 192

"Keep That Oil A-Rolling," 108, 235

Kelly, George "Machine Gun," 178

Kimes, George, 178, 179

Kimes, Matthew, 178–79

King, Jeffery S., 181

King, Martin Luther, Jr., 44

Kingston Trio, 255

Klein, Joe, 7, 12, 23, 24, 33, 34, 55, 91, 96–97, 136, 152, 206, 209, 211, 223, 224, 240, 274n

Korson, George, 125

Ku Klux Klan (KKK), 136, 144–45, 236

Kumrids, 210

LaChapelle, Pete, 270n

LaFollette Committee, 89, 131

LaGuardia, Fiorello, 108, 109–10

Lampell, Millard, 139, 227, 232, 233

Lange, Dorothea, 51, 61, 67, 82, 132

Lead Belly (Huddie Ledbetter), 31, 139–40, 154, 155–56, 246

Ledger, 157, 210

Leventhal, Harold, 34, 35

Lewis, John L., 205, 207, 234, 245, 248, 250

Lieberman, Robbie, 12

Life and Death of Pretty Boy Floyd, The, 181

Light, The, 213

Lincoln, Abraham, 196–97, 240

Lindbergh, Charles, 245

"Little Darling, Pal of Mine," 26

Little Red School House Chorus, 42

Logsdon, Guy, 52, 100, 112, 159

Lomax, Alan, 10, 25, 34, 49, 73, 75–76, 127, 143, 153, 168, 174, 176, 185, 191, 199, 220, 229, 231, 232, 282n

Lomax, Bess, 31

"Lonesome Road Blues" ("I'm Goin' Down That Road Feelin' Bad"), 72, 73, 74

Loney, George, 136

"Long and Lonesome Chain," 141, 154

Longhi, Jimmy, 242, 274n

Lorentz, Pare, 51

Los Angeles Times, 87, 254

"Lost John," 154

"Ludlow Massacre," 117–18

"Lumber is King" ("Lumber's th' Life"), 101–3

Lynching, 155–61

Lynn, Loretta, 43

Malone, Bill, 175

Marcus, Greil, 45, 177, 255

Marrs, Ernie, 27, 37

Marsh, Dave, 12, 89, 129, 206, 222, 250–51, 274n

Martinez, Alberto O., 39

Marx, Karl, 206

"Matthew Kimes," 179

McDonald, Country Joe, 40–41, 181, 255

McElvaine, Robert, 206

McGhee, Brownie, 139, 140–41

McGovern, George, 44

McGuire, Matthew, 231

McMurtry, Larry, 181

McWilliams, Carey, 4, 60, 132, 138

Mechanization, 66–67, 103

Meeropol, Abel, 155

Mellencamp, John, 255

Mermaid Avenue, 253

Merriam, Frank, 79, 269n

Merrill, Robert, 119

Merriweather, Anne May, 224, 225

"Michigan IO," 100

Midwest Labor, 235

Mighty Hard Road, A, 11

Miller, Bob, 61

"Miners' Kids and Wives" ("Waiting at
the Gate"), 123–24

"Miner's Song" ("Dig My Life Away"),
112–13

Minstrels of the Dawn, 43

Mooney, Tom, 180, 216

Morgan, Ruth, 185

Morning News, 184

"Mr. Tom Mooney Is Free," 180, 216

"Muleskinner Blues," 104

"Murder of Harry Simms, The," 112

"My Pretty Snow-Deer," 211

"My Song Is My Weapon," 12

"My Sweetyold CIO," 250

Nash, Jay, 180

National Association for the Advancement
of Colored People (NAACP), 43, 143,
150, 155, 156, 162, 163

National Industrial Recovery Act
(NIRA), 212

National Labor Relations Act (NLRA), 212

National Labor Relations Board
(NLRB), 212

National Maritime Union (NMU), 206,
241–43, 247

National Miners Union, 220

Nazareth, 255

Nelson, Laura, 136

Nelson, Lawrence, 136

New Yorker, The, 8

New York Times, 30, 180

New York Times Book Review, 8

"New York Town," 108

"Nigger Blues," 138

"1913 Massacre," 114–15, 118

Nixon, Richard, 44

"No Depression in Heaven," 217

"No Disappointment in Heaven," 217

Now Let Us Praise Famous Men, 90

Ochs, Phil, 41

Odetta, 38, 255

Ogan, Sarah, 111, 112, 125, 219

"Oh, Freedom," 191

"Oh, Susannah," 73

"Oh My Lovin' Brother," 26

Oil Workers International Union
(OWIU), 107, 108, 118, 235

"Oklahoma Hills," 15

"Old Rachel," 50

Olsen, Culbert, 180

On a Slow Train through California, 218

"On Bloody Rags," 141, 192

101 Woody Guthrie Songs, 42

"Only a Miner," 11

Orozco, José Clemente, 156

Ossana, Diana, 181

Palmer, A. Mitchell, 216

Parchman prison, 153

"Pasture of Plenty," 15, 89–90

Paull, Irene, 101, 235

Paxton, Tom, 41
"People's Army" ("You Are the People's Army"), 141, 142
People's Artists, 248
People's Songs, 119
People's Songs, 246, 248
People's World, 11, 87, 96, 139, 215, 216, 217, 222
Pepper, Claude, 143
Peter, Paul, and Mary, 10, 41, 255
Phillips, Wendell, 196
"Pictures from Life's Other Side," 49
Pilot, 242
Pipe-Smoking Time, 228
"Pittsburgh," 106
Place, Jeff, 32
Poll Tax, 142–43
"Poll Tax Chain" ("Bloody Poll Tax Chain"), 128, 141, 143–45, 146, 152–53, 157, 191
Populist Party (PP), 207–8
"Poor, Hard-Working Man Blues," 66, 97–98
Powers, Bill, 172
Pretty Boy, 181
Pretty Boy Floyd, 181
"Pretty Boy Floyd," 15, 180, 181–86
"Pretty Polly," 89
Price, Victoria, 162
"Prisoner's Song, The," 153
Pursuit of Happiness, 228
Purvis, Melvin, 180
Puzzled America, 225–26

Quantrill, William Clarke, 173
Quin, Mike, 96, 139, 180, 215–16

Race of Singers, A, 12
Rage Against the Machine, 255
"Ragged Hungry Blues," 112
"Raggedy, Raggedy," 63
Ramblin' Man, 12
Raper, Arthur, 161

Reagan, Ronald, 46
Reagon, Bernice, 45
"Rebel Girl," 226
"Redwing," 225
Reece, Florence, 221
Republican Party, 247, 249
Reuss, Richard, 7, 10, 137
Rice, Thomas Dartmouth, 145
Richmond, Al, 215
Richmond, Howie, 34
Robbin, Edward, 11, 96, 130, 139, 180, 206, 214–15, 233, 251
Robertson, Flora, 69
Robinson, Earl, 139, 221
Rockefeller, John D., 108
Rodgers, Jimmie, 59, 70, 71, 76
Rodnitzky, Jerome, 43, 260n
Rogers, Will, 8, 11, 75, 76, 199
"Roll On, My Union," 236
"Roll On Columbia," 101, 231
"Roll the Union On," 5
Romeika, Joseph, 146, 148, 150
Roosevelt, Eleanor, 198
Roosevelt, Franklin, 28, 218, 245–46
Rorty, James, 268
Ross, Benjamin, 192
Rothstein, Arthur, 51

Santa Monica Social Register Examine 'Er, 137
Schmidt, Cella, 54
Scottsboro Boys, 161–62, 180
"Scottsboro Boys," 162
Scruggs, Lester, 255
Seeds of Man, 13, 164
Seeger, Charles, 139, 232
Seeger, Pete, 7, 9, 10, 30, 34, 35, 36, 37–38, 39, 40, 42, 44–45, 75, 101, 139, 146, 181, 220, 223, 224, 232, 233, 234, 235, 246, 255, 263n, 264n, 265n
"Sharecropper Song," 64

Shaw, Robert Gould, 197
"She Came Along to Me," 227, 238
Shelton, Robert, 10, 11
Shull, Lynwood L., 150–51
Silber, Irwin, 39
"Silicosis is Killing Me," 125
Sinatra, Frank, 255
Sinclair, Upton, 86, 218
Sing Out!, 9, 35, 38
"66 Highway Blues," 75, 223
"Slavery Grave," 141, 146, 192
"Slipknot," 159, 161, 162, 192, 254
Smith, Edwin, 107, 118, 235
Smith, George, 98
Smith, Jerry J., 39
Smith, Kate, 22, 23
Smith Act (Alien Registration Act), 28
Socialist Party (SP), 208–9, 210, 216
"Solidarity Forever," 250
"So Long, It's Been Good to Know You"
    ("Dusty Old Dust"), 9, 24, 25, 53–56, 57,
    59, 176, 238
Songs for John Doe, 232
Songs for Political Action, 32
Songs to Grow On, 32–33
"Song to Woody," 255
Sonkin, Robert, 73, 166, 178
Southern Commission on the Study of
    Lynching, 155
Southern Tenant Farmers Union (STFU),
    63, 232
Spirit of '43, The, 198
Spivak, John L., 153
Springsteen, Bruce, 46, 255
"S.S. NMU," 243–44
"Stagger Lee," 177
"Stagolee," 178, 282n
Stalin, Joseph, 245
Starr, Belle, 171, 173, 178
"Star-Spangled Banner," 20, 23
Steele, Elmer, 184

Steinbeck, John, 14, 56, 74, 82, 126, 257
Stein, Walter, 132, 138
Stekert, Ellen, 11
Still, William, 196
Stott, William, 14
"Strange Fruit," 155, 156
"Streets of Laredo, The," 148
Sugar, Maurice, 221
"Sunny Cal," 69
Sweet Honey in the Rock, 42

Taft, Robert, 146, 277n
Taft-Hartley Act, 247, 248, 277n
"Tale a Feller Told Me, A," 141–42, 157, 192
"Talking Dust Bowl," 51, 72, 76
"Talking Meanness" ("Mean Talking
    Blues"), 128
"Talking Merchant Marine," 243
"Talking Miner" ("Talking Centralia"),
    120–21
"Talking Subway Blues," 108
Talking Union, 227, 232
"Talking Union," 232
Taylor, Paul, 61, 132
Tenant Farming, 61–65
*Ten Twenty-Five Cent Songs by Woody
    Guthrie*, 31, 36, 244
Terkel, Studs, 8, 67, 181
Terrill, Ray, 178
Terry, Sonny, 31, 140–41, 154
"That Union Feeling," 207, 219
They Shall Not Die, 163
"They Shall Not Die," 162
Thinking of Woody Guthrie, 40
"Thirty Days in the Workhouse," 154
"This Could Never Happen in My Dear
    Old Sunny South," 163
"This Land Is Their Land," 36–37
This Land Is Your Land, 32
"This Land Is Your Land" ("God Blessed
    America"), 6, 15, 19–21, 26–27, 28, 30–36,

37, 38–39, 41–47, 48, 50, 57, 87, 221, 244, 253, 254

This Land Is Your Land: The Asch Recordings, Vol. 1, 31

"This Morning I Am Born Again," 217, 244

"This Train Is Bound for Glory," 146

Thompson, Florence, 82

Thurmond, Strom, 249

Tisa, John, 290n

Todd, Charles, 72, 166, 178

Tolan Committee, 89, 131

"Tom Joad," 67, 98, 190–91, 220

Tragedy of Lynching, The, 161

Transport Workers Union (TWU), 108, 109, 110, 235

"Trenton Frameup," 163

Trenton Six, 163

Tribute to Woody Guthrie, A, 38–39

Trilling, Lionel, 90

Tripp, Thomas Alfred, 55

"Troubles of Mine," 211

Troup, Bobby, 74

Truman, Harry, 17, 36, 146, 247, 248, 249

Tubman, Harriet, 13, 16, 192, 194, 195, 196–97, 202

Turpin, Dick, 170

Tweedy, Jeff, 253

Twelve Million Black Voices, 236

"Twenty-One Years," 153

"Uncle Stud," 250

Unemployed Unions, 233

"Union Maid," 224, 225, 226, 227, 232

"Union's My Religion," 240, 245

"Union Spirit," 240

"Union Train," 245

United Automobile Workers (UAW), 235, 247

United Cannery, Agricultural, Packing and Allied Workers of America (UCAPAWA), 213–14

United Electrical Workers, 246

United Mine Workers of America (UMW), 116, 212, 245, 248

Vanguard Records, 40

Van Ronk, Dave, 36

Vietnam Songbook, The, 39

"Vigilante Man," 188, 220, 239

Village Voice, 39

Vincent, Leo, 211

Vision Shared, A, 42

"Wabash Cannonball, The," 107, 143

Wagner, Robert, 212

Wallace, Henry, 146, 249

Wallis, Michael, 181

"Washington Talkin' Blues," 102

Watson, Doc, 42

We, the People, 228

We Are Many, 113

Weatherwax, Seema, 261n

Weavers, 9, 35, 55

"Welcome the Traveler Home," 112

Werner, Craig, 164

"When the Curfew Blows," 160–61, 164–65

"When the World's on Fire," 26

"When You're Down and Out," 187, 234

"Where Are You Going My CIO?," 249–50

"Which Side Are You On?," 5, 111, 232

White, Josh, 155–56

Whitman, Walt, 10, 126, 251

"Whoopie Ti Yi Yo" ("Get Along Little Doggies"), 100

"Why We Come to California," 69

Wiggins, Ella May, 221

Wilco, 170

Wilgus, D. K., 11

"Will Rogers Highway," 75–76

Wilson, Woodrow, 4, 118, 208

Without Sanctuary, 157

Wood, Bob, 224

Wood, Ina, 224, 225
Woodward, C. Vann, 136, 142
Woodward, Isaac, 150–51, 153
Woody Guthrie: A Life, 12, 33
Woody Guthrie and Me, 11
Woody Guthrie Folk Songs, 10, 35
Woody Guthrie: Hard Travelin', 42
Woody Sez, 11
"Wreck of the Old '97," 36
Wright, Richard, 236

X, 255

Yip! Yip! Yaphank, 22
"You Are My Sunshine," 26
"You Fascists Bound to Lose," 236
"You Gotta Go Down and Join the
 Union," 248
Young, Israel, 32
Younger, Cole, 173
Yurchenco, Henrietta, 11

Zinn, Howard, 43

Permissions

The following organizations have kindly allowed me to quote from Woody Guthrie's song lyrics held under their copyright.

Woody Guthrie Publications

"1913 Massacre" by Woody Guthrie. Copyright 1961 (renewed) by Woody Guthrie Publications, Inc. "66 Highway Blues" by Woody Guthrie and Pete Seeger. Copyright 1967 (renewed) by Woody Guthrie Publications and Stormking Music, Inc. "A Tale a Feller Told Me" by Woody Guthrie. Copyright 1965 (renewed) by Woody Guthrie Publications, Inc. "Another Man Done Gone" by Woody Guthrie. Copyright 1998 by Woody Guthrie Publications, Inc. "Bet on Wallace" by Woody Guthrie. Copyright 2002 by Woody Guthrie Publications, Inc. "Billy the Kid" by Woody Guthrie. Copyright 1961 (renewed) by Woody Guthrie Publications, Inc. "Blinding of Isaac Woodard" by Woody Guthrie. Copyright 1965 (renewed) by Woody Guthrie Publications, Inc. "Bonnie Black Bess ("Unwelcome Guest") by Woody Guthrie. Copyright 1998 by Woody Guthrie Publications, Inc. "Calamity Jane" by Woody Guthrie. Copyright 2004 by Woody Guthrie Publications, Inc. "California Gold" by Woody Guthrie. Copyright 2002 by Woody Guthrie Publications, Inc. "California! California!" by Woody Guthrie. Copyright 2001 by Woody Guthrie Publications, Inc. "Chinese and the Japs" by Woody Guthrie. Copyright 2001 by Woody Guthrie Publications, Inc. "Christ for President" by Woody Guthrie. Copyright 1990, 1998 by Woody Guthrie Publications, Inc. "Cowboy's Philosophy" by Woody Guthrie. Copyright 2002 by Woody Guthrie Publications, Inc. "Don't Kill My Baby and My Son" by Woody Guthrie. Copyright 1967 (renewed) by Woody Guthrie Publications, Inc. "Farmer Labor Train" by Woody Guthrie. Copyright 2000 by Woody Guthrie Publications, Inc. "Farther Away" by Woody Guthrie. Copyright 2001 by Woody Guthrie Publications, Inc. "Ferguson Brothers Killing" by Woody Guthrie. Copyright 1990 by Woody Guthrie Publications, Inc. "The Final Call" by Woody Guthrie. Copyright 2001 by Woody Guthrie Publications, Inc. "Go Down and See" by Woody Guthrie. Copyright 2002 by Woody Guthrie Publications, Inc. "Gotta Keep 'Em Sailing" by Woody Guthrie. Copyright 2001 by Woody Guthrie Publications, Inc. "High Balladree" by Woody Guthrie. Copyright 1990 by Woody Guthrie Publications, Inc. "If I Was Everything on Earth" by Woody Guthrie. Copyright 2001 by Woody Guthrie Publications, Inc. "I'll Say It's Hard Times" by Woody Guthrie. Copyright 1964 (renewed) by Woody Guthrie Publications, Inc. "I'm Looking for That New Deal Now" by Woody Guthrie. Copyright 1967 (renewed) by Woody Guthrie Publications, Inc. "Indian Corn Song" by Woody Guthrie. Copyright 2002 by Woody Guthrie Publications, Inc. "Jesse James and His Boys" by Woody Guthrie. Copyright 1967 (renewed) by Woody Guthrie Publications, Inc. "Johnny Harty" by Woody Guthrie. Copyright 1995 by Woody Guthrie Publications, Inc. "Join That A. F. of L." by Woody Guthrie. Copyright 2001 by Woody Guthrie Publications, Inc. "Jolly Banker" by Woody Guthrie. Copyright 1964 (renewed) by Woody Guthrie Publications, Inc. "Keep That Oil A-Rollin'" by Woody Guthrie. Copyright 2001 by Woody Guthrie Publications, Inc. "Long and Lonesome

CPSIA information can be obtained at www.ICGtesting.com
Printed in the USA
LVOW13s2139080714

393490LV00001B/199/A